BASIC LOGIC

BASIC LOGIC

PROFESSOR ROBERT J. YANAL

WAYNE STATE UNIVERSITY

West Publishing Company

St. Paul • New York • Los Angeles • San Francisco

Copyediting Rosalie Koskenmaki
Design Linda Beauvais, Destiny 2
Composition Rolin Graphics
Cover design Roslyn M. Stendahl, Dapper Design, Minneapolis, MN
Cover painting GOTTLIEB, Adolph.
Descending Arrow. 1956.
Oil on canvas, 8 x 6′.
Collection, The Museum of Modern Art, New York.
Gift of the artist.

50 W. Kellogg Boulevard
P.O. Box 64526
St. Paul, MN 55164-1003

Printed in the United States of America
96 95 94 93 92 91 8 7 6 5 4 3 2 1

Library of Congress Cataloging-in-Publication Data

Yanal, Robert J.
Basic logic.
Includes index.
1. Logic. I. Title.
BC108.Y33 1988 160 87-34510
ISBN 0-314-64284-6

To my parents,
John and Elizabeth Yanal

PREFACE

About the Book

If there is any justification for the appearance of yet another introductory logic book, it is that the flourishing field of informal logic has become increasingly complex and disunified. Perhaps *Basic Logic* can offer a traditional, yet non-technical and straightforward alternative.

Basic Logic focuses entirely on the evaluation of arguments, more accurately, of justifications. It attempts to present, as the title suggests, the basic elements of deductive and inductive logic on an introductory level.

The book progresses from distinguishing justification from other things to argument diagrams that both facilitate a fine-grained method for the analysis of arguments and allow rules to be presented easily later. Here the most important foundation of logic is learned. For until the student is practiced in demonstrating what statement(s) is offered in support of what other statement(s) and whether there is a chain of reasons or an independent series of reasons, all the rest of logic—Modus Ponens, the Genetic Fallacy, and so on—will be for naught. Besides which, a logic course should have the minimal effect of preparing the student for hearing when a justification is being given and what is justifying what.

The traditional order of deductive before inductive logic is preserved in *Basic Logic*, for the reason that it is perhaps better for students to know what the "perfect" (deductively valid) justifications are in order to grasp what the "imperfect" (inductively valid) justifications are striving for. This is not, however, an absolutely compelling reason. Part Three may easily be taught before Part Two.

About the Exercises

Working on problems is as essential for learning logic as it is for learning arithmetic, and *Basic Logic* recognizes this by presenting a considerable number of exercises. The exercises usually run upwards in level of difficulty, from easier to harder problems. Teachers may want to take this into account when assigning problems.

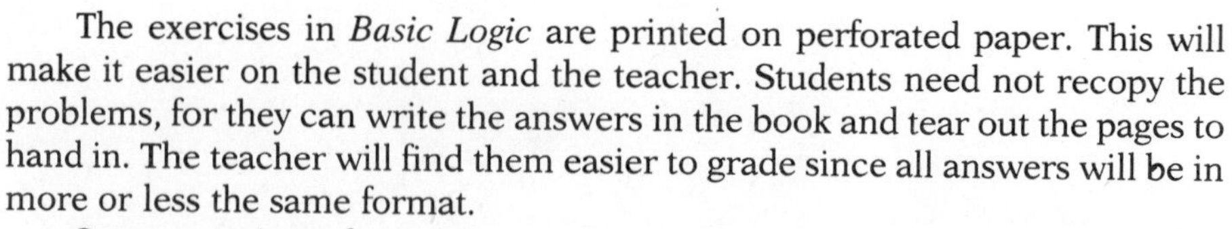

The exercises in *Basic Logic* are printed on perforated paper. This will make it easier on the student and the teacher. Students need not recopy the problems, for they can write the answers in the book and tear out the pages to hand in. The teacher will find them easier to grade since all answers will be in more or less the same format.

Some exercises, chosen more or less at random, are answered in the book. These are marked with a star (*). It is hoped that this tactic will provide model answers, hence produce better results for the unanswered questions.

Acknowledgments

I owe the ideas on the dependent/independent distinction in the Appendix to Chapter 2 to Barbara Humphries. Larry Powers pointed out the problems with Weak and Strong arguments as discussed in the Appendix to Chapter 3. Mike McKinsey convinced me that, despite rife doctrine, "or" is always weak. Larry Lombard made many good suggestions about causal arguments, not all of which I could accept without complicating the book beyond the introductory level.

In addition, suggestions were made, anonymously, by the following reviewers, who are here unmasked: Jeffrey Berger, Community College of Philadelphia; Fred J. Blomgren, Monroe Community College; James H. Buchanan, University of Akron; Michael Burke, Indiana University, Indianapolis; Henry N. Carrier, Brevard Community College; Steve Giambrone, University of Southwestern Louisiana; John Martin, University of Cincinnati; Douglass D. McFerran, Los Angeles Pierce College; Darryl Mehring, Metropolitan State College; John Peterson, University of Rhode Island; Leslie C. Read, Sacramento City College; Ben Starr, Modesto Junior College; Kenneth Stern, State University of New York at Albany; James D. Stuart, Bowling Green State University; and R. G. Wengert, University of Illinois, Urbana. All these people caught errors in the manuscript or suggested ways to improve it. The book is much better for their advice.

My editor at West, Clark Baxter, nursed the writing along with intelligence and wit, and Laura Carlson, the book's production editor, dealt cheerfully with art museums, arrow diagrams, and anxious authors.

Finally, I would like to thank Larry Spencer for his help in manuscript preparation, but mainly for his encouragement during the writing of *Basic Logic*.

CONTENTS

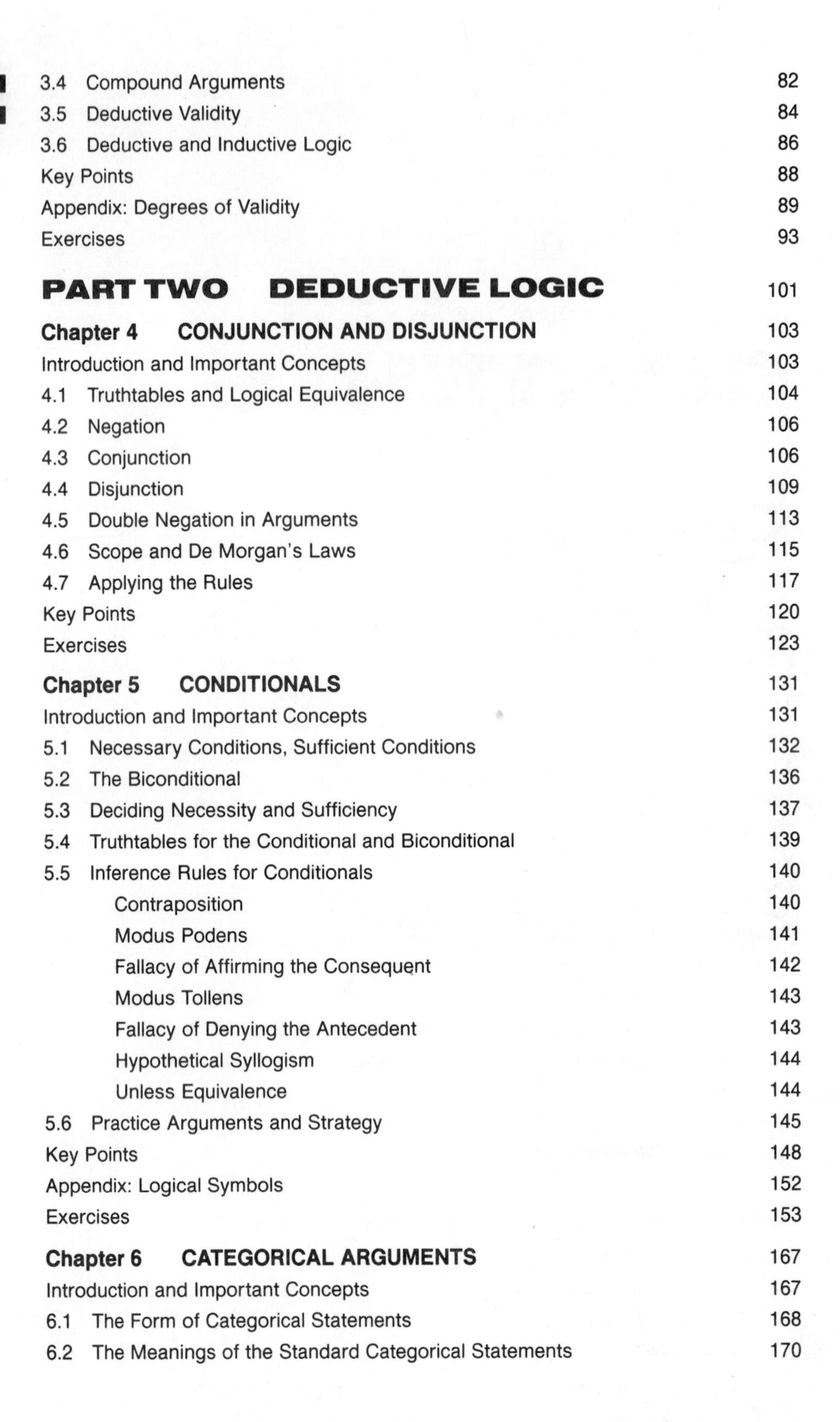

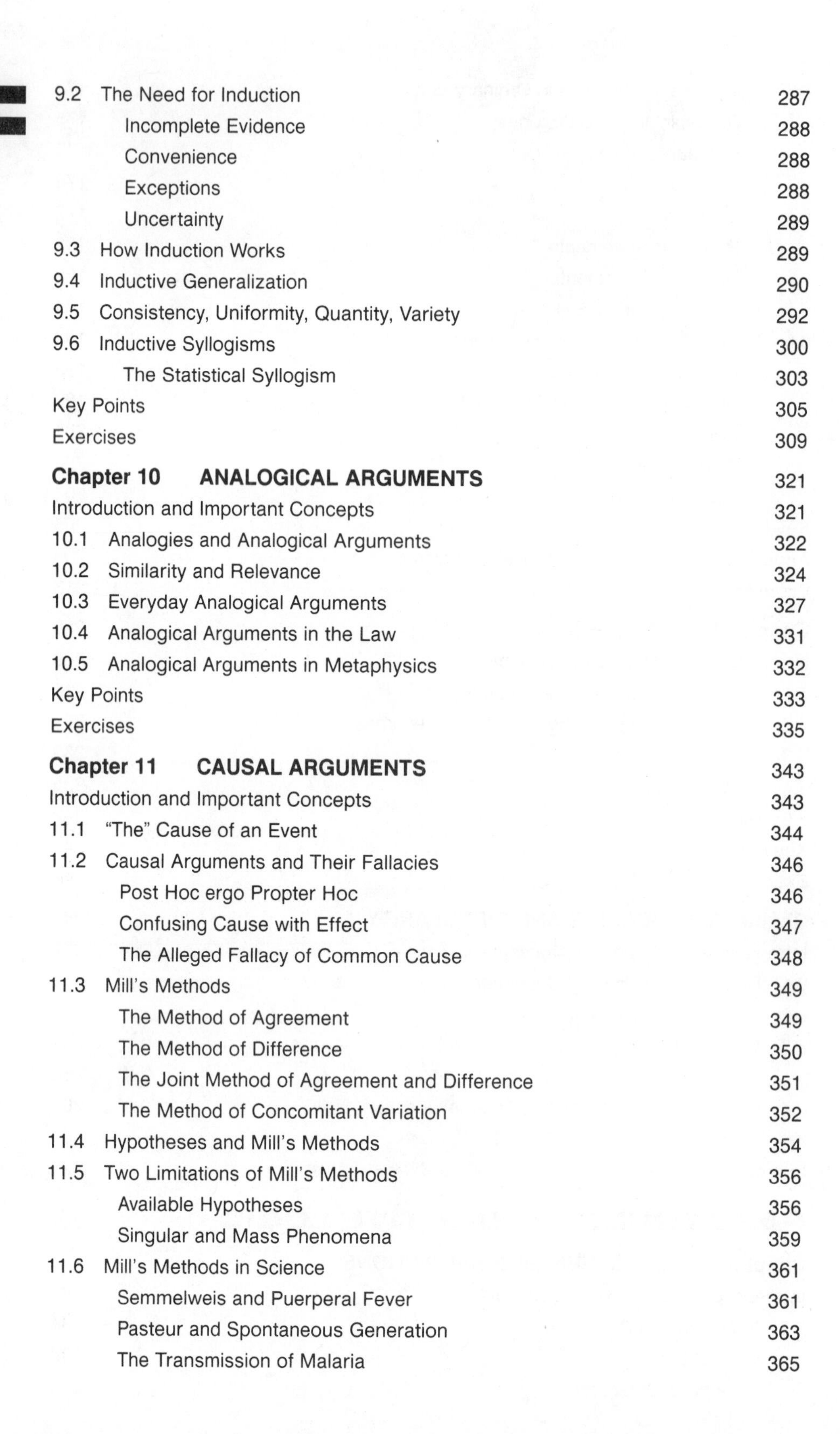

PART ONE

BASICS

CHAPTER 1

ARGUMENTS

Logic is the study of arguments. More precisely, logic is a set of rules to determine whether an argument is good or bad. What "good" and "bad" mean with respect to arguments is discussed in Chapter 3, and the rules for evaluating arguments begin with Chapter 4. This chapter will show you what an argument is, some of the uses of argument, the parts of an argument, and what kinds of discourse are ***not*** *arguments. These are the most important concepts in this chapter:*

LOGIC

ARGUMENT
(and its synonyms)

STATEMENT

PREMISE
(and its synonyms)

CONCLUSION
(and its synonyms)

REASONING INDICATOR
(be able to recognize one)

JUSTIFICATION
especially as distinguished from . . .

EXPLANATION

1.1 What Is an Argument?

First, note the spelling. The verb "to argue" ends with an "e" but the noun "argument" drops that "e." A logic student never writes "arguement." Second, there are several senses of "argument" in English that are not used in logic (and not used in this book). "Argument" can mean something like "a strong disagreement" or even "a shouting match," as in "John and Mary had a violent argument; they kept me awake all night." We ignore this sense of "argument" in logic. Sometimes "argument" is made to mean "statement" or "claim," as in "The senator argued that prayer should be allowed in public schools." This sense is closer to the logical sense of "argument" but still not on the mark.

The logical sense is this: An **ARGUMENT** is any piece of discourse (any communication by speech or writing) in which evidence in the form of statements is given for the truth of other statements. There are a number of other terms that are roughly synonymous with "argument." Here is a partial list:

(a piece of) reasoning

(making an) inference

justification (or justifying a statement)

producing evidence for your claim (or your belief)

drawing consequences

The term we shall use most throughout this book is "argument," but be prepared to encounter these other terms as well.

We'll begin with some simple examples of arguments. You say to me, "It's cold." "How do you know?" I ask. You may then be able to produce evidence for your statement. You might, for example, say, "The radio said the temperature at the airport was ten degrees" or "I can see icicles on the roof of the house across the street" or "I just stuck my head out the door and it felt cold." Any one of these produces evidence for your statement, "It's cold," and, of course, all of them together produce a lot of evidence for your statement. In effect, you have given an argument that can be restated like this:

> *Since the radio said the temperature at the airport was ten degrees, and I can see icicles on the roof of the house across the street, and I just stuck my head out the door and it felt cold, I conclude that it's* cold.

You will be given a number of examples of arguments in the following sections. While it is the main business of logic to evaluate arguments—to pick out the good ones from the bad—we must postpone this task temporarily. In other words, do not worry (yet) whether the example (or exercise) arguments are good or bad. Just try for the present to see why they are arguments.

1.2 Why Argue?

Argument serves at least three goals: (1) to EXTEND OUR KNOWLEDGE, (2) to PERSUADE, and (3) to see what consequences follow if we make certain assumptions (HYPOTHETICAL REASONING).

1. Here's an example of how argument extends our knowledge. The Polish astronomer, Copernicus (1473–1543), reasoned this way:

Since the planets are seen at varying distances from the earth, the earth is not the center of their orbit.

Copernicus used the observation that the planets are seen at varying distances from the earth as evidence for a further statement, namely that the earth is not the center of their orbit (thus contradicting the widespread belief that the other planets revolved around the earth). In effect, Copernicus moved from something we knew to something we didn't (yet) know, thus extending our knowledge.

Sherlock Holmes often engaged in the sort of reasoning that extends knowledge. Dr. Watson, A. Conan Doyle's fictional narrator, tells this story (Holmes speaks first):

"You have come in by train this morning, I see."

"You know me, then?"

"No, but I observe the second half of a return ticket in the palm of your left glove. You must have started early and yet you had a good drive in a dog-cart, along heavy roads, before you reached the station."

The lady gave a violent start, and stared in bewilderment at my companion.

"There is no mystery, my dear madam," said he, smiling. "The left arm of your jacket is spattered with mud in no less than seven places. The marks are perfectly fresh. There is no vehicle save a dog-cart which throws up mud in that way, and then only when you sit on the left-hand side of the driver."[1]

From certain observations (the woman was holding a return ticket, the left arm of her jacket was spattered with fresh mud), Holmes reasons to two conclusions (she took a train this morning and she rode in a dog-cart). And Holmes' inference is confirmed by the woman in question: "'Whatever your reasons may be, you are perfectly correct,' said she. 'I started from my home before six, reached Leatherhead at twenty past, and came in by the first train to Waterloo.'" In other words, Holmes reasons from certain facts he knew (by simple, though careful, observation) to other facts he did not (yet) know.

2. Another function of argument is to persuade. Here is an argument dealing with a highly controversial topic:

Much of the early research in which the [IQ] scores of Blacks were compared to the existing norms is misleading. For example, the average IQ of Black

[1]Sir Arthur Conan Doyle, "The Adventure of the Speckled Band."

> *schoolchildren from Florida, Georgia, Alabama, Tennessee, and South Carolina was found to be 80.7, while the norms of White children* nationwide *is 100. However, White schoolchildren from the same five southeastern states were not tested at that time, although it is known that the average IQ for Whites in that region is lower than the national average. Therefore, it is an abuse of statistics to argue, as many have, that such data are evidence for a 16- to 20-point difference between Blacks and Whites.*[2]

Here there are *two* statements for which evidence has been produced: that much early research into the IQ scores of blacks and whites is misleading and that it is an abuse of statistics to argue that certain data are evidence for an IQ difference between blacks and whites. Mr. Ehrlich and Ms. Feldman are presumably trying to persuade their readers that there is no evidence for a national IQ difference between blacks and whites.

Here is another example of an argument whose function is to persuade:

> *Just as we need more police to deal with traffic problems than we did 75 years ago, so we need more [Supreme] Courts to deal with cases.* (Former Chief Justice Warren Burger)

Former Justice Burger is attempting to persuade you that there should be more than one Supreme Court by posing an analogy between an increase in traffic problems and an increase in cases before the Supreme Court (see Chapter 10 on analogical arguments).

3. An argument usually begins with a piece of knowledge or a belief of the arguer. However, sometimes an argument begins with assumptions that may not be known or even believed to be true. The arguer wonders what will follow *if* those assumptions were made. We call this hypothetical reasoning. For example, suppose Jack and Jill are planning a two-day ski weekend. They know some things but not others. Jill reasons like this:

> *We each have $200 to spend on the weekend. We know that it will cost us $25 apiece in gas to get there and back. Let's assume that the room will cost us $50 each for the whole weekend, that we can eat for $20 a day, and that lift fees will be $15 a day. That would leave us $55 each for incidental expenses. So, it looks as though $200 each will get us through the weekend.*

Jill is reasoning from certain assumptions: *If* I'm right about the expenses for the room, food, and lift fees, then my conclusion will be right.

Hypothetical reasoning may begin with a definition. Since it is often the case that a definition is neither known nor believed to be true, but rather stipulated or granted for the sake of argument, reasoning from a definition can be considered to be hypothetical reasoning. An example:

> *One way to define straight pool itself is to consider it as the only pool game requiring transitions from one rack to the next.*

[2]Paul R. Ehrlich and S. Shirley Feldman, *The Race Bomb* (New York: The New York Times Book Co., 1977, p. 122.

Accordingly, your ability at the game will always be equal to your ability to make those transitions: breaking the balls, and positioning yourself for future break shots.[3]

It is as if Mr. Fels is asking his readers to grant him his definition of "straight pool," and granting it, Mr. Fels reasons to a point about the most important ability in playing the game.

The purposes of hypothetical reasoning are perhaps obvious. Often we do not have sufficient knowledge to begin a pattern of reasoning; we must make certain assumptions. We may not know, for example, what expenses will be on a vacation. So we draw out the consequences of some assumptions. Or, we pose a definition and draw consequences from it.

1.3 The Parts of Arguments

Since an argument is, at the minimum, discourse that advances some statement(s) on the basis of the reason or evidence given by some other statement(s), the primary component of an argument is the statement. **A STATEMENT** is what is expressed by language only when what is expressed can be either true or false. For our purposes here, we will take a statement to be what is expressed by the speaker (or writer) —the person's meaning—when what the speaker (or writer) means can be true or false.

Statements must be capable of being either true or false. This is because, in reasoning, logic is used to track the transmission of any truth in the initial statements to the conclusion. Not every piece of language expresses a statement because not every piece of language expresses something that is either true or false. None of these are statements, for none of them can be true or false:

Darn it!

Go to the store and buy a quart of milk.

Why did you set five places at the table?

The square root of two is wet.

Accordingly, such pieces of language cannot be used in reasoning.

[3]George Fels, *Mastering Pool* (Chicago: Contemporary Books, Inc., 1977), p. 9.

Here are some typical statements:

7 + 5 = 12.

Baseball is played with twenty-three players on each side.

All whales are mammals.

Alaska is warm during February.

Ammonia mixed with chlorine bleach gives off a poisonous gas.

These are statements because they are capable of being true or false, not because they are true. "Baseball is played with twenty-three players on each side" is false, but it is still a statement.

An argument must at the minimum use one statement as evidence for the truth of another. Therefore, an argument must at the minimum contain no fewer than two statements.

The statement (or statements) used as the basis for other statements is usually called the **PREMISE**, although other terms can be used:

reason(s)

the evidence

what's given

the assumption(s)

The statement (or statements) that is based on the premise is usually called the **CONCLUSION**, although other terms can also be used:

what is derived

what is inferred

what is implied

what is proved

Any argument has at least one premise and at least one conclusion.

A note on word usage: "Imply" and "infer" are sometimes confused. It is a grammatical error to say, "His remark inferred that she sold it," or "I implied from his remark that she sold it." The correct form is, "His remark implied that she sold it," and "I inferred from his remark that she sold it." Here's one way to keep them apart. "Imply" is like "throw" and "infer" is like "catch." You or your premises imply something (like throwing). Someone else infers something from you or your premises (like catching).

Although the term "premise" suggests something that comes first and "conclusion" suggests something that comes last, this is not always the case in arguments. Here are two identical arguments. The first is stated with the premise coming *first:*

Because no two snowflakes form under absolutely identical conditions, no two snowflakes are alike.

Now we'll restate it with the premise *last:*

No two snowflakes are alike, because no two snowflakes form under absolutely identical conditions.

How can you tell which statement in an argument is functioning as the premise, which as the conclusion?

Often, although not always, an argument contains reasoning indicators. A **REASONING INDICATOR** is a term (or terms) that appears BEFORE statements in arguments. A reasoning indicator tells the reader or hearer which statements are premises, which are conclusions. Here is a fairly complete list of each:

Premise Indicators

because	*follows from*
since	*assuming (that)*
for	*supposing (that)*
for the reason(s) (that)	*may be inferred from*
given (that)	*may be deduced from*
on account of	*as derived from*

Conclusion Indicators

therefore	*entails that*
thus	*suggests that*
it follows that	*demonstrates that*
it may be inferred that	*accordingly*
hence	*shows that*
so	*is a reason for*
implies that	*this is why*

To see how reasoning indicators work, let's look at some simple examples. In each case, the conclusion has been underlined and any reasoning indicators have been circled:

(Since) it is snowing, it is also cold.

We need to continue restrictions on imported cars, (for) this will prevent even more unemployment in the American car industry.

(Because) taxes are already too high, we need to reduce military spending.

There is nothing sacred about these ways of stating those arguments. Any one of them could be restated in any number of different ways. Here are some restatements. Again, the conclusion is underlined and any reasoning indicators are circled:

It is cold, (since) it is snowing.

(Because) we need to prevent even more unemployment in the American car industry, we need to continue restrictions on imported cars.

Taxes are already too high. (Therefore,) we need to reduce military spending.

Match these examples against the list of reasoning indicators. Make sure you see why the statement that is underlined as the conclusion in each case really is the conclusion.

In the preceding examples, the same statements ("It is snowing," "We need to prevent even more unemployment in the American car industry," and "Taxes are already too high") were always the premise in their respective arguments. Similarly, the same statements ("It is cold," "We need to continue restrictions on imported cars," and "We need to reduce military spending") always functioned as the conclusion in their respective arguments. These arguments were written twice to show the different ways you can say one and the same argument using different reasoning indicators.

This may give the false impression that some statement must somehow *always* be a premise. In fact, one and the same statement may sometimes function as a premise, sometimes as a conclusion, and sometimes as neither. It all depends on how the statement is used. Suppose a critic says.

Poetry is untranslatable.

By itself, this is just a statement—something that is either true or false—and not an argument. (An argument needs at least two statements.) That is, by itself, "Poetry is untranslatable" is *neither* a premise *nor* a conclusion. But suppose our critic thinks this statement stands in need of justification. The critic will then give this argument supporting it. (The conclusion is underlined, and the reasoning indicator is circled.)

I. Because the nuances of the meaning of a word cannot be carried intact from one language to another, poetry is untranslatable.

In this argument, the statement "Poetry is untranslatable" functions as the conclusion of the critic's argument. But the critic could have assumed this statement to be true, and used it to argue for another statement (again, the conclusion is underlined and the reasoning indicator is circled):

II. Poetry is untranslatable. So, to grasp the meaning of a poem, you must read it in its original language.

In argument I, "Poetry is untranslatable" is the conclusion. In argument II, "Poetry is untranslatable" is the premise. (And the bare statement "Poetry is untranslatable" by itself is not an argument at all, hence neither premise nor conclusion.)

Unfortunately, the parts of arguments are not always clearly expressed. There are four general difficulties. (1) Not all statements are expressed by declarative sentences. (2) Not all statements in a passage that contains an argument are part of the argument. (3) Not everything that looks like a reasoning indicator is one. (4) Not all arguments contain reasoning indicators.

In our discussion of these difficulties, we will have to rely at least occasionally on the imprecise notions of interpretation and context. Not everything in logic is cut and dried.

1. While the most straightforward way of expressing a statement is by a declarative sentence,

She had a broken arm.

there are other ways of expressing this statement. For example, someone might say,

Given her broken arm, she couldn't have lifted that heavy box.

This is an argument. There is a premise indicator, "given", but what follows it is not a statement as written. However, remember that we were to identify a statement with what the speaker/writer meant to express. The above argument is shorthand for:

Given that she had a broken arm, she couldn't have lifted that heavy box.

One of the first things you should do with a piece of reasoning is to identify clearly the statements expressed in it. This may involve restating the argument so that it contains declarative sentences, just as we had to restate "Given her broken arm" as "Given that she had a broken arm."

Another way of expressing statements is through sentences that have the grammatical form of questions:

Who knows whether there really is a God who is all powerful, all knowing, and all good? Therefore faith, not knowledge, is required for belief in such a God.

This expresses the following speaker meaning, with the statements written explicitly as declarative sentences:

No one knows whether there really is a God who is all powerful, all knowing, and all good. Therefore faith, not knowledge, is required for belief in such a God.

2. Arguments may occur within longer pieces of discourse. Not everything that is said around an argument is part of the argument. Real-life arguments often require restatement in order to exhibit explicitly the statements that compose them. In this example from the trial of Jeffrey MacDonald for the murder of his wife and two children, Prosecutor Jim Blackburn made this argument to the jury in his summation. Dr. MacDonald had claimed and testified that his wife and children were murdered by a Charles Manson–like group of hippies. The point at issue here is that Dr. MacDonald had testified that the murderers had stabbed his wife with a Geneva Forge knife that was found on the scene of the crime. Prosecutor Blackburn disagrees:

I suggest that the Geneva Forge knife didn't kill anybody. If [MacDonald] pulled it out of [his wife's] chest, why does the evidence suggest that there was no significant amount of blood on that knife? Perhaps, because it didn't go in that chest—it nicked the defendant's arm.[4]

This argument contains a sentence that has the grammatical form of a question but that is used to express a statement. It also contains some phrases that are extraneous to the argument. Boiled down to its primary elements, the argument can be restated like this:

The Geneva Forge knife didn't kill anybody, for the evidence suggests that there was no significant amount of blood on the knife. So the knife wasn't in

[4]As quoted by Joe McGinniss, *Fatal Vision* (New York: G. P. Putnam's, 1983), p. 574.

the wife's chest. The explanation for the blood is that it nicked the defendant's arm.

This is, of course, not the only way to restate the argument. In restating pieces of reasoning, you must try to capture the original intent: What did the maker of the argument intend to express? This is a process of interpretation, and there are no mechanical rules for interpretation: It is an art, not a science.

3. Sometimes what appear to be reasoning indicators turn up in contexts where no reasoning is going on:

> *I've been sitting here for two hours.*
>
> *She's been in Florida since the beginning of May.*
>
> *He walked over to the easel and began to paint. He was thus occupied when she arrived.*

Although "for," "since," and "thus" are often reasoning indicators, they do not indicate reasoning in the above examples. None of the above three examples is an argument, for none contains statements made on the basis of other statements.

4. Not only is there discourse that contains semblances of reasoning indicators, there is reasoning that contains no reasoning indicators at all:

> *The accused was found with the jewels in his pocket. How can you believe that he didn't steal them?*

The best interpretation of this passage is that it is a piece of reasoning, which can be restated like this:

> *The accused was found with the jewels in his pocket. This gives you good reason to believe that he stole them.*

A more complicated example is given below:

> *Anglers opposed to snagging [the practice of using barbed, unbaited hooks to snag fish in their bellies or backs] consider it immoral. They say snaggers:*
>
> - *Violate a doctrine of "fair chase," of enticing a fish to strike a lure or bait.*
> - *Take other fish illegally.*
> - *Leave tangled messes of monofilament line and snag hooks.*
> - *Leave smelly salmon carcasses to rot on the riverbanks, thrown away after valuable eggs are stripped from females to be sold illegally, or because the fish's deteriorated physical condition makes it unfit for food.*[5]

[5]Tom Opre, "Snagging," *The Detroit Free Press*, Feb. 17, 1985, p. B1.

There are no true reasoning indicators in this passage. Yet this is a piece of reasoning: four reasons that purport to justify the statement that snagging is immoral. (Note that the "because" in the last reason does not indicate a subinference: It gives an explanation of why snaggers leave carcasses to rot on riverbanks, but no evidence that this explanation is true.)

1.4
How Many Statements?

It is important that you be able to count statements, not only to determine whether something is a piece of reasoning but, if it is, to determine what its components are. While it might seem to be a trivial matter to count to two—the minimum number of statements an argument must have—there are problems you should be aware of.

How many statements are made in each of these examples?

It is raining and the picnic is cancelled.

Either it is raining or the picnic is cancelled.

If it is raining, then the picnic is cancelled.

The first makes two statements: "It is raining" and "The picnic is cancelled." The next two make only *one* statement each for purposes of counting statements in reasoning.

Perhaps another example will show why. If I say to a student,

You got a C on the final, but you will still fail the course.

then I have said *both* that this student did get a C on the final *and* that he will fail the course. I have made *two* statements. However, if I say,

Either you get a B or better on the final or you will fail the course.

then I have made only *one* statement, not two. I have not stated that he will get a B or better on the final and I have not stated that he will fail the course. Similarly, if I say,

If you get a C or lower on the final, then you will fail the course.

I have not stated that he got a C nor that he will fail the course. I have made *one* statement.

The rule is this. *CONJUNCTIONS make separate statements. DISJUNCTIONS and CONDITIONALS do not make separate statements.* Here is a fairly complete list of terms that conjoin, disjoin, and make a conditional:

Conjunctions

and	*It is raining and the sun is shining.*
but	*It is raining but the sun is shining.*

although	*Although it is raining, the sun is shining.*
while	*It is raining while the sun is shining.*
(even) though	*Even though it is raining, the sun is shining.*
	Disjunctions
or	*It is raining or the sun is shining.*
either. . . or	*Either it is raining or the sun is shining.*
	Conditionals
if	*If it is raining, the sun is not shining.*
if. . . then	*If it is raining, then the sun is not shining.*
unless	*Unless it is raining, the sun is shining.*
when(ever)	*When(ever) it is raining, the sun is not shining.*
is contingent upon	*I'll buy the house contingent upon a satisfactory report from the inspector.*
is sufficient for	*A satisfactory report from the inspector is sufficient for my buying the house.*
is necessary for	*A satisfactory report from the inspector is necessary for my buying the house.*

These terms are not *exactly* equivalent. "And" and "but," for example, do not mean exactly the same thing. But for our purposes, a conjunction joins statements that can be counted separately, while a disjunction or a conditional joins statements that cannot be counted separately.

These facts about conjunctions, disjunctions, and conditionals have consequences both for determining when reasoning is going on and for picking out its components. For example, the following is not an argument:

If you mix ammonia with chlorine bleach, you will produce a poisonous gas.

It makes only one statement, and an argument must have at least two statements. However, conditionals can figure in reasoning:

If you mix ammonia with chlorine bleach, you will produce a poisonous gas. (So) don't do it.

This is an argument with one statement as its premise, one other as its conclusion.

Suppose you are asked to underline the conclusion of this piece of reasoning:

Lee mostly eats and sleeps. So, either she is in the kitchen or in the bedroom.

The conclusion is "Either she is in the kitchen or in the bedroom." The *right* way to do it is:

Lee mostly eats and sleeps. (So,) either she is in the kitchen or in the bedroom.

One *wrong* way would be something like:

Lee mostly eats and sleeps. (So,) either she is in the kitchen or in the bedroom.

The wrong way says that from the premise, "Lee mostly eats and sleeps," you have drawn the conclusion, "She is in the kitchen." But you have not drawn that conclusion. You have drawn the much better conclusion, "Either she is in the kitchen or in the bedroom."

1.5 Sequences of Statements

Not everything, of course, is a piece of reasoning. In fact, non-reasoning is more common than reasoning. It is often the case that you can read pages of material or listen to many minutes of radio or TV talk before you encounter a piece of reasoning.

The first and most obvious kind of non-reasoning is the MERE SEQUENCE OF STATEMENTS:

> *On April 13, 1888, Alfred Nobel, a Swedish chemist and industrialist who twenty-one years earlier had mixed a capricious, extremely powerful oil called nitroglycerin with kieselguhr, a diatomaceous earth, to create a baton-shaped explosive he called dynamite, woke to read his own obituary in a French newspaper. The notice, inadvertently run in place of the obituary of an older brother, who had died the previous day, described Nobel as a "merchant of death," whose work with explosives was responsible, to a great extent, for Europe's accelerating arms race.*[6]

Mr. Di Salvatore has not, in this passage, engaged in any reasoning. He has merely put forward as true a number of statements. There is no evidence offered that any of these statements is true, nor does he draw any conclusions on the basis of these statements. (To say that he has offered no evidence is not, of course, to say that what he says is wrong or false.)

It is occasionally not clear whether a piece of discourse is an argument or a sequence of statements. Suppose a Republican member of congress is addressing a group of economists. She is quoted in a newspaper as saying:

> *Free trade between nations will be preserved. Foreign imports will not be tariffed.*

Her remarks—if we know nothing else about the context—can be interpreted as an argument or as two independently asserted statements. And if it is an argument, it can be interpreted two ways: with the first statement as evidence for the second ("Because free trade between nations will be preserved, foreign imports will not be tariffed"), and with the second statement as evidence for the first ("Since foreign imports will not be tariffed, free trade between nations will be preserved"). Which of the three interpretations is correct? The answer is that there is no way to decide *from an inspec-*

[6]Bryan Di Salvatore, "Vehement Fire," *The New Yorker*, April 27, 1987, p. 44.

tion of her words alone. Each interpretation is equally right—which is to say that we don't know if it is an argument.

Whether a piece of discourse is reasoning depends on its maker's intentions. Reasoning indicators can go far to establish what those intentions are. And the Republican member of congress who uttered those remarks may have had the intention to use one as a reason for the other. But the reason we don't know if those statements as they stand are reasoning is that this intention, if it was present, is nowhere in evidence. The statements can make sense interpreted as a piece of reasoning, but whether they should be so treated hangs on information about the legislator's intentions, information that is not available.

Moral: In your own speaking and writing, make clear whether you are giving argument, and what your premises and conclusion are.

1.6 Justification and Explanation

The distinction between justification and explanation is important, although notoriously hard to draw precisely. A **JUSTIFICATION** is an attempt to show that some statement is true by giving other statements in support of it. In effect, "justification" is synonymous with "argument." An **EXPLANATION** is an attempt to show why something happened. Most important, *explanations are not justifications, hence not arguments.*

Consider the following statement:

The pipes burst because the water froze.

Is it an argument? True, it does contain the term "because," which often functions as a reasoning indicator, but we already know that sometimes such appearances are deceiving. However, in saying that the pipes burst because the water froze I am merely making a statement. I have not justified my statement. Hence I have given no argument. I have merely advanced an explanation, which may or may not be true. Now, I may have reasoned toward my statement, but my statement *in itself* is merely a claim about a causal connection between the water's freezing and the pipes' bursting. I could, perhaps, produce evidence for it:

There was water in the pipes, and the pipes go very near an outside wall. It got down to zero last night. And water expands when frozen. So the pipes burst because the water froze.

And now I have produced a justification, i.e., an argument.

Here is a short newspaper item:

> *John B. Ford III, president and general manager of the Detroit Grand Opera Association, which has brought the Metropolitan Opera to Detroit each spring for the past 26 years, has warned association supporters that future Met visits are in jeopardy, and the Detroit association itself may dissolve.*
>
> *In a letter this week, Ford laid out the association's financial picture, and noted that the tour's marketability has declined because of "obscure or unpopular selections" and lack of big-name stars.*[7]

As John Guinn reports it, Mr. Ford does not make an inference. He states that the marketability of the Metropolitan Opera Tour has declined because of obscure and unpopular selections and lack of big-name stars. Mr. Ford probably has evidence that these are the reasons for the decline in the Met's marketability in Detroit, but this evidence is not given in this text. Therefore the text contains no piece of reasoning. Again, some reasoning could probably be given, perhaps something like this:

> *Whenever the Met has brought obscure or unpopular operas or operas without big-name stars, both ticket sales and donations have fallen off. And so we can see that the tour's marketability has declined because of such factors.*

Personal explanations—individuals' stated reasons why they do (or have done or will do) something—are not justifications. In his speech to the Athenian court, Socrates (as recounted by Plato) says this:

> *Someone may wonder why I go about in private giving advice and busying myself with the concerns of others, but do not venture to come forward in public and advise the state. I will tell you why. You have heard me speak at sundry times and in divers places of a superhuman oracle or sign which comes to me, and is the divinity which Meletus ridicules in the indictment. This sign, which is a kind of voice, first began to come to me when I was a child; from time to time it forbids me to do something which I am going to do, but never commands anything. This is what deters me from being a politician.*[8]

Socrates is not making any inferences. He is telling us his motives. He may have direct knowledge that these in fact are his motives. Or he may have inferred that these must be his motives (in a process similar to what you go through when you wonder, "Now why did I do that?"). In either event, there is no reasoning—no evidence—in the above passage. We might construct an argument that Socrates' explanation is correct. We might perhaps reason:

> *Socrates summed up his philosophy in the words, "Know thyself." We may therefore infer that he would have accurate self-knowledge of his motives. Besides, Socrates was known as honest and truthful. So when he says that*

[7] John Guinn, "Future Met visits are in jeopardy," *Detroit Free Press*, Feb. 21, 1985, p. 16A.

[8] Plato, *The Apology of Socrates*, trans. Jowett.

his motive for not serving the state is that he hears a superhuman oracle that forbids but never commands, we have good reason for believing that this is his motive.

The lesson to be drawn is that the term "because" is ambiguous. Sometimes it functions as a reasoning indicator—when "because" has the sense of "here is a reason or piece of evidence for something." Sometimes it functions as a causal or explanatory term—when "because" has the sense of "here is the cause or the explanation of something." Careful reading and judicious interpretation are sometimes required to tell the difference.

The problem with distinguishing justification from explanation is that each often takes the same form, for example,

A *because* B.

How can we tell whether a justification (an argument) is being given or whether an explanation is being stated? One rule of thumb is this: If the context is such that the truth of *A* is in question—I say to you "*A* because *B*" and it is apparent that you are not willing to grant the truth of *A* (I am trying to persuade you of the truth of *A*)—then "*A* because *B*" is a justification. But if the context is such that the truth of *A* is taken for granted—we both agree that *A* is true (so I can hardly be trying to persuade you of the truth of *A*)—then what I am doing is explaining why *A* is true.

Here is an illustration of this rule of thumb. I say to you:

New highways interrupt the natural drainage of wilderness land, thus creating new swamps.

Is it an explanation of why new swamps are turning up or a justification that new swamps are being created? (To put it another way: Is it an argument or not?)

Suppose we assume that you know that new swamps have been created (and I know that you know). Then I will in all likelihood be attempting to *explain why* new swamps have been created. I could hardly be attempting to justify my claim—to persuade you of its truth—if we both agree that it's true. On the other hand, suppose we assume that you do not know that new swamps have been created (and I know that you don't know this). Then I will in all likelihood be attempting to *justify* the statement that new swamps have been created.

How would we know in practice? Suppose the passage in question appears in this context:

The National Wildlife Service has recently produced statistics to show that the number of swamps is actually increasing. [New highways interrupt the natural drainage of wilderness land, thus creating new swamps.]

Now the passage in brackets looks most like an explanation, for the first sentence would appear to state that there is evidence for the truth of "new swamps are being created." Hence the second sentence is unlikely to be a justification that the statement is true. Suppose however that the passage in brackets appears in this context:

Usually when a population expands into wilderness areas, the effects are not good for the natural wildlife. But not always. [New highways interrupt the natural drainage of wilderness land, thus creating new swamps.]

Now it appears that the passage in brackets is a justification, i.e., an argument, for it looks like an attempt to persuade the reader of the truth that new highways create new swamps.

There is one other clue for distinguishing an explanation from an argument. This is what we might call a principle of charity. If something makes better sense as one than the other, read it in its best light. Someone says,

I've been taught since childhood that there is a heaven and a hell, and that's why I believe in heaven and hell.

Now this might be an *excellent explanation of why* I believe in heaven and hell. It is, however a *terrible justification that* my belief is true. (In fact, thinking it is a *good justification* will be discussed in Chapter 12 as a mistake in reasoning called the "Genetic Fallacy.")

Sometimes it will be clear whether a piece of discourse is either a justification or an explanation (or neither), but sometimes it will not. In exercises, where you are asked to decide between justification or explanation, it will occasionally be appropriate to answer "borderline." Keep in mind, though, that the basic question you want to ask is whether the best interpretation of a passage is that some statement is being used to prove the truth of some other statement. If so, it is a justification. If not, it isn't.

1.7 Reasoning in Context

Now that you know what an argument is, the next step is for you to be able to spot one. It is one thing for an argument to be highlighted as an example; it is another to pick one out of a larger context. This section will not teach you anything new. It will, however, give a few illustrations (with some discussion) of reasoning in larger contexts.

We will adopt this convention for present purposes. Brackets will mark the beginning and end of a piece of reasoning. As before, the conclusion of the argument will be underlined and any reasoning indicators circled.

Our first example comes from an article on the federal debt:

In 1979, despite widespread support for tax reductions, nearly two-thirds of those interviewed in a Gallup poll declared that they would willingly forgo a tax cut if that would help the federal government avoid incurring a larger deficit. [Since most people are quick to admit that they find the whole issue of

> *debts and deficits quite incomprehensible, it seems probable that much of the public abhorrence of them stems from the thrall exerted by vast numbers.]. . . Our national debt today comes to about six thousand dollars per person. . . .* [9]

Dr. Heilbroner begins with a statement about the results of a 1979 Gallup poll. He then introduces another statement—that most people quickly admit that they find the issue of debts and deficits incomprehensible—as the premise of an argument. From this premise, he deduces the conclusion that the public's abhorrence of deficits and debts comes from the fascination exerted by huge numbers. Dr. Heilbroner concludes with another statement—really an illustration of "vast numbers"—about what our national debt amounts to per person.

In this next example, we shall see how many statements are advanced before an argument is made. The issue concerns the Family Rights and Privacy Act, also called the Buckley Amendment. Among other things, the Buckley Amendment grants students the right to see their letters of recommendation, unless they explicitly waive their right. In her letter to the editor of the Proceedings and Addresses of the American Philosophical Association, Professor Diana Ackerman writes:

> *I think it clearly* is *good to enable people to know what information about them is officially recorded for use in decisions that can shape their whole professional futures. Arguments against access to one's recommendations, like arguments against access to one's own medical records, are a distressing mixture of presumptuous paternalism, self-interested desires to avoid arguments and explanations, and affirmation of one's supposed "inability" to deal professionally on an open and honest basis with the people one is writing about. I find these a pretty shabby bunch of reasons. But philosophers who disagree can always lobby for the Buckley Amendment to be repealed. This would be a far more honorable course than the current underhanded attempts to subvert it. Philosophers who respect students' rights, on the other hand, can make their letters available to students who do sign the waiver. [This is not dishonest, as the waiver says not that the student has not seen his letter, but merely that he waives his right to do so.]* [10]

Professor Ackerman begins by stating her belief that it is good to enable people to know certain information. Note that this belief is not supported by a reason. She proceeds to describe and disparage—not argue against—arguments that have been offered against access to letters of recommendation. She says that these arguments are "shabby," but does not say why—again, no argument. After suggesting a course of action for philosophers who respect students' rights (to allow students to see their letters of recommendation even if the students have waived their rights to see them), she gives an argument that this would not be dishonest. Her reason is that the waiver says merely that the student waives the right to see the letter, not that the student has not seen it.

[9] Robert Heilbroner, "The Deficit," *The New Yorker*, July 30, 1984, p. 47.

[10] *Proceedings of the American Philosophical Association*, May 1983, p. 729.

For our last example, here is a passage from a book on a very timely subject:

> *As we go along, I will be familiarizing you with Computerese. Computerese is so unique that it could rightly qualify as the world's 297th language. [It's a tough language to crack, too. So much of the jargon is defined by other jargon which is defined by still more jargon.] Sometimes it's eight and nine layers deep. Some of the Computerese words are used because they're accurate, specific, scientific terms. . . . Other terms are abstract and, at heart, meaningless.*[11]

You might be tempted to pick out "Computerese is so unique" or "Some of the Computerese words are used because they're accurate, specific, scientific terms" as pieces of reasoning—the former because it contains a semblance of a reasoning indicator ("so"), the latter because it has a "because." But "Computerese is so unique" is no more a piece of reasoning than "It rained so hard." The other is less obviously not an argument. But it seems best read as an explanation. Mr. McWilliams is just *stating* that some Computerese words are used because they're accurate, specific, scientific terms, but has presented no evidence that this explanation is correct. However, there is a justification of the statement that computerese is a tough language to crack given by the statement that so much of its jargon is defined by other jargon. So this passage contains an argument, even though within the argument there are no reasoning indicators.

KEY POINTS

An argument is any piece of discourse (any communication by speech or writing) in which evidence in the form of statements is given for the truth of another statement.

- Synonyms for argument include: reasoning, inference, justification, producing evidence, drawing consequences.
- Arguments serve three goals: They extend our knowledge; they persuade; they draw out consequences from assumptions (hypothetical reasoning).

A statement is what is expressed by language only when what is expressed can be either true or false. "All whales are mammals" is a statement; "Darn it!" is not.

- The statement or statements used as the basis for other statements is called the premise (or reason, evidence, what's given, the assumptions).

[11] Peter A. McWilliams, *The Word Processing Book* (Los Angeles: Prelude Press, 1982), p. 27.

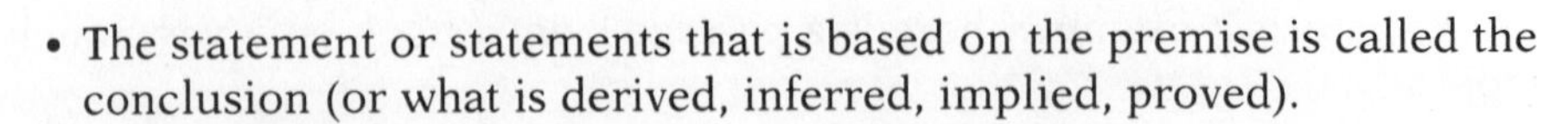

- The statement or statements that is based on the premise is called the conclusion (or what is derived, inferred, implied, proved).
- Every argument must contain at least two statements, one functioning as the premise, the other as the conclusion.
- Not all statements are expressed by declarative sentences. Sometimes rewriting is required.
- Not all statements in a passage that contains an argument are part of the argument.
- Conjunctions (e.g., "and") make separate statements.
- Disjunctions (e.g., "or") and conditionals (e.g., "if. . . then") do not assert separately or individually their parts.
- In particular, a simple conditional is not in itself an argument.

Often, although not always, an argument contains reasoning indicators. A reasoning indicator is a term or terms that appears before statements in arguments, and tells the reader or hearer which statements are premises or which are conclusions.

- Not everything that looks like a reasoning indicator is one.
- Not all arguments contain reasoning indicators.

A justification is an attempt to show that some statement is true by giving some other statement(s) in support of it. An explanation is an attempt to show why something happened.

- Explanations are not arguments.
- Context determines whether a piece of discourse is an explanation or a justification (or neither).
- One rule of thumb for determining whether an explanation or a justification is being given is this. If the truth of something is at issue, it is probably being justified. If the truth of something is taken for granted, it is probably being explained.
- Another rule of thumb for distinguishing justification from explanation is the principle of charity. If something makes better sense as an explanation than as a justification, read it as an explanation.

EXERCISES

A. Answer these questions. Some multiple choice questions have more than one right answer. Circle ALL correct answers.

A1. Which of these is *not* a purpose of argument?

- **a.** To extend knowledge
- **b.** To persuade someone else
- **c.** To draw out the consequences of accepting some statement(s)
- **d.** To see what the facts add up to
- **e.** To get your own way

A2. Which of these does *not* (at least roughly) mean "premise"?

- **a.** Reason
- **b.** Evidence
- **c.** What is inferred
- **d.** What is assumed
- **e.** The first statement(s) in an argument

A3. Which of these does *not* (at least roughly) mean "a piece of reasoning"?

- **a.** Argument
- **b.** The drawing of an inference
- **c.** Seeing what follows
- **d.** Criticizing

A4. A conditional:

- **a.** is not itself an argument
- **b.** can be the premise of an argument
- **c.** can be the conclusion of an argument

A5. "Everyone wants to reduce the federal budget, yet no one is willing to make sacrifices" is:

- **a.** a disjunction
- **b.** an argument
- **c.** a conjunction
- **d.** a conditional
- **e.** none of the above (we haven't covered it yet)

A6. Write "P" if the term is a premise indicator, "C" if it is a conclusion indicator, and "N" if it is neither:

- ***a.** If ___*N*___
- ***b.** Because ___*P*___
- **c.** Since ______
- **d.** Accordingly ______
- **e.** It follows that ______
- **f.** All ______
- **g.** I will prove that ______
- **h.** Whereas ______
- **i.** The evidence is ______
- **j.** No one cares that ______
- **k.** Or ______
- **l.** Thus ______
- **m.** I conclude that ______
- **n.** Assuming ______
- **o.** It is false that ______

A7. The *premise* of "He bought steak and potatoes. That means that he'll be cooking tonight" is:

- **a.** "He bought steak."
- **b.** "He bought potatoes."
- **c.** "He'll be cooking tonight."
- **d.** None of the above.

A8. The *conclusion* of "He just shaved his beard. If you want to see him, look in the den" is:

- **a.** "He just shaved his beard."
- **b.** "You want to see him."
- **c.** "Look in the den."
- **d.** "If you want to see him, look in the den."
- **e.** None of the above.

A9. "The milk spoiled because you left it out" isn't a piece of reasoning because:

- **a.** We don't know whether you really did leave it out.
- **b.** "Because" is never a reasoning indicator.
- **c.** It's an explanation.
- **d.** This is a trick question. It is a piece of reasoning.

A10. A mistake in reasoning shows:

- **a.** You haven't really reasoned at all.
- **b.** The argument you made is not good.
- **c.** A tragic flaw in character.

PRESTON MINI MARKET

34 PRESTON ROAD
BRIGHTON
M**62190 TID****0240
AID : A0000000031010
VISADEBIT

VISA DEBIT

ICC PAN SEQ 00

SALE

CARDHOLDER COPY

PLEASE KEEP THIS RECEIPT
FOR YOUR RECORDS

AMOUNT 131.98

Verified by PIN

THANK YOU
23:02 30/12/18

AUTH CODE: 399329

PRESTON MINI MARKET
34 PRESTON ROAD
BRIGHTON
M**62190 TID****0240
AID : A0000000031010
VISADEBIT
VISA DEBIT
**** **** **** 0178
ICC PAN.SEQ 00

SALE
CARDHOLDER COPY
PLEASE KEEP THIS RECEIPT
FOR YOUR RECORDS

AMOUNT £31.98
Verified by PIN
THANK YOU
23:02 30/12/18
AUTH CODE: 399329

B. Using "Federal deficits are high" as the premise and "Interest rates will continue to rise" as the conclusion, write the argument five different ways, using five different argument indicators.

***B1.** *Because federal deficits are high, interest rates will continue to rise.*

B2.

B3.

B4.

B5.

C. For each of the following:

(1) Answer "Argument" or "Not an argument" or "Can't tell."

(2) Be prepared to justify your answer. For example, if you say it is not an argument, is this because it is a mere sequence of statements? Because it is a causal or explanatory statement? Because the context leaves it ambiguous?

(3) If it is an argument, circle any reasoning indicators and underline its conclusion.

***C1.** If oxen and horses had hands, and could paint with their hands, and produce works of art as men do, horses would paint the forms of the gods like horses, and oxen like oxen, and make their bodies in the image of their several kinds. (Xenophanes)

Not an argument. Just a statement (a conditional).

C2. Unemployment will increase. Taxes are bound to go up.

C3. May reasoned that she was bound to be promoted soon.

C4. May is bound to be promoted soon in view of the fact that she is doing such excellent work.

C5. Failing to vote in an election is just as much a choice as voting for a particular candidate.

C6. The governor is going to help the farmers because he told them so in his speech last night.

C7. Reason does not influence actions; only emotion does.

C8. A tree falling in the wilderness with nobody around to hear it will make no sound. There can be no auditory sensation unless there is a perceiver to have it.

C9. Only pure studies in form have true artistic worth. So landscape paintings, for example, do not have true artistic worth.

C10. A massage after exercise feels wonderful. There's nothing like it in the world.

C11. Business is good for Widgets, Inc. Their sales so far this year are 25 percent higher than last year at this time.

C12. Joe is rich, smart, and handsome, whereas his friend Jim is poor, dumb, and ugly.

***C13.** Whereas Mr. Jones is incompetent to manage his own affairs, the court will appoint a legal guardian.

Argument

C14. Judy cannot swim as fast as Joan.

C15. As there seems to be a consensus on the matter, I hereby adjourn the meeting.

C16. Whenever he gets drunk, he loses his money.

C17. He's drunk again. I guess this means that he'll lose his money.

C18. Nobody knows the trouble I've seen. And nobody cares.

C19. Creationists cannot account for all the physical facts. But neither can Evolutionists.

C20. Evolution is a scientific theory because it is testable in a laboratory.

C21. Because inflation is down, interest rates will keep steady or decline.

C22. If you are in the market for a car, then buy now; for interest rates will go up soon.

C23. Joe argued that interest rates will keep steady or decline. Jane argued that interest rates are bound to go up.

C24. It is unfair to allow students to take tests late, for they would have more time to study than students who took the tests on time.

C25. Socialism is inefficient in view of the fact that it encourages laziness.

C26. Since there are laws of logic, correct reasoning is not a matter of "what sounds right."

C27. If aspirin upsets your stomach, you should avoid taking it. So, if you have a headache, try a non-aspirin pain reliever.

C28. Without a government, everyone would be constantly at war with everyone else. It follows that government is necessary for peaceful living.

C29. Music cannot depict particular situations, events, locales, or characters. This proves that music cannot tell a story.

C30. Music cannot tell a story. So don't try to find one when you listen to it.

C31. In 1957, among the thirty-three nations that chose not to exercise the death penalty, the number of murders never increased. Thus, capital punishment simply does not appear to serve as a deterrent. (Norman Mailer)

C32. Since the planets are seen at varying distances from the earth, the earth is not the center of their orbit. (Copernicus)

C33. Killing a person is immoral, so abortion is immoral.

C34. A three-month-old fetus is not a person. Surely you would agree.

***C35.** Even if you do not have the cash to pay your bills you are still responsible for paying them. Responsibility for debts is not contingent on your ability to pay them.

Most likely an argument.

D. The following contain statements that are expressed in nonstandard ways: by mere phrases, rhetorical questions, etc.

(1) If any of the following is an argument, rewrite it in straightforward indicative sentences in some straightforward way, like "*Premise*, therefore *Conclusion*" or "*Conclusion* because *Premise*." Underline the conclusion.

(2) If it is not an argument, just say so and say why it isn't.

***D1.** Of course he's guilty. Didn't he admit that he threatened to kill her? (Example due to Monroe Beardsley)

Argument. He's guilty because he admitted that he threatened to kill her.

D2. Given the general prevalence of violence, governments will have to become stronger or suffer collapse.

D3. Noise at night in your apartment means eviction for you.

D4. Can you really expect me to pass you? You cheated on the exam!

***D5.** [Wayne] Williams's appeal from his life sentence is heading toward the U.S. Supreme Court, which has not recently been an abounding reservoir of hope for the criminally convicted. His case, all the same, remains under judicial review, a circumstance that would have made a five-hour broadcast proclaiming his guilt altogether disgraceful. *The Atlanta Child Murders* conveys an impression of Williams's innocence without being bold enough to affirm it; and, given that redeeming aspect, it cannot be called any worse than relatively disgraceful. (Murray Kempton, "Misjudgment at Atlanta," a review of the CBS docu-drama, *The Atlanta Child Murders,* in *The New York Review of Books,* March 14, 1985, p. 31.)

Contains this argument: Given that The Atlanta Child Murders *conveys an impression of Williams's innocence without being bold enough to affirm it, it cannot be called any worse than relatively disgraceful.*

D6. Your mother says she loves your father, so why does she have contempt for men who remind her of him? Her feelings are mixed. (Sonya Friedman, *Men Are Just Desserts.* New York: Warner Books, 1983, p. 51.)

D7. According the G'Zells [a couple who surgically changed a goat into a 'unicorn'], the unicorn is neither a single species nor a mere myth, but the product of a 'lost art' they've discovered—and even patented. But many animal lovers are not mollified. ASPCA leaders have called for a detailed disclosure of exactly how the operation is performed—and have promised to lobby for a federal law prohibiting the public display of altered beasts. 'Where do we draw the line? If humans mutilate animals for cheap thrills,' fumes ASPCA director John Kullberg, 'What's to stop us from playing around with eye sockets and making a Cyclops?' ("A Unicorn—Or a Goat?" *Newsweek,* April 22, 1985, p. 32.)

E. Here are some longer pieces of discourse. If any contains an argument or arguments, then: bracket the beginning and end of the argument, circle any argument indicators, and underline the conclusion. If a discourse contains no arguments, say so.

E1. Song and dancing were parts of the worship of the Greek gods. Contests in music and poetry were held at the shrine of Apollo in Delphi. Civic festivals with 'games' were similarly developed, notably the festival of Athena at Athens. And all these contests were means of gaining honor. (John A. Garraty and Peter Gay, eds., *The Columbia History of the World.* New York: Harper & Row, 1972, p. 149.)

***E2.** The Fisher Space Pen with its sealed pressurized ink cartridge was selected by NASA (after rigorous testing) for use on all manned Apollo flights because it is the only pen that will write satisfactorily in the gravity-free void, the blazing heat, the freezing cold of Outer Space. Fisher Space Pens were actually used extensively by the Astronauts on all flights to the Moon. They were also purchased by the Russian Government and used by the Cosmonauts on the Soyuz 3, 4, and 5 flights.

[Nitrogen-powered, the ink in the replaceable Space Pen cartridge is positively fed to the tungsten carbide ball by gas pressurized at 50 p.s.i. (So) it will write at any angle, even up, without pumping.] It starts to write instantly, as soon as the ball starts rolling, and won't skip no matter how fast you write. [It is also the cleanest ball pen ever developed (because) virtually no excess ink ever escapes its high-precision stainless steel socket.] (Advertising brochure with Fisher Space Pen)

Note: The first sentence, "The Fisher Space Pen with its sealed pressurized ink cartridge was selected by NASA (after rigorous testing) for use on all manned Apollo flights because it is the only pen that will write satisfactorily in the gravity-free void, the blazing heat, the freezing cold of Outer Space," despite the fact that it contains a "because," seems best interpreted as an explanation *of why the pen was selected by NASA, not a justification (i.e., not an argument).*

E3. 'People say, how come he's not angry, and bitter, and mad, and accusatory, and I'm not because all those things are negative,' said Beckham, 37. 'There's nothing you can do about the past. You can only affect the future.' (From an article by Larry Olmstead in the *Detroit Free Press,* September 2, 1984.)

E4. Proteins are burned for energy if the diet does not supply enough calories from carbohydrates and fats. Thus, you can gain weight from eating excess calories in the form of protein just as from eating too many carbohydrates or fats. But eating more protein than your body requires is economically unwise: foods that provide primarily carbohydrates or fats are cheaper sources of calories. (Tim Davis, "Facts About Fast Food," *Consumers' Research,* August 1984, p. 13.)

E5. Television advertising by MCI repeatedly urges telephone users to begin saving "5% to 40%, even 50%" on long distance bills. Some long-distance customers are finding ways to save even more. They simply are walking away from their bills altogether. (Bob Woletz, "Money Rolling Out," *Forbes*, September 10, 1984, p. 142.)

E6. [Frank] Harvey [an American journalist in Vietnam] saw the war in straightforward terms: 'The United States is presently a world leader and I believe we intend to keep it that way. . . . We are prepared to fight, if necessary, to hold onto what we've got and get more. In Vietnam. In South America. Anywhere.'

Reporting like this had been quite adequate in the Second World War, where the issues were more clearly discernible. Vietnam was a new kind of war and required a new kind of war correspondent. It was an interdisciplinary war, where complex political issues intruded on the military aspects, where battle success was necessary but where battle success alone was insufficient, a war where unwarranted optimism, propaganda, and news management could deeply obscure the issue. (Philip Knightly, *The First Casualty*, New York: Harcourt Brace Jovanovich, 1975, pp. 385–386.)

E7. For nearly two decades millions of late-night television addicts have watched with hypnotic fascination as Ronco Teleproducts super-hyped its wares. Who can forget the fast-talk commercials for the Pocket Fisherman, the Smokeless Ashtray or the venerable (It slices! It dices!) Veg-O-Matic? (*Newsweek*, Feb. 13, 1984, p. 174.)

E8. Advertising exists only to purvey what people don't need. Whatever people do need they will find without advertising if it is available. This is so obvious and simple that it continues to stagger my mind that the ad industry has succeeded in muddying the point. (Jerry Mander, *Four Arguments for the Elimination of Television*, New York: William Morrow & Co., 1978, p. 126.)

E9. Anyone who has ever giggled himself into the hiccups knows how the initial giddiness turns to annoyance at the body's uncontrollable rebellion —and how, after not very long, annoyance can give way to the worry that they may never end. No one on earth knows more about this alarming state of mind than 92-year-old Charles Osborne of Anthon, Iowa. One November day in 1922, on a farm near Union, Nebraska, while helping lift a 350-pound hog, Osborne began to hiccup. He hasn't stopped since. (*Newsweek*, Feb. 18, 1985, p. 12.)

E10. To many well-informed contemporaries [in 1793] it was only a question of time before the French would be defeated, the Republic overthrown, and the monarchy restored. That this did not happen was due above all to the lack of unity among the allies. Indeed, Prussia and Austria were busy with the partitioning of Poland in 1793 and 1795 when they should have been concentrating on the defeat of France, and so it turned out that Poland helped to save the French Republic. (John A. Garraty and Peter Gay, eds., *The Columbia History of the World,* New York: Harper & Row, 1972, p. 769.)

F. Find one clear instance of an argument in a source other than this textbook. Look in the daily newspaper, magazines, nonfiction, other textbooks, etc. Copy it verbatim, circle any argument indicators, underline its conclusion, and rewrite it, if necessary, to display its premise(s) and conclusion(s) as declarative sentences.

CHAPTER 2

ARGUMENT DIAGRAMS

The simplest structure of an argument is one statement as premise, and another as conclusion. But reasoning can be quite complicated, involving multiple premises and conclusions. The notational device of the first chapter—underlining the conclusion—is inadequate for showing the structure of complicated arguments. To be in the best position to apply the rules of logic to evaluate arguments, it is often helpful to analyze arguments into their simplest components. Divide and conquer, as the saying goes. This chapter will teach you a diagrammatic method of doing this to arguments. These are the most important concepts in this chapter:

THE BASIC STRUCTURE

DEPENDENT REASONS
especially in contrast with. . .

INDEPENDENT REASONS

SIMPLE ARGUMENTS
especially in contrast with. . .

COMPOUND ARGUMENTS

DIVERGENT CONCLUSIONS
especially in contrast with. . .

CHAIN ARGUMENTS

2.1
The Basic Structure

The simplest structure an argument can have is one statement as premise and one other as conclusion. The most basic argument diagram, then, is this:

Premise

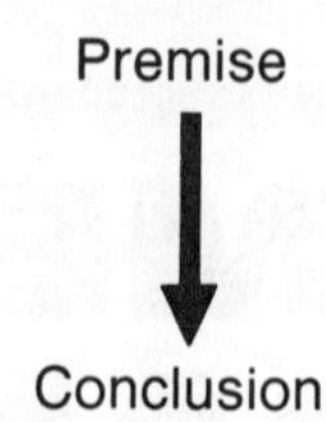

Conclusion

The arrowhead points *from* the premise *to* the conclusion. The correct diagram of the following example (the conclusion is underlined and any reasoning indicators are circled),

Since there are icicles hanging from the roof, it is cold outside.

is this:

There are icicles hanging from the roof.

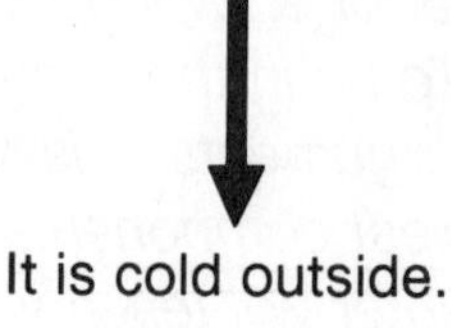

It is cold outside.

but *not* this:

It is cold outside.

There are icicles hanging from the roof.

The second misrepresents which statement is functioning as the premise. The direction of the arrow is crucial in argument diagrams. We can call this the FULL TREATMENT DIAGRAM.

There is another way of doing argument diagrams, which involves bracketing and numbering the statements so as to avoid having to rewrite all the statements.

Since (1) ⟨there are icicles hanging from the roof⟩, (2) ⟨it is cold outside⟩.

Having numbered the component statements, we can more easily do the argument diagram:

(1)

(2)

We'll call this the SHORT-CUT METHOD.

Both methods say the same thing. The full treatment is useful when some component of an argument needs to be rewritten:

Given her broken arm, she couldn't have lifted it.

This example would be best accorded the full treatment:

She had a broken arm.

She couldn't have lifted it.

There are other occasions when the full treatment is preferable: when arguments are complicated and it would be better to see their component statements displayed. We will slip in and out of the full treatment as the occasion demands.

Since the argument diagram in effect takes the place of reasoning indicators, you should not include them in your diagram. Also, circling the reasoning indicators and underlining the conclusion will now be optional, since the argument diagram does the same task. Neither should you include any remarks and asides that are not, strictly speaking, part of the inference. This example,

On the whole, forasmuch as certain of the lower animals also dream, it may be concluded that dreams are not sent by God.[1]

can be diagramed like this:

Certain of the lower animals also dream.

Dreams are not sent by God.

These are the only portions of the discourse that actually exhibit the reasoning. The other portions are, for our purposes, irrelevant. You have an alter-

[1]Aristotle, "On Prophesying by Dreams," trans. J. I. Beare.

native of putting aside the irrelevant parts in numbering your statements in a short-cut diagram:

> *On the whole forasmuch as (1) ⟨certain of the lower animals also dream,⟩ it may be concluded that (2) ⟨dreams are not sent by God.⟩*

And your diagram is simply:

2.2 Dependent and Independent Reasons

There can be more than one reason given for a conclusion. But reasons can "fit together" differently. Here are two examples:

> Example A. *Going over 55 m.p.h. is against the law and you shouldn't go against the law. So you shouldn't go over 55 m.p.h.*

> Example B. *Going over 55 m.p.h. is against the law. Besides, it's unsafe. So you shouldn't go over 55 m.p.h.*

The examples are superficially similar, but there is a difference between them. Example A contains dependent reasons; Example B contains independent reasons.

Reasons are **DEPENDENT** when together they make the overall strength of the argument MUCH GREATER than they would considered separately. Example A, whose reasons are dependent, should be diagramed like this (remember that you can treat conjunctions as separate statements):

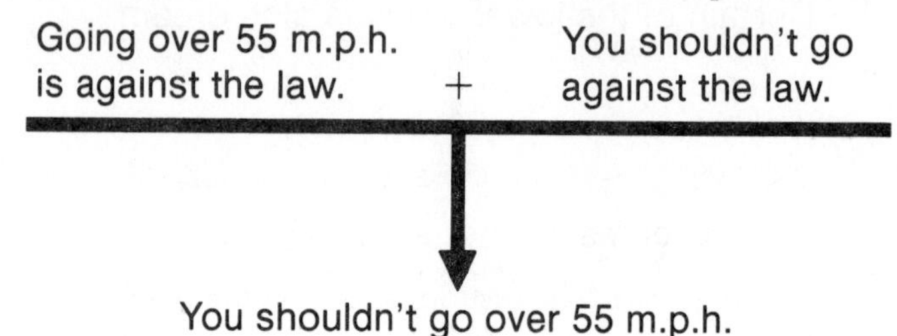

Reasons are **INDEPENDENT** when together they DO NOT make the overall strength of the argument much greater than they would considered separately. Example B contains independent reasons, and should be diagramed like this:

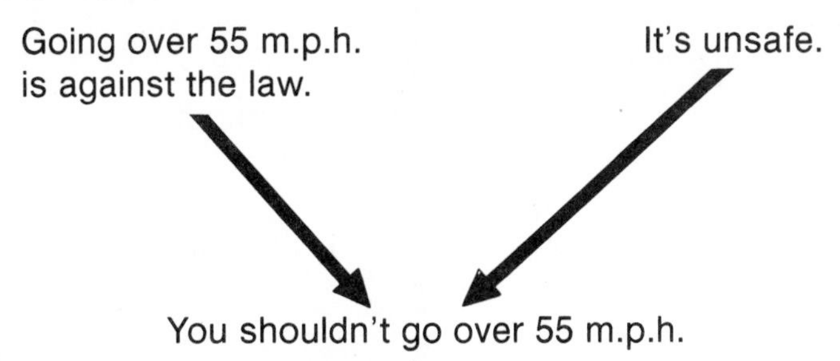

There are other ways of characterizing the dependent/independent reason distinction. Reasons are DEPENDENT when they:

- fill in each other's logical gaps (i.e., support each other)
- are in the same line of thought
- present one unified piece of reasoning (i.e., form one argument).

Notice that Example A contains reasons that exhibit these signs of dependent reasons. The reasons in Example A are "Going over 55 m.p.h. is against the law" and "You shouldn't go against the law." These fill in each other's logical gaps, they are in the same line of thought, and they present one unified argument. In fact, it is this last feature that is shown when dependent reasons are diagramed with one arrow. Reasons are INDEPENDENT when they:

- do not fill in each other's logical gaps (i.e., do not support each other)
- are not in the same line of thought
- present separate pieces of reasoning (i.e., form more than one argument).

The reasons in Example B are independent: "Going over 55 m.p.h. is against the law" and "It's unsafe" do not fill in each other's logical gaps, they are not in the same line of thought, and they present two arguments (hence each independent reason has its own arrow to show it as a separate inference).

Independent reasons could be put on two separate diagrams, for they are really two arguments. That is, Example B could (with additional work) be diagramed like this:

Going over 55 m.p.h. is against the law.

↓

You shouldn't go over 55 m.p.h.

AND

[Going over 55 m.p.h.] is unsafe.

↓

You shouldn't go over 55 m.p.h.

This brings us to another characterization of pieces of reasoning: some are simple and some are compound. **SIMPLE ARGUMENTS** contain one inference, i.e., one arrow. **COMPOUND ARGUMENTS** are pieces of reasoning that contain more than one simple argument, and thus contain more than one inference, i.e., have more than one arrow. Example A is a simple argument; Example B is compound. We could combine these two examples and produce another compound argument:

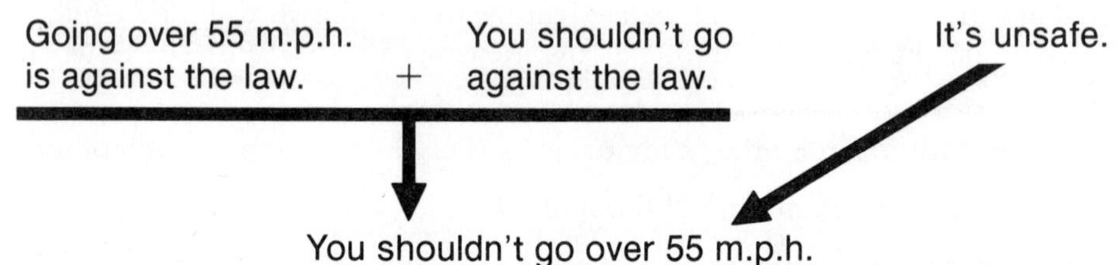

This is a compound argument, composed of two simple arguments. Each simple argument is identified by its arrow.

For another example of the dependent/independent distinction, consider this case. You are involved in determining the color of crows. You see crow after crow, and each of them is black. Let's suppose you observe 100 crows. You then engage in a piece of reasoning that goes something like this:

> *Crow #1 is black. Crow #2 is black. . . . Crow #100 is black. So all crows are black.*

Now each of these reasons supports each other, each is in the same line of thought, and together they present one unified piece of reasoning. But most important, together they make the argument much stronger than each considered independently. That one crow is black gives only the slightest reason to think that all crows are black. If these were independent reasons, we would have 100 separate inferences, each from a single crow's being black to all crows' being black—and each would offer only the slightest reason to believe the conclusion. But together—considering all 100 observations

—we have much better evidence for "All crows are black." So these reasons are dependent:

Crow #1 is black + Crow #2 is black + . . . + Crow #100 is black.

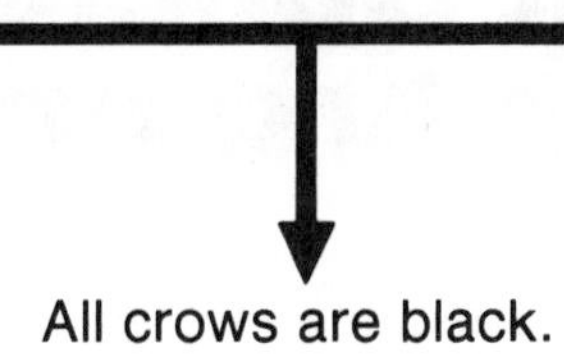

All crows are black.

But if we were to introduce another piece of evidence of a different kind, a statement that does not fill in logical gaps in our observations, we would have a compound argument. Suppose we argued as follows:

> *Crow #1 is black. Crow #2 is black. . . . Crow #100 is black. In addition, the encyclopedia tells me that all crows are black. So all crows are black.*

We would diagram it like this:

Crow #1 is black.

\+

Crow #2 is black.

\+

. . .

\+

Crow #100 is black.

The encyclopedia tells me that all crows are black.

All crows are black.

This is a compound argument with premises, 100 of which are dependent and one of which is independent (from the others).

It is important to remember that premises that are linked conceptually can still be independent. In this example,

> *(1) ⟨It will enhance your job prospects if you have basic computer skills.⟩ Besides, (2) ⟨jobs in computers pay well.⟩ Therefore (3) ⟨you should learn to use a computer.⟩*

the premises seem more conceptually related than, say, the crow observations and the encyclopedia information of the preceding example, but they are still independent, for they do not make the argument much stronger considered together than they would considered separately. Therefore they ought to be diagramed like this:

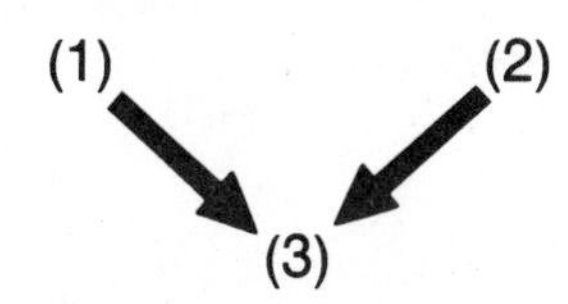

2.3 Divergent Conclusions and Chain Arguments

Arguments can have more than one conclusion, just as they can have more than one premise. And multiple conclusions can be related to each other in one of two ways.

We'll begin again with two clear examples:

Example C. *He's drunk again. This means he won't be at work. Moreover, he won't be fit to talk to.*

Example D. *He's drunk again. This means he won't be at work, and therefore won't be able to pay his bills.*

Example C advances two conclusions on the basis of one reason. Furthermore, its conclusions are divergent. Two (or more) conclusions are **DIVERGENT** when each is inferred separately from the same premises. The way to diagram an argument with divergent conclusions is this:

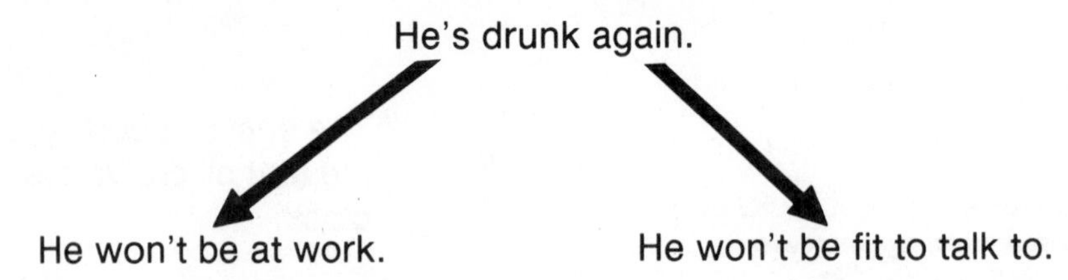

This diagram says: From the premise, "He's drunk again," the arguer has inferred two separate statements: "He won't be at work" and "He won't be fit to talk to." This is a compound argument, and could, with a little more effort, be diagramed like this:

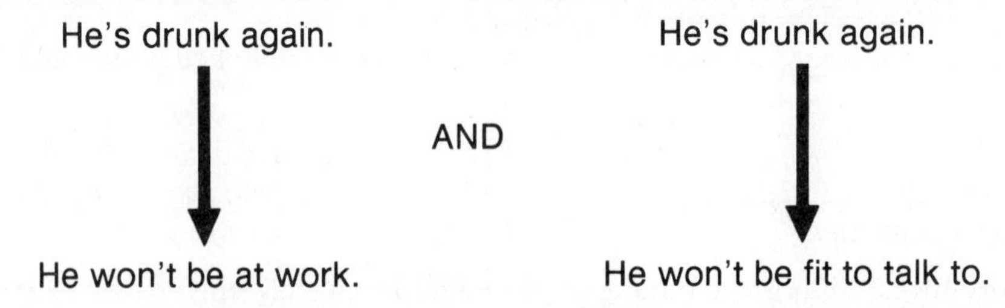

Example D is different. It is a chain argument. In a **CHAIN ARGUMENT**, one conclusion is advanced on the basis of premise(s), and that conclusion is then used as the reason for yet another conclusion. We can represent Example D this way:

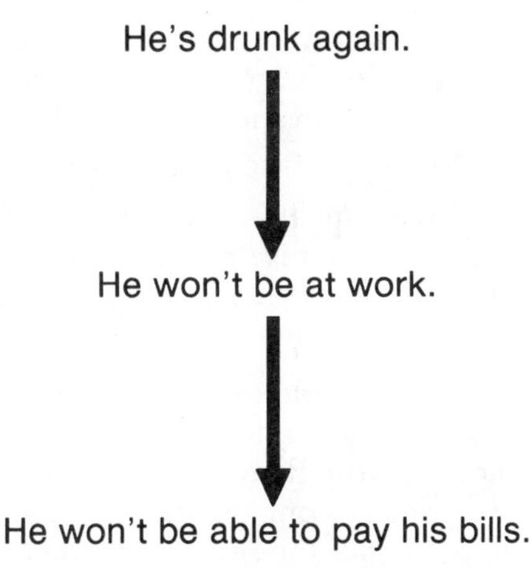

This says: From the premise "He's drunk again," the reasoner has drawn one conclusion, "He won't be at work," and then has used this conclusion as the reason for yet another statement, "He won't be able to pay his bills." It is a compound argument and could be written like this:

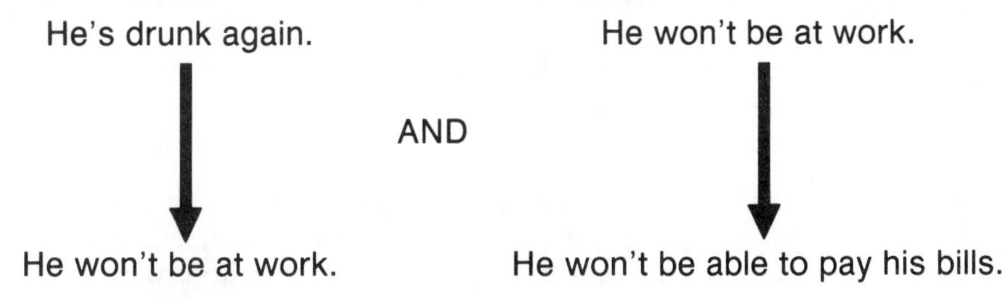

2.4 Strategies and Practice in Diagraming

The preceding discussions canvassed all the structures pieces of reasoning may exhibit. Most of the examples were fairly straightforward. Unfortunately, real-life arguments often do not wear their structure on their sleeves. Some strategizing and practice are required to diagram them correctly. It also sometimes happens that the structure of an argument is ambiguous, and you should be cautioned that in such cases there may be no single correct diagram. We will work through some more complicated examples in this section. First, however, here are some strategies in diagraming an argument:

- Make sure you are dealing with a piece of reasoning. Doing a diagram of some piece of discourse says that it is an argument. Diagraming a nonargument is therefore a mistake.
- If you are dealing with an argument, it is best to find its conclusions first. If it helps, circle any reasoning indicators. If there is more than

one conclusion, ask yourself whether one of the conclusions is advanced on the basis of another (then it is a chain argument) or whether each conclusion is advanced separately (in which case the conclusions are divergent).

- When you've located the conclusion(s), you may assume that some of what's left over is/are the premise(s). Determine how the premises are related to each other. Are some dependent on one another? Are some independent of one another? Is there a mixture of both?
- Remember that you may separate statements that are conjoined together, but you may not separate statements that are disjunctions or conditionals. In fact, it is usually best to separate conjunctions: If you do not, and keep reasons or conclusions "and-ed" together, you may be unable to display whether the reasons are dependent or independent, or whether the conclusions are divergent or chain together.
- Keep in mind that, as in interpreting whether a piece of discourse is an argument, you are trying to get at the reasoner's intentions. What is the best way, given the evidence available to you, of representing the structure of the arguer's thought? Usually there is an answer, although sometimes an argument's structure is ambiguous. Be guided by charity: Interpret an argument to be the best the words allow.
- Remember that not everything that is said during a piece of reasoning belongs to the reasoning as such. Extraneous remarks, asides, and other irrelevant comments should be omitted in an argument diagram. Remember, too, that the arrows take the place of reasoning indicators, and so do not include the reasoning indicators in the diagram.

We will work our way through some examples. Here's our first:

Your mother says she loves your father, so why does she have contempt for men who remind her of him? Her feelings are mixed.[2]

You must locate the conclusion first. Ask yourself: What statement is being justified in this argument? It is, "Her [i.e., your mother's] feelings are mixed." What of the two remaining statements? They are evidence for the conclusion, i.e., they are the premises of this argument. But how are they related to each other—dependently or independently? They are dependent, since together they produce a much stronger argument than each does considered alone. Further, since one of the premises is in the form of a question, we should use the full treatment method to display all premises as declarative statements. The diagram:

[2]Sonya Friedman, *Men Are Just Desserts* (New York: Warner Books, 1983), p. 51.

Your mother says she loves your father. + She has contempt for men who remind her of him.

↓

Her feelings are mixed.

The hardest part of this diagraming problem is to decide whether the premises are independent or dependent. Sometimes you can check your work by reading the diagram back to yourself to see if your diagram captures the intent of the argument. Suppose you diagramed the premises *incorrectly* as independent:

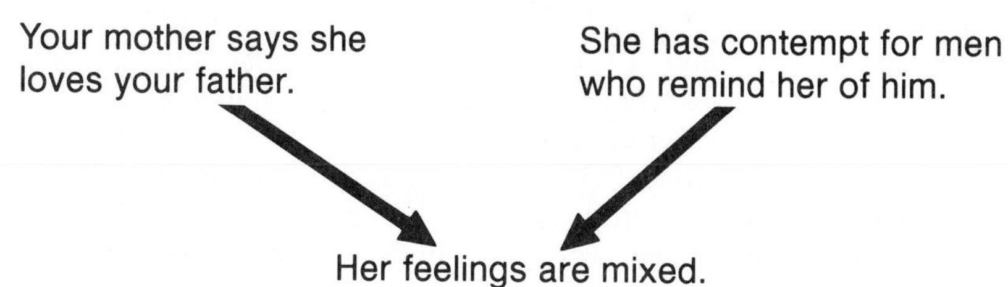

Now you have a compound argument with two simple arguments. One of its simple arguments says:

Your mother says she loves your father.

↓

Her feelings are mixed.

But this is nonsensical: It would be irrational to conclude that your mother's feelings are mixed from the premise that she loves your father! Since diagraming the premises as independent produces a sub-argument that was in all likelihood not intended by its author, you can see that you are dealing with dependent premises.

Next we will deal with a passage that contains multiple separate arguments: Sherlock Holmes's reasoning (quoted in Chapter 1). As the statements here are straightforward, we can use the short-cut method, and so we'll number them right off:

> *"(1) ⟨You have come in by train this morning, I see.⟩"*
>
> *"(2) ⟨You know me, then?⟩"*
>
> *"No, but (3) ⟨I observe the second half of a return ticket in the palm of your left glove.⟩ (4) ⟨You must have started early⟩ and yet (5) ⟨you had a good drive in a dog-cart, along heavy roads, before you reached the station.⟩"*
>
> *(6) ⟨The lady gave a violent start, and stared in bewilderment at my companion.⟩*

> *"(7) ⟨There is no mystery, my dear madam,⟩" said he, smiling. "(8) ⟨The left arm of your jacket is spattered with mud in no less than seven places.⟩ (9) ⟨The marks are perfectly fresh.⟩ (10) ⟨There is no vehicle save a dog-cart which throws up mud in that way, and then only when you sit on the left-hand side of the driver.⟩"*[3]

First, Holmes makes this inference:

Notice that (2) is irrelevant to the *inference* (although not to the style of writing, in which Conan Doyle often presents Holmes's audience as being startled by his powers of reasoning).

The reader might wonder why we numbered statement (2) if it, in the end, does not figure in the diagram. If you knew in advance that (2) is irrelevant, you could have simply ignored it. The point is that since the numbering of statements will usually be done before the diagram, you will sometimes end up rejecting statements that you already numbered. This remark also applies to statements (6) and (7).

Next, Holmes embarks on another piece of reasoning: an attempt to justify (4) and (5). Here again you should look at the various statements to see which are actually playing a role in the argument (i.e., which are really being presented as evidence). Statements (6) and (7) are there for "literary" value, for neither of them give any "facts." Holmes's evidence for (4) and (5) is really (8), (9), and (10). However, we have to determine the internal structure among all these statements. Notice first that (4) claims that the woman started early, while (5) claims that she took a dog-cart. There is separable evidence for each of these statements. (8) and (10) form evidence for (5) but not for (4). (She could have started late and still had those same mud spatters.) The evidence for (4) is that the marks are fresh, i.e., statement (9). Yet (9) is not disconnected from the rest of the argument, for we must also join it to the fact that these mud spatters are from her ride in the dog-cart. The complete diagram of the second argument:

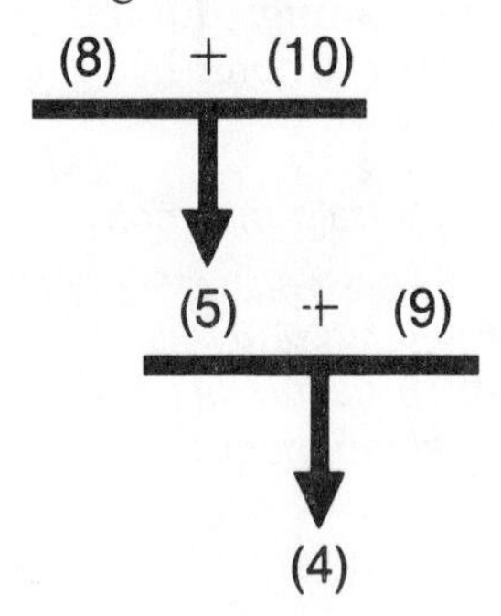

[3]Sir Arthur Conan Doyle, "The Adventure of the Speckled Band."

Here is another argument from Chapter 1. This, too, lends itself to the short-cut method, and so we'll begin by numbering its statements (and circling the one reasoning indicator):

> *(1) ⟨Much of the early research in which the [IQ] scores of Blacks were compared to the existing norms is misleading.⟩ (2) ⟨For example, the average IQ of Black schoolchildren from Florida, Georgia, Alabama, Tennessee, and South Carolina was found to be 80.7, while the norms of White children* nationwide *is 100.⟩ (3) ⟨However, White schoolchildren from the same five southeastern states were not tested at that time, although it is known that the average IQ for Whites in that region is lower than the national average.⟩ Therefore, (4) ⟨it is an abuse of statistics to argue, as many have, that such data are evidence for a 16- to 20-point difference between Blacks and Whites.⟩*[4]

The best first step is to find the conclusion. There is a conclusion indicator preceding (4), and (4) is *a* conclusion; but also look at (1). (1) seems to be a conclusion too, for it appears to be justified by what follows. We will momentarily postpone the question of just how (1) and (4) are related to each other, but now that we know (1) and (4) are conclusions we can begin to see that (2) and (3) are evidence for statements (1) and (4). So what we now know is that (2) and (3) will appear above and pointing to (1) and (4). Concentrate on the relation between (2) and (3). They are dependent, for together they make the argument much stronger than each considered independently. Thus we have:

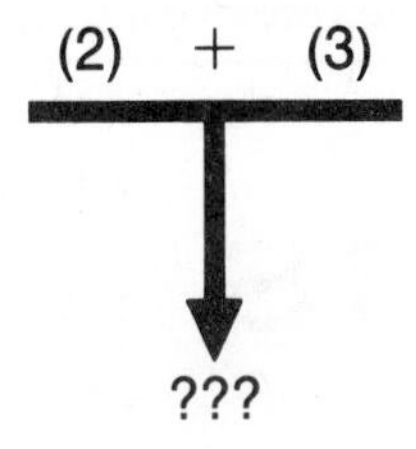

How are we to put in (1) and (4)? The argument is ambiguous, allowing for several readings. One reading is to treat (1) and (4) as *divergent conclusions*, like this:

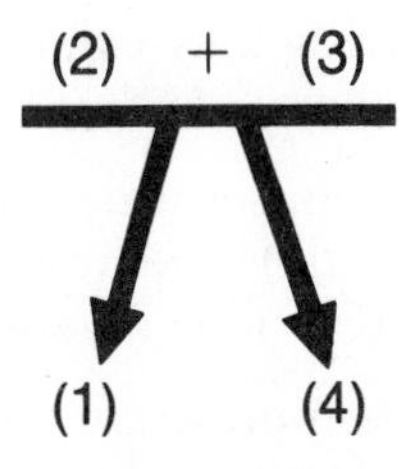

[4]Paul R. Ehrlich and S. Shirley Feldman, *The Race Bomb* (New York; The New York Times Book Co., 1977), p. 122.

Another reading treats (4) and (1) and *chaining together,* with (4) as the first sub-conclusion, and (1) as the ultimate conclusion—a reading slightly justified by the fact that the authors have stated (1) first, perhaps signaling it as their main point. On this reading we would have:

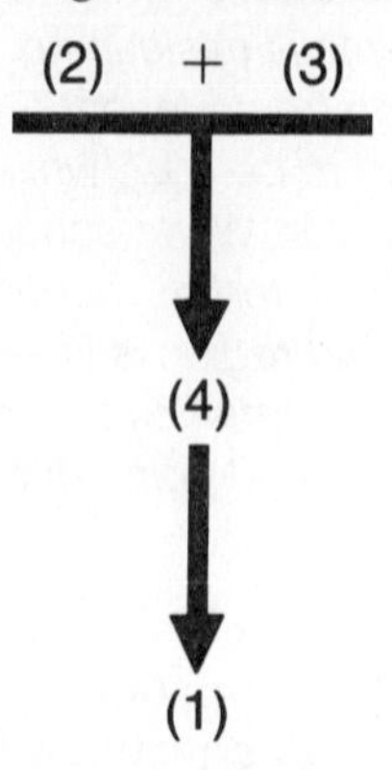

This second reading says that from the evidence in (2) and (3), the authors have first concluded that it is an abuse of statistics to argue that certain data are evidence for an IQ difference between blacks and whites, and on the basis of that conclusion have further advanced the claim that much early research done on comparative IQ scores is misleading.

Go over these examples until you understand why the diagrams go as they do. The best way to learn, however, is to try your hand at diagraming. The exercises that follow this chapter will give you a number of diagraming problems of increasing difficulty.

KEY POINTS

Argument diagrams are a teaching tool:

- They show what parts of the argument support what other parts, which is another way of saying they exhibit the premise(s) and conclusion(s) of the argument.
- They show how multiple premises are related to each other (dependently or independently), and how multiple conclusions are related to each other (whether they diverge or chain together).
- They also show how many simple arguments there are in any compound argument. The number of arrows equals the number of simple arguments.

Some arguments have more than one reason:

- Two (or more) reasons are dependent when they make the overall strength of an inference much greater than when considered independently and summed. Several dependent reasons and one conclusion make one unified simple argument.

- Two (or more) reasons are independent when they are not dependent, that is, when they form two (or more) separate simple arguments within one compound argument.

Some arguments have more than one conclusion:

- Divergent conclusions are inferred separately from the same premise(s). A compound argument with divergent conclusions will have at least as many simple arguments as there are divergent conclusions.
- Multiple conclusions chain together when one conclusion is drawn and then is itself used as the justification for another conclusion.

Strategies in Diagraming:

- See if any statements will have to be rewritten (because they are given in the form of questions or phrases, for example). If so, use the full treatment; if not, try the short-cut method.
- In separating your statements in either method, obey the rules for separating statements.
- Find the conclusion(s) first. Locate and circle any reasoning indicators, if this helps you.
- If you extract the conclusion, look at the remaining statements. If any are irrelevant to the inference, discard them in considering how to draw your diagram.
- Determine how the premises are related to one another: are they independent or dependent?
- Determine how any multiple conclusions are related to one another: do they diverge or chain together?
- Make a trial run of your diagram, and read it back to yourself to see whether it accurately represents the arguer's intentions. If not, try again.
- If the argument is genuinely ambiguous—two (or more) different diagrams seem equally equipped to capture the structure of the argument —point this out.

Appendix: The Dependent/Independent Distinction

This section may be omitted for the sake of simplicity. However, for those interested, it contains a slightly more formal account of the dependent/independent distinction.

First, it is necessary to say something about summing probabilities. Suppose a reason, *R1*, is brought forward to support a conclusion, *C*; and suppose that *R1* lends 0.3 probability to *C*. This diagram results:

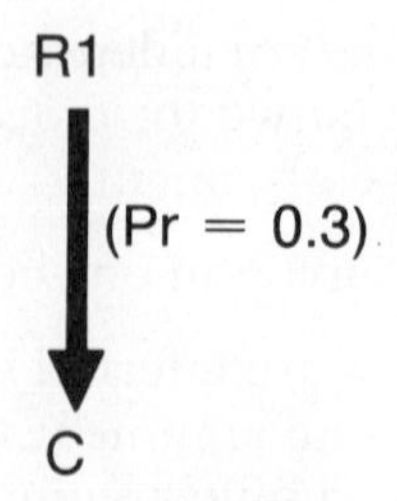

Next, suppose that another reason, *R2*, is brought forward in support of the same conclusion, *C*; and also suppose that *R2* lends 0.4 probability to *C*.

Obviously, *C* is supported by two reasons whose probability together is greater than the probability of either one individually. But how much greater? It would be an error to simply add the probability of each reason (0.3 + 0.4), thereby coming to the conclusion that *C* is now supported with 0.7 probability. Here's why. If we know *R1*, then we have 0.3 certainty that *C* is true. Certainty can be thought of as 1.0 probability. In other words, knowing that *C* is true on the basis of knowing that *R1* is true is the same as knowing *C* with probability 0.3 times 1.0 (= 0.3). Therefore, merely knowing that *R1* is true leaves us with 0.7 (= 1.0 minus 0.3) of uncertainty. Now, when *R2* (which, remember, lends 0.4 probability to *C*) is brought forward, we have decreased our uncertainty by 0.4. We now know 0.4 times 0.7, or 0.28 more than we knew before. In total, we know the conclusion with 0.3 (the probability of *R1*) plus 0.28 (the probability of *R2* times the remaining "unknown" left over from 0.3), which equals 0.58. To put it into a nonstandard diagram:

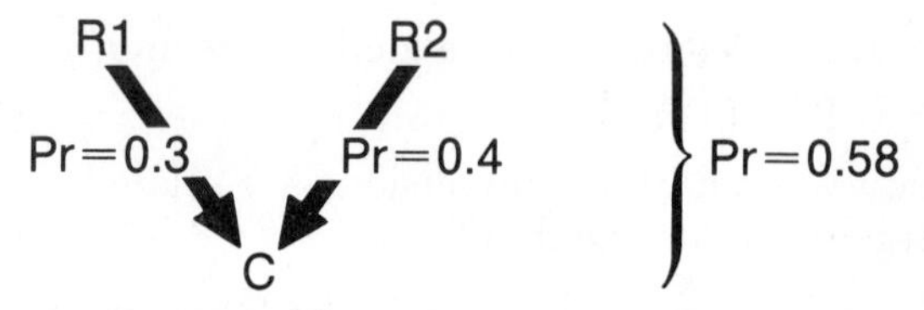

We shall call this the "ordinary" way of summing probabilities.

Here is a concrete example of an ordinary summing of probabilities. It is highly artificial, but will make the point. Suppose it is known that three out of every ten apples in Farmer Brown's orchard are Grade A. Suppose also that you have a device that detects the presence of Grade A apples. Unfortunately, this device is right only half the time. You are presented with an apple from Farmer Brown's orchard, and you test it with your detecting device. The device shows it to be Grade A. You present this argument:

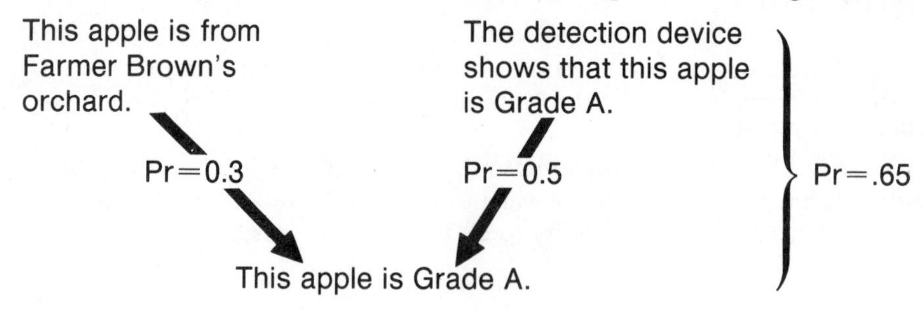

The probabilities sum in the ordinary way: 0.3 plus 0.35 (which is 0.5 times the "unknown," 0.7) equals 0.65. *When probabilities sum in the ordinary way, reasons are independent.*

Next consider this example. Suppose you know this to be true: "He's either in the kitchen or in the bedroom." Suppose you also know this to be true: "He's not in the bedroom." You now formulate this argument:

> *He's either in the kitchen or in the bedroom, and he's not in the bedroom. So, he's in the kitchen.*

Should these reasons be represented as dependent or as independent?

Suppose (what will turn out to be wrong) that they are independent. This would mean that the probabilities should sum in the ordinary way. Try it:

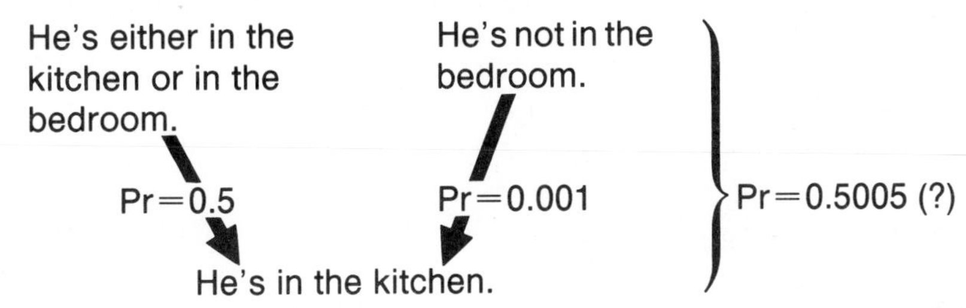

But surely the argument has a strength of greater than 0.5005 probability! Using the probability 0.5 for the first premise, and the cooked-up probability 0.001 for the second, the ordinary sum of the two would be 0.5 plus (0.001 times 0.5), or 0.5005. However, the two premises together yield a probability of 1.0 to the conclusion. That is, if you know that he's either in the kitchen or in the bedroom, and if you know that he's not in the bedroom, then you know *for certain* that he's in the kitchen.

When probabilities do not sum in the ordinary way—when they "jump" in this fashion—reasons are DEPENDENT. Therefore, the correct diagrammatic representative of that argument would be:

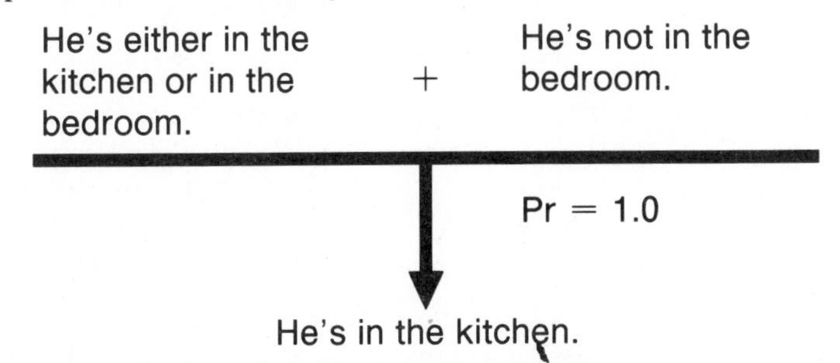

One characterization of the difference between dependent and independent reasons given earlier was that reasons are dependent when the support they lend to the conclusion together is much stronger than the support each lends to the conclusion alone. This section attempted to give a more formal explanation of this phenomenon.

EXERCISES

Diagram each argument in the following sets of problems. The problems are arranged in three groups of difficulty: Easier (A), Medium (B), and Hard (C).

1. If any passage is not or does not contain an argument, say so and go on to the next problem.

2. Decide whether the short-cut or full treatment is better. If the argument contains anything that has to be rewritten, it is better to give it the full treatment—or at least to rewrite the statements that need it and number the others.

3. If you are going to use the short-cut method, separate and number the statements. Keep the rules for separating statements in mind.

4. Find the conclusion(s). If it helps, circle any reasoning indicators.

5. Try to decide what relation the pieces of evidence (the premises) bear to each other and to the conclusion(s).

6. Try a diagram, building up from the conclusion(s). Leave out any irrelevant statements.

7. Read your diagram back to yourself to see if you've correctly captured the meaning and structure of the original passage.

***A1.** Of course he's guilty. Didn't he admit that he threatened to kill her? (Example due to Monroe Beardsley)

He admitted that he threatened to kill her.

He's guilty.

A2. How do I know Connors won't win? He won't be playing because he has the flu!

A3. He got an A+ so he must have cheated!

A4. Since they want Creationism taught in public schools, contemporary Creationists cannot present their view as based on religious faith. (Philip Kitcher, *Abusing Science: The Case Against Creationism*. The MIT Press, 1982, p. 26.)

A5. We have found that a ribbon, regularly re-inked with lubricant ink, does not lose its suppleness—hence the ribbon does not fray, hence it can be used over & over again. (Informational brochure for the "MacInker" ribbon re-inker.)

A6. If an idea presents itself to us, we must not reject it simply because it does not agree with the logical deductions of a reigning theory. (Claude Bernard)

A7. Although you said that Threadbare was out of town, you cannot really believe this since you phoned his office several times and were seen at his house.

A8. Although highly popular at aquariums, dolphins are formidable rivals of anglers because they consume large quantities of fish.

A9. In 1957, among the 33 nations that chose not to exercise the death penalty, the number of murders never increased. Thus, capital punishment simply does not appear to serve as a deterrent. (Norman Mailer).

A10. No two snowflakes are alike because no two snowflakes form under absolutely identical conditions. (*Nova*: "The Shape of Things.")

***B1.** Since (1) ⟨morals have an influence on action⟩, it follows that (2) ⟨they cannot be derived from reason⟩; and that because (3) ⟨reason alone can never influence action.⟩ (David Hume)

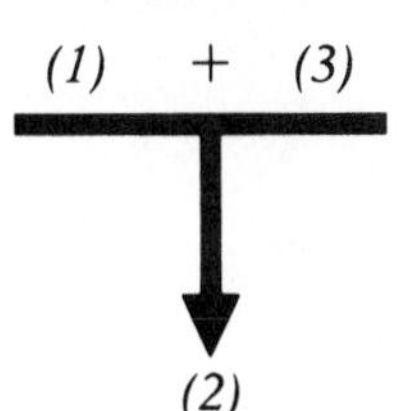

B2. The distinctive look of an E-COM letter carries a lot of weight with recipients. The bold blue stripe conveys a sense of urgency. So the message inside is conveyed effectively. (Advertisement)

B3. Because space does not permit designation of student lounges in libraries other than the Law Library, and because food and drink can damage library materials, eating and drinking are not allowed (in the library). (Policy Statement, Wayne State University Libraries)

B4. Oh Officer, I didn't realize I was speeding. I've had such a bad week. My boss is on my back and my wife is ill. Surely you can let me go this time.

B5. Anglers opposed to snagging [the practice of using barbed, unbaited hooks to snag fish in their bellies or backs] consider it immoral. They say snaggers:

- Violate a doctrine of "fair chase," of enticing a fish to strike a lure or bait.
- Take other fish illegally.
- Leave tangled messes of monofilament line and snag hooks.
- Leave smelly salmon carcasses to rot on the riverbanks, thrown away after valuable eggs are stripped from females to be sold illegally, or because the fish's deteriorated physical condition makes it unfit for food. (Tom Opre, "Snagging," *The Detroit Free Press,* Feb. 17, 1985, p. B1.)

B6. Beware! Waterfowl Hunting Takes Place in the Marsh: September, October, November, December. A Hazard, Therefore, Exists. Enter At Your Own Risk. (Sign in a marsh outside Leamington, Ontario.)

B7. Diogenes Laertius, in his *Life of Plato,* cites Plato's will verbatim. The will is interesting for two things. It indicates that when Plato drew it up, he was not wealthy, though also not in great poverty. Its total silence about the buildings, grounds, and contents of his school, the Academy, pretty well proves that by this time Plato had ceased to be the owner of the Academy. (Gilbert Ryle, "Plato," in Paul Edwards, ed., *The Encyclopedia of Philosophy.* New York: Macmillan & The Free Press, 1967, V, p. 314.)

B8. There is plainly a point where raising taxes is counter-productive, driving out more revenue than it brings in, and Detroit has probably reached it. But the city's ability to cut taxes as a means of attracting and holding residents is limited, since people's decisions to invest or to move out also depend on their perceptions of safety, public services and the quality of life, and providing all of those things costs money. Detroit is battling forces nobody else has figured out how to beat, either. Until someone does, the city has to go on scrimping and struggling until its tax base and fortunes turn. (Editorial, *Detroit Free Press,* Sept. 2, 1984.)

B9. There is a simple way to test astral projection. In your absence, have a friend place a book face up on a high and inaccessible shelf in the library. Then, if you ever have an astral projection experience, float to the book and read the title. When your body reawakens and you correctly announce what you have read, you will have provided some evidence for the physical reality of astral projection. But, of course, there must be no other way for you to know the title of the book, such as sneaking a peek when no one else is around, or being told by your friend or by someone your friend tells. To avoid the latter possibility, the experiment should be done "double blind"; that is, someone quiet unknown to you who is entirely unaware of your existence must place the book and judge whether your answer is correct. To the best of my knowledge no demonstration of astral projection has ever been reported under such controlled circumstances with skeptics in attendance. I conclude that while astral projection is not excluded, there is little reason to believe in it. (Carl Sagan, *Broca's Brain*. New York: Ballantine Books, 1979, p. 56.)

B10. Every so often, an idea pops up with superficial appeal that ultimately collapses of its own weight. I think this fate awaits "comparable worth": the notion that different jobs can be rated equal and paid equally; in practice, it's intended to raise women's wages and offset alleged sex discrimination. The Civil Rights Commission voted 5–2 against comparable worth last week. I think the vote's correct because, if widely adopted, comparable worth would raise prices, hurt low-skilled workers and ultimately harm the economy. (Robert J. Samuelson, "The Myths of Comparable Worth," *Newsweek*, April 22, 1985, p. 57.)

***C1.** (1) ⟨American business has yet to learn a fundamental lesson: you can buy in any language, but you cannot sell in any language.⟩ . . . (2) ⟨In New York City alone there are more than 10,000 Japanese salespeople, almost all of whom speak English.⟩ (3) ⟨In contrast, only a handful of the approximately 1,000 American salespeople in all of Japan speak Japanese.⟩ (4) ⟨It should be obvious which nation will do a better job of selling its products, and why.⟩ (Paul Simon, "Is America Tongue-Tied?" *Academe,* March-April 1983, p. 11.)

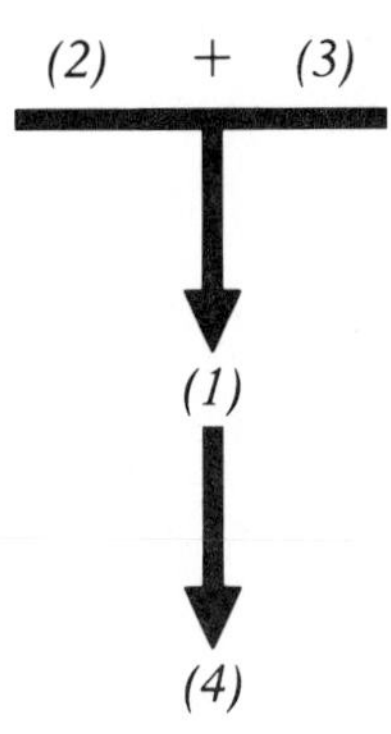

C2. Bulk mail pays its own way. Whenever I think about it, I'm reminded of the schmoos in "Li'l Abner": they multiplied rapidly and supplied all man's needs. Like the schmoo, one piece of bulk-rate mail regenerates itself many times over. Not only do you place your order using the prepaid envelope, but the company will spend postage money again fulfilling it and then again in billing you. If you take five months to pay for your purchase, and you are sent five reminders, you are responsible for generating quite a few letters out of one piece of junk mail.

So when you see me coming with a pouch full of circulars, don't bemoan my fate. I love it. Bulk-rate mail plays an important part in generating the revenue that in turn provides my salary. (Romaine Worster, "A Letter Carrier's Last Word," *Newsweek,* Feb. 18, 1985, p. 11.)

C3. While all forms of tobacco use can be addictions, cigarette smoking is especially so. Most cigarette smokers inhale the smoke into their lungs, where a high concentration of nicotine passes into the pulmonary veins and travels to the brain within seven seconds. By comparison, heroin injected into a vein in the arm requires about 14 seconds to reach the brain. Thus, with each puff, the cigarette smoker administers a rapid, concentrated dose of nicotine to the brain, achieving a measure of gratification that may be stimulating, relaxing, or satisfying in some way. And this act is repeated hundreds of times a day, more frequently than any other form of drug-taking. ("Gum to Help You Stop Smoking," *Consumer Reports*, August 1984, p. 244.)

C4. We believe that cichlids are intelligent fish—not in the limited sense that they can learn a particular skill but that they betray some of those attributes that make humans the successful animals that they are. Cichlids exhibit an awareness of their surroundings, a definite alertness, and what we might inadequately describe as inquisitiveness.

C5. Today, then, there can be no doubt that the Fifth Amendment privilege is available outside of criminal court proceedings and serves to protect persons in all settings in which their freedom of action is curtailed in any significant way from being compelled to incriminate themselves. We have concluded that without proper safeguards the process of in-custody interrogation of persons suspected or accused of crimes contains inherently compelling pressures which work to undermine the individual's will to resist and compel him to speak where he would not otherwise do so freely. (Justice Earl Warren, delivering the majority opinion in *Miranda* v. *Arizona* (U.S. Supreme Court, 1966). The Fifth Amendment privilege referred to is: "No one . . . shall be compelled in any criminal case to be a witness against himself.")

C6. My third point is that as an instrument of educational or social reform retirement is too blunt. It is rather more like a lead pipe than a scalpel. Suppose, as a commission, that you succeed in creating incentives to early retirement. Who retires? Who knows? The weakest faculty? The strongest? Probably—and it is all a big guess—the faculty that have least need for an institutional relationship. This means those who have the most going on outside the university. The best will leave. The worst will stay. (William Graebner, "Trouble in River City," *Academe*, January-February 1985, p. 17. The issue addressed is the proposal made by various commissions on higher education that the problem of "too many faculty" in some departments should be solved by inducing early retirement.)

C8. I can't offer statistical studies on the deterrent effect of the [exclusionary] rule. What I can offer, however, is my testimony that I have watched the rule deter, routinely, throughout my years as a prosecutor. When an Assistant United States Attorney, for example, advises an FBI agent that he lacks probable cause to search for bank loot in a parked automobile unless he gets a better "make" on the car; or that the agent has a "staleness" problem with the probable cause to believe that the ski masks used in the robbery are still in the suspect's friend's apartment; or that he should apply for a search warrant from a magistrate and not rely on the "consent" of the suspect's sister to search his home—the rule is working. The principal, perhaps the only, reason those conversations occur is that the assistant and the agent want the search to stand up in court. (Stephen Sachs, "The Exclusionary Rule: A Prosecutor's Defense," in John Arthur and William Shaw, eds., *Readings in the Philosophy of Law*. Englewood Cliffs, NJ: Prentice Hall, 1984. p. 454. The exclusionary rule is supposed to protect our 4th Amendment right against "unreasonable search and seizure." The rule says that evidence gathered through an unreasonable search and seizure must be excluded at a trial.)

C9. When varieties intermediate between two other forms occur, they are much rarer numerically than the forms they connect. . . . I think we can understand why intermediate varieties should not endure for very long periods.

For any form existing in lesser numbers would run a greater chance of being exterminated than one existing in larger numbers; and in this particular case the intermediate form would be eminently liable to the inroads of closely allied forms existing on both sides of it. (Charles Darwin, *On the Origin of Species*. Cambridge, MA: Harvard University Press, p. 176.)

CHAPTER 3

EVALUATING ARGUMENTS

You have been introduced to reasoning: what it is, what it isn't, and to its varieties of structure. In this chapter we come (at last) to the main topic of this book: logic. We will be mainly concerned in this chapter with describing the general features of logic: what it evaluates, how it evaluates, and its varieties. In one way, this chapter is still introductory, for you will not yet be given any of the specific rules of logic. That is the role of all succeeding chapters. But you will learn what questions logic sets out to answer. The main concepts you should acquire from this chapter are:

SOUND and UNSOUND ARGUMENT

DEGREES OF VALIDITY
DEDUCTIVELY VALID
STRONG
MEDIUM
WEAK

FALLACY

LOGICAL POSSIBILITY and IMPOSSIBILITY

DEDUCTIVE and INDUCTIVE LOGIC

3.1 The Two Parameters of Evaluation

Perhaps the most important lesson you should learn from this chapter is that any piece of reasoning has two separate and independent aspects that must be evaluated before the argument can be said to be good or bad. These are: the strength of the evidential support, and the accuracy of the evidence.

Let's begin with a simple example. You say,

Gilbert lives in Rio de Janeiro, so I guess he speaks Portuguese.

You've given an argument: From a premise or piece of evidence (Gilbert lives in Rio de Janeiro), you've drawn an inference (that Gilbert speaks Portuguese). Diagramed, your argument looks like this:

Gilbert lives in Rio de Janeiro.

He speaks Portuguese.

Is this a good argument? You must look at two separate parameters.

First, how well does the evidence (the premise) support the conclusion? That is, if Gilbert really lives in Rio de Janeiro, does this lend strong or weak support to the conclusion that the conclusion is true? Logicians call this the **DEGREE OF VALIDITY** of the argument, though there are other terms roughly synonymous:

amount of support given by the premise(s)

strength of the evidence

how well the evidence justifies

the rationality of believing the conclusion given the premise(s)

There is a second question to be asked before the argument can be said to be good: Is it true that Gilbert lives in Rio de Janeiro? We can call this the TRUTH OF THE PREMISE(S), though other terms are roughly synonymous:

accuracy of the evidence

reliability of the reasons

You can see that the ordinary English term "good argument" is refined in logic. To see the refinement better, consider a bad argument. An argument can be bad for one of two different reasons. The evidence for its conclusion as presented by its premises can be false. Or, the evidence (the premises) can be true, but not support the conclusion very well. So, a good argument must do both: The evidence for its conclusion as presented by its premises must be true AND the premises must strongly support their conclusion.

To illustrate this, return to our sample argument:

Gilbert lives in Rio de Janeiro.

He speaks Portuguese.

This argument would be bad EITHER if it's false that Gilbert lives in Rio OR if the fact that he lives in Rio is not very convincing evidence that he speaks Portuguese. Conversely, then, the argument would be good only when it's true that Gilbert lives in Rio AND this fact strongly supports the conclusion that he speaks Portuguese.

It bears repeating that these two parameters of argument evaluation are quite independent of one another. Some premise may offer next to no support for its conclusion, yet still be true or accurate. In this silly example,

President Reagan supports a strong defense.

Traffic fatalities will decrease in the U.S.

the premise is quite true, but it offers no support for the conclusion. (Who would deny that President Reagan supports a strong defense? Yet who would think that this was any evidence one way or the other for a decrease in traffic fatalities?) In this other silly example,

The Galapagos Islands are made of green cheese.

The surface of the Galapagos is soft and squishy.

The premise is clearly and incontrovertibly false. Yet if it were true, it would offer good evidence for its conclusion.

Each silly example is a bad argument, but each is bad in a quite different way. The "President Reagan/traffic fatalities" argument is bad because the premise, even though true, offers no support for its conclusion: in other words, its degree of validity is low. The "Galapagos Islands/green cheese" argument is bad because its premise is false, even though its degree of validity is high.

Since the ordinary English terms "good argument" and "bad argument" are not sufficiently refined, logic substitutes the technical terms "sound" and "unsound" in their place. A **SOUND** argument contains only true premises AND these premises strongly support their conclusion. A sound argument is a good argument. Conversely, an **UNSOUND** argument EITHER contains one or more false premises OR these premises do not strongly support their conclusion (or both). An unsound argument is a bad argument.

The "Galapagos Islands/green cheese" argument.

The Galapagos Islands are made of green cheese.

↓

The surface of the Galapagos is soft and squishy.

is unsound because it contains a false premise. The "President Reagan/traffic fatalities" argument,

President Reagan supports a strong defense.

↓

Traffic fatalities will decrease in the U.S.

is unsound because its premise does not strongly support its conclusion, that is, it is of a low degree of validity.

Here is an example of a clear case of a sound argument. Consider the ever popular

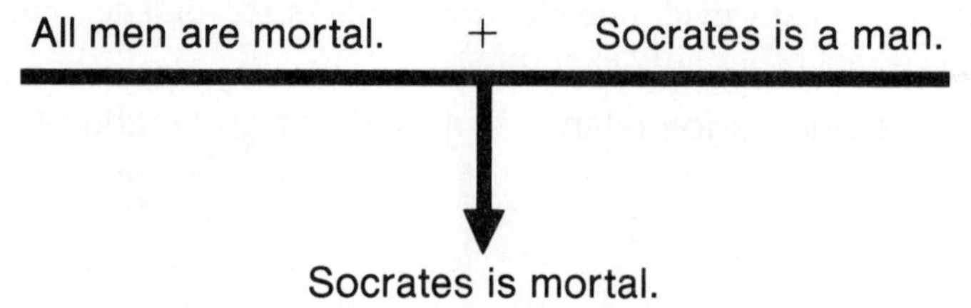

This argument is sound because all its premises are true AND they strongly support their conclusion (its degree of validity is high).

Note that these uses of the terms "valid" and "sound" are somewhat special. In English it is common to call a statement "valid" or "sound" when you mean it is true or acceptable. However, in the special sense the science of logic gives to these terms, a mere statement cannot be valid or sound (or invalid or unsound). "Valid" and "sound" apply strictly to *arguments*.

3.2
Degrees of Validity

We have spoken above of a sound argument as one in which all of its premises are true AND strongly support their conclusion. The degree of support the premises of an argument give to their conclusion is called the **DEGREE OF VALIDITY** of the argument. We must give a clearer sense to the notion of the premises of an argument "strongly" (or "weakly") supporting their conclusion.

First, recall that the issue of the degree of support the premises of an argument lend their conclusion is completely independent of the truth or falsity of those premises. The premise in this argument,

The Galapagos Islands are made of green cheese.

↓

The surface of the Galapagos is soft and squishy.

strongly supports its conclusion, even though that premise is false, while the premise in this argument,

President Reagan supports a strong defense.

↓

Traffic fatalities will decrease in the U.S.

hardly supports its conclusion at all, even though that premise is true.

This means that we can evaluate the degree of validity of an argument without concerning ourselves with the truth of its premise(s). In fact, to evaluate the degree of validity of an argument we simply suppose or assume that the premises are true. We ask ourselves a question like this: If the premises of this argument are true—or given these premises—how well do they support their conclusion?

Now, the business of logic as such is to assess the degree of validity of an argument. Logic as such does not inquire into the actual truth or falsity of the premises of an argument. Actual truth or falsity is a matter for science or ordinary observation or whatever—but not for logic proper. This, in effect, means that the business of logic proper is only half of the question of sound-

ness! To put the point more visually, consider the arrow of the arrow diagrams. The arrow symbolizes an inference, and logic proper attempts to tell us how strong or weak that inference is, i.e., what its degree of validity is:

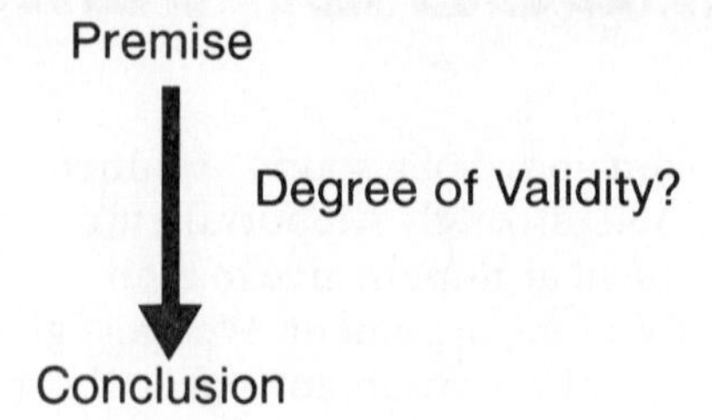

Since the premises of a simple argument can offer varying degrees of logical support, it will be helpful to have some terms to indicate those degrees. These terms describe the DEGREES OF VALIDITY of arguments, or (to say the same thing in other words) the DEGREES OF LOGICAL SUPPORT the premises of an argument can offer their conclusion:

DEDUCTIVELY VALID (DV). A simple justification is Deductively Valid if, supposing its premises to be true, its conclusion must be true as well. The evidence in a deductively valid argument is perfect and complete. Deductively Valid arguments are, logically, the strongest possible arguments. If their premises are true, the truth of their conclusion is a sure thing.

STRONG (S). A simple justification is Strong just in case while supposing its premises to be true, its conclusion is very likely to be true as well. The premises of a Strong justification, if true, give you very good reason to believe that the conclusion is true. If the premises of a Strong argument are true, the truth of the conclusion is a good bet.

MEDIUM (M). A simple justification is Medium just in case while supposing its premises to be true, its conclusion has about as much chance of being true as it has of being false. The premises of a Medium justification, even if true, do not give you a compelling reason to believe that the conclusion is true. It would be unwise to bet that the conclusion of a Medium argument is true, even if its premises are true.

WEAK (W). A simple justification is Weak just in case while supposing its premises to be true, its conclusion has little or no chance of being true. The premises of a Weak argument provide little reason to believe the conclusion. It would be a terrible bet to bet that the conclusion of a Weak argument is true, even if its premises are true!

Some simple examples are in order. Note that the assessment of the validity of the argument (in abbreviation: "DV," "S," "M," or "W") is written by the arrow. This is appropriate, since it is the strength of the logical inference from premises to conclusion that we are assessing—and the arrow symbolizes an inference.

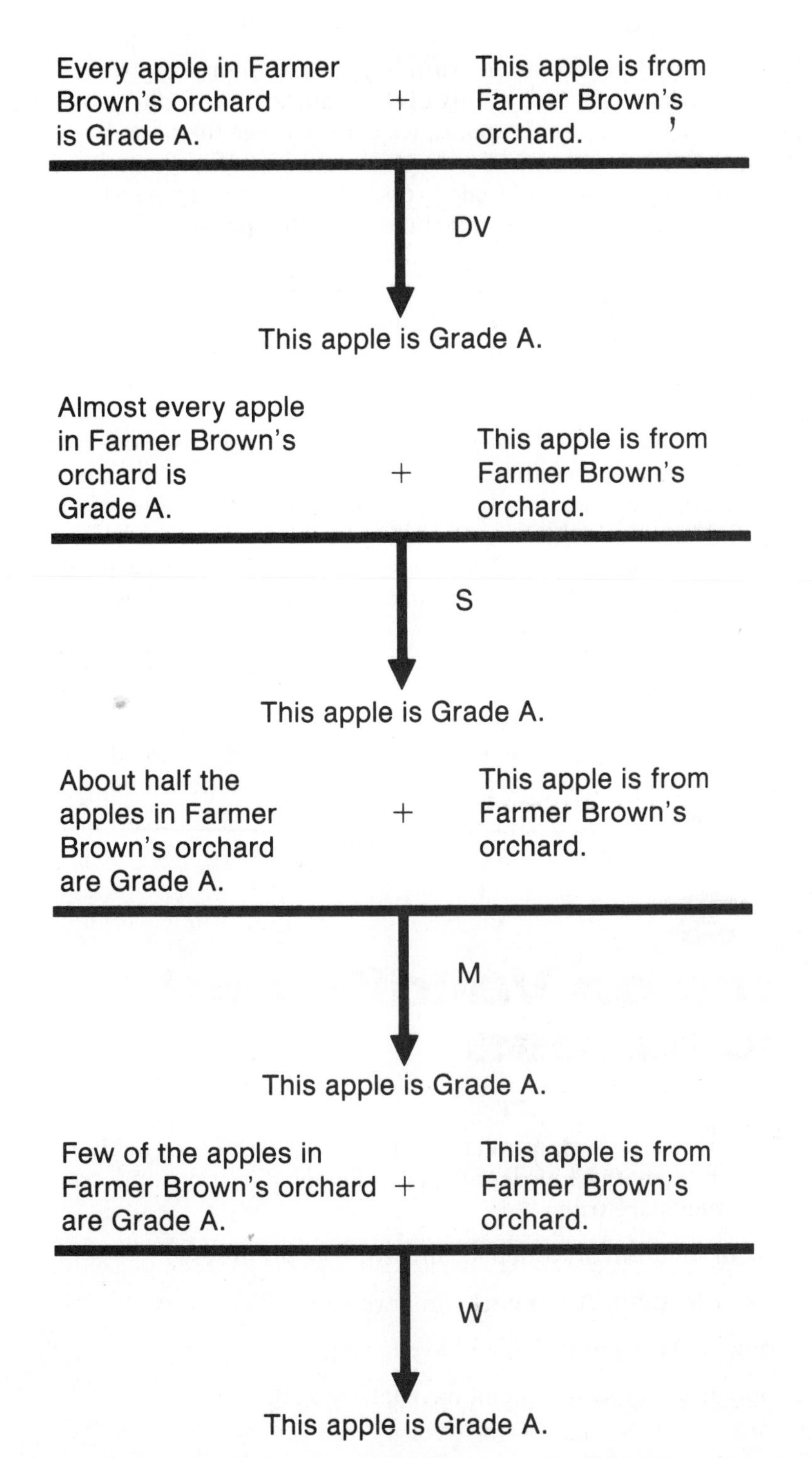

Notice that each assessment of validity in each of the preceding simple justifications was done by supposing the premises to be true—or, to put it another way, by disregarding the actual truthvalue of the premises. For we have graded the degree of validity of each of the preceding arguments without knowing anything about the truth or falsity of their premises. However, although we can assess the validity of the arguments without knowing anything about Farmer Brown's apples, we cannot judge the overall soundness of the arguments unless we know the truth or falsity of the premises. But we have finished the business of logic proper, for all logic proper does is to inquire after degrees of validity, not the truth of the premises.

Earlier it was said that the premises of a sound argument had to give strong support to their conclusion. Having defined and illustrated the various degrees of validity, we can make this definition a little more precise. A **SOUND** argument contains only true premises AND is either STRONG or DEDUCTIVELY VALID. Arguments whose degree of validity falls below Strong cannot be sound.

Arguments below Strong—arguments whose premises offer only Medium or Weak support for their conclusion(s)—cannot be considered good arguments. The premises simply do not offer compelling evidence to believe in the truth of their conclusions. Consider the third ("About half the apples") and fourth ("Few of the apples") arguments. Their premises hardly offer sufficiently strong evidence that a certain apple from Farmer Brown's orchard is Grade A.

One of the purposes of reasoning is to extend our knowledge: We want to be able to have good grounds for believing something (for example, that a certain apple is or isn't Grade A). Only arguments that are at least Strong give us good grounds. Only when there is a fairly "tight" logical fit between premises and conclusion is it rational to believe the conclusion on the basis of the premises.

3.3 More on Validity and Soundness

You should resist the temptation to confuse truth with a high degree of validity and falsehood with a low degree of validity. That is, try to understand why these statements are true:

- Weak or Medium arguments can have true premises.
- Weak or Medium arguments can have true conclusions.
- Strong or DV arguments can have false premises.
- Strong or DV arguments can have false conclusions.

Here's the first silly example again, this time with its degree of validity evaluated:

President Reagan supports a strong defense. (True)

↓ Weak

Traffic fatalities will decrease in the U.S.

It is known that the premise is true. Have we made a mistake in calling it "Weak"? Must we revise our estimation of its validity upwards? No. The argument is still Weak, for all this assessment claims is that the premise offers little or no support for its conclusion. That it happens to be true is irrelevant to assessing validity. Also, do not be tempted to think that the premise is false just because it happens to be in a Weak argument.

Let's reconsider the second silly example, this time with the assessment of its validity written in:

The Galapagos Islands are made of green cheese. (False)

↓ Strong

The surface of the Galapagos is soft and squishy.

It is known that the premise is, as a matter of fact, false. Does this mean we must revise our estimate of its validity downwards—that the argument is only Medium or Weak? No. Saying the argument is Strong implies only this: Were the premise true it would give you very good reason to believe in the truth of the conclusion. And you would certainly not change your mind about the surface of the Galapagos—that is, decide that the premise must be true after all—just because the statement that the Galapagos Islands are made of green cheese turns up in a Strong argument!

Let us now talk about conclusions. Here is yet another silly example. You have an ordinary gaming die—"die" is the singular of "dice"—in your hands, you close your eyes, roll it, and make this awful argument:

I'm rolling an ordinary die.

↓ Weak

A three turns up. (True)

You, of course, have only a one-in-six chance of rolling a three: hardly rational to bet that you'll roll a three given only that you're rolling an ordinary die. But suppose you do get a three! That is, your conclusion turns out to be true. Must you revise your estimate of the argument's strength upwards? No. The argument is still Weak. And you certainly won't deny that a three turned up, if it really turned up, just because it was not predictable.

Consider this variation. You're still rolling an ordinary die. You close your eyes, roll, and make this unhelpful but quite reasonable prediction:

I'm rolling an ordinary die.

↓ Strong

A one, a two, a three, a four,
or a five is turning up. (False)

But suppose you roll a six! Your conclusion turned out to be false. Must you revise your estimate of the argument downwards to account for this unexpected occurrence? No. The argument is still Strong, even though its conclusion is false.

Furthermore, although considerations of truth and falsity do play a role in the complete assessment of the quality of an argument, such considerations must be used in the right way. The first silly example is unsound *because its degree of validity is below Strong:*

President Reagan supports a strong defense.

↓ W, Unsound (because Weak)

Traffic fatalities will decrease in the U.S.

We need go no further in looking at the truth of its premises. And it is still unsound even when we discover (or grant) that its premise is true. The second silly example is unsound *because it has a false premise:*

The Galapagos Islands are made of green cheese.

↓ S, Unsound (because false premise)

The surface of the Galapagos is soft and squishy.

This needs two steps. Having decided the primary question of logic proper, its degree of validity, we must proceed to ask whether its premise is true; and the answer, of course, is that the premise is not true. Hence it is unsound.

But do not let considerations of the truth or falsity of the conclusion enter the picture. In the first dice example,

I'm rolling an ordinary die.

↓ W, Unsound (because Weak)

A three is turning up. (True)

the argument is Weak and thus Unsound, even though the conclusion (we're still supposing) is true! In the second dice example,

I'm rolling an ordinary die.

↓ S, Sound (because premise true and strongly supports conclusion)

A one, a two, a three, a four, or a five is turning up. (False)

the argument is Strong. It is also Sound as long as you've made the premise true by actually rolling an ordinary die—even though the conclusion has turned out to be false when you roll that unexpected six! False conclusions do not change the Soundness of an argument. Remember what arguments are doing. They are giving you evidence (the premises) to believe something else (the conclusion). That an argument is Sound means that the evidence not only strongly justifies the conclusion but the evidence is also accurate. But a Strong argument is not a perfect argument. You can still go wrong—that is, come to believe a falsehood—with a Sound argument when it is Strong.

Do not be misled, therefore, into thinking you can infer the logical strength of an argument from the truth or falsity of its parts. Nor can you infer the truth or falsity of the parts of an argument from the mere knowledge of its degree of validity. Here is all that logic proper guarantees (these are simple, not compound, arguments):

If the argument is **DV,** this is IMPOSSIBLE:

Premises — True
Conclusion — False

If the argument is **Strong,** this is UNLIKELY:

Premises — True
Conclusion — False

Logic makes no guarantees about any other possibilities. If the premises are false, logic cannot make any predictions about the truth of the conclusion. If the argument is M or W, logic cannot make any predictions about the truth of the conclusion.

It is time to introduce a term that will play a large role in our study of logic. A **FALLACY** is an error in reasoning. An argument that commits a fallacy is **FALLACIOUS.** And a fallacious argument is unsound. We will study a number of fallacies throughout the rest of this book—for a preview, turn to the entry for "fallacy" in the Glossary at the end of the book—but for the moment it will suffice to say that there are two sorts of fallacies corresponding to the two parameters of argument evaluation. **LOGICAL FALLACIES**, the larger subject, are committed when there is some error in reasoning such that the argument turns out to be WEAK. **FALLACIES OF SOUNDNESS** are committed when a false premise is used. (See Chapter 7, "Falsehoods," for fallacies of soundness.)

3.4 Compound Arguments

We have been discussing validity and soundness with respect to simple arguments. How do these concepts function in compound arguments? (See Chapter 2 for the distinction.) In this example,

If I get an A on the final exam, I will get an A in the course. And I got an A on the final exam. Besides, the fortune teller told me I would get an A in the course. The conclusion is obvious: I'll get an A in the course.

there are two simple justifications that will be seen when the argument is diagramed:

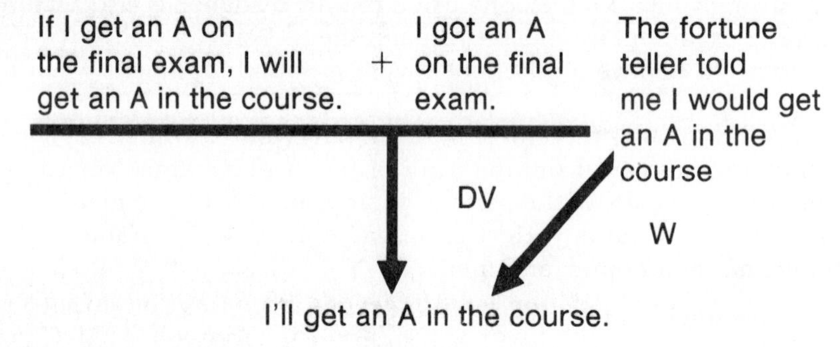

The logical strength of each simple justification must be assessed. This compound argument, then, contains one Deductively Valid simple justification and another that is Weak. Notice that the fortune teller simple justification has no bearing on the logical strength of the other simple justification, and vice versa. The DV argument cannot strengthen the W argument; the W argument cannot weaken the DV argument. There is, in effect, no answer to the question whether the logical strength of the entire compound argument is sufficiently strong. There are only assessments of the logical strength of its component simple arguments. It would make no sense to "average" the two simple justifications and call the whole compound M, for the compound contains no argument of degree of validity M. You have a DV argument and a W argument and that is the end of it.

In addition, the truth of the premises in simple justifications can vary independently. Suppose the following are true: "If I got an A on the final exam, I will get an A in the course" and "I got an A on the final exam." Then this is the overall assessment of the compound argument:

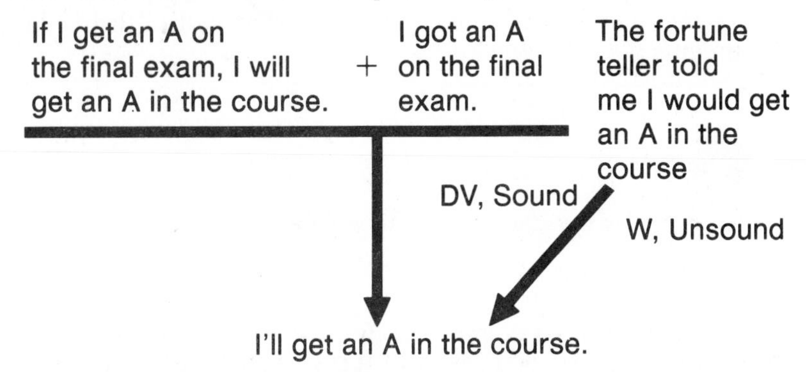

(Can you see why the second justification is unsound, even when no assumptions were made about the truth of its premise?) You might say, "But this is no overall assessment of soundness. There are two judgments." However, this is as far as we can go when some part(s) of a compound argument are sound while some other part(s) are unsound: there simply is no "averaging" in such circumstances, and no other answer than that one part is sound, the other part unsound.

Suppose we have a chain argument, for example:

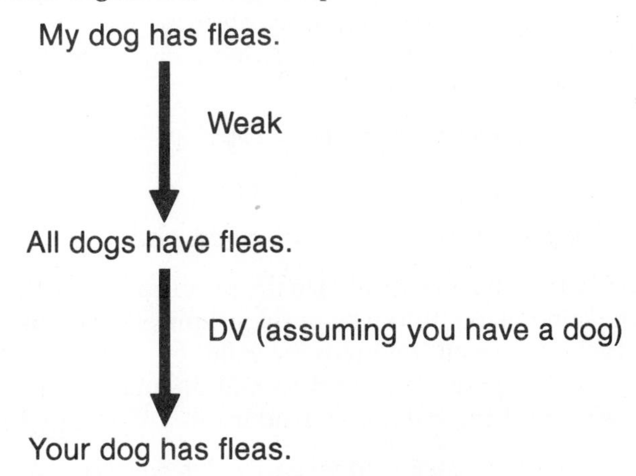

The first argument in the chain, "My dog has fleas, therefore all dogs have fleas," is Weak. It will be specifically discussed in Section 9.5 as the fallacy of hasty generalization, though for present purposes it is sufficient to point out that one dog having fleas is a Weak reason to believe that all dogs have fleas. But the weakness of the first argument does not diminish the strength of the second argument. "All dogs have fleas, so your dog has fleas" is still DV. However, since we have only a Weak reason to believe the premise of the second argument to be true, we do not have a reason to believe that the second argument is Sound.

This will be important later, for it is often the case that a number of different reasons are produced in favor of a conclusion (i.e., a number of simple arguments are advanced for one conclusion). And it is often the case that some of these are sound, and others not. Be careful not to throw out the Strong arguments with the Weak.

3.5 Deductive Validity

The science of logic had its beginnings in the West in a group of writings called the *Organon* by Aristotle (384-322 B.C.). The *Organon* dealt with the deductive validity of the categorical syllogism (discussed in Chapter 6), and indeed for most of its history logic has been concerned almost entirely with the study of categorical syllogisms. Even after logicians in the twentieth century made sophisticated developments in logic that went beyond the topics covered in Aristotle's *Organon*, the thrall of deductively valid arguments held sway. For deductively valid arguments offer perfect evidence for their conclusions, and anything less than deductive validity was considered shabby in comparison.

In fact, there is a variety of terms that has come into use because of logic's concentration on deductively valid arguments. Each of these means the same thing:

The argument is deductively valid.

The premises entail *the conclusion.*

The conclusion follows from *the premises.*

Similarly, the questions "Do the premises entail the conclusion?" and "Does the conclusion follow from the premises?" are just different ways of asking, "Is the argument deductively valid?"

It is important to understand the perfection of the evidence in deductively valid arguments. Consider this DV argument:

John is a bachelor. Therefore he has no wife.

"Bachelor" is by definition "a male who has no wife." Therefore the premise of this argument cannot be true and its conclusion false. There is a contradiction in supposing that (1) John is a bachelor and (2) he has a wife, for (1) means that he has no wife while (2) contradicts (1). Accordingly, the argument is DV.

In another kind of example of Deductive Validity, we meet the same phenomenon:

No mammals are cold-blooded creatures. Therefore no cold-blooded creatures are mammals.

The premise asserts a complete separation between mammals and cold-blooded creatures. It says you will never find a creature that is both cold-blooded and a mammal. But this is precisely what the conclusion says. It, too, says that there is a complete separation between cold-blooded creatures and mammals. Thus it would be a contradiction to hold the premise true (a complete separation between cold-blooded creatures and mammals) and to deny the conclusion (which denial would say that there is not a complete separation). It is logically impossible for there to both be and not be a complete separation between mammals and cold-blooded creatures. And so the argument is DV.

Next consider an example of a Strong argument:

John just fell from the forty-fourth floor of a skyscraper, and has landed on hard concrete. Therefore John is hurt.

What is the degree of validity of this argument? We have excellent reason to believe that its conclusion is true. But is it Deductively Valid? No. It is Strong. If an argument is DV, it is logically impossible for its premises to be true and its conclusion false. A state of affairs is **LOGICALLY IMPOSSIBLE** just in case it implies a contradiction. A **CONTRADICTION** is a state of affairs that both happens yet doesn't happen. It is describable only as "X and not X." If it does not imply a contradiction it is **LOGICALLY POSSIBLE**. Now there is no contradiction in supposing that (1) John fell from the forty-fourth floor, (2) he has landed on hard concrete, and (3) he is not hurt. The state of affairs described by the conjunction of (1), (2), and (3) is therefore logically possible. (1), (2), and (3) are not like "X and not X." It is extremely unlikely for (1), (2), and (3) to all be true together, but not logically impossible. In other words, it is not logically impossible for the premises to be true and the conclusion false.

A similar example will make the same point:

Mary's car has a gasoline engine, and her car is completely out of gas. Therefore her car won't start.

This argument, too, is at best Strong. It is not Deductively Valid, for it is not logically impossible for the premises to be true and the conclusion false. To put this point in other words: The state of affairs described by (1) Mary's car has a gasoline engine, (2) her car is out of gas, and (3) her car will start does not imply a contradiction. It may be a violation of the laws of nature as we know them, but it is not a contradiction.

This is why the evidence in DV arguments can be considered perfect: There cannot be any slip or gap between premise and conclusion. If you are getting the feeling that DV arguments are merely spinning their wheels, repeating in the conclusion what has already been said in the premises, then you are on the right track. For that is precisely why DV arguments are DV: The conclusion just draws out what has already (somehow) been stated in the premises.

Take care, then, in assessing an argument as DV. Do not be misled by evidence that is extremely strong. Unless the evidence entails the conclusion—unless it is logically impossible for the premises to be true while the conclusion is false—the argument is not deductively valid.

3.6 Deductive and Inductive Logic

The terms "deductive" and "inductive" are usually held to be important in learning logic, although exactly what they mean is disputed.

A well-respected dictionary (*Webster's New World Dictionary of the American Language*, 2d College Edition, Simon & Schuster, 1982) defines "deductive" as "reasoning. . . from the general to the specific" and defines "inductive" as "reasoning from . . . individual cases to a general conclusion." This captures some of what is meant by "deductive" and "inductive." A typical deductive argument moves from the general to the specific, for example,

All dogs are furry, and Max is a dog. So Max is furry.

We've reasoned from some premise about all dogs (the general) to a conclusion about Max (a specific dog). A typical inductive argument moves from the specific to the general, for example,

This dog, and this, and this are furry. So all dogs are furry.

Beginning with specific cases, we reason to a general conclusion.

But, some deductive arguments move from the general to the general:

No dogs are cats, so no cats are dogs.

And some inductive arguments move from the specific to the specific:

Crow #1 is black, crow #2 is black, . . . , Crow #100 is black, so the next crow I see will be black.

So reasoning from the general to the specific cannot be definitional of all deductive arguments, and reasoning from the specific to the general cannot be definitional of all inductive arguments.

Some logic textbooks define a deductive argument as an argument whose conclusion must be true if its premises are true; and define an inductive argument as an argument whose premises even if true allow for the possibility of a false conclusion. But this definition of deductive arguments is a definition of deductively *valid* arguments, and does not allow for the possibility of an argument that is deductive yet not deductively valid. The following should be counted as a deductive argument even though its maker slipped and produced a deductively invalid argument:

All holidays are days off, so all days off are holidays.

while the following should be considered an inductive argument, even though it is technically deductively valid:

95% of all dogs die by the age of eighteen. So Fido (my dog) will probably die by the age of eighteen.

(The argument is technically deductively valid because of the "probably" in its conclusion. That 95% of all dogs die by eighteen just means that my dog will *probably* die by eighteen).

Other logic texts draw the distinction another way: A deductive argument is an argument whose maker intends to be Deductively Valid; an inductive argument is an argument whose maker intends to be at best Strong. On this conception, "All holidays are days off, so all days off are holidays" is a deductive argument (though deductively invalid) if the arguer tried for Deductive Validity, while "95% of all dogs die by the age of eighteen, so Fido will probably die by the age of eighteen" is an inductive argument (although deductively valid) if the arguer aspired only to a Strong argument.

This conception has some plausibility, although we ought to note that many people who make arguments simply try to make the best argument they can without intending it to be (specifically) Deductively Valid or Strong. Does this mean that some arguments are neither deductive nor inductive?

In addition, what will we make of this example? This argument is commonly held to be both deductive and fallacious:

If the plane landed on time, he will be at the meeting at 9 A.M. And he is at the meeting at 9 A.M. So the plane landed on time.

This argument commits the fallacy of affirming the consequent (see Chapter 5), and is not deductively valid. Yet the premises give us *some* reason to believe the conclusion. So the argument has an inductive aspect. Does this mean some arguments are both deductive and inductive?

It is an odd distinction indeed when, on one way of reading it, some arguments are neither deductive nor inductive, and on another way of reading it, some arguments are both.

In truth, however, the more important distinction is not between deductive and inductive arguments but between deductive and inductive logic.

Deductive logic, which we will treat in Part Two, gives rules to apply to arguments to decide whether those arguments are deductively valid or not. If the argument is not deductively valid, deductive logic has no more to say about it, for deductive logic is interested only in a yes-or-no answer to "Is this argument DV?"

Inductive logic, treated in Part Three, will give some rules for helping us to decide how strong an argument is, if it is known already that it is not deductively valid. By its nature, inductive logic is fuzzier than deductive logic. The rules of deductive logic are applied in an all-or-nothing fashion. We will know for certain whether an argument is DV. In contrast, as you will see, the rules of inductive logic allow for a certain latitude and even disagreement (yes, disagreement in logic) in judging the degree of validity of inductive arguments. You will be told that a sample must be "large enough" to draw the conclusion, but will be given no hard and fast rules for determining how large is "large enough."

KEY POINTS

There are two separate and independent parameters in evaluating an argument:

- The primary question is the degree of validity of the argument: How strong is the evidential relation between premises and conclusion?
- The next question is the truth of the premises.

There are four degrees of validity: Deductively Valid, Strong, Medium, and Weak.

- Only Deductively Valid and Strong arguments produce a sufficiently strong logical relation between premises and conclusion to be worthy of further consideration.
- An argument is Sound when and only when it is either Deductively Valid or Strong and all its premises are true.

It is important not to confuse the degree of validity of an argument with the truth or falsity of any of its parts.

- Deductively Valid or Strong arguments can have false premises or false conclusions.
- Medium or Weak arguments can have true premises or true conclusions.

- The only guarantees logic makes is that in a DV argument you cannot have true premises and a false conclusion, and that in an S argument you are unlikely to have true premises and a false conclusion.

Compound arguments are composed of simple arguments. It is the simple arguments whose validity and soundness is assessed. The degree of validity of one simple argument cannot affect the degree of validity of another simple argument in the same compound. Ditto with soundness.

A DV argument is one in which it is logically impossible for the premises to be true and the conclusion false.

- This means that, strictly speaking, an argument is DV only when you can derive a contradiction by assuming the premises true and the conclusion false.
- Other arguments, however Strong, are not DV unless they entail a contradiction in this way.

It is difficult, if not impossible, to distinguish deductive from inductive arguments. The more important distinction is between deductive and inductive logic.

- Deductive logic produces rules that give a yes-or-no answer to the question, "Is this argument DV?"
- Inductive logic produces rules that may give some help in answering the question, "How strong is this argument?

Appendix: Degrees of Validity

The term "degrees of validity" will strike some as badly chosen, for classically an argument is either valid or not, period, with no "degrees" in between. There are other choices of terminology that could have been made. *Basic Logic* could have opted for "deductive validity" and "inductive validity," neither of which come in "degrees." The problem with that option is that it leaves no name for the arguments that are what *Basic Logic* calls "Medium." "Strength of evidential support" could have been used instead of "degrees of validity" (and of course what "degree of validity" means is "strength of evidential support"). "Valid" would then be reserved only as a name for deductively valid arguments. This seemed a waste of such a seminal term. "Valid" is not peculiar to the nomenclature of logic. It occupies a prominent place in ordinary discourse, and as such deserves a prominent place in the evaluative vocabulary of any logic text.

The fact is that some change in the classic meaning of "valid" or "sound" must be made in any text (or course) dealing with both deductive and inductive logic. In the classic sense, "valid" means "deductively valid" and soundness requires deductive validity. "One million crows were observed in locales around the world, each was black, and so all crows are black" is not (deductively) valid, hence not sound. But this is an unacceptable use of "sound," for soundness ought to map onto (or explicate) what is called in ordinary discourse a "good" argument. The decision was made, then, to bring the evaluative terminology in *Basic Logic* as close as possible to ordinary discourse and to make it encompass both deductive and inductive logic without sharp breaks. This required changing the classic meaning of "valid" and "sound." The gains seem to outweigh the loss, which in any event will be felt only by the classic logician.

There is a problem with what arguments to call Weak. The example in 3.2 of a Weak argument was:

I. Few apples in Farmer Brown's orchard are Grade A, and this is an apple from his orchard. So it's Grade A.

This argument is certainly bad, but it differs from the more usual kind of argument we would call Weak:

II. I've picked one apple from Farmer Brown's orchard and it's Grade A. So all apples from his orchard are Grade A.

The premises of I subtract likelihood from its conclusion, while the premises of II add likelihood (however slight) to its conclusion.

The difference is something like this. Consider the argument "P therefore Q". Suppose there is some initial (a priori or natural or background) probability for Q, say, 1/2, but P, were it to happen, would lower the probability of Q to, say, 1/10. This is the situation in (I). Now, let the initial probability on Q be 1/100. But this time P, were it to happen, would raise the probability for Q to 1/10. This is the situation in (II). *Basic Logic* calls an argument Weak not because some fact lowered the initial probability of an event, but because that fact gives only slight reason to believe that the event will (or did) occur.

There is a similar situation, though in reverse as it were, about what arguments to call Strong. Again, consider "P therefore Q." Suppose the initial probability on Q is 98/100, but P, were it to happen, would lower the probability of Q to, say, 89/100. The argument "P therefore Q" should still be counted Strong, even though the fact of P makes Q less likely. Again, *Basic Logic* deems an argument Strong not because the fact mentioned in the premise raises the likelihood of an event, but because the premise gives good reason to believe in the conclusion.

There are other problems. I say that this argument is Weak:

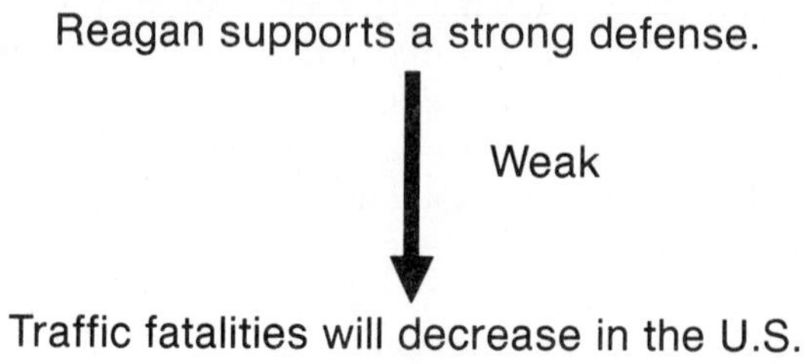

Reagan supports a strong defense.

↓ Weak

Traffic fatalities will decrease in the U.S.

But then is this argument Strong?

Reagan supports a strong defense.

Traffic fatalities will *not* decrease in the U.S.

We cannot count it as Strong, for the premise simply has nothing to do with the conclusion.

Regarding simple and compound arguments, we have another difficulty. Suppose we have this chain argument, with the probability each premise lends to its respective conclusion marked in:

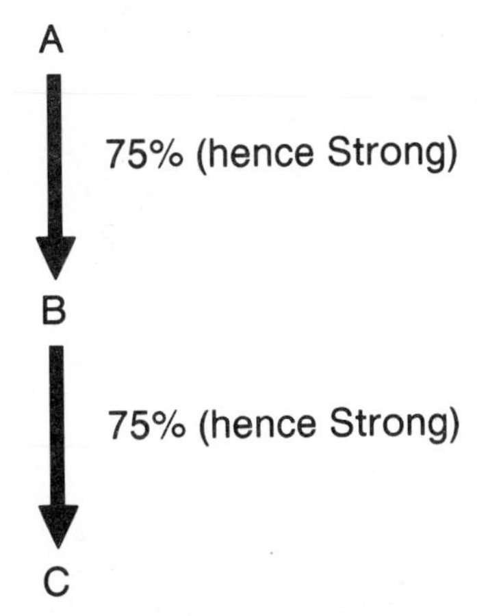

Suppose *A* is true. So "*A* therefore *B*" is Sound. What of "*B* therefore *C*"? We can't assume that *B* is true, so the soundness of "*B* therefore *C*" can't be evaluated. This concurs with what was said in 3.4. Here's an attempt at the overall degree of probability of the above argument: $.75 \times .75 = .56 =$ Medium. How could an argument each of whose parts—*A* so *B*, *B* so *C*—is Strong be less than Strong overall? Is it because, as 3.4 suggests, there is no "overall" argument, *A* so *C*? This seems ad hoc, although certainly in the case discussed in 3.4 (getting an A because of an A on the final, because of the fortune teller) there does not seem to be one "overall" argument.

EXERCISES

A. Circle ALL correct answers. Some questions have more than one.

A1. You know that a certain argument is Strong. This is a measure of

- **a.** its soundness
- **b.** its degree of validity
- **c.** the truthvalue of its conclusion

A2. You know that a certain argument is Sound. So you must also know

- **a.** that all its premises are true
- **b.** that at least one of its premises is true
- **c.** that it is deductively valid
- **d.** that its conclusion is true

A3. You know that a certain argument is Medium. So you also know

- **a.** that its conclusion cannot be true
- **b.** that some of its premises are false
- **c.** that it is unsound
- **d.** none of the above

A4. You know that the conclusion of a certain argument is true. So you also know

- **a.** that it must be at least Strong if not Deductively Valid
- **b.** that its premises are also true
- **c.** that it is sound
- **d.** none of the above

A5. You have an argument with two dependent premises, and you know that one of the premises is false. So you also know

- **a.** that it cannot be sound
- **b.** that it cannot be Deductively Valid or Strong
- **c.** that its conclusion is false
- **d.** none of the above

A6. You have an argument with two dependent premises, and you know that each premise is true and that the argument is Deductively Valid. So you also know

- **a.** that it is sound
- **b.** that its conclusion is true
- **c.** none of the above

A7. You have an argument that you know is Deductively Valid but that also has a false conclusion. So you also know

- **a.** that it must have at least one false premise
- **b.** that this is a trick question because such an argument is impossible
- **c.** none of the above

A8. You have an argument that you know is Strong (no better), but that has a false conclusion. So you also know

- **a.** that it must have at least one false premise
- **b.** that this is a trick question—such an argument is impossible
- **c.** none of the above

A9. A certain compound argument has two simple arguments as parts. One simple argument is Strong, the other Weak. The logical strength of the entire compound argument is

- **a.** Medium
- **b.** Strong
- **c.** Weak
- **d.** none of the above

A10. A certain compound argument has two simple arguments as parts. One simple argument is Deductively Valid, the other Strong. However each simple argument has one false premise. Now you know

- **a.** that the entire compound argument is sound
- **b.** that the entire compound argument is unsound
- **c.** that the entire compound argument is somewhere between Strong and Deductively Valid
- **d.** that this is a trick question—there can be no overall assessment of the soundness of a compound argument

B. Answer the questions for each of the following. Some of the multiple choice questions may have more than one correct answer. Circle ALL correct answers

B1. Joe's car battery is dead.

Joe's car won't start.

1. Assess the logical strength of the inference, and write it on the diagram.

2. This inference is
   - **a.** Sound
   - **b.** Unsound
   - **c.** Not enough information to tell

B2. No marsupials are mammals.

No mammals are marsupials.

(If you don't know what a marsupial is, look it up in a dictionary or encyclopedia.) This justification is
   - **a.** Sound
   - **b.** Unsound
   - **c.** Not enough information to tell, even with a dictionary

B3. All cats are mammals.

All mammals are cats.

1. Assess the degree of validity of this inference, and write your answer on the diagram.

2. This inference is
   - **a.** Sound
   - **b.** Unsound
   - **c.** Not enough information to tell

B4. If interest rates go down in January, then housing construction goes up in May. + Interest rates are going down in January.

DV

Housing construction goes up in May.

An economist makes this argument in January. At the end of May, it turns out that housing construction did not go up. What should you conclude?

- **a.** The argument was Deductively Valid in January, but not at the end of May.
- **b.** The argument is still Deductively Valid at the end of May.
- **c.** The argument must have a false premise.
- **d.** The argument is unsound.
- **e.** It is a Deductively Valid and Sound argument with a false conclusion.

B5.

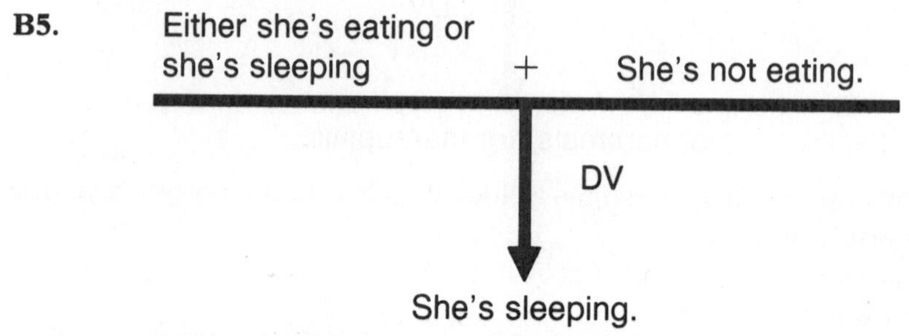

1. Suppose you know that she's not sleeping.
   - **a.** Then the argument isn't DV after all.
   - **b.** Then the argument is unsound.
   - **c.** Then one of the premises is false.
   - **d.** Then she really is eating.

2. Suppose you know that she is sleeping.
   - **a.** Then the argument is sound.
   - **b.** Then each of the premises is true.
   - **c.** Not enough information to tell whether a. or b.

B6. Almost all her daytime activities consist of either eating or studying.

↓ Strong

She's either in the library or in the kitchen. + She's not in the kitchen.

↓ Deductively Valid

She's in the library.

1. Given these evaluations of each simple justification in this compound argument, and given that she is in the library, which of these must be true?

- **a.** Each simple justification must be sound.
- **b.** The compound argument as a whole must be sound.
- **c.** Not enough information to tell whether a. or b.

2. Given the justifications of each simple argument, but now given that she is not in the library, which of these must be true?

- **a.** The simple justification from "Almost all her daytime activities consist of either eating or studying" to "She's either in the library or in the kitchen" is unsound.
- **b.** The other simple justification is unsound.
- **c.** The compound argument as a whole is unsound.
- **d.** There is not enough information to decide.

B7. The weather report says there's an 80% chance of rain today.

The *Farmers Almanac* (published six months ago) predicts rain today.

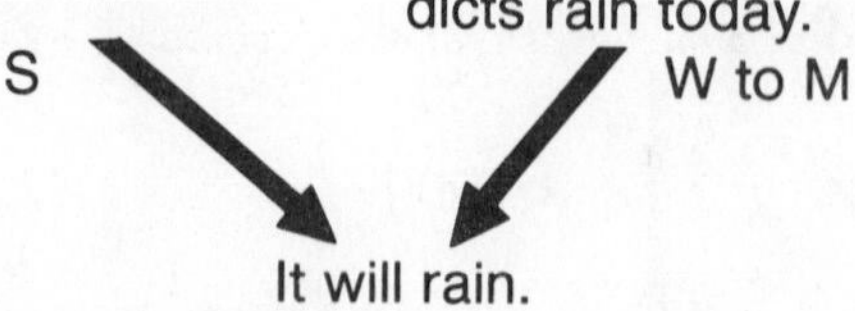

1. Given that the premises are true and that the evaluations of validity are correct, which of these must be true?

a. There is a Sound argument that it will rain and an Unsound argument that it will rain.
b. The Weak to Medium argument weakens the Strong argument.
c. The Strong argument strengthens the Weak to Medium argument.

2. Suppose it does not rain. Continue to assume that the premises are true and that the evaluations of validity are correct. Which of these—there may be more than one—must be true?

a. Neither of the arguments is sound.
b. That it didn't rain is not surprising in view of the fact that the compound argument contains a Weak to Medium simple justification that must have weakened the Strong simple justification.
c. These suppositions are inconsistent. There could not be a false conclusion if one of the simple justifications is Strong, and all the premises are true.
d. None of the above.

3. If you answered d. to 2, how could the conclusion be false, even though the compound argument contains all true premises and at least one Strong justification?

B8.

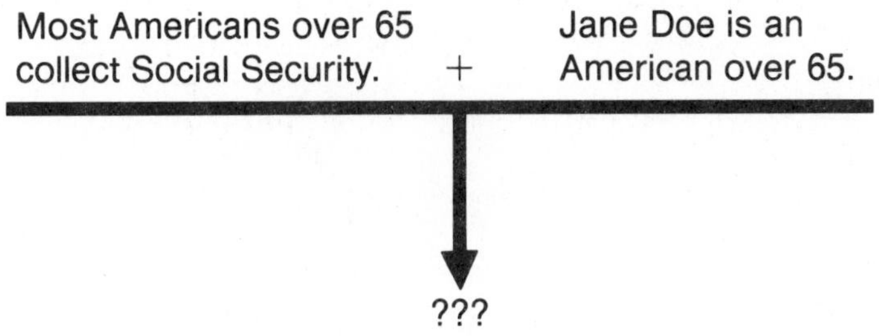

Most Americans over 65 collect Social Security. + Jane Doe is an American over 65.

↓

???

Assume that the premises are true.

1. Which conclusion will make the argument strongest?

- **a.** Jane Doe collects Social Security.
- **b.** Jane Doe does not collect Social Security.
- **c.** Jane Doe probably collects Social Security.

2. Which conclusion will make the argument weakest?

- **a.** Jane Doe collects Social Security.
- **b.** Jane Doe does not collect Social Security.
- **c.** Jane Doe probably collects Social Security.

PART TWO

DEDUCTIVE LOGIC

CHAPTER 4

CONJUNCTION AND DISJUNCTION

There is a logic of statements that turns on the meanings of "and," "or," "not," and "if . . . then." Arguments composed of statements containing such terms are deductively valid or invalid depending on whether they capture or violate their sense. We will introduce truthtables, which give the meanings of these terms, and some rules for deductive validity (postponing "if . . . then" until the next chapter). The important concepts in this chapter include:

SIMPLE and COMPOUND STATEMENTS

TRUTHTABLES

LOGICAL EQUIVALENCE

NEGATION

CONJUNCTION

DISJUNCTION

SCOPE

4.1 Truthtables and Logical Equivalence

This section sets out some preliminaries to the study of the logic of statements.

A **SIMPLE STATEMENT** is a positive statement that contains no other statements as parts. These are examples of simple statements:

She is at home.

She is at the library.

Florida is warm.

Florida is sunny.

You drink more than three ounces of liquor.

Your are legally drunk.

A **COMPOUND STATEMENT** is a statement that contains one or more positive statements as meaningful parts. Here are some examples of compound statements:

She is not at home.

She is either at home or at the library.

Florida is warm because it's sunny.

If you drink more than three ounces of liquor, then you are legally drunk.

A compound statement is created from simple statements by using connectives, such as "not," "or," "because," "if. . . then," and others. In this chapter and the next we will be interested in **TRUTHFUNCTIONAL CONNECTIVES**:

not (and other negation connectives)

and (and other conjunction connectives)

or (and other disjunction connectives)

if (and other conditional connectives)

A **TRUTHFUNCTIONAL CONNECTIVE** is a term that (a) is defined by a truthtable (see below) and (b) determines the truthvalue of a compound statement given the truthvalues of its simple statements. This means, for example, that if we know the truthtable for "and," whether "Florida is warm in February" is true or false, and whether "Florida is sunny in February" is true or false, then we will know whether "Florida is warm and sunny in February" is true or false.

A truthtable assumes there are two truthvalues, true (T) and false (F). It also assumes that a statement is either one or the other (although this is part of the definition of a statement, i.e., a piece of discourse that is either true or false). A truthtable presents an array of *possibilities* of truthvalues for simple statements. A truthtable does not assert that a simple statement is true, nor does it assert that it is false.

It will be helpful to use variables in giving truthtables. The letters "P" and "Q" will stand for any simple statement whatsoever.

Two (or more) statements are **LOGICALLY EQUIVALENT** when they are true and false under exactly the same circumstances, and two statements are true and false under exactly the same circumstances when their truthtables are exactly the same. We will express a logical equivalence with a double-headed arrow:

This means that you will get a Deductively Valid argument going from top to bottom and going from bottom to top. This is to say that both these arguments are deductively valid:

After a brief encounter with negation, you will be introduced to certain rules for deductive validity. For example, you will be told that this is a valid rule:

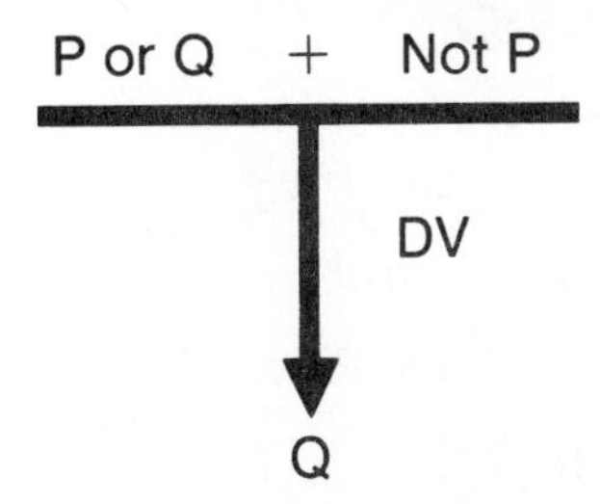

This means that *any argument that has this form is deductively valid,* whether the premise is "She's at home or in the library" or "The Democrat will barely win or will lose by a huge majority" or whatever.

4.2 Negation

Before explaining conjunction and disjunction, a few words must be said about negation. The simplest truthtable is for negation, usually expressed by "not":

P	Not P
T	F
F	T

This reads: When "*P*" is true, "Not *P*" is false; and when "*P*" is false, "Not *P*" is true.

There are a few ways to express negation in English:

It is raining.	*It is not raining.*
He will come.	*He won't come.*
Sugar is toxic.	*Sugar is nontoxic.*
There are ghosts.	*It's false that there are ghosts.*

The truthtable for "not" says that if the statement in the left column is true, it's negation (the statement in the right column) is false; and vice-versa (if the right-hand statement is true, then the left-hand statement is false). Although we are using some of the language and instruments of logic (validity, truth-tables), the operation of negation is very commonsensical.

Mostly, negation does not function by itself in arguments, but operates on the truthvalues of the simple parts of conjunctions, disjunctions, and conditionals.

4.3 Conjunction

The truthtable for "and" states that a conjunction is true only when all its simple statements are true:

P,	Q	P and Q
T	T	T
T	F	F
F	T	F
F	F	F

The truthtable for conjunction accurately reflects ordinary English. If I say, "You are subject to a fine and imprisonment," then what I say is true only when it is true that you are subject to a fine and you are subject to imprisonment.

Besides "and" there are several other ways to express conjunction in English:

Conjunctions

and	*It is raining and the sun is shining.*
but	*It is raining but the sun is shining.*
although	*Although it is raining, the sun is shining.*
while	*It is raining while the sun is shining.*
(even) though	*Even though it is raining, the sun is shining.*

These are not exactly the same in English, but for logical purposes they are equivalent: Each asserts that two simple statements are both true. That is, any conjunction—"*P* and *Q*," "*P* but *Q*," "*P* although *Q*," and the rest—asserts that "*P*" is true and asserts that "*Q*" is true.

Filling out a truthtable for compound statements containing both conjunction and negation connectives is easy. Problem: Write out a truthtable for

It is windy, yet not sunny.

We'll abbreviate the simple statement "It is windy" as "*W*," and "it is sunny" as "*S*" (and remember that "yet" is conjunction):

W *and not* S

The truthtable:

W,	S	W and not S
T	T	F (F)
T	F	T (T)
F	T	F (F)
F	F	F (T)

The truthtable for "*W* and not *S*" is under the "and." The truthvalues in parentheses are the truthvalues for "not *S*." The first line says that when both "*W*" and "*S*" are true, then "not *S*" is false, and "*W* and not *S*" is false. And so on.

Using the truthtable for conjunction, we can determine the truthvalue of compound statements. Suppose we know (or it is given) that

"It is sunny" is True.

"It is windy" is False.

Then we can say, for example, that

"It is sunny and windy" is False.

"It is sunny but not windy" is True.

How so? Consider the truthtable. Let "*S*" abbreviate "It is sunny" and "*W*" abbreviate "It is windy":

	S, W	S but W	S but not W
	T T	T	F (F)
"S" is T, "W" is F →	T F	F	T (T)
	F T	F	F (F)
	F F	F	F (T)

The truthtable tells us that when "*S*" is T and "*W*" is F (the second row), "*S* but *W*" is F. The truthvalues in parentheses under "Not *W*" are the opposite of "*W*." The second row tells us that when "*S*" is T and "Not *W*" is T, "*S* but not *W*" is T.

We will learn two rules for conjunction. The first is an equivalence:

CONJUNCTION ORDER (CO)

P and Q

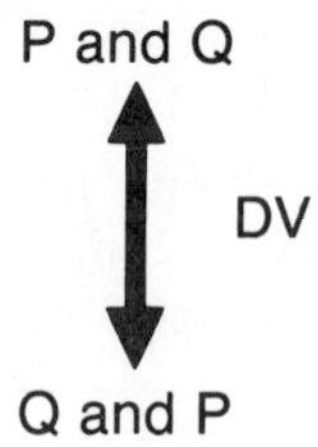

Q and P

This rule is fairly obvious. It simply says that, logically, it makes no difference in which order you state a conjunction. For example:

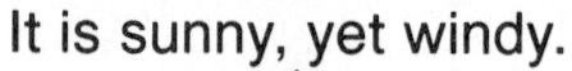

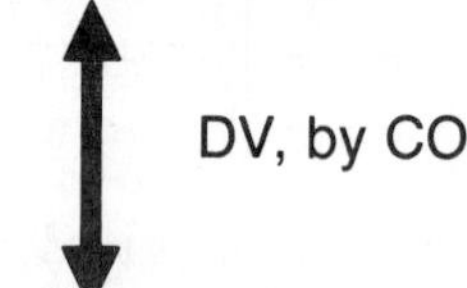

It is windy, yet sunny.

The second rule is almost equally obvious:

SIMPLIFICATION (SIMP)

P and Q

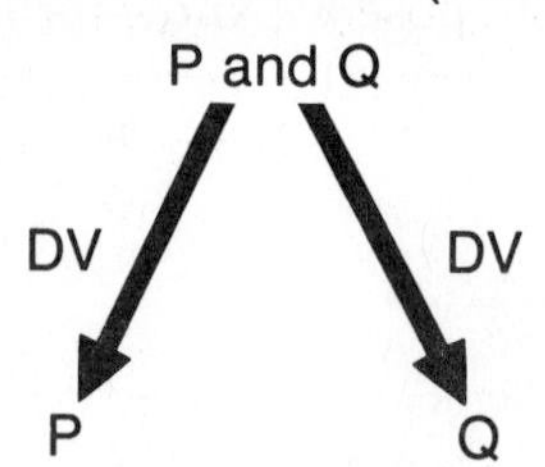

Simplification simply states that if "P and Q" are true, then "P" must be true and that "Q" must be true. For example:

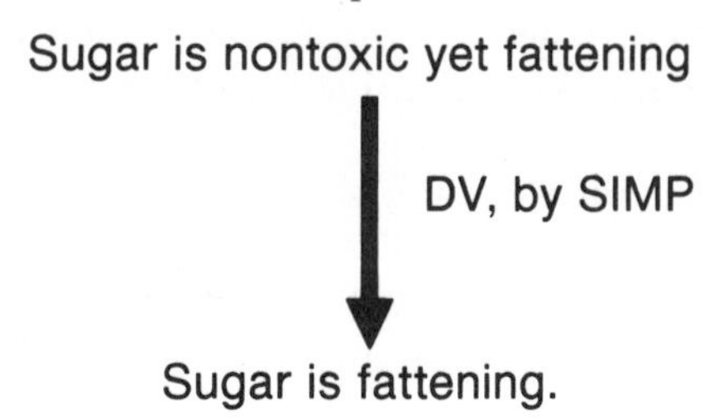

Each simple statement in a conjunction is a **CONJUNCT**. The two rules for conjunction, then, can be expressed like this: The order of conjuncts in a conjunction is irrelevant (CO); and a conjunction entails any of its conjuncts (SIMP).

4.4 Disjunction

The truthtable for "or" requires some explanation. The standard logical definition of "or" (in "*P* or *Q*") is "Either *P* or *Q* or both." Thus a disjunction is taken to be false only when all its simple statements are false:

P,	Q	P or Q
T	T	T
T	F	T
F	T	T
F	F	F

This sense of "or" is equivalent to "and/or": Notice the first line of the truthtable: "*P* or *Q*" is true even when both disjuncts are true. This "and/or" sense is intended when, for example, someone says "He's likely to turn up late or broke" (implying "or both").

But suppose I say, "He's in New York or he's in San Francisco." Surely I can't imply "or both" if I have any idea where New York and San Francisco are.

The sense of "or" given in the truthtable is sometimes called "weak 'or'" ("and/or"), for it allows "*P* or *Q*" to be true when both simple statements are true. It is also sometimes said that the "or" of "He's in New York or he's in San Francisco" is a "strong 'or'," implying "but not both." Are there really two different "or's" in English? Or is the "but not both" just something understood by the hearer?

If we can distinguish between what a statement (in itself) means from what kinds of expectations or beliefs it arouses, we can see that "but not both" is not a part of the meaning of the statement but rather part of the expectations or beliefs surrounding the statement. Since we all know someone can't be in both New York and San Francisco, the temptation is to think that the "or" is different. But this isn't sufficient evidence to think that the "or" is different. "Today he is in Toledo or in Detroit." Since Toledo is a relatively short (about one and a half hour) drive from Detroit, he could be in both today.

It is odd to hold that the meaning of "or" changes depending on whether we're talking about New York/San Francisco or Detroit/Toledo. It is more plausible to hold that the expectations or beliefs surrounding a statement change. In other words, "or" always means what it means in its truthtable definition.

There aren't many ways to express disjunction in English:

	Disjunctions
or	*It is raining or the sun is shining.*
either. . . or	*Either it is raining or the sun is shining.*

And that seems to be about it.

Writing a truthtable for disjunctions that contain negations is not difficult. Problem: Write a truthtable for

Either it's windy or it's not sunny.

Abbreviating "It's windy" as "*W*" and "It's sunny" as "*S*," we arrive at this,

Either W *or not* S.

the truthtable for which is:

W,	S	W or not S
T	T	T (F)
T	F	T (T)
F	T	F (F)
F	F	T (T)

The first line says that when "*W*" is true and "*S*" is true, then "not *S*" is false and "*W* or not *S*" is true. And so on.

Given the truthtable for "or," we can say, as we did for conjunction, whether a disjunction is True or False. Suppose we are given (again):

"It is sunny" is True.

"It is windy" is False.

Then we know that:

"It is either sunny or windy" is True.

"It is either not sunny or windy" is False.

We know this by looking at the truthtable. Again, let "*S*" abbreviate "It is sunny" and "*W*" abbreviate "It is windy":

	S, W	S or W	Not S or W
	T T	T	(F) T
"S" is T, "W" is F →	T F	T	(F) F
	F T	T	(T) T
	F F	F	(T) T

We will learn two rules for disjunction. The first is an equivalence, and matches CO:

DISJUNCTIVE ORDER (DO)

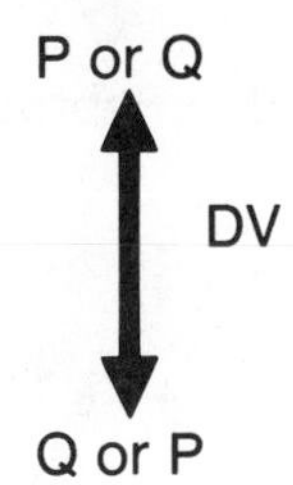

For example:

It's either not sunny or windy.

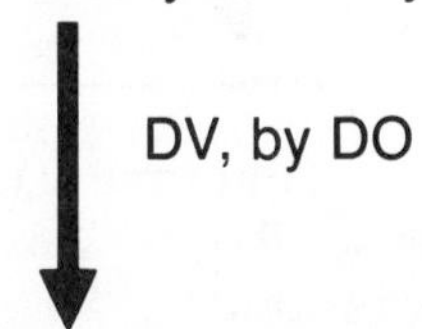

It's either windy or not sunny.

The second is an important rule for many arguments in ordinary language:

DISJUNCTIVE SYLLOGISM (DS)

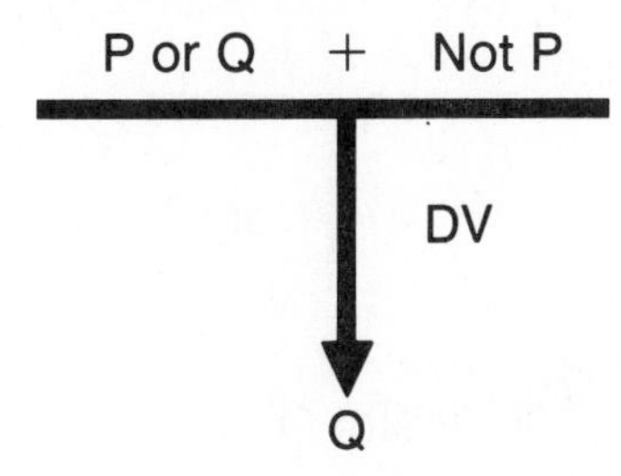

Here is an example of a valid disjunctive syllogism:

I was told that my ad would appear in either the January edition or the February edition. It hasn't appeared in January's. So it will appear in the February edition.

It is valid by DS. Its structure can be better indicated in an argument diagram with a little bit of shorthand:

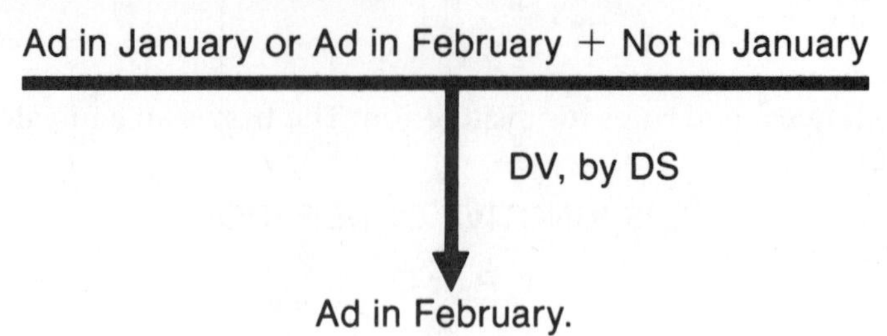

Note that there is no disjunctive version of simplification. Neither of these arguments is DV:

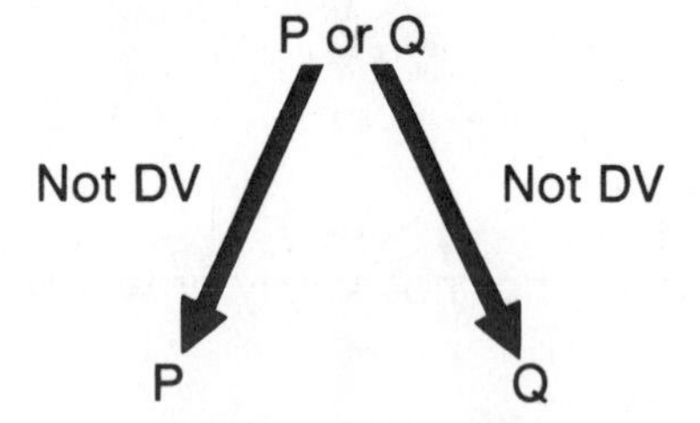

Since "*P* or *Q*" can be true if only one of the disjuncts is true, you cannot infer "*P*" from "*P* or *Q*" because "*P* or *Q*" may be true yet "*P*" be false. Hence this example is deductively invalid:

I know it's true that either we'll be on time or he'll be angry. So we'll be on time.

This sort of argument is unlikely to be made. However, there is another kind of deductively invalid argument that may be heard:

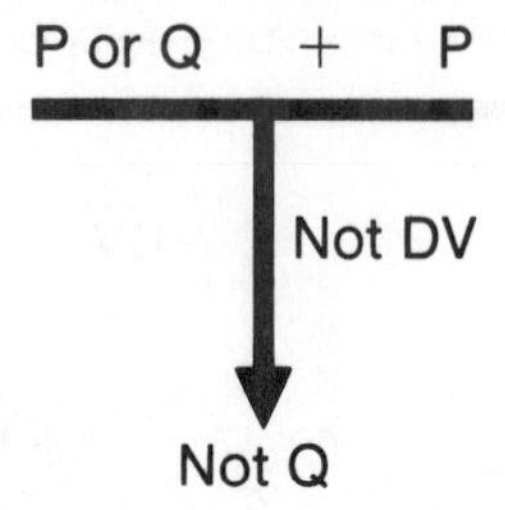

Since "*P* or *Q*" may be true when both simple statements are true, you cannot validly infer that just because one turns out to be true, the other will be false. For example, this is deductively invalid:

I've heard that he'll put a Christmas tree outside or inside. I see he has one outside. So he hasn't put one inside.

Even if it's true that he will put a Christmas tree outside or inside, it doesn't deductively follow that he hasn't put one inside just because he has one outside—he could (weak "or," remember) have put one both outside and inside. Perhaps an argument diagram with a little shorthand will help:

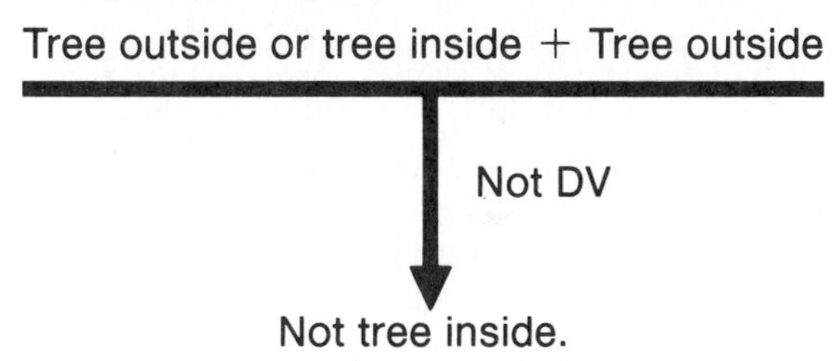

Each simple part of a disjunction is a **DISJUNCT**. The rules for disjunction can be expressed this way: The order of disjuncts in a disjunction is irrelevant (DO); the denial of one disjunct entails the other (DS); a disjunction does not entail any one of its disjuncts; and the affirmation of one disjunction does not entail the denial of the other.

4.5 Double Negation in Arguments

The truthtables for "*P*" and "Not not *P*" are the same:

P	Not (not P)
T	T (F)
F	F (T)

You can see that double negation just reverses the truthvalues yet again. If "*P*" is true, then "Not *P*" is false, and if "Not *P*" is false, then "Not not *P*" must be true again. When two statements are logically equivalent, one may be deductively inferred from the other. Therefore we have this rule of inference:

DOUBLE NEGATION (DN)

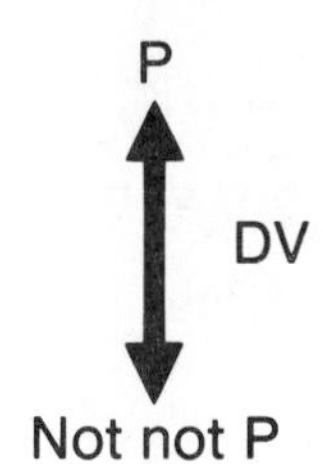

There are few natural arguments in English that rely solely on DN for their validity. One could imagine something like this argument occurring in a context in which one person has asserted that sugar is nontoxic and another wishes to deny it:

> *You say sugar is nontoxic. Well, sugar is toxic. So it is* not *nontoxic!*

This argument is DV because of DN. But while DV, its soundness is at issue since which person is right about sugar depends on the truth or falsity of "Sugar is toxic." (See Circular Reasoning in Chapter 7.)

Mostly DN is used to yield or cancel out double negatives in the application of other rules. For example, this is a valid inference:

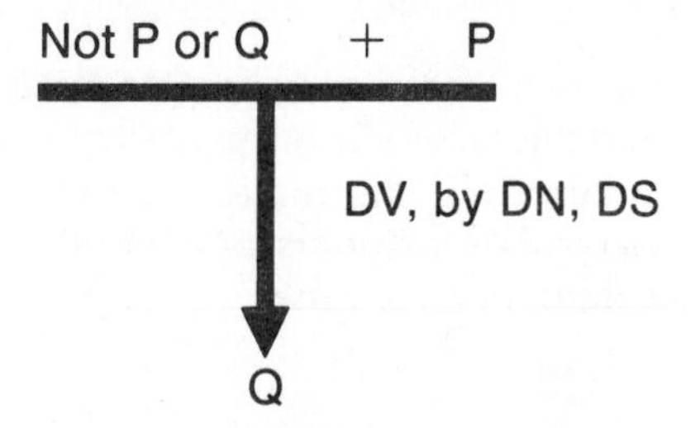

The validity of this inference depends on the equivalence of "*P*" and "Not not *P*" to apply DS. DS, in effect, says that an argument is deductively valid if one premise is a disjunction and another premise denies one of the disjuncts. "*P*" by DN is "Not not *P*," and "Not not *P*" denies "*P*." A concrete example:

> *Either she won't go or she'll borrow the money. But she's going. So she'll borrow the money.*

An argument diagram in detail and using some shorthand will show this argument DV:

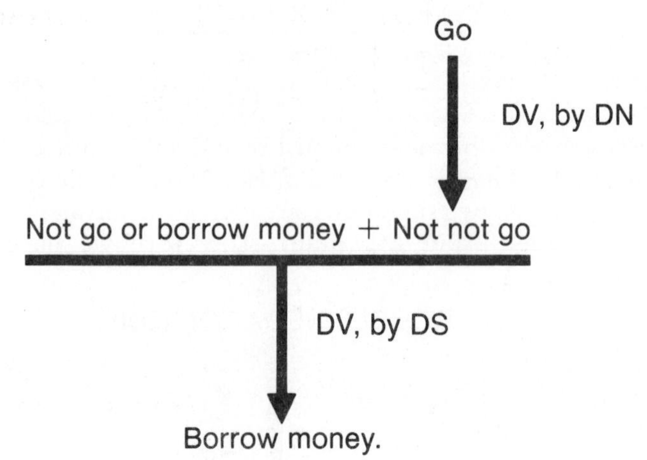

4.6
Scope and De Morgan's Laws

The scope of negation—of "not"—is what it negates. There is a difference between

(A) Not P *and* Q.

(B) Not P *and not* Q.

*(C) Not (*P *and* Q*).*

In (A) only the first conjunct is denied; in (B) each conjunct is denied; and in (C) the whole conjunction is denied. That is, the scope of "not" in (A) is "*P*"; the scope of the first "not" in (B) is "*P*" and of the second "not" is "*Q*"; the scope of "not" in (C) is "*P* and *Q*."

Truthtables will show that these are not equivalent:

P, Q	Not P and Q	Not P and not Q	Not (P and Q)
T T	(F) F	(F) F (F)	F (T)
T F	(F) F	(F) F (T)	T (F)
F T	(T) T	(T) F (F)	T (F)
F F	(T) F	(T) T (T)	T (F)

The truthvalues in parentheses are the truthvalues of the negated simples—e.g., when "*P*" is T, "Not *P*" is F. The truthvalues outside parentheses are the truthvalues of the entire compound sentence. None of these are true and false in exactly the same cases. (Verify this for yourself.) Therefore they are not equivalent.

We now have to see how ordinary English shows scope. (A) is no problem, for example:

(A) This is not salary, yet it is taxable.

(B) typically uses "neither. . . nor," for example:

(B) This is neither salary nor is it taxable.

Do not get confused because "neither. . . nor" sounds like "either. . . or." "Neither *P* nor *Q*" denies "*P*" and denies "*Q*." (C) is cumbersome to express in ordinary English. We have to say something like:

(C) This is not both salary and taxable.

And remember that (A), (B), and (C) are not equivalent.

Differences in the scope of "not" can happen in disjunction:

(D) Either not P *or* Q.

(E) Either not P *or not* Q.

(F) Not (either P *or* Q*).*

These are not equivalent as a truthtable test will show:

P, Q	Not P or Q	Not P or not Q	Not (P or Q)
T T	(F) T	(F) F (F)	F (T)
T F	(F) F	(F) T (T)	F (T)
F T	(T) T	(T) T (F)	F (T)
F F	(T) T	(T) T (T)	T (F)

Here are some ordinary English examples:

(D) Either you don't make the sale or you'll be fired.

(E) Either you don't make the sale or you won't be fired.

(F) It's not true that either you make the sale or you'll be fired.

You can see that it is cumbersome to express (F) in ordinary English.

Using the truthtables for conjunction, disjunction, and negation, we can say what the truthvalue of compound statements is. For example, we are again given:

"It is sunny" is True.

"It is windy" is False.

On this basis, we can say that:

"It is neither sunny nor windy" is False.

"It is not both sunny and windy" is True.

"It is either not sunny or not windy" is True.

Truthtables will show this. Abbreviating "It is sunny" with "*S*" and "It is windy" with "*W*":

	S W	Neither S nor W = Not W and not W	Not (S and W)	Not S or not W
	T T	(F) F (F)	F (T)	(F) F (F)
→	T F	(F) F (T)	T (F)	(F) T (T)
	F T	(T) F (F)	T (F)	(T) T (F)
	F F	(T) T (T)	T (F)	(T) T (T)

De Morgan's Laws (named for Augustus De Morgan, nineteenth-century British mathematician and logician) state equivalences between "and" and "or." They are:

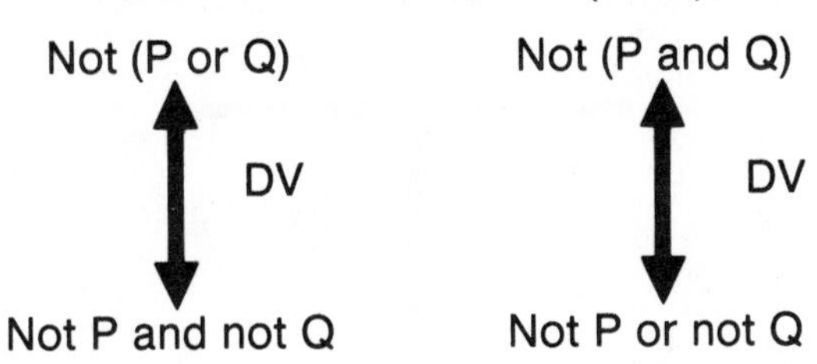

For example, each of the following arguments is deductively valid by DeM:

This is neither salary nor taxable. (Not P *and not* Q*) So it isn't either salary or taxable. (Not (*P *or* Q*))*

*It's not both salary and taxable. (Not (*P *and* Q*)) So it's either not salary or not taxable. (Not* P *or not* Q*)*

4.7 Applying the Rules

Besides learning the inference rules, you must be able to apply them to arguments. This involves seeing what form the parts of an argument have. Is the premise an "either. . . or"? Is the conclusion a conjunction or the denial of a conjunction? And so on. Also, you will sometimes have to apply more than one rule at the same time.

Our first example:

She's at home, because either she's at home or at the library, and she's not at the library.

We can do better if we set out the premises and conclusion in a little bit of shorthand:

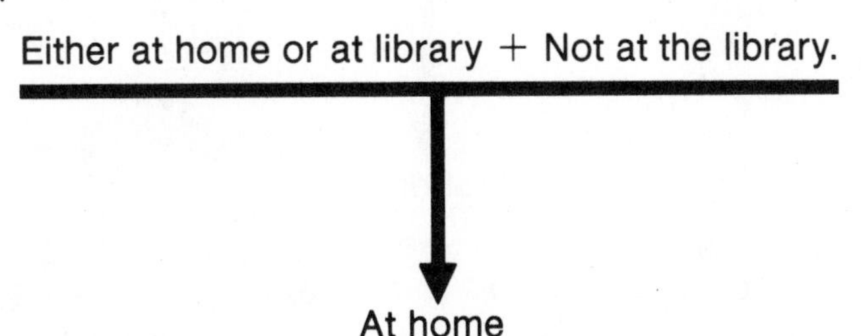

Two rules are relevant here: DO and DS. The form DS was given is:

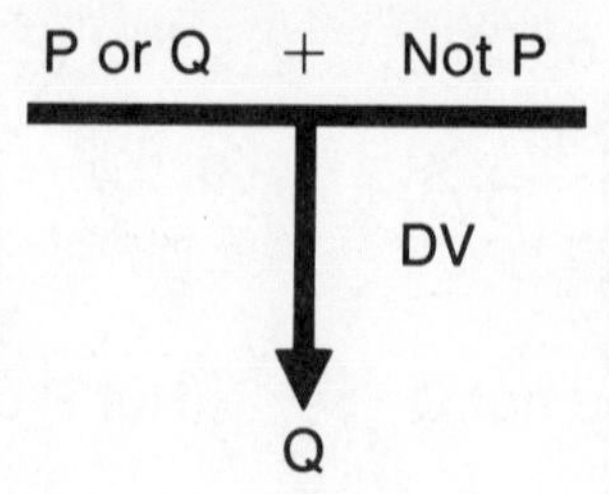

But the argument at issue has the second disjunct denied. Well, use DO to make it the first disjunct and the argument is valid by DO and DS. We can write it like this:

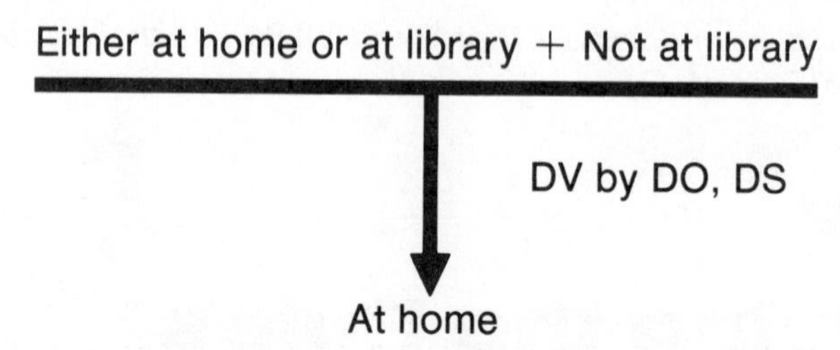

Or if you chose not to do an argument diagram, you could have written it like this:

> *She's at home, because either she's at home or at the library, and she's not at the library. DV by DO, DS.*

Here is a slightly more complicated example:

> *This amount in your paycheck is not both bonus and wages. It's wages. So it's not bonus.*

Set it out in shorthand:

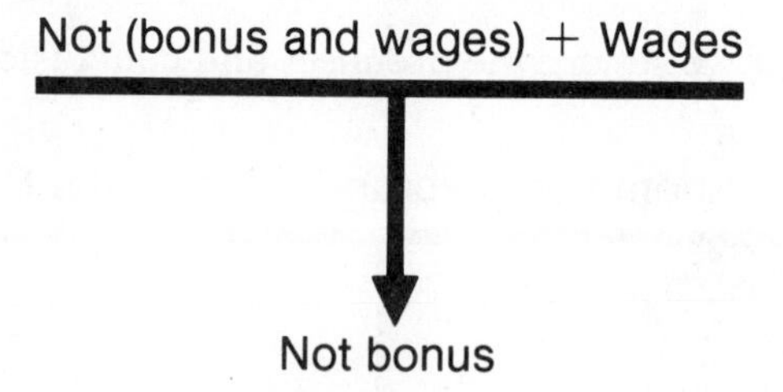

The first premise, "Not (bonus and wages)," means by DeM "Not bonus or not wages." By DO, we can derive "Not wages or not bonus." The second premise, "Wages," entails by DN "Not not wages." Thus we've gotten:

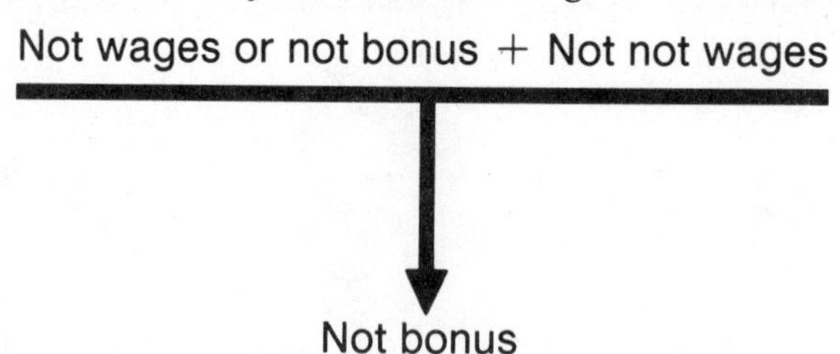

The second premise, "Not not wages," denies "Not wages," and so by DS we can validly infer the conclusion. This argument is valid according to four valid rules of inference:

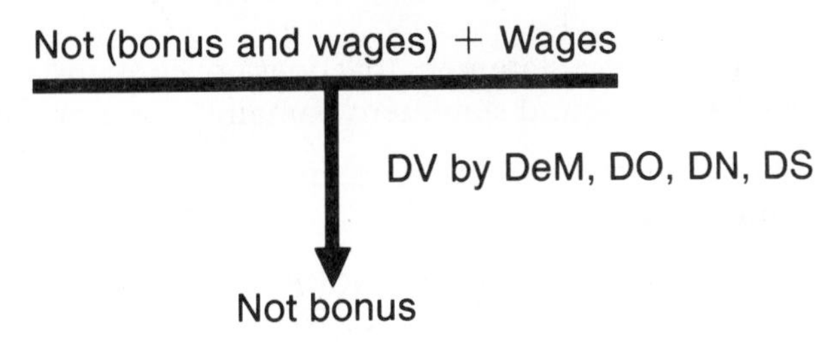

This is about as complicated as the exercises will get.

Invalid arguments are treated in a similar fashion, except that their mistakes often have no name. For example,

You'll either fail the exam or pass the course. And since you've passed the course, you haven't failed the exam.

Putting it into shorthand we have:

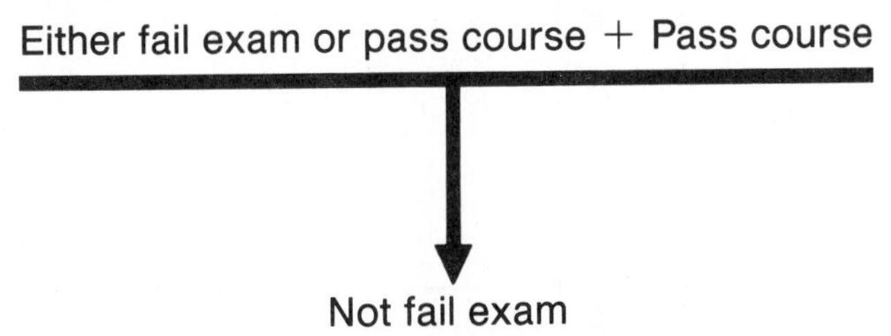

But we cannot apply DS here. This is an instance of the invalid argument form:

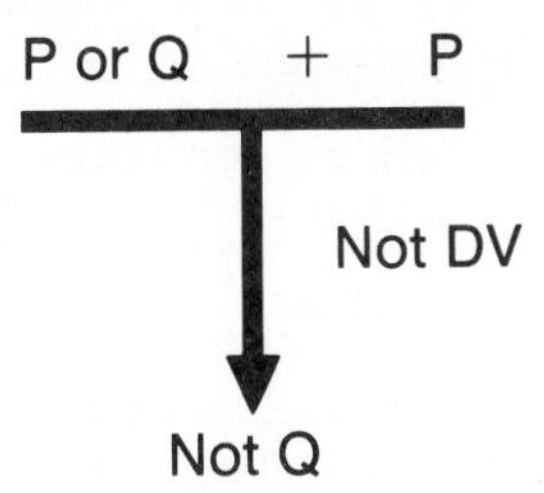

The "or" of the first premise is weak: You'll either fail the exam or pass the course or both. Just because you've passed the course (as the second premise asserts—and suppose this to be true), it doesn't follow that you haven't failed the exam. So you write:

You'll either fail the exam or pass the course. And since you've passed the course, you haven't failed the exam. Not DV

KEY POINTS

A simple statement is a statement that does not contain "and," "or," "not," or "if. . . then." A compound statement contains one more of these terms.

A truthtable gives the conditions under which a compound statement is to be counted as True or False.

P	Not P
T	F
F	T

P, Q	P and Q
T T	T
T F	F
F T	F
F F	F

P, Q	P or Q
T T	T
T F	T
F T	T
F F	F

Given the truthtables for "and," "or," and "not," and given the knowledge of fact (or just given some facts), we can determine the truthvalues of compound conjunctions and disjunctions.

- Given, for example, that "He's a gentleman" is True, while "He's a scholar" is False, we know that
- "He's not a gentleman" is False.
- "He's a gentleman and a scholar" is False.
- "He's a gentleman or a scholar" is True.

Two statements are logically equivalent when they have exactly the same truthtable (i.e., are true or false under the same circumstances). When two statements are logically equivalent, each may be inferred from the other with deductive validity. DN, CO, DO, and DeM are logical equivalences.

The valid inference rules we have learned in this chapter are:

CONJUNCTION ORDER (CO)

P and Q

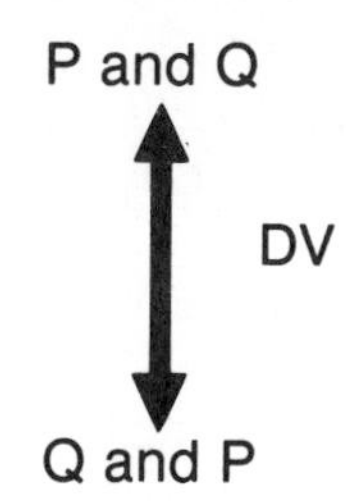

Q and P

SIMPLIFICATION (SIMP)

P and Q

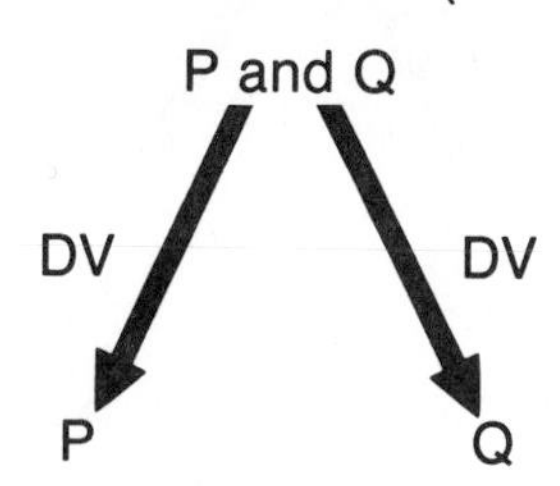

P Q

DISJUNCTIVE ORDER (DO)

P or Q

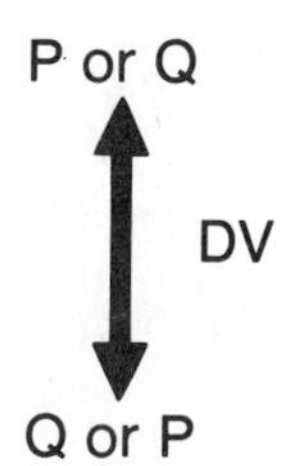

Q or P

DISJUNCTIVE SYLLOGISM (DS)

P or Q + Not P

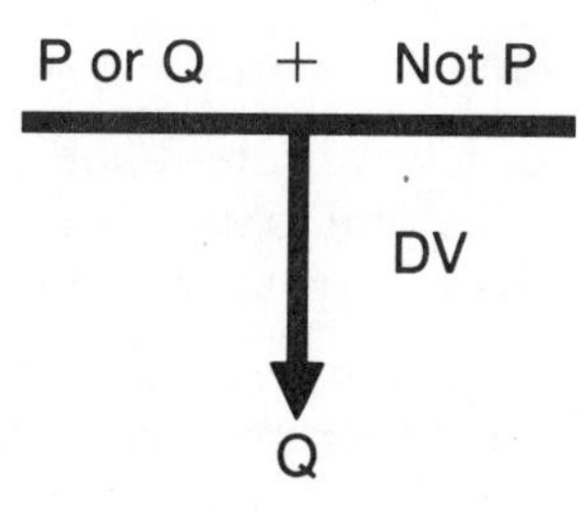

Q

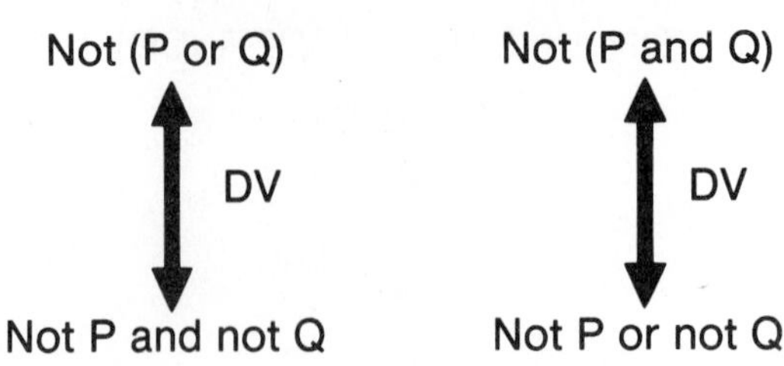

Two invalid inferences were mentioned:

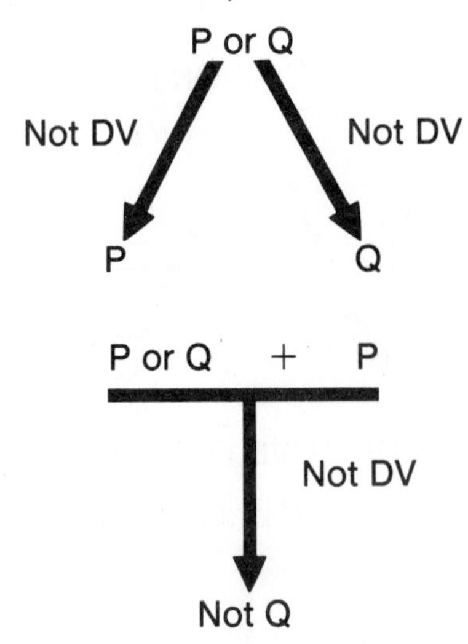

Be aware of scope, that is, what the "not" ranges over. It is especially important to distinguish:

> It is not both sunny and windy. = Not (sunny and windy).
>
> It is not sunny and not windy. = Neither sunny nor windy.
>
> It is not sunny but it is windy. = Not sunny and windy.

Some arguments make use of several rules to be deductively valid. In dealing with arguments, it is often helpful to use shorthand style in assessing the validity of such arguments. That is, try to take an argument like:

> *This bread either lacks enough yeast or enough sugar. But I know I put enough yeast in it. So it doesn't have enough sugar.*

into:

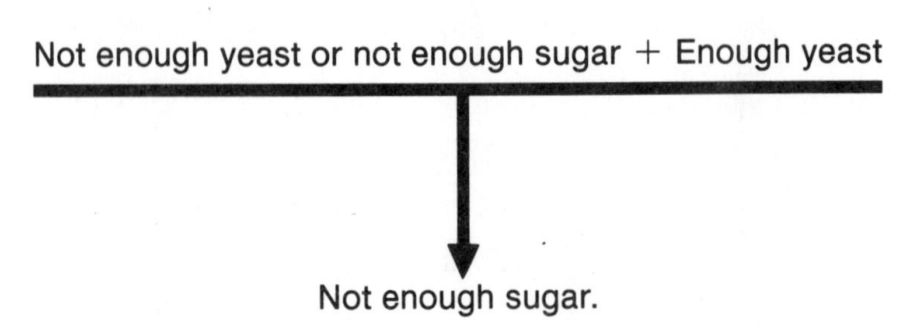

EXERCISES

A. Using as simple statements,

Waldo will flunk out.

Waldo will make $1 million.

write a conjunction of these in six different English sentences.

***A1.** *Waldo will flunk out, yet he'll make $1 million.*

A2.

A3.

A4.

A5.

A6.

B. You are trying to deal with your taxes. Here are the facts:

"You earn $20,000 a year" is True.

"You have no interest paid to you" is True.

"You own your own home" is False.

You must decide whether certain rules—B1 through B11—apply to you. (What the rules are doesn't matter for this exercise.) Which of the rules applies to you (given the facts)?

(1) If a statement is true, the rule applies. Answer "Yes."

(2) If a statement is false, the rule does not apply. Answer "No."

*B1. You earn less than $20,000 a year.

NO

B2. You own your own home.

B3. You earn less than $20,000 a year and have no interest paid to you.

B4. You either earn less than $20,000 a year or you own your own home.

B5. You have at least $100 paid to you in interest or you don't own your own home.

B6. You have no interest paid to you but you earn at least $20,000 a year.

B7. You don't both earn $20,000 a year and own your own home.

B8. You neither own your own home nor earn less than $20,000 a year.

B9. You earn $20,000 a year and have no interest paid to you and don't own your own home.

B10. Either you don't own your own home or you earn less than $20,000 a year or you have at least $100 in interest paid to you.

B11. Either you own your own home or you don't.

C. Circle ALL correct answers. (Some problems have more than one.)

C1. When two statements, say "*P*" and "*Q*," are logically equivalent, this means

- **a.** "*P*" entails "*Q*."
- **b.** "*Q*" entails "*P*."
- **c.** "*P*" and "*Q*" will each have the same truthtable.
- **d.** The relation between "*P*" and "*Q*" is only a single-headed arrow.

C2. If a rule says this:

then we know:

- **a.** "*P*" deductively entails "*Q*."
- **b.** "*Q*" deductively entails "*P*."
- **c.** The argument "*P*, therefore *Q*" is deductively valid.
- **d.** The argument "*P*, therefore *Q*" is sound.

C3. The rule DS says:

- **a.** An argument is valid if it has a disjunction as a premise, a denial of one of the disjuncts as another premise, and the other disjunct as a conclusion.
- **b.** An argument is valid if it has a disjunction as a premise, an affirmation of one of the disjuncts as another premise, and the denial of the other disjunct as a conclusion.
- **c.** None of the above.

C4. "It's sunny but windy" is logically equivalent to

- **a.** It's sunny.
- **b.** It's windy.
- **c.** It's windy and sunny.
- **d.** It's false that it's neither windy nor sunny.
- **e.** None of the above.

C5. "Either you pass the exam or you fail the course" is logically equivalent to

- **a.** Either you fail the course or you pass the exam.
- **b.** You pass the exam.
- **c.** You fail the course.
- **d.** Either you fail the course or you pass the exam or both.
- **e.** It's false that you will both not pass the exam and not fail the course.
- **f.** None of the above.

C6. "It's not both sunny and cloudy" is logically equivalent to

- **a.** It's neither sunny nor cloudy.
- **b.** It's either not sunny or not cloudy.
- **c.** It's not both cloudy and sunny.
- **d.** It's either sunny or cloudy.
- **e.** None of the above.

C7. "The party is not either black tie or white tie" is logically equivalent to

- **a.** The party is neither black tie nor white tie.
- **b.** The party is not black tie and it is not white tie.
- **c.** The party is not both black tie and white tie.
- **d.** The party is black tie and white tie.
- **e.** None of the above.

C8. This is false: The milk is not sour but the bread is stale. So?

- **a.** Either the milk is not sour or the bread is not stale.
- **b.** Either the milk is sour or the bread is not stale.
- **c.** The milk is not sour, yet the bread is stale.
- **d.** None of the above.

C9. "It's night but I can't see the stars" asserts that

- **a.** It's night.
- **b.** I can't see the stars.
- **c.** Both a. and b.
- **d.** None of the above.

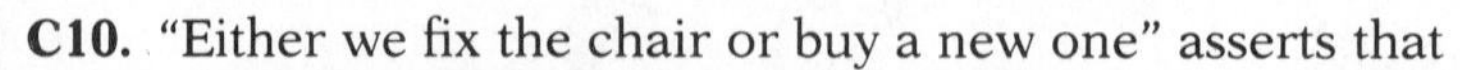

C10. "Either we fix the chair or buy a new one" asserts that

a. We fix the chair.
b. We buy a new one.
c. Both a. and b.
d. None of the above.

C11. Brian says to Paul, "Either we'll go to Mackinac Island or visit my sister in Traverse City." Later Paul receives a postcard from Brian, posted from the Grand Hotel on Mackinac Island. Assume that this proves that Brian was on Mackinac Island. Assume that what Brian said to Paul is true. What should Paul deductively conclude?

a. Brian did not visit his sister in Traverse City.
b. Maybe Brian visited his sister in Traverse City; maybe he didn't.

D. Each of the following arguments has a missing premise or a missing conclusion. Supply the missing part so as to produce a deductively valid argument according to the rule(s) given.

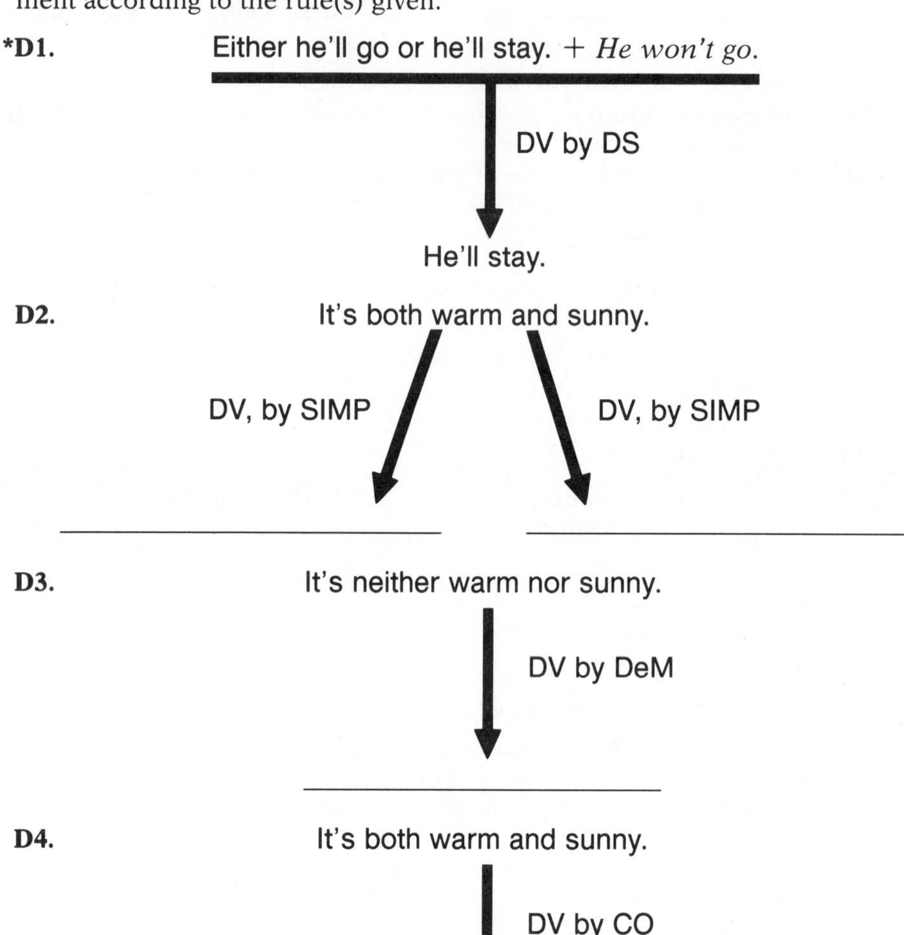

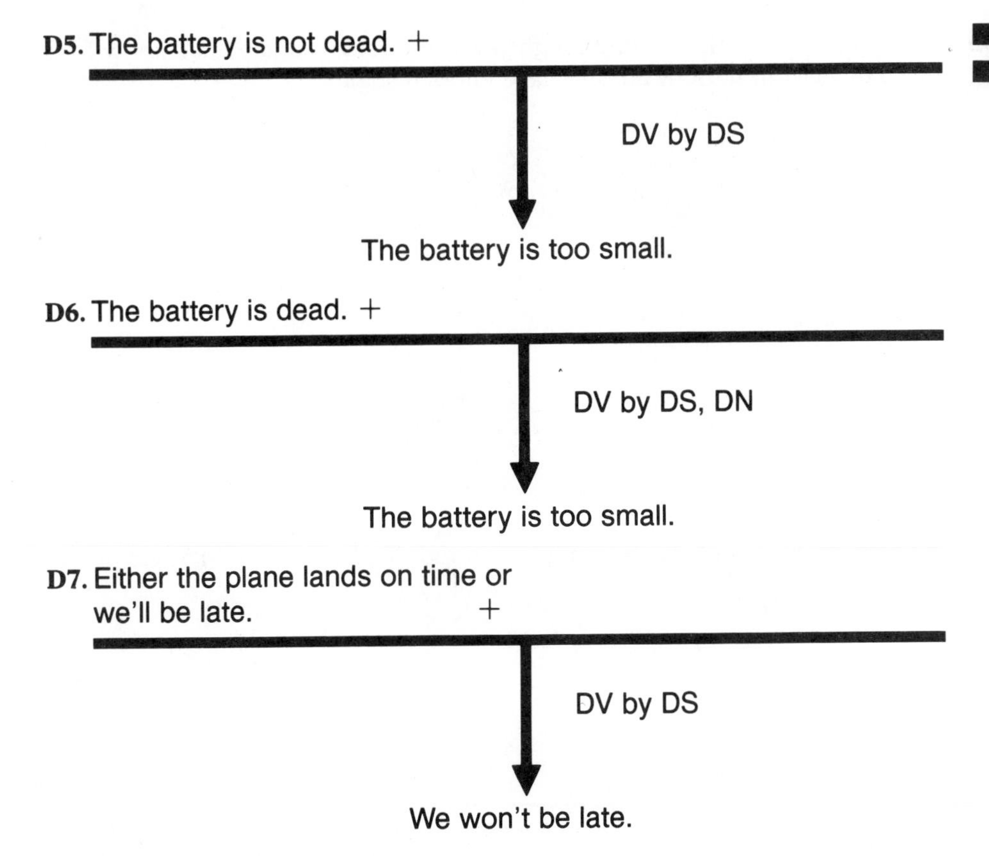

E. Here are some arguments.

(1) Diagram each in a "shorthand" style.

(2) Decide whether each is deductively valid or not, and why—state the rule(s).

(3) Occasionally you will be asked if the argument is sound.

***E1.** You're either my friend or my enemy. Since you're not my enemy, you must be my friend. Deductively Valid? Why? Sound?

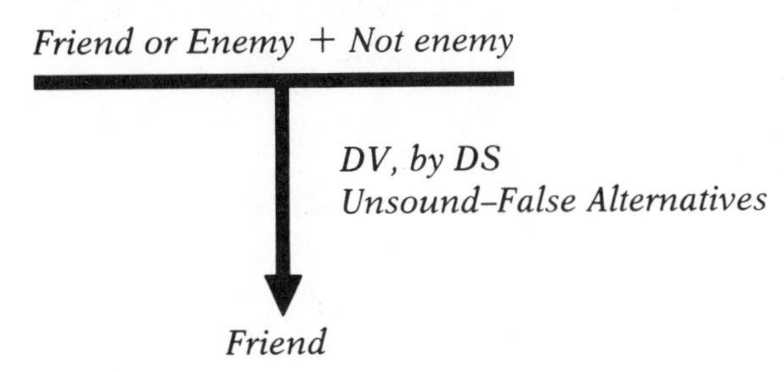

E2. This bread lacks either enough yeast or enough sugar. But I know I put enough yeast in it. So it doesn't have enough sugar.

E3. He'll arrive on time, but in a bad mood. So, he'll arrive in a bad mood.

E4. He'll arrive on time or in a good mood. So, he'll arrive in a good mood.

E5. You haven't come in first, although we know you've come in first or second. So you've come in second.

E6. You've come in first. We knew you'd come in first or second. So you haven't come in second.

E7. He's neither broke nor unemployed. So he's not broke.

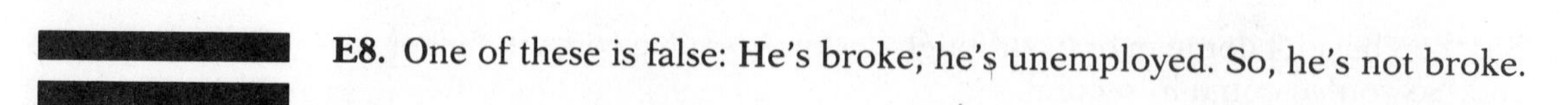

E8. One of these is false: He's broke; he's unemployed. So, he's not broke.

E9. We knew yesterday that this painting is by Rembrandt or by one of his students. Today we discover that Rembrandt didn't paint it, nor did Vermeer. So, it's by one of Rembrandt's students.

E10. Only some terriers are yappy because either all terriers are yappy or only some are, and not all terriers are yappy.

CHAPTER 5

CONDITIONALS

This chapter studies conditionals, most commonly expressed as "if. . . then" statements. It complements the previous chapter on conjunction and disjunction, and completes our study of the logic of statements. The conditional, as you will see, is a more complicated statement form than either conjunction or disjunction. The most important concepts in this chapter include:

The CONDITIONAL
— and different ways to express one

ANTECEDENT and CONSEQUENT
—especially as they express

NECESSARY and SUFFICIENT CONDITIONS

The BICONDITIONAL

These RULES for conditionals:
CONTRAPOSITION
MODUS PONENS
MODUS TOLLENS
HYPOTHETICAL SYLLOGISM
UNLESS EQUIVALENCE

These FALLACIES:
of AFFIRMING THE CONSEQUENT
of DENYING THE ANTECEDENT

5.1 Necessary Conditions, Sufficient Conditions

Although we call the conditional an "if. . . then" statement, there are several other ways of expressing the conditional. The following are all equivalent, that is, they each say the same thing:

If P *then* Q. *(If it's an ant, then it's an insect.)*

If P, Q. *(If it's an ant, it's an insect.)*

Q, *if* P. *(It's an insect, if it's an ant.)*

You can see that "then" is optional.

The **ANTECEDENT** of a conditional is the statement that follows "if"; the **CONSEQUENT** of a conditional is the statement that follows "then" (if there is a "then") or that follows "only if" (if there is an "only if"):

If <u>*ANTECEDENT*</u>, *then* <u>*CONSEQUENT*</u>.

If <u>*ANTECEDENT*</u>, <u>*CONSEQUENT*</u>.

<u>*CONSEQUENT*</u>, *if* <u>*ANTECEDENT*</u>.

It does not matter which is *written* first, antecedent or consequent ("If *P* then *Q*", and "*Q*, if *P*" are equivalent). But it is crucial that the antecedent remain the antecedent, and the consequent remain the consequent. You cannot "switch" statements around in a conditional. (There is no rule for conditionals corresponding to Conjunctive or Disjunctive Order.) None of the following are valid:

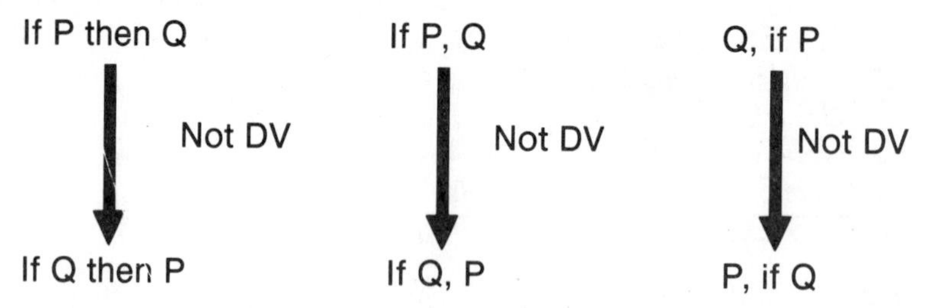

The example we have been using will confirm this. We move from a truth to a falsehood—which cannot happen if the argument is DV:

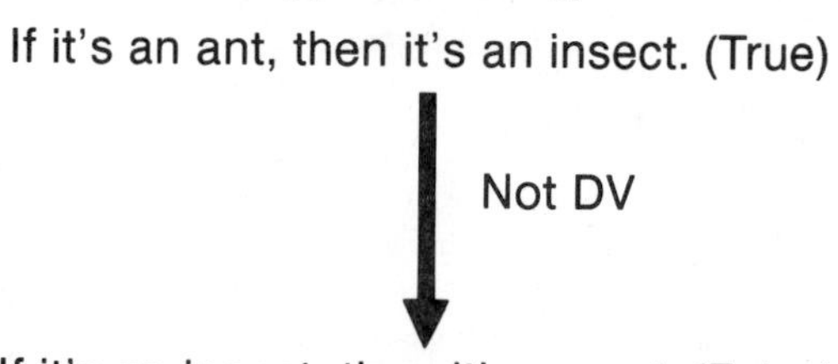

A conditional is primarily used to state sufficient or necessary conditions.

A **SUFFICIENT CONDITION** for something else (*P*) is a condition (circumstance, fact, event) that, if true, will bring about *P*. A **NECESSARY CONDITION** for something else (*P*) is a condition (circumstance, fact, event) that, if true, makes *P* possible (or that *P* needs in order to happen).

We say that a sufficient condition for being married is going through a legally sanctioned marriage ceremony. Going through a legally sanctioned marriage ceremony is a condition that, if it happens, will bring about the state of being married. We say that a necessary condition for being married is getting a marriage license. Getting a marriage license is a condition that, if true, makes being married possible (or which being married needs in order to happen). We can express these facts in another way, by using "if. . . then" statements:

If two people have gone through a legally sanctioned marriage ceremony, then they're married.

Two people are married only if they have a marriage license.

Each of the following is equivalent:

If P *then* Q. *(If it's an ant, then it's an insect.)*

P *only if* Q. *(It's an ant only if it's an insect.)*

P *is a sufficient condition for* Q. *(Being an ant is a sufficient condition for being an insect.)*

Q *is a necessary condition for* P. *(Being an insect is a necessary condition for being an ant.)*

The most important facets to remember are these:

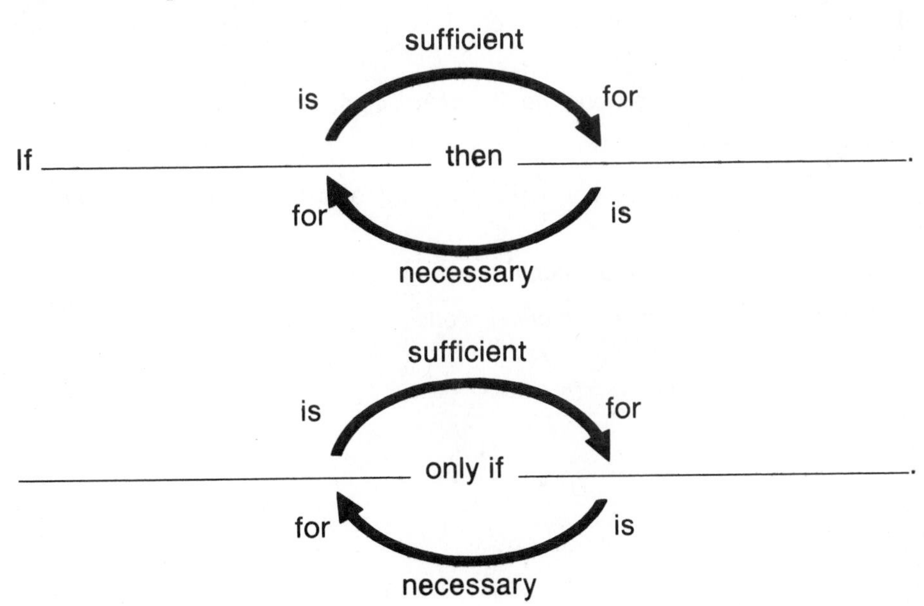

While "If P then Q" and "P only if Q" are equivalent in meaning, they have different rhetorical force. "If P then Q" tends to emphasize the sufficiency of P for Q, while "P only if Q" tends to emphasize the necessity of Q for P. (This is somewhat like emphasizing words in sentences. "She is *his* aunt" and "She is his *aunt*" both mean the same, although each emphasizes a different aspect of the same fact.)

There are various kinds of statements of necessary or sufficient conditions. There are *legal conditions*, for example,

> *Being convicted of second-degree murder is sufficient to receive a twenty-five year prison term.*
>
> *It is necessary to have a valid driver's license to legally operate a motor vehicle.*

Rules (other than those of law) often give necessary or sufficient conditions:

> *A passing grade on the final exam is sufficient for passing the course.*
>
> *In bridge it is necessary to bid and make six of anything to get the bonus for a small slam.*

Causal conditions are also statable in terms of necessity or sufficiency:

> *A sufficient condition for enlivening dry yeast is to soak it in warm milk.*
>
> *To get from New York to Los Angeles in less than a day it is necessary to take a plane.*

Necessary or sufficient conditions also state parts of the *meanings of words:*

> *To be a bachelor, it is necessary that you be unmarried.*
>
> *It is sufficient to have floating ship wreckage to have flotsam on the water.*

The *plans or intentions of persons* can be expressed in terms of necessary or sufficient conditions:

> *It's necessary that you lend me $5 before I'll go to the movie.*
>
> *Your word is sufficient for me to believe it.*

There are also what we can call, for want of a better term, *wild conditionals:*

> *There's food in the refrigerator, if you're hungry.*
>
> *If he's innocent, then I'm a monkey's uncle.*

We can rewrite the previous examples in different ways:

THIS is equivalent to	*THIS*
Being convicted of second-degree murder is sufficient to receive a twenty-five year prison term.	*If you're convicted of second-degree murder, then you receive a twenty-five year prison term.*
It is necessary to have a valid driver's license to legally operate a motor vehicle.	*You can legally operate a motor vehicle only if you have a valid driver's license.*
A passing grade on the final exam is sufficient for passing the course.	*If you get a passing grade on the final exam, then you'll pass the course.*
In bridge it is necessary to bid and make six of anything to get the bonus for a small slam.	*You get the bonus for a small slam only if you bid and make six of anything.*
A sufficient condition for enlivening dry yeast is to soak it in warm milk.	*If you soak dry yeast in warm milk, then it will enliven.*
To be a bachelor, it is necessary that you be unmarried.	*You are a bachelor only if you are unmarried.*
It is sufficient to have floating ship wreckage to have flotsam on the water.	*If you have floating ship wreckage, then you have flotsam on the water.*
It's necessary that you lend me $5 before I'll go to the movie.	*I'll go to the movie only if you lend me $5.*
There's food in the refrigerator if you're hungry.	*Your being hungry is a sufficient condition for there being food in the refrigerator.*
If he's innocent, then I'm a monkey's uncle.	*A sufficient condition of my being a monkey's uncle is his innocence.*

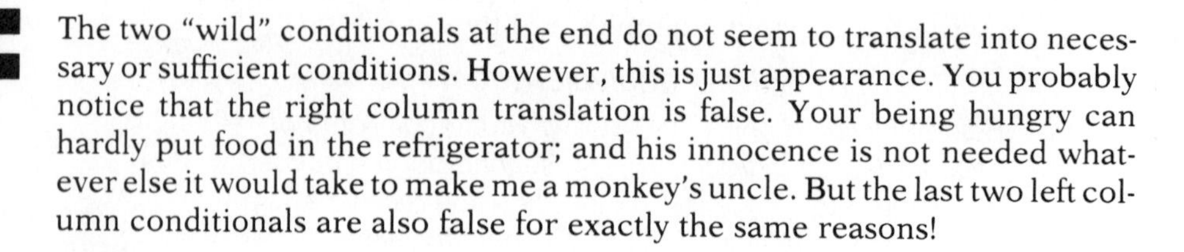
The two "wild" conditionals at the end do not seem to translate into necessary or sufficient conditions. However, this is just appearance. You probably notice that the right column translation is false. Your being hungry can hardly put food in the refrigerator; and his innocence is not needed whatever else it would take to make me a monkey's uncle. But the last two left column conditionals are also false for exactly the same reasons!

5.2 The Biconditional

Besides conditionals, there is something called a biconditional. A **BICONDITIONAL** expresses necessary AND sufficient conditions. The phrase "if and only if" (whose standard logic abbreviation is "iff") is a biconditional. The following are equivalent:

P *if and only if* Q.

P *iff* Q.

If P *then* Q *and if* Q *then* P.

Notice especially the third line above. It says not only is "*P*" sufficient for "*Q*" ("If *P* then *Q*"), but "*P*" is also necessary for "*Q*" ("If *Q* then *P*"). It also says the same about "*Q*." The biconditional is typically used to express definitions, for example:

Something is a vixen if and only if it is a female fox.

Something is an artwork if and only if it is a beautiful object created by some person(s).

The first is clearly true: Any dictionary will verify it. The second is more controversial: Some would claim that not all beautiful objects created by persons are artworks. (Is a beautiful dress an artwork?) The point, however, is that each *claims* to state necessary and sufficient conditions. The first claims that being a female fox is necessary and sufficient for being a vixen. The second claims, correctly or not, that being a beautiful object created by some person(s) is necessary and sufficient for being an artwork. Thus:

THIS is equivalent to THIS which is equivalent to THIS

Something is a vixen if and only if it is a female fox.	*If it is a vixen then it is a female fox, and if it is a female fox then it is a vixen.*	*Being a female fox is necessary and sufficient for being a vixen.*

Something is an artwork if and only if it is a beautiful object created by some person(s).

If it is an artwork then it is a beautiful object created by some person(s), and if it is a beautiful object created by some person(s) then it is an artwork.

Being a beautiful object created by some person(s) is necessary and sufficient for being an artwork.

5.3 Deciding Necessity and Sufficiency

Remember that the order is:

ANTECEDENT is sufficient for CONSEQUENT.

CONSEQUENT is necessary for ANTECEDENT.

The conditional,

If P *then* Q.

states that *P* is sufficient for *Q* and that *Q* is necessary for *P*. Not every statement is true, and conditionals are no exception. Each of these is a conditional:

If it lays eggs, it's a mammal.

It's a marsupial only if it flies.

But each is false: Laying eggs is not sufficient for being a mammal, and flying is not a necessary condition for being a marsupial. If a conditional is false, then there is something wrong about what sufficient or necessary conditions it presents.

In order to decide whether some statement is a sufficient condition or a necessary condition or both or neither for another statement, you must form conditionals and decide whether they are true or false. Here are four pairs:

A	*B*
It's a hairbrush.	*It's a brush.*
It's a flower.	*It's a rose.*
It's an engine-driven, two-wheeled vehicle.	*It's a motorcycle.*
It's a radio.	*It's stereophonic.*

The problem is whether the *A* statement is sufficient, or necessary, or both (necessary and sufficient), or neither for the *B* statement. Form conditionals and decide if they're true:

It it's a hairbrush, then it's a brush. (True)

If it's a brush, then it's a hairbrush. (False)

"It's a hairbrush" turns up as the antecedent in a true conditional, with "It's a brush" as a consequent. So "It's a hairbrush" is sufficient for being a brush. But being a hairbrush is not necessary for being a brush; there are paint-brushes, clothes brushes, etc. We also see this when we see that the second conditional is false. The second pair is the opposite:

If it's a flower, then it's a rose. (False)

If it's a rose, then it's a flower. (True)

"It's a flower" is not sufficient for being a rose (the first conditional is false), but it is necessary (the second conditional is true). The third pair yields two true conditionals:

If it's an engine-driven, two-wheeled vehicle, then it's a motorcycle. (True)

If it's a motorcycle, then it's an engine-driven, two-wheeled vehicle. (True)

So being an engine-driven, two-wheeled vehicle is sufficient *and* necessary for being a motorcycle. Or, in other words, this biconditional is true:

It's an engine-driven two-wheeled vehicle if and only if it is a motorcycle. (True)

Statement *A* of the fourth pair is neither sufficient nor necessary for statement *B*, because *both* conditionals are false:

If it's a radio, then it's stereophonic. (False)

If it's stereophonic, then it's a radio. (False)

5.4 Truthtables for the Conditional and Biconditional

The truthtable for the conditional, called by logicians the "material" (or "truthfunctional") conditional, is:

P,	Q	If P then Q
T	T	T
T	F	F
F	T	T
F	F	T

As a concrete example of a conditional, consider this:

If the headlights are left on all night, the car won't start in the morning.

The first two lines of the truthtable for the conditional seem straightforward. The first line says: When both antecedent and consequent are true—when both "The headlights are left on all night" and "The car won't start in the morning" are true—the whole conditional should be counted as true. The second line says: When the antecedent is true and the consequent false—when the headlights were left on all night, but the car did start in the morning—then the whole conditional should be counted as false.

The third and fourth lines seem odd. They say that when the antecedent of a conditional is false—in our example, when it is false that the headlights were left on all night—then the whole conditional should be counted as true, regardless of whether the consequent is true (third line) or false (fourth line). Why?

The material conditional concentrates on how we *falsify* conditionals. The truthtable for "if. . . then" in effect says: Assume a conditional to be true, unless shown false; and a conditional will be shown false only when the antecedent is true (or happens) but the consequent is false (or fails to happen).

Here is another illustration of this falsification aspect of the truthtable for the conditional. I say to you:

If you cook tonight, then I'll cook tomorrow.

Suppose you cook tonight. Suppose I do not cook tomorrow. (In other words, suppose the antecedent is true but the consequent is false.) We would all count my original statement as false (or a lie or a deception). Next, suppose you do not cook tonight—that is, suppose the antecedent false. Now it doesn't matter what I do tomorrow. Either I cook or I do not, that is either I make the consequent true or I make the consequent false. But in *neither* case do you have warrant for claiming that what I orginally said is false (or a lie or a deception)—which is tantamount to assuming my original conditional statement, "If you cook tonight, then I'll cook tomorrow," as true. (Remember, we're assuming only two truthvalues: True or False.)

There is another reason for adopting the above truthtables as defining "if. . . then." We want to have different truthtables. Suppose we were to count the last two instances, the controversial ones, as false, that is:

P, Q	If P then Q	
T T	T	
T F	F	
F T	F	←
F F	F	←

Then we would in effect say that "and" and "if. . . then" mean the same, because the truthtable just above is the same as the truthtable for conjunction. But "and" and "if. . . then" do not mean the same thing. Hence, those last two lines are made true in the table for the material conditional.

The truthtable for the biconditional is more straightforward:

P, Q	P if and only if Q
T T	T
T F	F
F T	F
F F	T

Since the biconditional claims an equivalence between two statements, it is true just when the two statements have the same truthvalue. The biconditional,

Something is a vixen if and only if it is a female fox.

is true when you have a vixen (and it is a female fox), and when you don't have a vixen (and it isn't a female fox). Should you produce a vixen that turns out not to be a female fox, or a female fox that turns out not to be a vixen, the biconditional would be false.

5.5 Inference Rules for Conditionals

Contraposition

While you cannot legitimately switch antecedent and consequent ("If it's an ant then it's an insect, so if it's an insect then it's an ant" is invalid), you can do so if you change the truthvalues of antecedent and consequent:

CONTRAPOSITION (CONTRA)

If P then Q

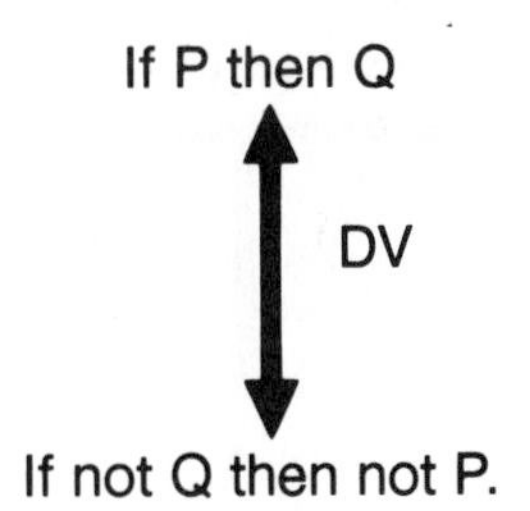

If not Q then not P.

Contraposition, in effect, says that when "*Q*" is stated as necessary for "*P*" ("If *P* then *Q*"), then when "*Q*" is false ("Not *Q*" is true) "*P*" will be false ("Not *P*" will be true) because the necessary condition for "*P*," namely "*Q*," fails to be true. Of course, contraposition will hold for all equivalences. For example,

P is a sufficient condition for *Q*.

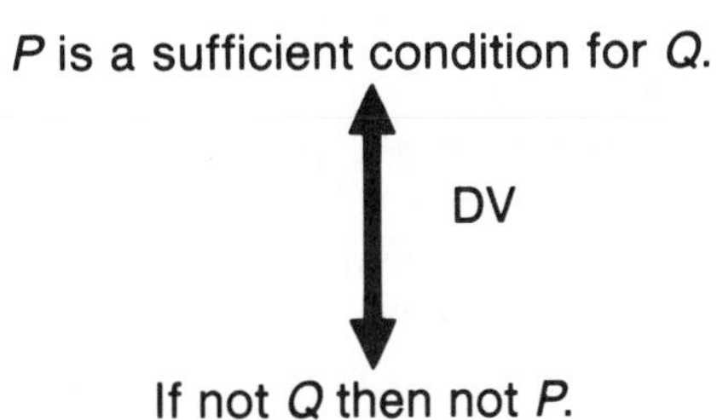

If not *Q* then not *P*.

And so on for the other conditional equivalences. This argument is valid by contraposition:

If it's an ant then it's an insect.

If it's not an insect then it's not an ant.

Modus Ponens

It is important to note that different sufficient conditions for the same thing may each be correct. That is, each of the following conditionals are true:

If I stick a pin into it, the balloon will burst.

If you stick a pin into it, the balloon will burst.

If I hold a lighted cigarette to its surface, the balloon will burst.

If an elephant steps on it, the balloon will burst.

And so on. This fact leads to an important derivation rule for conditionals, and explains why some other inferences do not work. The rule was known by the medieval logicians, and is called by its Latin name:

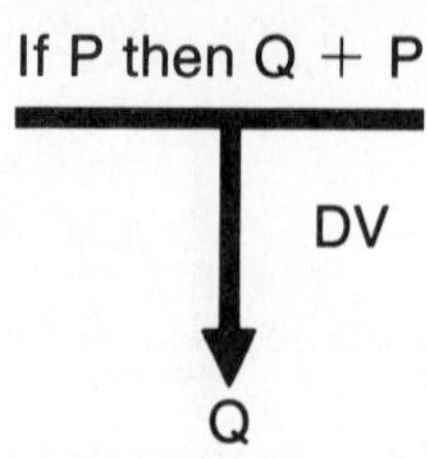

Modus Ponens ("the affirming mode") is a crucial inference rule for conditionals. It says that if "If *P* then *Q*" is true (which means that "*P*" is sufficient for "*Q*"), and if "*P*" is in addition true (which means that the sufficient condition for "*Q*" has happened), then "*Q*" will be true too. For example,

> *If I stick a pin in the balloon, then it bursts. And I did stick a pin into it. So it burst. (DV, by MP)*

Fallacy of Affirming the Consequent

But there is an inference that may be tempting to make, but which is *not* deductively valid. It is called:

THE FALLACY OF AFFIRMING THE CONSEQUENT

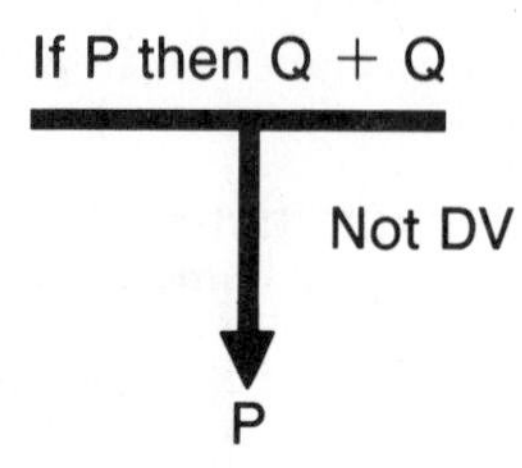

Don't forget that there can be many sufficient conditions for the same thing. Suppose you were to argue as follows:

> *It's true that if you stick a pin into the balloon, then it will burst. I see that the balloon has burst. Therefore you stuck a pin into it. (Not DV)*

The conclusion doesn't necessarily follow. Even if the premises are true. there could be many ways for the balloon to have burst: You could have held a lighted cigarette to its surface, for example.

Modus Tollens

A close cousin of MP is Modus Tollens ("the denying mode"):

MODUS TOLLENS (MT)

If P then Q + Not Q

DV

Not P

This says that if it really is true that "*P*" is sufficient for "*Q*" (i.e., that "If *P* then *Q*" is true), and also that "*Q*" hasn't happened (i.e., that "Not *Q*" is true), it will follow that "*P*" hasn't happened (i.e., that "Not *P*" is true). For example,

If an elephant steps on it, the balloon will burst. But the balloon hasn't burst. So an elephant hasn't stepped on it. (DV, by MT)

Fallacy of Denying the Antecedent

There is an inference that has a surface resemblance to MT but that is deductively *invalid:*

THE FALLACY OF DENYING THE ANTECEDENT

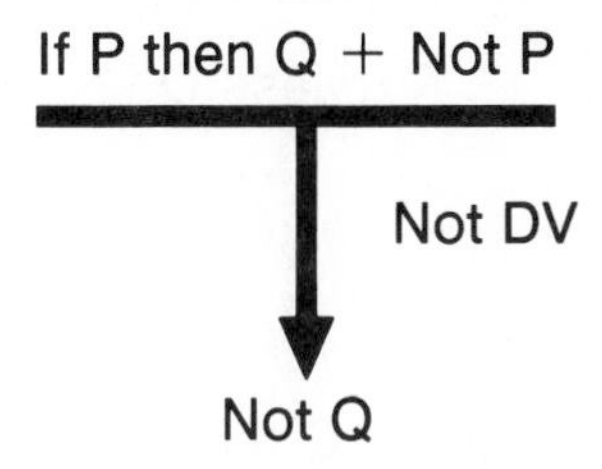

Suppose you were to argue like this:

If an elephant stepped on it, the balloon will burst. But an elephant couldn't have stepped on it. (There are no elephants for miles around; the balloon is in a very small room; etc.) So the balloon hasn't burst. (Not DV)

This is an instance of the fallacy of denying the antecedent. It is an invalid argument. True, if an elephant stepped on it, the balloon would burst. True, an elephant couldn't have stepped on it. But it will not follow that the balloon hasn't burst, for as you so well know by now there are many sufficient conditions for bursting a balloon besides elephants.

Helpful Hint: It is best to understand the principles—the logic—behind MP and MT and the fallacies. However, in case of memory failure, this may help. The valid rules are MP and MT. MP in effect affirms the antecedent (AA), and MT in effect denies the consequent (DC): AADC. Remember "*A*ll *A*dolescents *D*rink *C*ola," a plausible *truth* for the *valid* rules. One fallacy affirms the consequent (AC), the other denies the antecedent (DA): ACDA. Re-

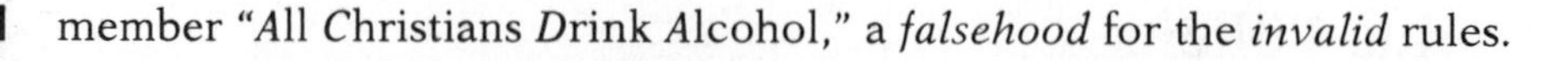

member "*A*ll *C*hristians *D*rink *A*lcohol," a *falsehood* for the *invalid* rules.

Hypothetical Syllogism

There is a rule for chaining conditionals together:

HYPOTHETICAL SYLLOGISM (HS)

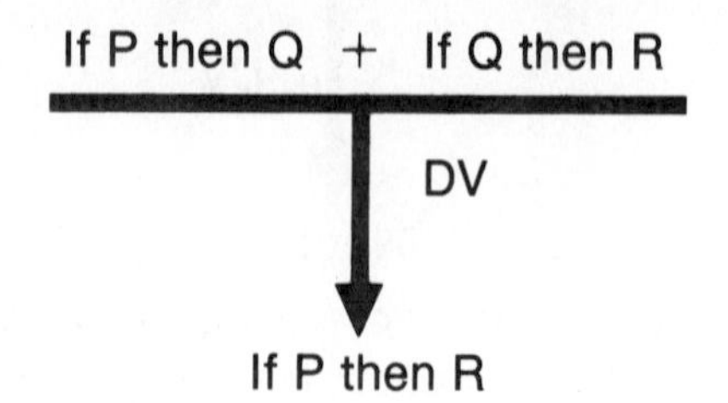

For example, you might argue:

If you leave the milk out, it will go sour. And if the milk goes sour, we won't have any for cereal tomorrow. So, if you leave the milk out, we won't have any for cereal tomorrow. (DV, by HS)

Unless Equivalence

"Unless" is actually a conditional:

UNLESS EQUIVALENCE (UNLESS EQ)

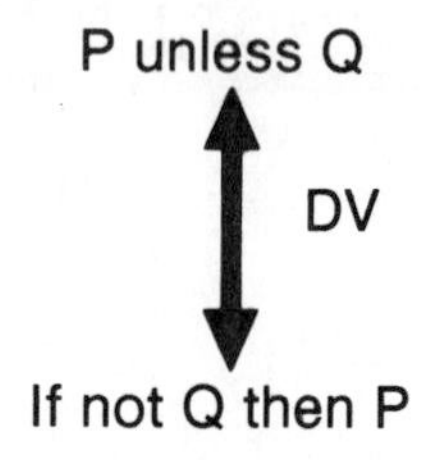

For example, these statements are equivalent:

We'll go on a picnic tomorrow unless it rains.

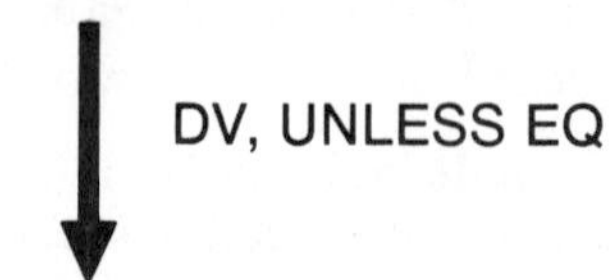

If it doesn't rain then we'll go on a picnic tomorrow.

We do not need special rules for "unless." Since we can translate "unless" statements into a conditional, we can use CONTRA, MP, MT, or HS to prove arguments containing "unless" statement valid or invalid. For example:

I was told that I would not pass the course unless I got at least a B on the final exam. Since I passed, I must have gotten at least a B on the final.

Using some shorthand, we can prove the argument valid in a few steps:

Not pass course unless got at least B on final.

↓ DV, UNLESS EQ

If not at least B on final then not pass course.

Now we can apply a few more rules:

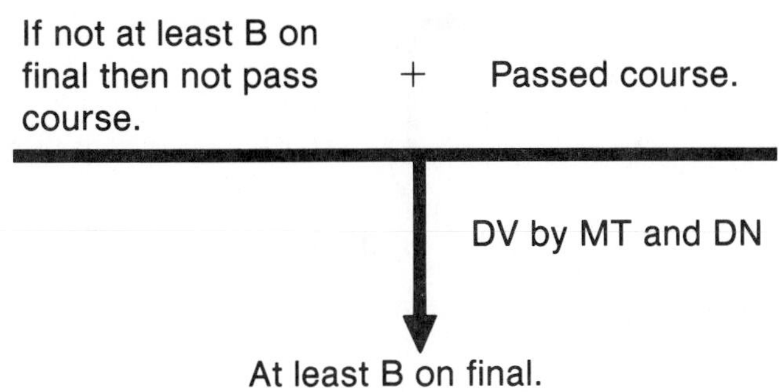

5.6 Practice Arguments and Strategy

While this chapter concentrated on conditionals, arguments involving conditionals are not independent of the rules for conjunction, disjunction, and negation. For example:

> *(1) If you get at least a B on the final, you'll pass Basketweaving 101. However, (2) even though you haven't passed Basketweaving 101, you've graduated. So, (3) you didn't get at least a B on the final.*

As always, it is crucial to see what form the various premises take. It is fairly obvious that (1) is a conditional, but you must recognize (2) as a conjunction and (3) as a negation. Try setting out the argument in "shorthand":

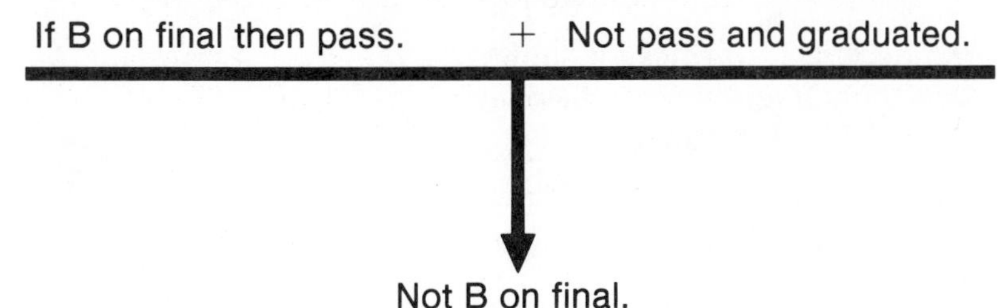

The rule SIMP for conjunction says that any conjunction, "P and Q," entails any one of its conjuncts. In the above argument, "Not pass and graduated" entails "Not pass," which allows you to apply MT:

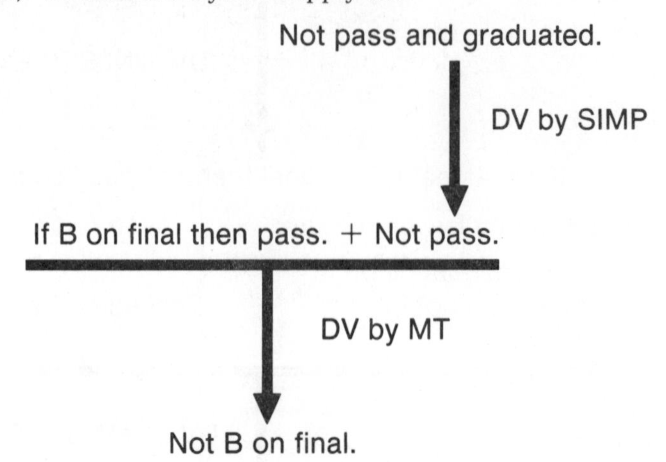

It is not absolutely necessary to go through the argument, diagraming it step by step, as above. You might be able to see the fact that the two rules show the argument valid, in which case you can simply state that like this:

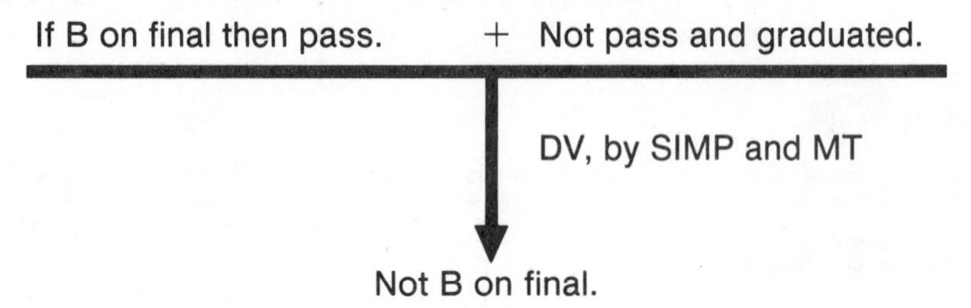

Contraposition (CONTRA) often plays a role in determining the validity of arguments, as in this next example:

We have power because the TV wouldn't be on if we didn't, and the TV is on.

As usual, the first thing to do is to determine the form of the argument using shorthand:

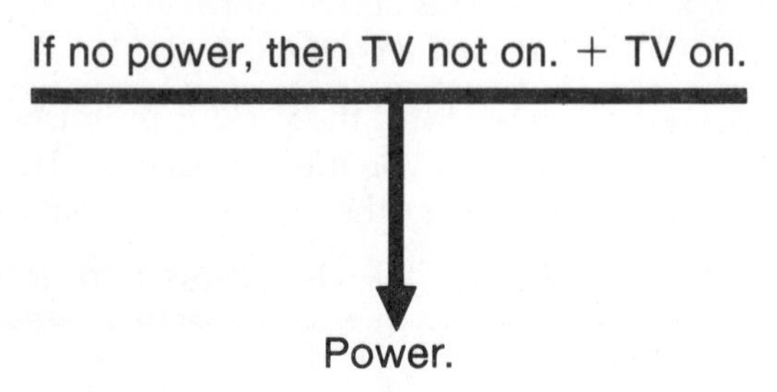

The next thing is to examine the argument to see which valid rules, if any, apply. This is an art that will improve with practice. You might look first to see if there's any way MP will apply. And MP will apply if the conditional is reversed by CONTRA:

If no power on, then TV not on.

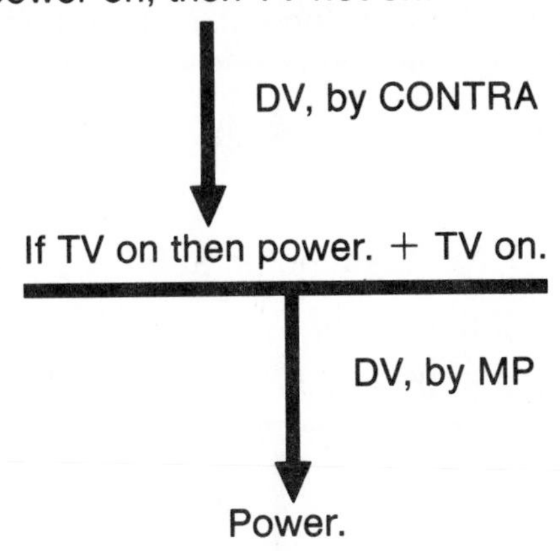

Or, if you can see this immediately:

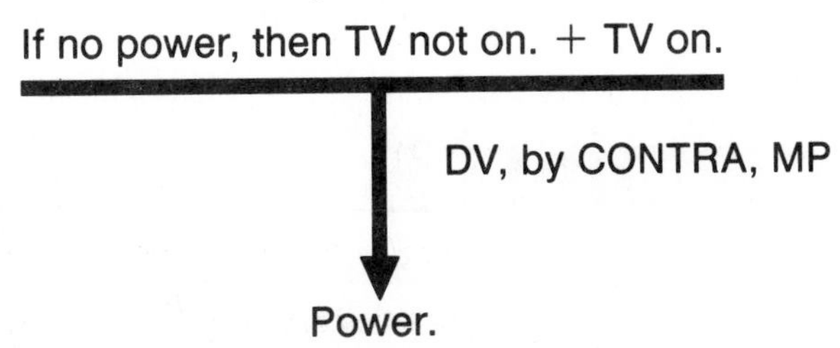

Double Negation (DN) sometimes plays a role in determining the validity of arguments, as in this next example:

If she put the roast in at 5, as you say, it wouldn't be done at 7. But it is done at 7. So she didn't put it in at 5.

The usual shorthand diagram first:

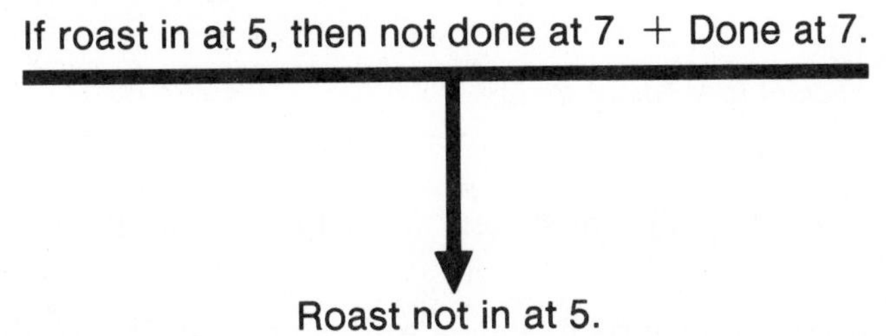

One thing you might notice about this argument is that "Done at 7" denies the consequent of the conditional, "not done at 7." This is so because of DN: "Done at 7" is equivalent to "Not not done at 7." When you see this, you can use MT. The step-by-step diagram:

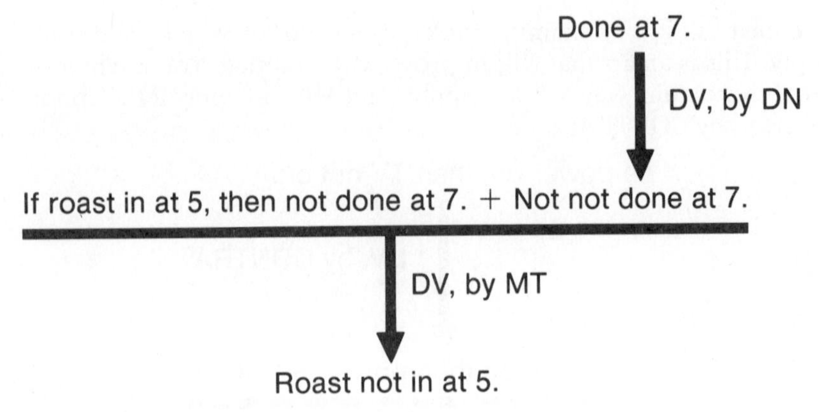

Or, if you can see this immediately:

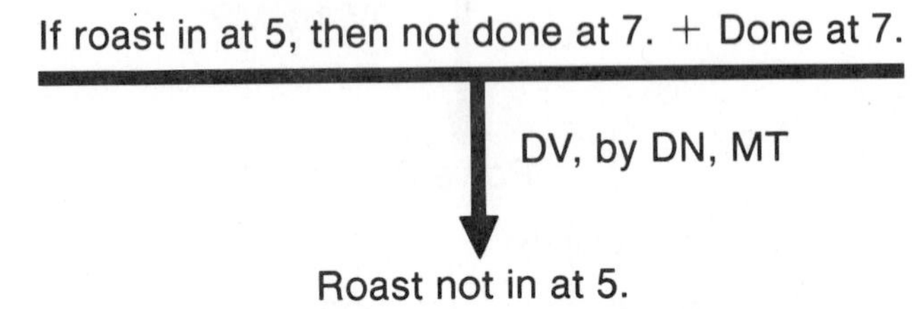

KEY POINTS

There are several ways to write a conditional. Each of these says exactly the same thing:

If P *then* Q.

If P, Q.

Q, *if* P.

P *only if* Q.

P *is (a) sufficient (condition) for* Q.

Q *is (a) necessary (condition) for* P.

What follows the "if" is the antecedent. What follows the "then" or the "only if" is the consequent.

- The antecedent purports to state a sufficient condition for the consequent.
- The consequent purports to state a necessary condition for the antecedent.

- Although the statements are logically equivalent, "If *P* then *Q*" emphasizes the sufficiency of "*P*" for "*Q*," while "*P* only if *Q*" emphasizes the necessity of "*Q*" for "*P*."

The biconditional purports to state sufficient *and* necessary conditions. Each of these is a biconditional, and each is equivalent to the others:

P *if and only if* Q.

P *iff* Q.

If P *then* Q *and if* Q *then* P.

To determine whether some statement, e.g., "It's an ant," is sufficient, or necessary, or both, or neither, for another statement, e.g., "It's an insect," form conditionals and determine which, if any, are true:

If it's an ant, then it's an insect. (True)

If it's an insect, then it's an ant. (False)

So "It's an ant" is sufficient but not necessary for "It's an insect" (or being an ant is sufficient but not necessary for being an insect).

The truthtable for the conditional is:

P,	Q	If P then Q
T	T	T
T	F	F
F	T	T
F	F	T

This is called "the material conditional." It assumes that an "if. . .then" statement is false only when the antecedent is true but the consequent is false (or doesn't happen). Thus it concentrates on falsification.

The truthtable for the biconditional is:

P,	Q	P if and only if Q
T	T	T
T	F	F
F	T	F
F	F	T

This says that each member of the biconditional should be true when each has the same truthvalue—after all, the biconditional just says that one condition is necessary and sufficient for the other—and false otherwise.

Here are the VALID RULES for conditionals:

CONTRAPOSITION (CONTRA)

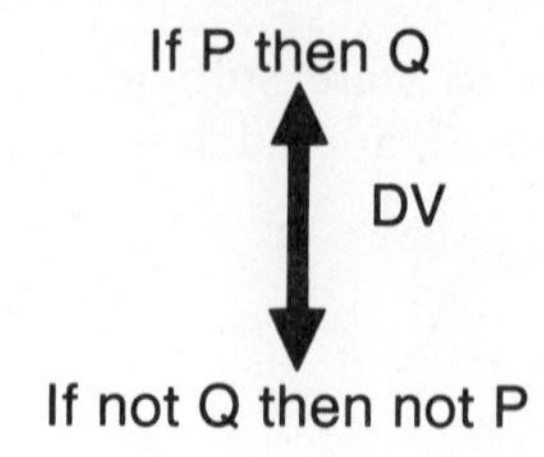

MODUS PONENS (MP)

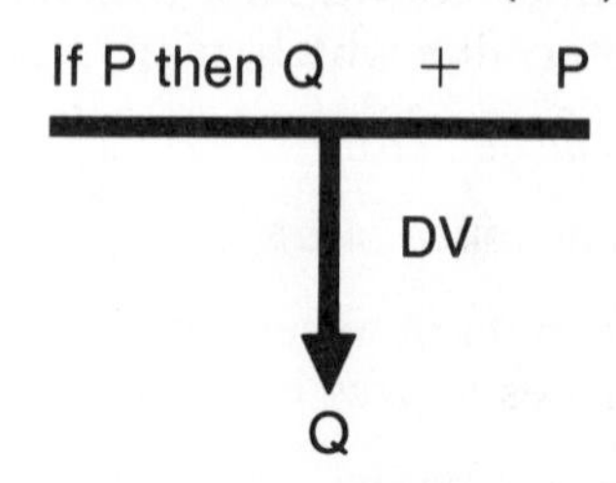

MODUS TOLLENS (MT)

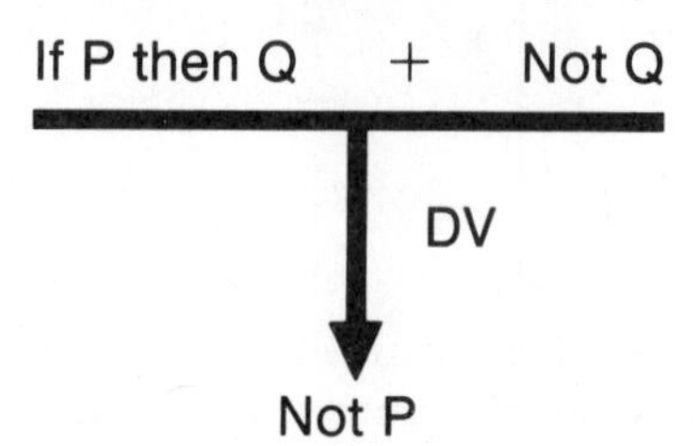

HYPOTHETICAL SYLLOGISM (HS)

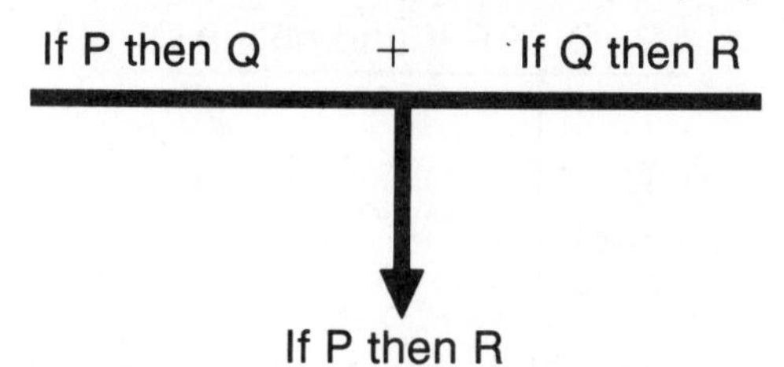

UNLESS EQUIVALENCE (UNLESS EQ)

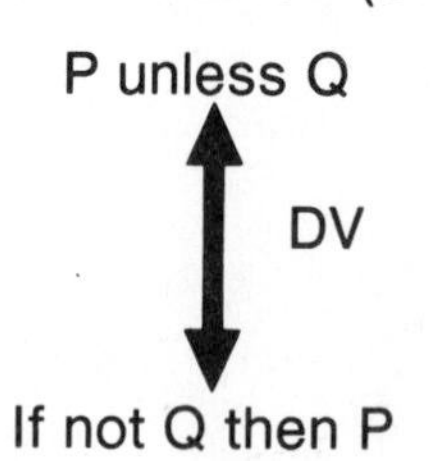

These are some INVALID INFERENCES:

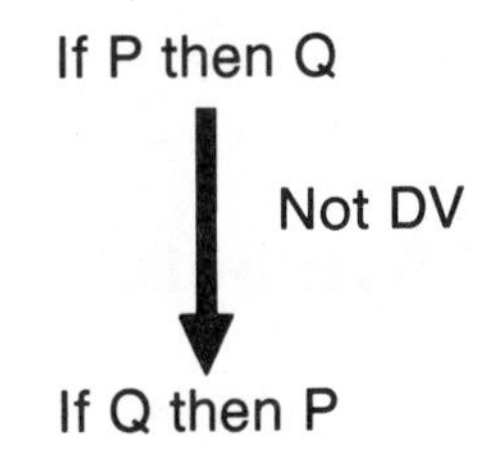

THE FALLACY OF AFFIRMING THE CONSEQUENT

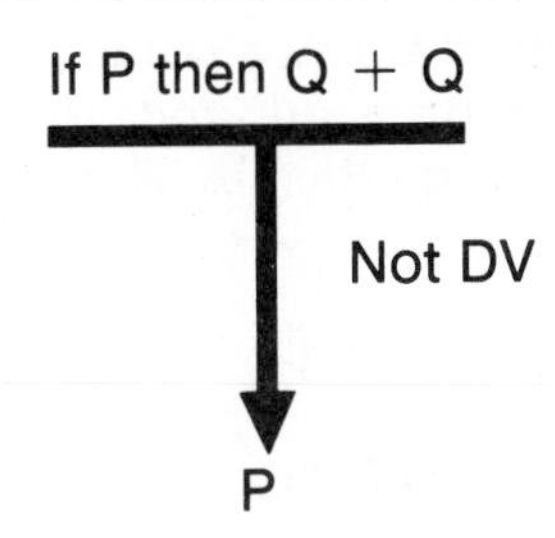

THE FALLACY OF DENYING THE ANTECEDENT

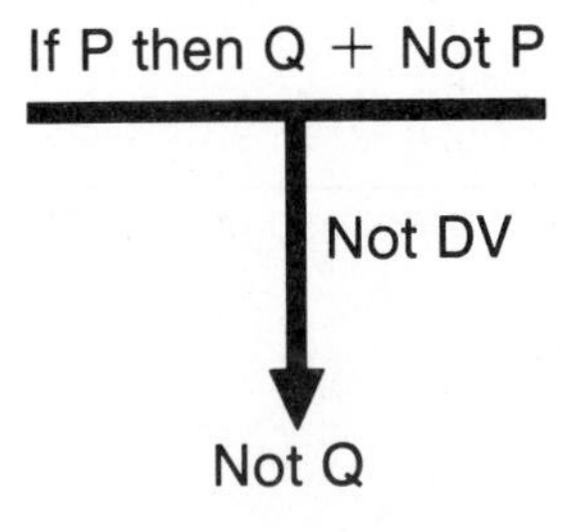

Remember that MP and MT are the *valid* rules

- MP affirms the antecedent (AA).
- MT denies the consequent (DC).
- AADC makes the likely *truth*, "All Adolescents Drink Cola."

Remember that there are two *fallacies* (*invalid* rules):

- One fallacy affirms the consequent (AC).
- Another denies the antecedent (DA).
- ACDA yields the *falsehood*, "All Christians Drink Alcohol."

To determine whether an argument is valid:

- Separate premise(s) from conclusion.
- Diagram the argument using shorthand.
- Inspect it to see if any valid rules apply immediately.
- If no valid rules apply immediately, see if using CONTRA or DN will

allow you to use MP or MT.

- If this doesn't seem to be working, check to see if the argument commits one of the fallacies.

Appendix: Logical Symbols

Some care has been taken, both in this and in the previous chapters, to keep problems and statements of the rules of inference as close to English as possible. However, modern symbolic logic has developed a notational scheme—actually several notational schemes—to abbreviate the truth-functional connectives. Here are two examples of alternative symbolism, one by Alfred North Whitehead and Bertrand Russell, *Principia Mathematica* (1910-1913), the other by Benson Mates, *Elementary Logic* (1965):

	Basic Logic	*Whitehead-Russell*	*Mates*
Negation	*Not* P	$\sim P$	$-P$
Conjunction	P *and* Q	$P \cdot Q$	$P \& Q$
Disjunction	P *or* Q	$P \vee Q$	$P \vee Q$
Conditional	*If* P *then* Q	$P \supset Q$	$P \rightarrow Q$
Biconditional	P *if and only if* Q	$P \equiv Q$	$P \leftrightarrow Q$

Symbolic notation also makes use of parentheses. What is said in *Basic Logic* as

Not both P *and not* Q

could be said symbolically as

$\sim(P \cdot \sim Q)$ *Whitehead-Russell*

$-(P \& -Q)$ *Mates*

Similarly, the rules of inference could be expressed more quickly using the symbols of modern logic, for example, Modus Ponens:

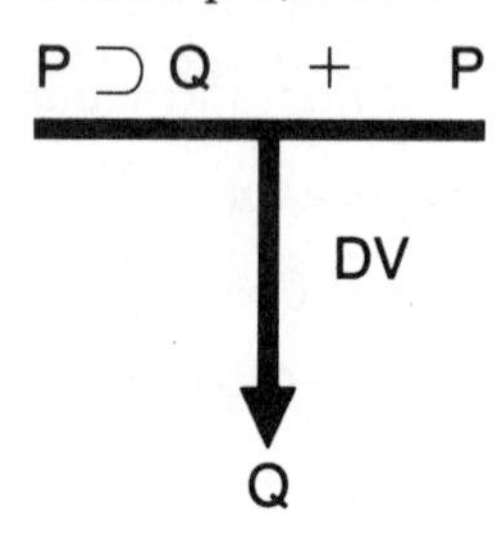

EXERCISES

A. Using "Inflation goes down" as the *antecedent* and "Stock prices rise" as the *consequent*, write a conditional six *different* ways (always keeping the antecedent as the antecedent).

***A1.** *If inflation goes down, then stock prices rise.*

A2.

A3.

A4.

A5.

A6.

B. Say whether the item in Column A is SUFFICIENT, or NECESSARY, or BOTH (necessary and sufficient), or NEITHER for the item in Column B.

A		B
***B1.** Being a flower	*NECESSARY*	Being a rose
B2. Being a rose	______	Being a flower
B3. Wearing clothes	______	Wearing slacks
B4. Being female	______	Being a feminist
B5. Being male	______	Being an uncle
B6. Having sexual intercourse	______	Becoming pregnant

B7. Writing ________________ Using a pen

B8. Moving your body ________________ Jumping up and down

B9. Putting paint on canvas ________________ Making art

B10. Going to college ________________ Studying French

B11. Studying French ________________ Studying the official language of Quebec

C. Using "If spending increases, then prices rise" as one premise, construct five arguments of the following sort, adding a second premise in each case.

***C1.** An argument that obeys MP.

If spending increases, then prices rise. + *Spending increases.*

DV, by MP

Prices rise.

C2. An argument that obeys MT.

C3. An argument that commits the fallacy of Affirming the Consequent.

C4. An argument that commits the fallacy of Denying the Antecedent.

C5. An argument that obeys HS.

D. Circle ALL correct answers. (Some questions may have more than one.)

D1. "If inflation goes down, then stock prices rise" asserts that

- **a.** Inflation goes down.
- **b.** Stock prices rise.
- **c.** Both a. and b.
- **d.** None of the above.

D2. "If inflation goes down, then stock prices rise" is equivalent to:

- **a.** "If stock prices rise, then inflation goes down."
- **b.** "If inflation doesn't go down, then stock prices don't rise."
- **c.** "If stock prices don't rise, then inflation doesn't go down."
- **d.** "Stock prices rising is necessary for inflation going down."
- **e.** "Stock prices rising is sufficient for inflation going down."
- **f.** "Inflation goes down, if stock prices rise."
- **g.** "Unless stock prices rise, inflation doesn't go down."

D3. Mrs. Spaulding, cleaning lady at the Princess Theater, overhears the star saying on opening night, "If the critics praise the play, it will be a hit." After the opening night performance, she overhears the producer saying, "It's a hit." What can she infer with certainty from these remarks?

- **a.** The critics praised the play.
- **b.** The critics did not praise the play.
- **c.** She'll get a raise.
- **d.** None of the above.

D4. Detective Sam Spade says, "If the fingerprints on the gun are the gunsel's then he shot the moll." But the lab reports show that the fingerprints on the gun are *not* the gunsel's. From Spade's remark and the lab reports, which you will assume to be true, what can you conclude with certainty?

a. The gunsel shot the moll.
b. The gunsel did not shoot the moll.
c. Neither of the above.

D5. "The existence of true love between two persons is a necessary condition for their having a satisfactory sexual relationship" deductively entails:

a. If true love exists between two persons, then they have a satisfactory sexual relationship.
b. If two persons have a satisfactory sexual relationship, then true love exists between them.
c. Neither of the above.

D6. "If you light the fuse then the dynamite will explode, and if the building didn't collapse, then the dynamite didn't explode." Given this, what deductively follows?

a. The building didn't collapse.
b. If the building collapsed, then you lit the fuse.
c. If you lit the fuse, then the building collapsed.
d. None of the above.

D7. Ms. R, president of R & R Travel Agency, gives this advice to Mr. S: "If Transylvania were a fun place I would have booked lots of trips there. But in my long career as a travel agent I have not booked lots of trips there. In fact, I've never booked even one trip there. So Transylvania is not a fun place." Which is correct?

a. If Ms. R's reasons are true, her conclusion must be true.
b. Even if Ms. R's reasons are true, her conclusion doesn't necessarily follow.

D8. "Keeping a minimum balance of $500 is sufficient to avoid service charges" means:

a. If you do not keep a minimum balance of $500, then you will not avoid service charges.
b. If you keep a minimum balance of $500, then you will avoid service charges.
c. If you have avoided service charges, then you must have a minimum balance of $500.
d. If you have not avoided service charges, then you have not kept a minimum balance of $500.

D9. The argument: "If the steaks are burned, then the fire was too hot. The steaks are burned. So the fire was too hot." However, suppose that in fact the fire was not too hot.

a. The argument cannot be DV.
b. The argument is DV by MP.
c. The argument must be unsound.
d. None of the above.

D10. The argument: "If you brought Aunt Mary roses, then she'll be happy. But you didn't bring her roses. So, she won't be happy." Suppose that in fact Aunt Mary isn't happy.

a. The argument must be DV.
b. The argument is not DV.
c. The argument is unsound.
d. None of the above.

E. Supply the missing part that is required to make the argument deductively valid by the rule(s) given.

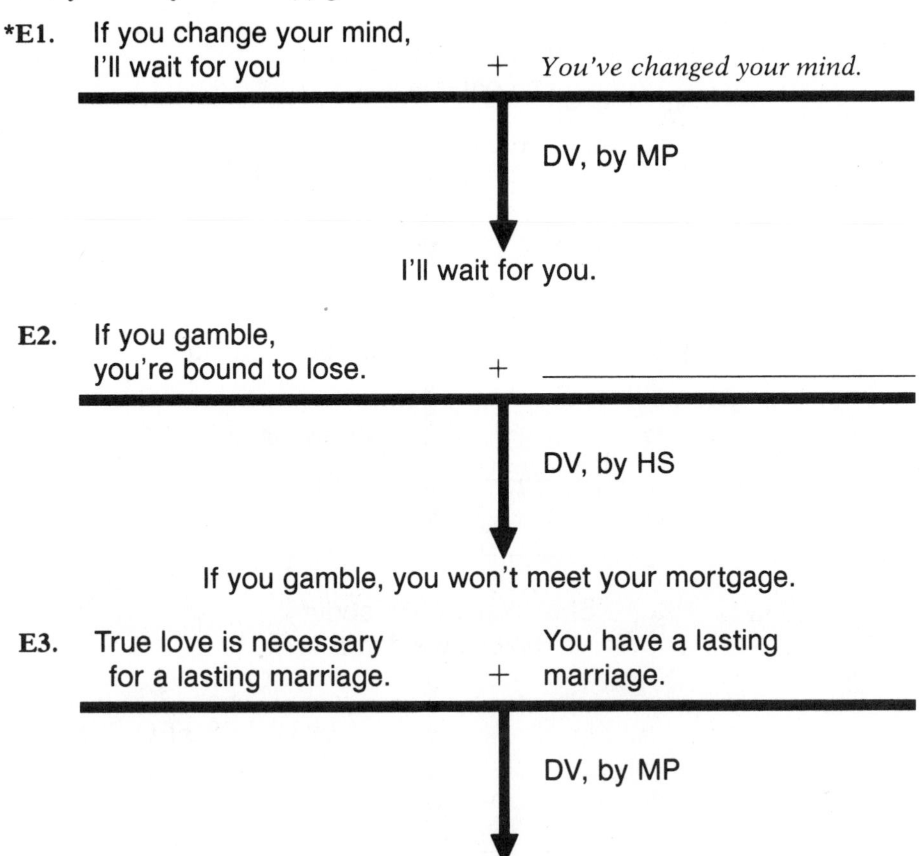

E4. Filling out this form is sufficient for applying. + But you haven't applied.

DV, by MT

____

E5. Bread will rise only if it contains yeast.

DV, by CONTRA

____

E6. We won't pay unless he stops shouting.

DV, by UNLESS EQ

____

E7. She'll keep quiet about it unless we don't.

DV, by UNLESS EQ, DN

____

E8. If we don't have enough sugar, then we can't make the cake. + We can make the cake.

DV, by MT, DN

____

F. Decide whether the following arguments are DV or not. Do a diagram for each in shorthand, and if it is valid state the relevant rule(s). If it is not valid, say why.

***F1.** If he has the king of spades, I'll make my bid. And he has the king of spades! So I'll make my bid.

If he has K of S I'll make my bid. + He has K of S.

DV, by MP

I'll make my bid.

F2. If he doesn't have the king of spades, I won't make my bid. But he has the king of spades! So I'll make my bid.

F3. If three out of four doctors recommend aspirin for headache, then you should take aspirin for headache. But three out of four doctors don't recommend aspirin for headache! So you shouldn't take aspirin for headache.

F4. If you have insufficient insurance, you're courting disaster. But you're not courting disaster. So you have sufficient insurance.

F5. If no one will ever find out, then it's OK to lie. But someone *will* find out! So it's not OK to lie.

F6. If you take Flight #427 to Boston, you'll arrive in plenty of time for the meeting. But you've missed Flight #427! So you won't arrive in plenty of time for the meeting.

F7. If you don't do it, he won't either. If he won't, no one will. So if you don't do it, no one will.

F8. You're subject to a fine and a prison term. If you're subject to a prison term, you'll lose your job. So you'll lose your job.

F9. (*Difficult*) If Mr. Bill took the 7 A.M. flight to Chicago and it landed on time, then he will be in Chicago by noon. But Mr. Bill is not in Chicago by noon. So either he didn't take the 7 A.M. flight or it didn't land on time.

F10. (*Difficult*) If you filed your tax returns on time, you've done your duty as a citizen. If you've done your duty as a citizen, you're to be praised. You've filed your tax returns on time. Therefore, you're to be praised.

G. These problems will make use not only of the rules for conditionals in this chapter, but also the rules for conjunction, disjunction, and negation from the chapter before. They are somewhat difficult. Decide whether the argument is DV.

***G1.** She has gloves and an overnight bag. If she has an overnight bag, she's going out of town. I conclude that she's going out of town.

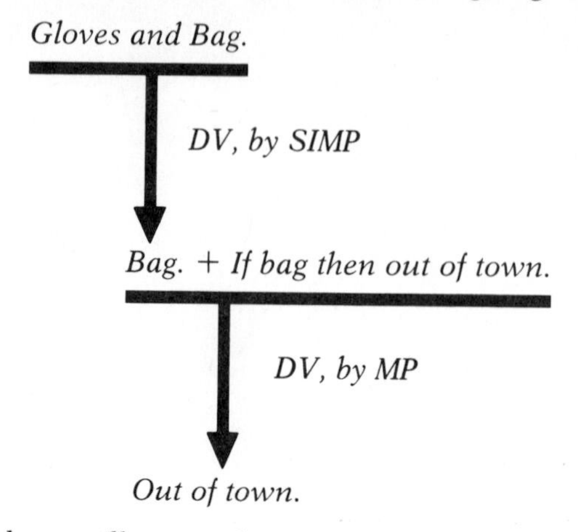

G2. Either we'll win or lose. But we can't lose! If we win, we'll be on easy street. So we'll be on easy street.

G3. If you're taking this course, you'll get a good job and a nice salary. You're taking this course. So you'll get a nice salary.

G4. If you don't manage on your meager wages, then you'll either starve or freeze. Since you're neither starving nor freezing, I guess you're managing on your meager wages.

G5. Either the terrorists' demands are met or the hostages are killed. If the hostages are not killed, their families will be most relieved. The terrorists' demands are being met, so I conclude that the hostages' families will be most relieved.

G6. If you had quit you would either have forfeited the entry fee or been barred from future matches. Since you haven't quit, you have neither forfeited the entry fee nor been barred from future matches.

CHAPTER 6

CATEGORICAL ARGUMENTS

Categorical arguments were the first subject of Western logic, studied by Aristotle (384-322 B.C.) in his logical works, which were called by a later editor the Organon *(the "tool"). Categorical arguments were also the principal subject for medieval logicians. Our study of categorical arguments will rely heavily on the work of a modern British logician, John Venn (1834-1923), who introduced a sort of pictorial method, now called Venn diagrams, for proving the deductive validity and invalidity of categorical arguments. Important concepts in this chapter include:*

CATEGORY and CLASS

CATEGORICAL STATEMENT
— and the standard forms . . .
A = *All A are B.*
E = *No A are B.*
I = *Some A are B.*
O = *Some A are not B.*

CLASSICAL and MODERN INTERPRETATIONS of A and E

EXISTENTIAL IMPORT of I and O

VENN DIAGRAMS
— how to read and use them

SYLLOGISM

STANDARD CATEGORICAL SYLLOGISM

SORITES

6.1 The Form of Categorical Statements

Much of our knowledge of the world is expressed by classifying or categorizing things, as a thing of this or that kind. We say, for example, that the flower before us is an iris, not a lily; that this animal is a marsupial, not a mammal; or that no acids are bases, but all acids have a ph factor of less than 7. That is, we assign things to classes or categories and assert or deny that some class is contained within another.

A **CATEGORY** or the more modern designation **CLASS** is simply a group or set of things. Examples of classes or categories are:

the class of roses

of red things

of pirates

of dangerous people

of Volkswagens

of statues

of students who study logic

Note that a different category name designates a different category. Thus the class whose members are

statues

is different from the class whose members are

statues by Michelangelo

which is different still from the class whose members are

statues by Michelangelo in Florence

And so on.

Our primary interest in categories is not merely in naming them, but in saying something about the relation of some category to another. In other words, we wish (sometimes) to say something about the relation between, for example, pirates and dangerous people. Are all pirates dangerous? No pirates dangerous? Only some? We want, sometimes, to make categorical statements.

A **CATEGORICAL STATEMENT** asserts or denies membership in a category or class. The medieval logicians who studied the logic of categories named four standard categorical statements according to whether the statement asserted or denied membership in a category. The Latin "Affirmo" ("I affirm") and "Nego" ("I deny") were used to form abbreviations. The standard categorical statements that *affirmed* membership in a category were called **A** and **I** after the vowels "*A*ff*I*rmo." These are:

A — *All* X *are* Y. *(E.g., All pirates are dangerous.)*

I — *Some* X *are* Y. *(E.g., Some pirates are dangerous.)*

The standard categorical statements that denied membership in a category were called **E** and **O** after the vowels "nEgO." These are:

E — *No* X *are* Y. *(E.g., No pirates are dangerous.)*

O — *Some* X *are not* Y. *(E.g., Some pirates are not dangerous.)*

We can define a **STANDARD CATEGORICAL STATEMENT** as any statement that is in exactly the form **A**, **I**, **E**, or **O**. Since these letters are standard and convenient, we will use them often. You should memorize what statement each stands for.

Besides the fact that some categorical statements affirm class membership and others deny it, there is another kind of division to be drawn. The **A** and **E** statements are *universal:* They affirm or deny something about all members of the subject class. The **I** and **O** statements are *particular:* They affirm or deny something about a *particular* member of the subject class. Thus we have:

	UNIVERSAL	*PARTICULAR*
AFFIRMATIVE	*All* X *are* Y.	*Some* X *are* Y.
NEGATIVE	*No* X *are* Y.	*Some* X *are not* Y.

These are the *standard* categorical statements. They are the constituents of the categorical syllogism (see 6.5), and are what mainly interested logicians from Aristotle to Venn. But **A**, **E**, **I**, and **O** are not the only statements we can make using categories. We can, for example, make any of these nonstandard categorical statements—nonstandard because they are not exactly reducible to the form **A**, **E**, **I**, and **O**:

There are no ghosts.

Socrates is a man.

Some novels are both artistic and popular.

We deal with the representation of these nonstandard statements mainly in 6.6. Now, on to the standard categorical statements.

6.2 The Meanings of the Standard Categorical Statements

The standard categorical statements, **A**, **E**, **I**, and **O**, are given exact and somewhat technical meanings. The interpretation of the particular categorical statements is this:

I	*Some* X *is* Y.	means	*There is at least one* X *and it is also a* Y.
O	*Some* X *is not* Y.	means	*There is at least one* X *and it is not a* Y.

For example,

Some pirates are dangerous.	means	*There is at least one pirate and he is dangerous.*
Some pirates are not dangerous.	means	*There is at least one pirate and he is not dangerous.*

You can see that "Some" means "There is at least one." Thus, you could confirm as true "Some pirates are dangerous" by producing one dangerous pirate. This is why the **I** and **O** statements are called particular.

Another feature of **I** and **O** statements is important. "Some" means "There is at least one" and "There is" means "There exists." **I** and **O** statements have what is termed "existential import." A categorical statement has **EXISTENTIAL IMPORT** when it deductively implies the existence of members of the subject class. (The subject class of "Some *X* is (not) *Y*" is *X*, i.e., the class named by the grammatical subject of the sentence.) Thus, these arguments are DV:

Some pirates are dangerous.

↓ DV

There is (exists) at least one pirate.

Some pirates are not dangerous.

There is (exists) at least one pirate.

This perhaps uninteresting fact about the particular **I** and **O** statements becomes contentious when interpreting the universal **A** and **E** statements.

The universal statements, **A** and **E**, are subject to two different interpretations. The CLASSICAL or ARISTOTELEAN INTERPRETATION is this:

A	*All* X *are* Y.	means	*If anything is an* X, *it is also a* Y, *and there is at least one* X.
E	*No* X *are* Y.	means	*If anything is an* X, *it is not a* Y, *and there is at least one* X.

For example,

All pirates are dangerous.	means	*If anything is a pirate, he is also dangerous, and there is at least one pirate.*
No pirates are dangerous.	means	*If anything is a pirate, he is not dangerous, and there is at least one pirate.*

On the classical reading, the universal **A** and **E** statements have existential import, for each ends by asserting the existence of members of the subject class (e.g., "There is at least one pirate. . ." or simply "There are pirates. . ."). Thus, on the classical reading, these arguments are DV:

All pirates are dangerous.

There is (exists) at least one pirate.

No pirates are dangerous.

There is (exists) at least one pirate.

However, John Venn gave the universal statements **A** and **E** what we call the modern interpretation. Before setting out Venn's interpretation, let me remind you that although a category or class can be named, it does not necessarily mean that that category has any members. I would assume that the category,

Toyotas personally owned by Lee Iacocca.

has no members. If a category has no members, it is said to be EMPTY; and if a category has members, it is said to be NON-EMPTY.

John Venn wondered whether universal statements deductively implied the existence of members of the subject class—he wondered, that is, whether **A** and **E** statements had existential import. He decided to take those statements as not necessarily asserting the existence of members of the subject class. This is the meaning he gave them. We will call it the MODERN INTERPRETATION:

A	*All* X *are* Y.	means	*If anything is an* X, *it is also a* Y.
E	*No* X *are* Y.	means	*If anything is an* X, *it is not a* Y.

For example,

All pirates are dangerous.	means	*If anything is a pirate, he is also dangerous.*
No pirates are dangerous.	means	*If anything is a pirate, he is not dangerous.*

Note that to say of anything "*if* it's an *X*" does not assert that *there is* something that's an *X*. These arguments are not DV on the modern interpretation:

All pirates are dangerous.

↓ Not DV (Modern)

There is at least one pirate.

No pirates are dangerous.

↓ Not DV (Modern)

There is at least one pirate.

The modern interpretation of **A** and **E** is sometimes at odds with ordinary English. A book on breeds of dogs tells you, "No Basenjis bark." You would be astonished if you later discovered that there were no such things as Basenjis—e.g., that they have been extinct for hundreds of years, or were a figment of the author's imagination. In other words, you naturally take "No Basenjis bark" to have existential import, i.e., to imply the existence of Basenjis.

However, this does not mean that the modern interpretation is wrong. For the classical interpretation is also sometimes at odds with ordinary English. You read in a history book, "No witches were burned in America in the twentieth century." But you do not conclude that, therefore, there are witches. Or, a store opens its doors for its first day of business. You enter it, and see a sign, "All who shoplift here are prosecuted." Since it's the store's first day of business, you should not conclude that there exist shoplifters here who have been prosecuted. In other words, you do not take "No witches were burned in America in the twentieth century" or "All shoplifters are prosecuted" to have existential import; yet you take them to be true nonetheless. You are really using the modern interpretation.

Modern logic prefers the modern interpretation, and *except where otherwise noted we will too.* In Chapter 4, in discussing the meaning of "or," it was suggested that we distinguish between the meaning of a statement and expectations or beliefs surrounding it. It is worth considering that distinction here. In general, when someone asserts "All *X* are *Y*" or "No *X* are *Y*" we expect the subject class to have members. Aristotle and the medievals thought this expectation was built into the meaning of those statements. Modern logic argues that the expectation of existence of members of the subject class is just that—an expectation that is generally satisfied, but not part of the *meaning* of **A** and **E** statements. You can always add existential import to the modern interpretation ("All witches have cats, and there are witches"). You cannot subtract existential import from the classical interpretation without contradicting yourself ("All witches have cats, but there are no witches" implies on the classical interpretation "There is at least one witch and there are no witches").

6.3 Categorical Statements in Ordinary English

The pure or standard form of the four categorical statements is:

A — *All* X *are* Y.

E — *No* X *are* Y.

I — *Some* X *are* Y.

O — *Some* X *are not* Y.

However, in ordinary speech and writing we often make categorical statements that are not in standard categorical form. We might say, for example, "Dogs have four legs," which is not strictly in standard categorical form. The standard categorical form of this ordinary English statement is, "All dogs are things with four legs," but this is stilted and sounds artificial. However, for purposes of checking the deductive validity of arguments that use categorical statements, we must be able to "translate" ordinary English into standard categorical form. We must do this for two purposes: first, to see whether the statement is an **A**, **E**, **I**, or **O** statement and, second, to see exactly which categories are being spoken of. (The second will be important when you come to labeling the circles of Venn diagrams.)

Here are some examples of universal statements in standard categorical form:

All X *are* Y.

All shoplifters are people who are prosecuted.

All Canadian whiskey is a substance subject to import duty.

All students are people required to take logic.

All shortcake is a food that contains baking soda.

No X *are* Y.

No shoplifters are people who are prosecuted.

No Canadian whiskey is a substance subject to import duty.

No students are people required to take logic.

No shortcake is a food that contains baking soda.

These examples are not in colloquial English. We would more naturally say, "All students are required to take logic" or "All shortcake contains baking soda." However, the strict categorical form allows us to see that the categories are "people required to take logic" or "foods that contain baking soda."

Here are some examples of **I** and **O** statements in standard categorical form:

Some X *are* Y.

Some pirates are dangerous.

Some dangerous pirates are sailors of the Atlantic.

Some pirates are good husbands.

Some X *are not* Y.

Some pirates are not dangerous.

Some dangerous pirates are not sailors of the Atlantic.

Some pirates are not good husbands.

Notice again that some of these sound stilted and artificial. For example, we would not say, "Some dangerous pirates are sailors of the Atlantic," but rather "Some dangerous pirates sail the Atlantic."

The ability to render ordinary English into standard categorical form is an important skill in dealing with categorical arguments. Actually, two skills are required: determining the categories spoken of, and determining whether the statement is of **A**, **E**, **I**, or **O** form (also called determining the quantifiers).

Determining the Categories

The trick here is to take an ordinary English categorical statement and, *without changing its basic meaning*, bring out the categories it speaks of. In other words, to write in standard categorical form you must try to fill in the blanks with names of categories:

All ________ are ________.

No ________ are ________.

Some ______ are ________.

Some ______ are not ______.

Here are some examples of such rewritings:

All citrus fruit contains vitamin C. → All citrus fruit are food that contains vitamin C.

Ralph's Market does not sell pink grapefruit. → No pink grapefruit are items sold by Ralph's Market.

Some Chinese dishes contain MSG. → Some Chinese dishes are things that contain MSG.

Some oranges don't taste sweet. → Some oranges are not things that taste sweet.

As you can see, such renderings require the use of artifices like "items sold by Ralph's Market" or "things that taste sweet."

Nonstandard Quantifiers

A standard quantifier is any of the terms "all," "no," or "some." Other quantifiers are nonstandard. Two common nonstandard universal quantifiers are "only" and "not all":

Only doctors are allowed to prescribe drugs. → All who are allowed to prescribe drugs are doctors.

Not all cans are returnable. → Some cans are not returnable.

Notice that the categories in "Only *X* are *Y*" are *reversed* into "All *Y* are *X*."

Some quantifiers are not translatable without substantial loss of meaning into strict categorical form. "Most" and "few" are two examples. Given the quantifiers of categorical logic, the only way we could render

Most sailors are good swimmers.

or

Few sailors are good swimmers.

into standard categorical form is to write

Some sailors are good swimmers.

for each. But this hardly captures what is meant. Similarly, if we were to try to translate

Thirty-five logicians like Chinese food.

into standard categorical form, the closest we could come is

Some logicians like Chinese food.

which is inadequate.

Moral: Not every statement can be rendered adequately into standard categorical form.

Missing Quantifiers

A **QUANTIFIER** is a term like "all," "no," "some," "most," and so on. It says how many things are being spoken of. "All" and "no" speak of every member of the class; "some" speaks of at least one member of the class. Sometimes quantifiers are missing. Examples:

1. *M.B.A.s make good salaries.*
2. *Dogs are mammals.*
3. *Nurses are not doctors.*
4. *Apartment buildings are hard to manage.*

To supply the missing quantifier, think what the speaker or writer is most likely to have meant. Sometimes there will be a clear-cut answer, sometimes not (but that is the speaker's or writer's problem, not yours).

Here are the best "translations" of 1–3:

1. *Some M.B.A.'s make good salaries.*
2. *All dogs are mammals.*
3. *No nurses are doctors.*

The speaker is unlikely to have meant *all* M.B.A.s but likely to have meant *all* dogs and *no* nurses. Number 4 is ambiguous:

4. *Some apartment buildings are hard to manage. (?)*

4. *All apartment buildings are hard to manage. (?)*

Each is plausible (unless you have the speaker or writer there to question), and so we cannot say there is *one correct* reading of number 4.

6.4
Venn Diagrams

Venn diagrams are the pictorial means by which we will represent the information content of a categorical statement. The rules of Venn representation are:

A CIRCLE represents a CLASS or CATEGORY.

A LABEL by the circle tells WHICH CATEGORY.

OVERLAPPING CIRCLES represent COMBINATIONS OF CLASSES.

SHADING IN represents DEFINITELY NOTHING THERE.

The ★ represents AN INDIVIDUAL.

The BAR represents EITHER HERE OR THERE, CAN'T TELL WHICH.

WHITE SPACE represents NO INFORMATION ABOUT THAT AREA.

Some sample diagrams all illustrate the rules in practice.

A Venn diagram is, first of all, a diagram representing the information content—the meaning—of a categorical statement. As a categorical statement deals with categories, the most prominent aspect of any Venn diagram is the circle that stands for a category (or class). For example, this represents the class of dogs:

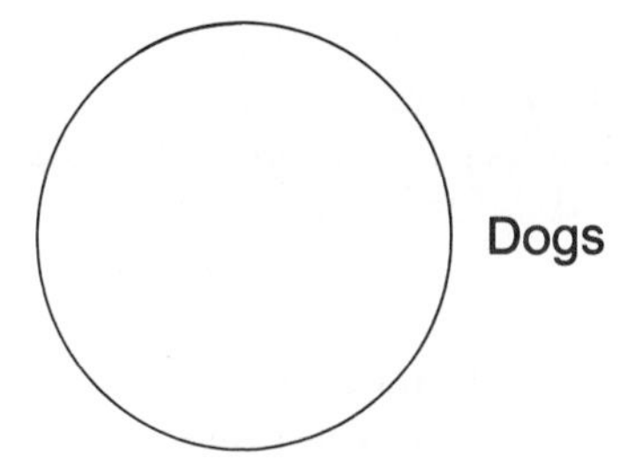

This represents the class of ghosts:

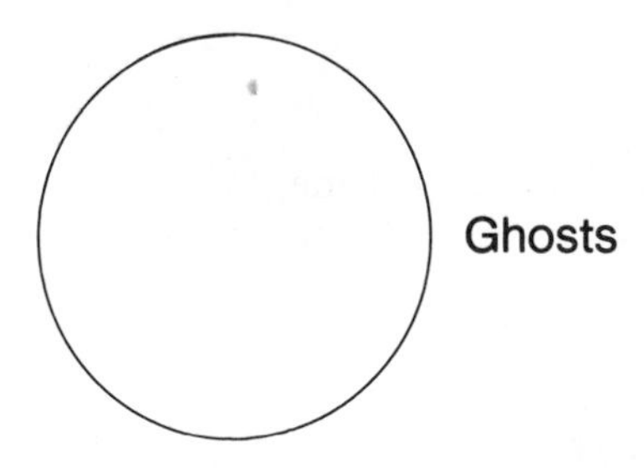

This represents nothing at all, for it is not labeled:

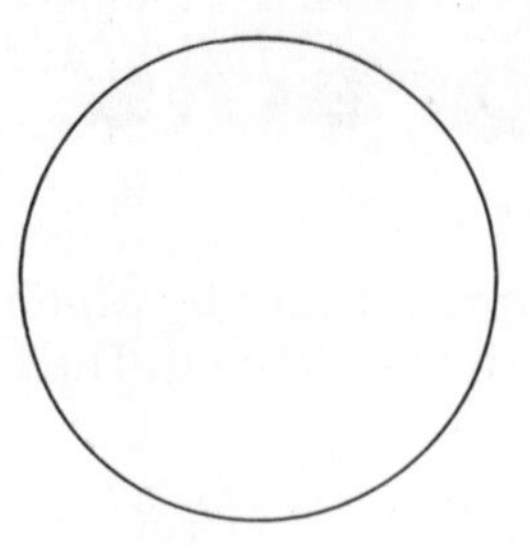

What class a certain circle stands for is determined by what that circle is labeled.

Venn diagrams have specific sectors representing specific classes. This diagram,

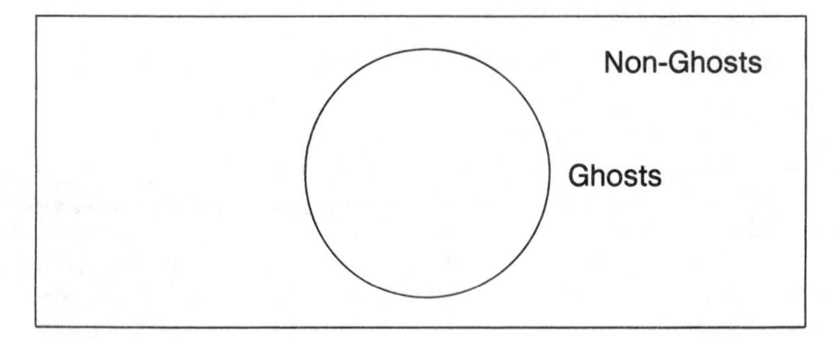

actually has *two* sectors: the class of ghosts (within the circle) and the class of non-ghosts (outside the circle).

Suppose we want to represent on a Venn diagram the information in the following nonstandard categorical statement:

There are no ghosts.

We would draw a circle, label it "ghosts," and shade it in because shading in, by convention, represents nothing there (i.e., that that class is empty):

There are no ghosts.

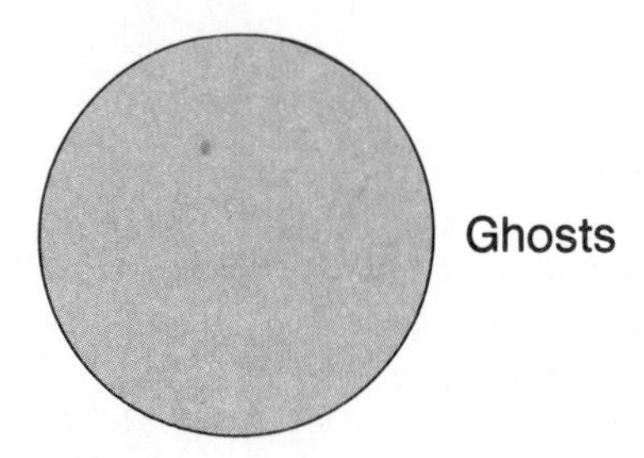

Do not become confused by the fact that shading in involves making marks in a circle (i.e., putting something there). Its conventional meaning is class emptiness: nothing there.

To illustrate how to use both areas of a one-circle Venn diagram, suppose we want to diagram

Nothing is nonmaterial.

Labeling the circle this way (below) means that the area *outside* the circle— the class of the nonmaterial — gets shaded in:

Nothing is nonmaterial.

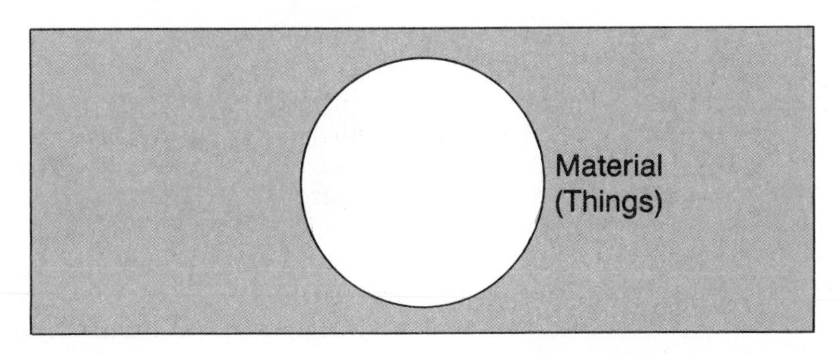

Here are some simple cases of using ★. By convention ★ means "there is something there, i.e., that class has at least one member." The statement,

Ghosts exist.

says that the class of ghosts has at least one member. On a Venn diagram, it would be rendered as:

Ghosts exist.

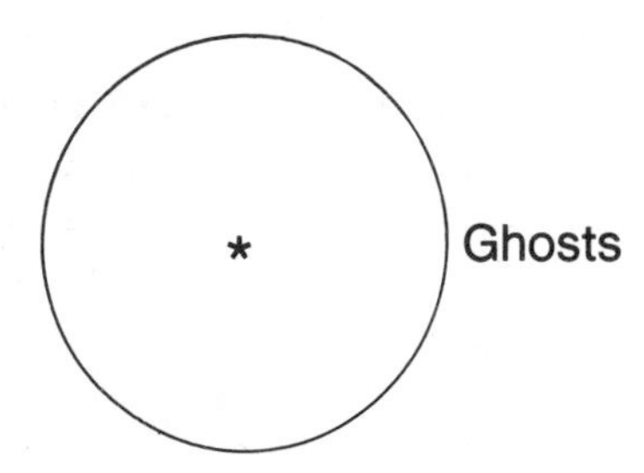

However, these nonstandard categorical statements are not as common as the standard categorical statements, if for no other reason than that we usually want to say something about the relation between *two* classes or categories.

To represent the information content of a categorical statement dealing with two categories, we need two intersecting circles. Our next series of examples will concern a series of propositions about the relation between the class of pirates and the class of thieves. Let us first familiarize ourselves with the areas of two-circle Venn diagrams:

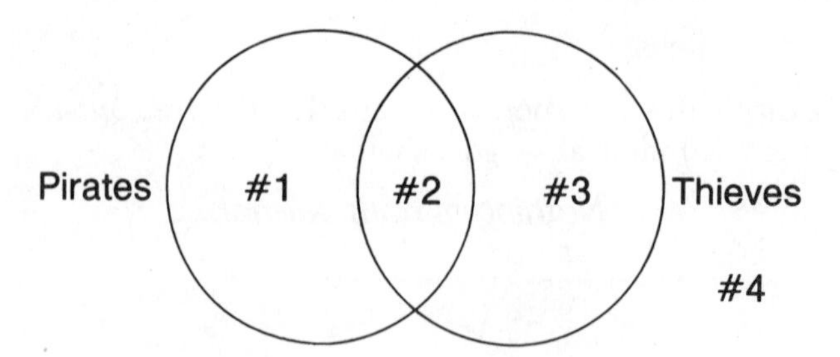

Note that there are *four* areas of the Venn diagram. These are created when circles overlap, and *represent different classes*. Area #1 represents the class of pirates who are *not* thieves. Area #2 represents the class of *both* pirates *and* thieves. Area #3 represents the class of thieves who are *not* pirates. And area #4 represents the class of things that are neither pirates nor thieves. (Make sure you see this before going on.)

As a bit of practice for what's coming next, we'll "translate" from the Venn diagram to English. This diagram:

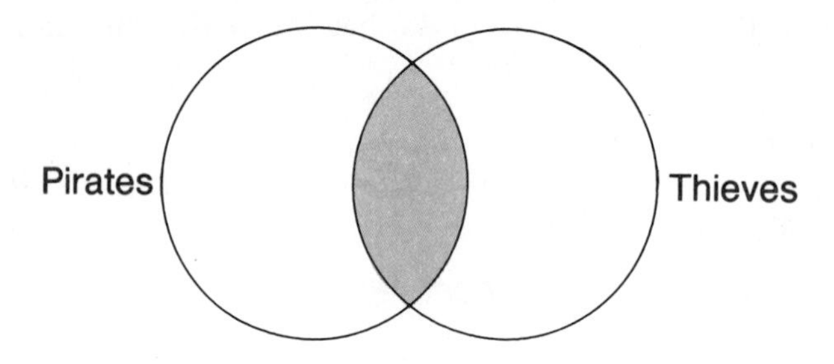

says

There no such thing as a pirate who is a thief.

while this diagram,

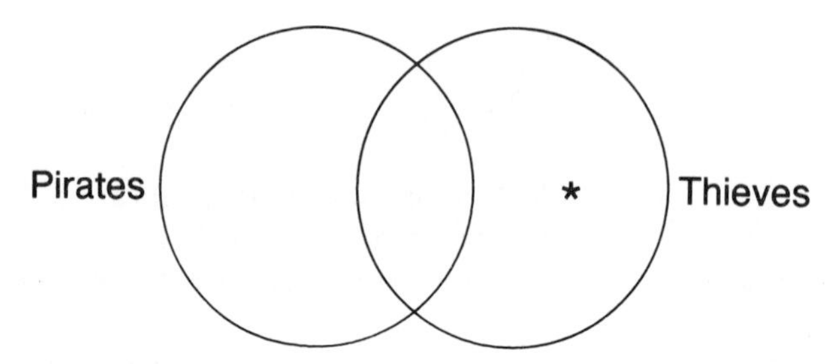

says

There's a thief who isn't a pirate.

We'll next go into detail about how to represent the four standard categorical statements.

Particular Statements

Remember that the **I** statement, for example,

Some pirates are thieves.

means

There is at least one pirate who is a thief.

and that the **O** statement, for example,

Some pirates are not thieves.

means

There is at least one pirate who is not a thief.

I and **O** statements, having existential import, are taken to assert the existence of at least one member of the class named by the subject. Since they assert the existence of at least one member (but do not say whether there is or is not more than one member), we represent their existential import with the ⋆ as follows:

Some pirates are thieves.

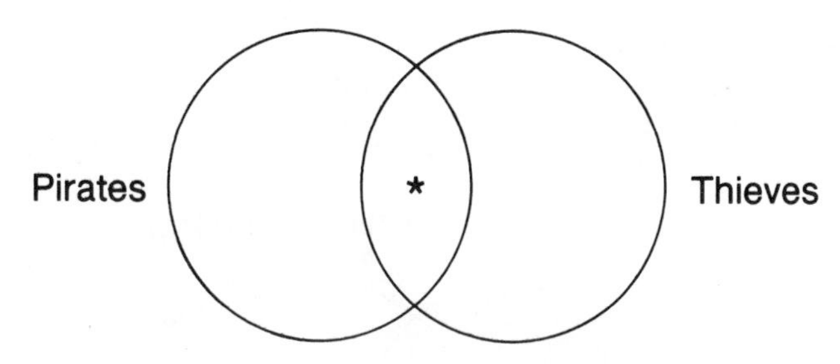

Some pirates are not thieves.

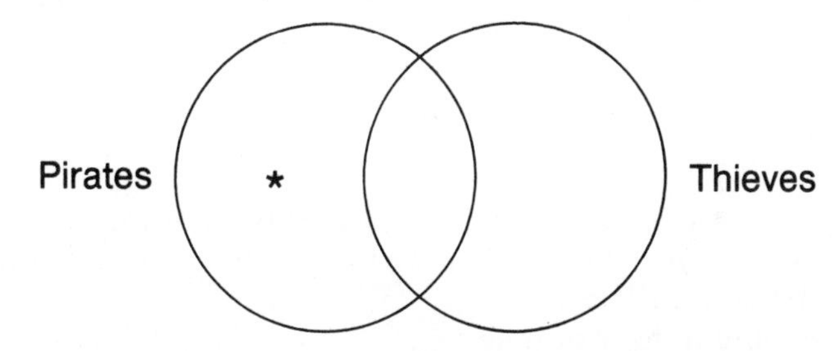

Notice where ⋆ is. In the **I** statement, "Some pirates are thieves," it falls into the area of *both* pirates *and* thieves, thus pictorially saying that there is one individual who is both a pirate and a thief. In the **O** statement, "Some pirates are not thieves," ⋆ falls into the area of pirates who are not thieves, thus pictorially saying that there is one individual who is a pirate but not a thief. Also notice that which circle is labeled what doesn't matter. This diagram could just as correctly represent

Some pirates are not thieves.

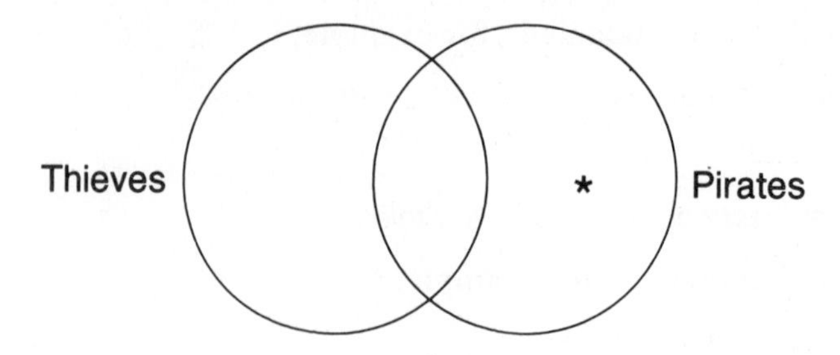

as long as * is in the area of pirates who are not thieves.

Universal Statements

The universal statement **A**, for example,

All pirates are thieves.

means (on the modern interpretation):

If anyone is a pirate, he is a thief.

Meditate on the meaning of the (modern) **A** statement. "All pirates are thieves" merely says "There's no such thing as a pirate who is not a thief." Or it says "The class of pirates who are not thieves is empty." On a Venn diagram:

All pirates are thieves. (Modern)

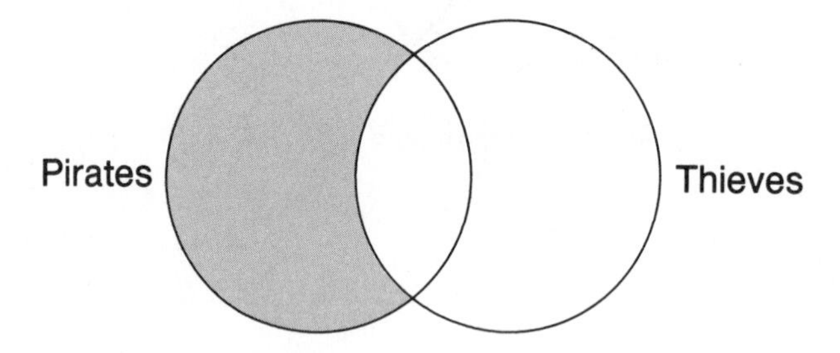

Notice that the class of things that are pirates but not thieves (area #1) is shaded in, that is, *empty*. If *all* pirates are thieves, then there is no such thing as a pirate who is not a thief.

The **E** statement, for example,

No pirates are thieves.

can be seen to mean, on the modern interpretation,

If anyone is a pirate, he is not a thief.

Put another way, "No pirates are thieves" says there is no such thing as someone who is both a pirate and a thief, i.e., that the class of people who are both pirates and thieves is empty. On a Venn diagram:

No pirates are thieves. (Modern)

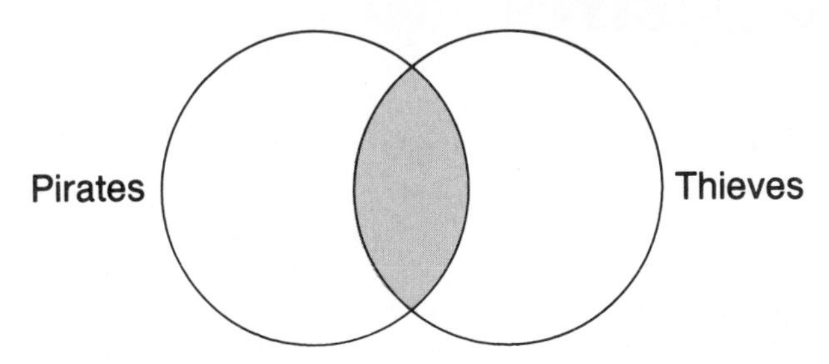

Notice here that the area of overlap—the class of both pirates and thieves, i.e., area #2—is shaded in, that is, *empty*.

In contrast, the classical interpretation of **A** and **E** would look like this on Venn diagrams:

All pirates are thieves. (Classical)

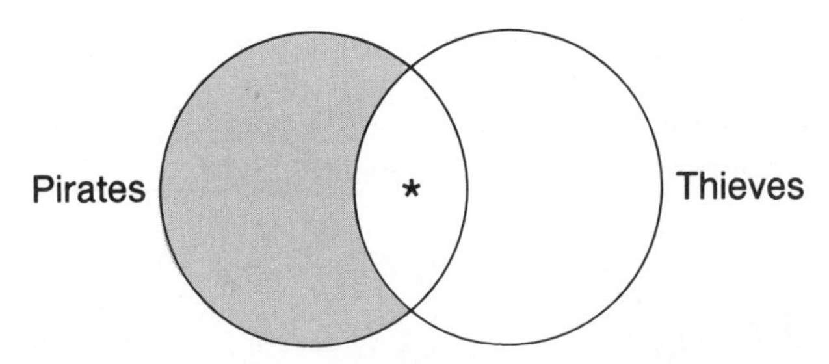

No pirates are thieves. (Classical)

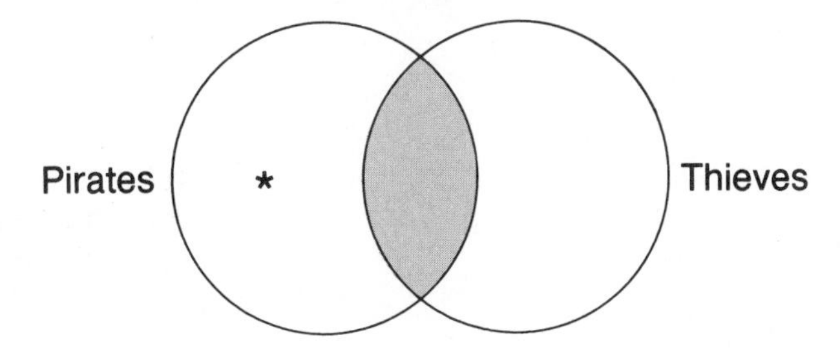

You will see that * is precisely what indicates the existential import of the classical interpretation, for * in area #1 says "and there are pirates," which is just what distinguishes the classical from the modern readings.

The classical interpretation will not be used in further problems unless otherwise indicated.

6.5 Testing Categorical Syllogisms

A **SYLLOGISM** is any argument with two premises and one conclusion. There are various kinds of syllogisms, both deductive and inductive. Here we will study the standard categorical syllogism. A **STANDARD CATEGORICAL SYLLOGISM** is a syllogism whose premises and conclusion are in standard categorical form, and that contains exactly three category (or class) terms. The term "standard categorical syllogism" denotes a kind of argument; it is not the only kind amenable to test by Venn diagrams, as the next section will show. However, the standard categorical syllogism will be the subject of this section.

This is an example of a standard categorical syllogism:

All pirates are cruel people, and all cruel people are people whose parents were cruel; so all pirates are people whose parents were cruel.

Suppose we want to test it for deductive validity. The first thing is to learn the parts of a three-circle Venn diagram. There are three categories or classes at issue: Pirates, Cruel People, and People Whose Parents Were Cruel. Therefore we need three circles and three labels:

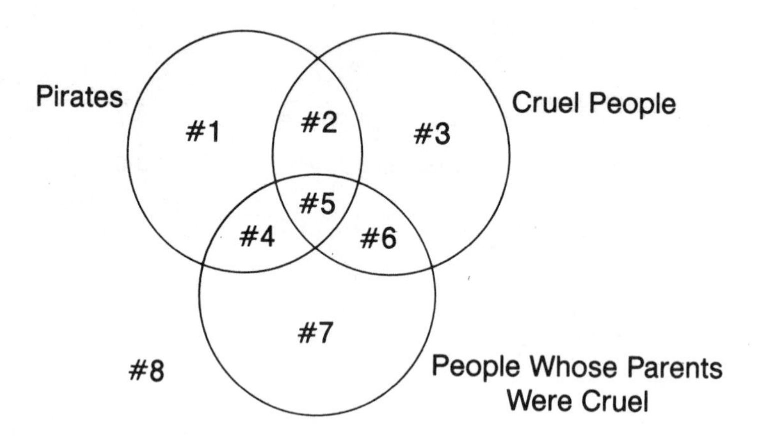

There are eight areas. Each must be read in relation to the others (as in the two-circle diagram). For example, area #1 is the class of pirates who were not cruel and are not people whose parents were cruel, and area #6 is the class of cruel people whose parents were cruel but who are not pirates. (As an exercise, name the remaining six sectors.)

The way to prove a standard categorical syllogism deductively valid or invalid is to diagram both premises on one diagram and see if the conclusion is thereby diagramed. Remember that an argument is deductively valid just in case it is impossible for the premises to be true and the conclusion false.

Also remember that deductive validity occurs when the conclusion is somehow already contained in the premises. The Venn diagram method of establishing deductive validity relies on this fact. If the argument is deductively valid, the conclusion will appear after only the premises have been diagramed. This shows that the conclusion was contained in the premises all along.

The first premise when diagramed looks like this:

All pirates are cruel people.

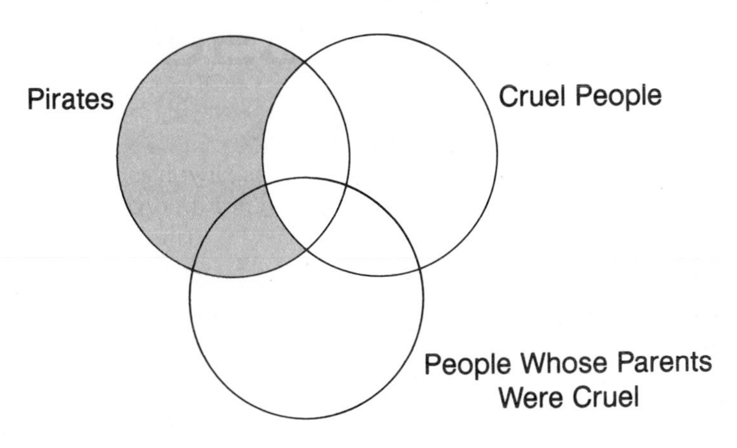

The second premise rendered onto the above yields this diagram:

All pirates are cruel people. All cruel people are people whose parents were cruel.

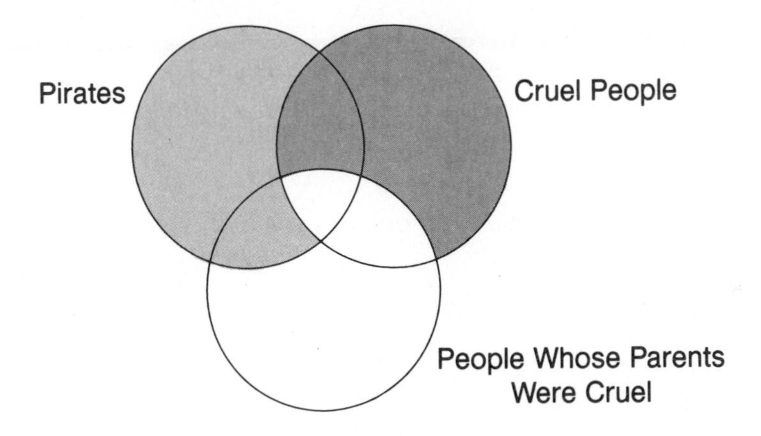

The argument is DV because the two premise diagram immediately above *shows* the conclusion, "All pirates are people whose parents were cruel." This is shown in areas #1 and #2, which are areas of pirates without parents who were cruel people; and both areas are shaded in, showing that there is no such thing as a pirate whose parents were *not* cruel.

It might help if you do a Venn diagram of the conclusion alone:

All pirates are people whose parents were cruel.

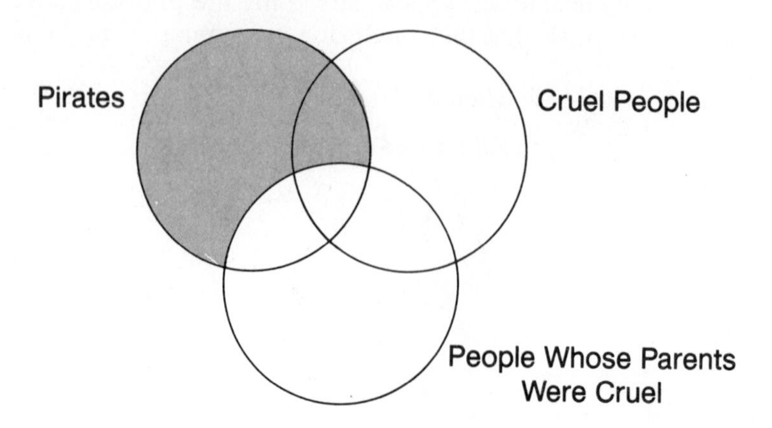

This shows what areas must be shaded in on the *testing* diagram for the conclusion to appear when only the premises are diagramed. Just remember that this is only an aid. *Do not diagram the conclusion onto the testing Venn diagram!* You want to see if the premises entail it. Putting the conclusion on (independently) will make *every* argument deductively valid: After all, if you put it there, how could it fail to turn up?

Here's another syllogism that we'll prove to be deductively invalid:

No used car dealers are completely honest people. + No completely honest people are loan sharks.

Deductively Invalid

No used car dealers are loan sharks.

The first premise is diagramed:

No used car dealers are completely honest people.

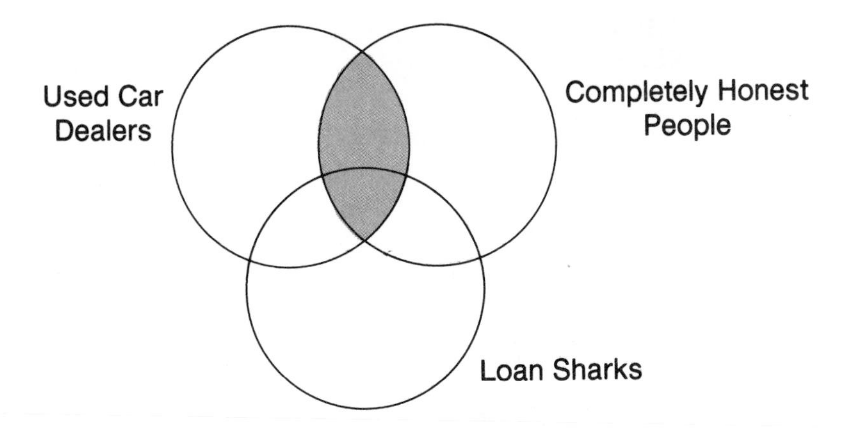

The second premise is put on the diagram along with the first:

No used car dealers are completely honest people. No completely honest people are loan sharks.

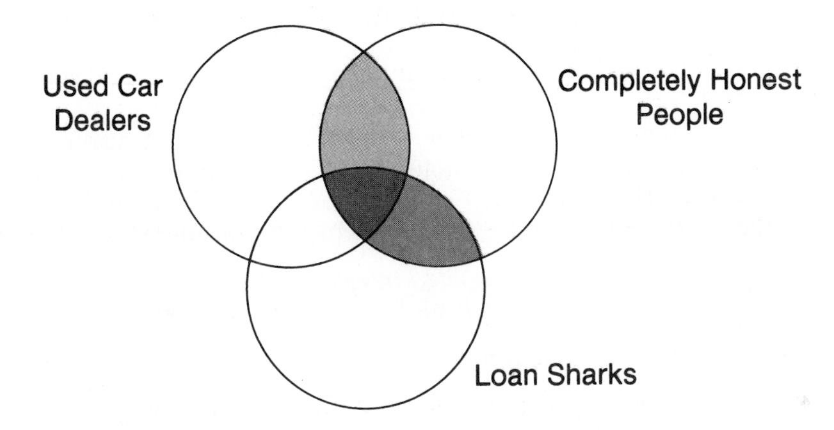

The diagram does *not* show area #4, the class of used car dealers who are loan sharks (but not completely honest people—although this is irrelevant for the present purpose) empty. If the conclusion had appeared it would show these areas empty:

No used car dealers are loan sharks.

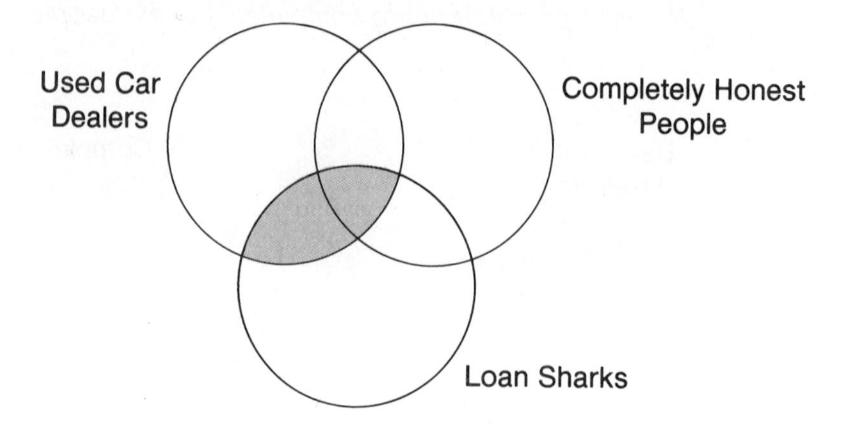

The premises therefore leave open the possibility that there are used car dealers who are loan sharks. That is, the conclusion does not appear on the diagram when only the premises are diagramed. This means that the conclusion is not necessarily true, given the premises. Remember that white space—an area that is neither shaded in nor contains ✲—represents no information. In the above diagram, we have no information about area #4. So, there could, for all we know from the premises, be a used car dealer who is a loan shark!

By the way, there is no such thing as a deductively valid standard categorical syllogism that has two negative (**E** or **O**) premises.

There is another notational device we must use for dealing with some categorical syllogisms that include particular premises, premises of the form **I** or **O**. This is the bar, "———", that connects two ✲s. The bar means "Either in this area or that; can't tell which." Consider this syllogism:

Some soft drinks are caffeinated beverages, but all soft drinks are sweetened. Therefore some caffeinated beverages are sweetened.

The first premise is diagramed like this:

Some soft drinks are caffeinated beverages.

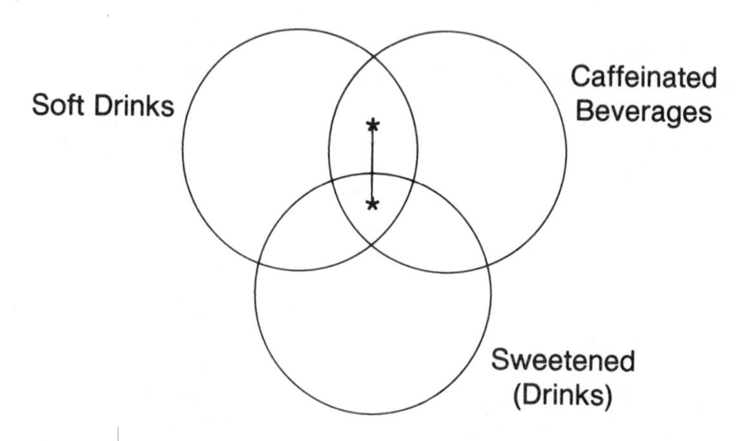

"Some soft drinks are caffeinated beverages" says that there is at least one thing that is both a soft drink and a caffeinated beverage. But the area of the diagram of things that are both soft drinks and caffeinated beverages is, on this three-circle diagram, actually two areas, #2 and #5. If you put * in #2, you've presupposed that the thing that is both a soft drink and caffeinated *is not* sweetened, and if you put * in #5, you've presupposed that the thing that is both a soft drink and caffeinated *is* sweetened. But you can't presuppose either of these things! The premise in itself doesn't specify *anything* about being or not being sweetened. Therefore we use the bar, which means, "Either in this area or that; not enough information to tell."

However, the diagram of the second premise, "All soft drinks are sweetened," clears up the ambiguity:

Some soft drinks are caffeinated beverages.
All soft drinks are sweetened.

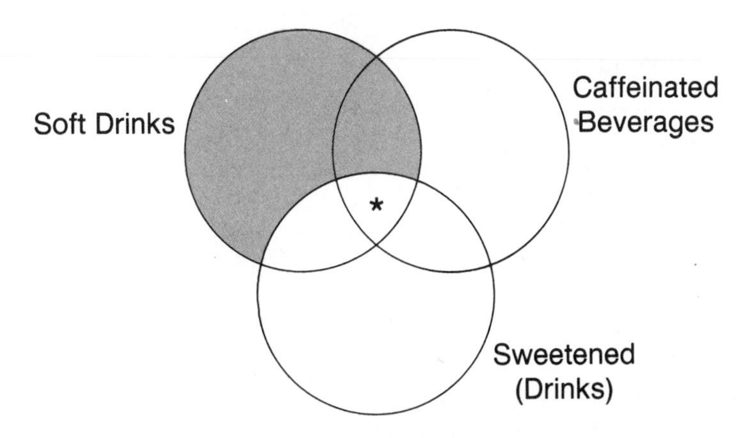

Now we know—if the second premise is true—that there is nothing in area #2 and definitely something in area #5. This is the area of things that are both soft drinks and sweetened (and caffeinated, too, but this is irrelevant now): that is, the conclusion, "Some caffeinated beverages are sweetened," appears when the premises alone are diagramed. So the argument is deductively valid. Here (just checking) is the diagram of the conclusion:

Some caffeinated beverages are sweetened.

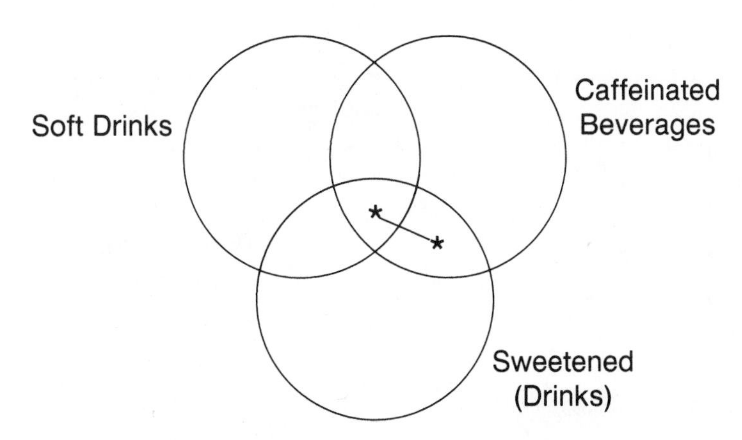

The bar in the conclusion diagram that connects the two *s simply means that for the conclusion to appear, a * must appear in one area or the other.

It might be noticed that had we diagramed the second premise first, we would not have had to use the bar. But then you wouldn't have seen how the bar works, in particular how a universal premise can show which sector * is in. The best advice for future problems is: *Diagram the universal premise first.*

Now for an invalid categorical syllogism:

Some French Canadians are separatists. Some separatists live in Toronto. So some French Canadians live in Toronto.

Diagram the first premise:

Some French Canadians are separatists.

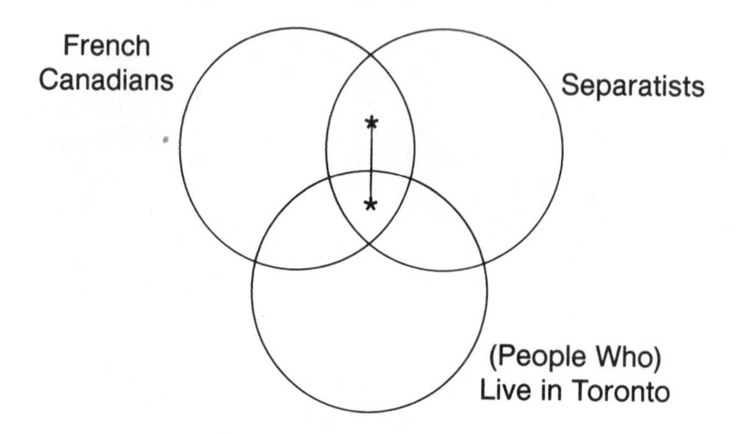

Diagram the second premise onto the same diagram:

Some French Canadians are separatists.
Some separatists live in Toronto.

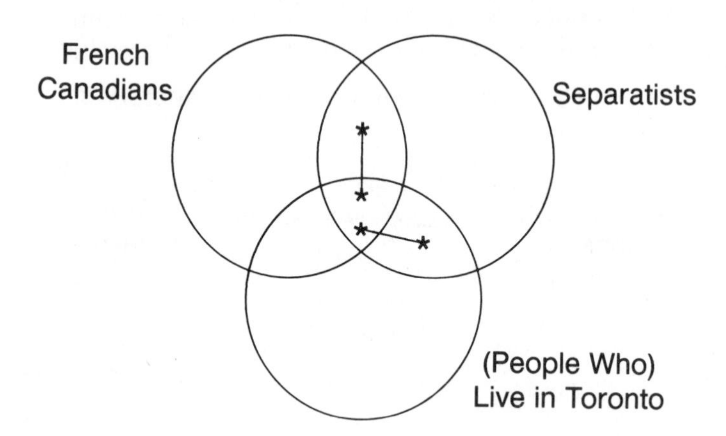

However the conclusion, "Some French Canadians live in Toronto," doesn't necessarily appear. For the premises to show that the conclusion deductively follows, there would have to be * *definitely* in either area #4 or #5, like this:

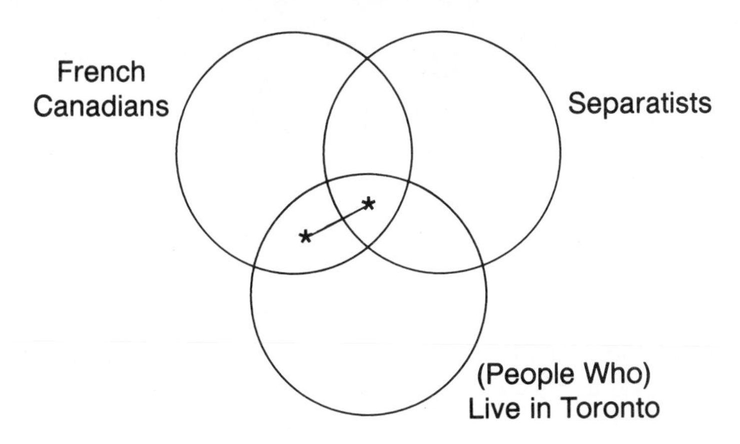

But in the testing diagram the conclusion doesn't appear when only the premises are diagramed, for on the testing diagram there isn't anything in #4, but there isn't *definitely* anything in #5 either. The possibility is open that one * is in #2, the other in #6, and nothing in #5. So the conclusion doesn't necessarily follow, and the argument is deductively invalid.

It is impossible to have a deductively valid standard categorical syllogism with two particular premises, that is, two premises of either **I** or **O** form.

One last reminder on Venn diagrams and validity: By diagraming premises on a Venn diagram, you are in essence supposing them to be true. The diagram is a picture of sorts of what, logically, the premises would "look like" if true. By seeing if the conclusion appears, you are in effect determining whether the conclusion is contained within the premises. If it is, then the argument is deductively valid. Of course, this is not the same as soundness, for one or both premises might be false.

Venn diagrams test the validity of the *form* of categorical syllogisms. This form is deductively valid:

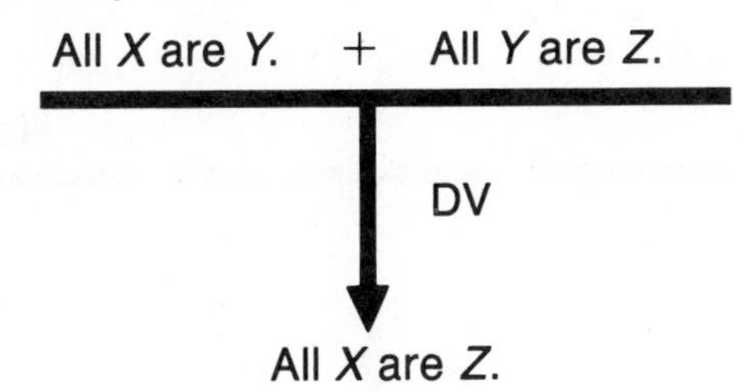

A Venn diagram will show this:

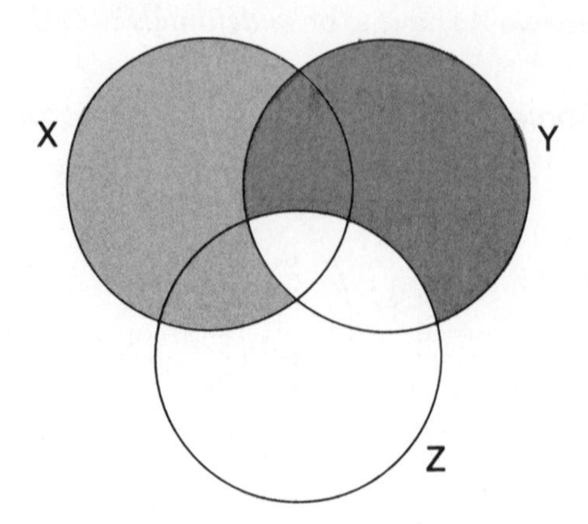

This means that any particular categorical syllogism that has this form will be deductively valid. For example, each of these syllogisms share this form; accordingly, each is DV:

All pirates are thieves, and all thieves are immoral. So all pirates are immoral.

All insects are animals with segmented bodies. All animals with segmented bodies have a head, thorax, and abdomen. Therefore all insects have a head, thorax, and abdomen.

You can extract a logical form from any categorical syllogism you've proved valid (or invalid). For example, earlier we proved this syllogism to be deductively invalid:

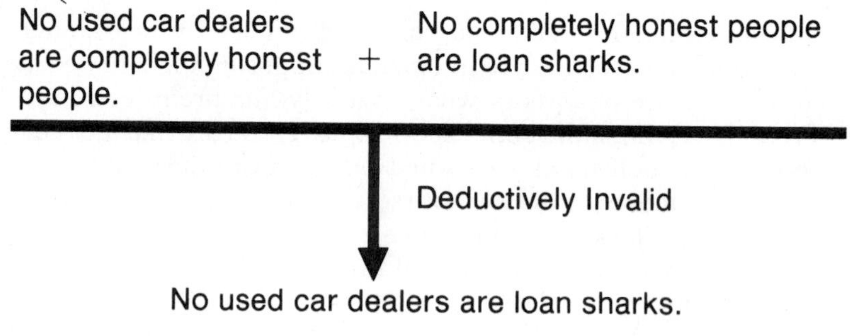

Its logical form is this:

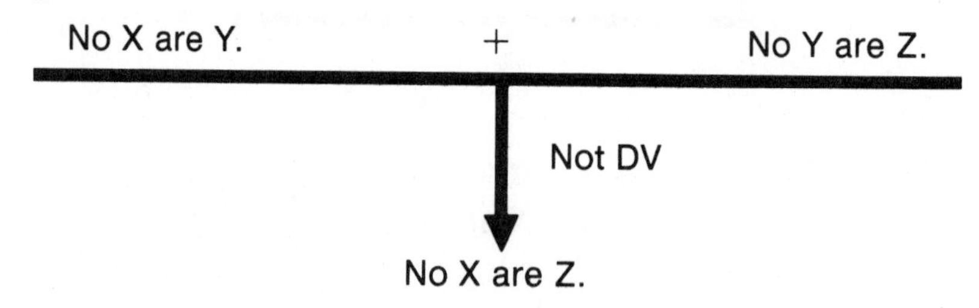

Any particular syllogism that shares this form will also be deductively invalid.

For more on the form of categorical syllogisms, see the Appendix to this chapter.

6.6 Testing Other Categorical Arguments

The standard categorical syllogism is not the only kind of categorical argument amenable to testing by Venn diagrams. We will discuss a number of different nonstandard categorical arguments, and use Venn diagrams to establish validity.

Immediate Inferences

An immediate inference is an argument with one conclusion deduced from one premise. This categorical argument is an immediate inference:

Some films are artworks.

Some artworks are films.

Why is it deductively valid? The Venn diagram of the premise:

Some films are artworks.

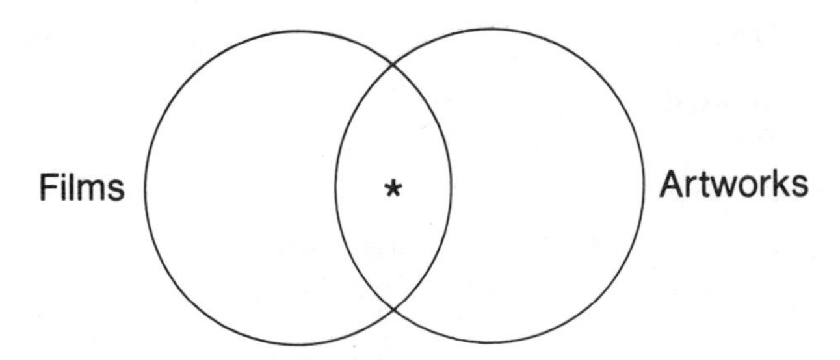

shows that the conclusion appears. There is a * in the area of things that are both films and artworks, thereby showing that some artworks are films. In effect, the diagrams for any **I** statement and its reverse, i.e., "Some *X* are *Y*" and "Some *Y* are *X*," are identical.

This also holds for any **E** statement. This argument is deductively valid:

No national parks are privately owned lands.

No privately owned lands are national parks.

as its Venn diagram shows:

No national parks are privately owned lands.

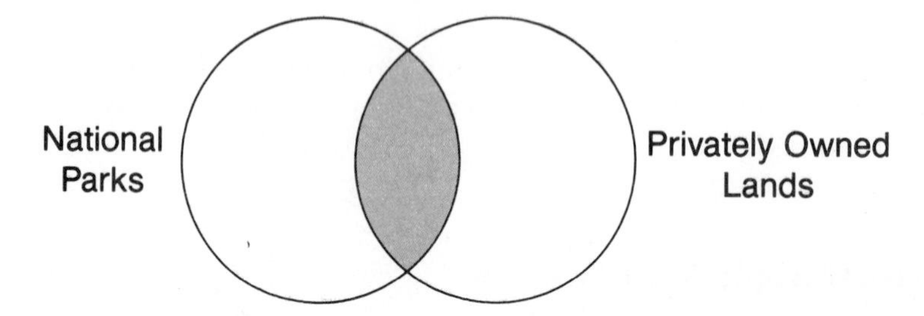

Again, the diagram of the premise is the diagram of the conclusion; so the conclusion appears when the premise alone is diagramed.

If two categorical statements have the same Venn diagram they are logically equivalent. We have just shown that switching around subject and predicate in any **E** and **I** statements yields the same diagram. Thus, we have shown these logical equivalences:

No *X* are *Y*.   Some *X* are *Y*.

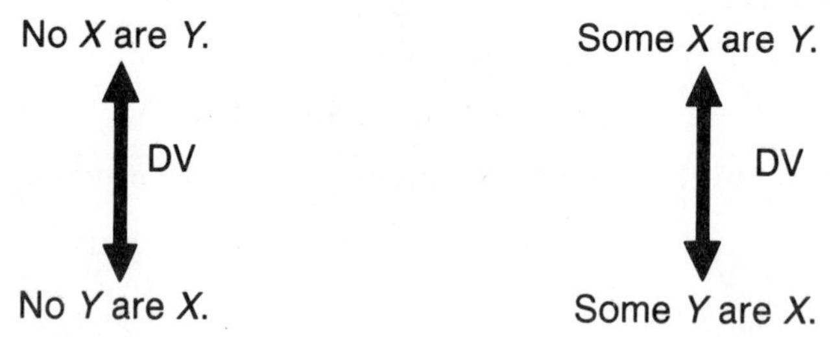

No *Y* are *X*.   Some *Y* are *X*.

The **A** and **O** categorical statements do not work like this. The obviously invalid argument below—obvious because the premise is clearly true and the conclusion clearly false—can be proven invalid with a Venn diagram:

All whales are mammals.

Not DV

All mammals are whales.

The diagram of the premise

All whales are mammals.

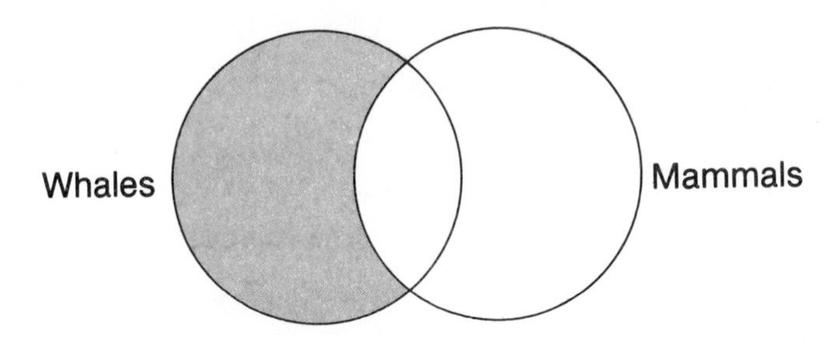

does not reveal the conclusion. For the diagram of the conclusion would be this:

All mammals are whales.

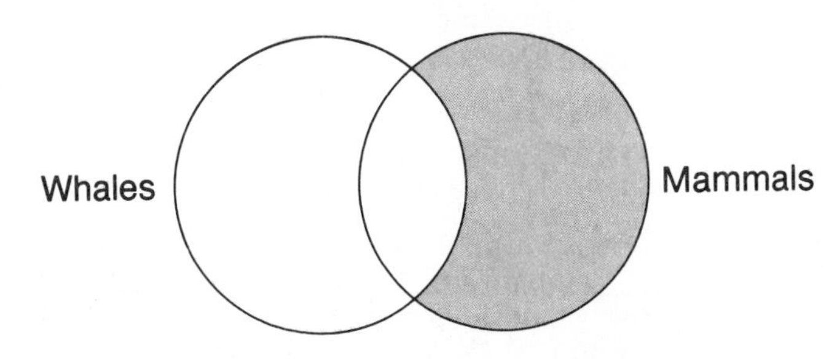

Here's an example of going from one **O** statement to its reverse:

Some flowers are not roses.

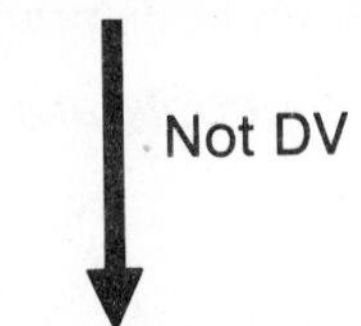

Some roses are not flowers.

The argument is, again, obviously invalid: We move from a truth to a falsehood. The Venn diagram of the premise

Some flowers are not roses.

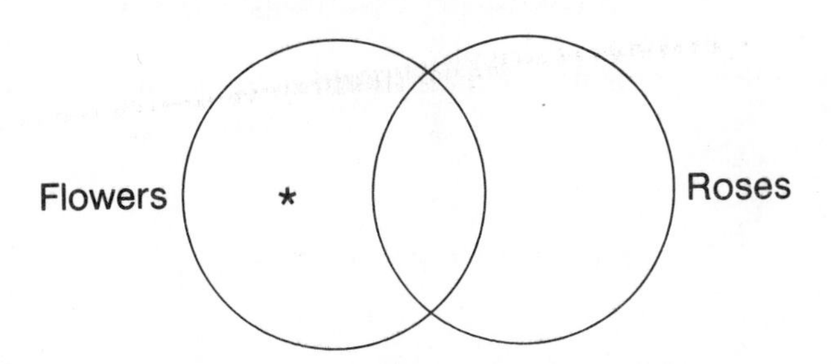

does not reveal the conclusion. The diagram of the conclusion should look like this:

Some roses are not flowers.

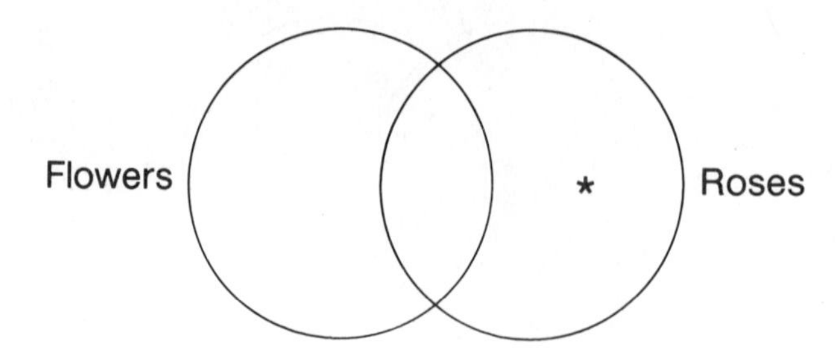

All this is to say that switching subject and predicate around in **A** and **O** categorical statements does not yield DV arguments.

There are some peculiarities with the meaning of the categorical statements. Some categorical arguments that may *appear* deductively valid are in fact deductively *in*valid. For example:

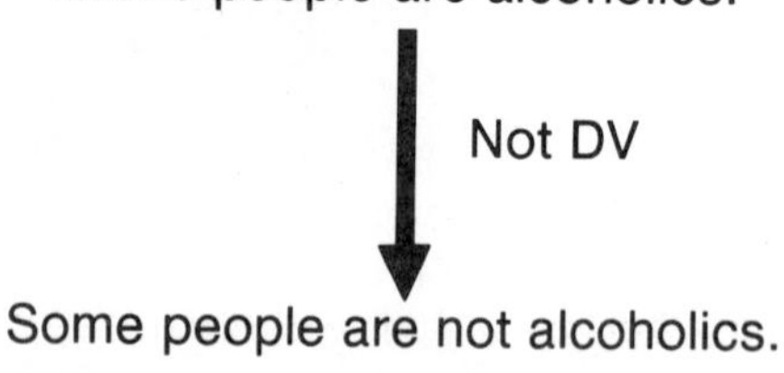

It might seem that the first implies the second. Why else would I say "Some people are alcoholics" if I didn't think that some were not? However, the argument is technically invalid. "Some *X* are *Y*" does not, by its meaning, rule out "All *X* are *Y*." The diagram of its premise

Some people are alcoholics.

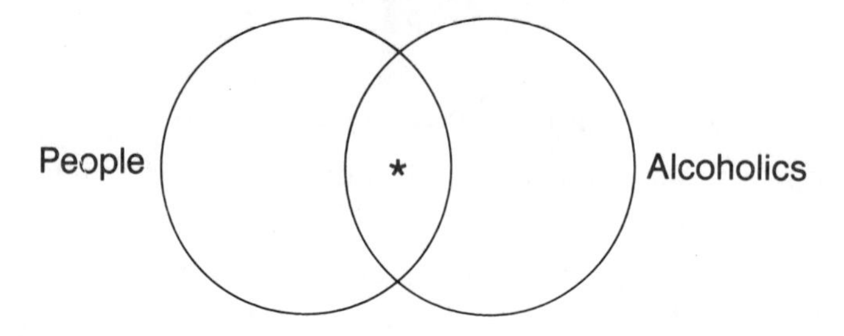

does not show the conclusion, which would be diagramed like this:

Some people are not alcoholics.

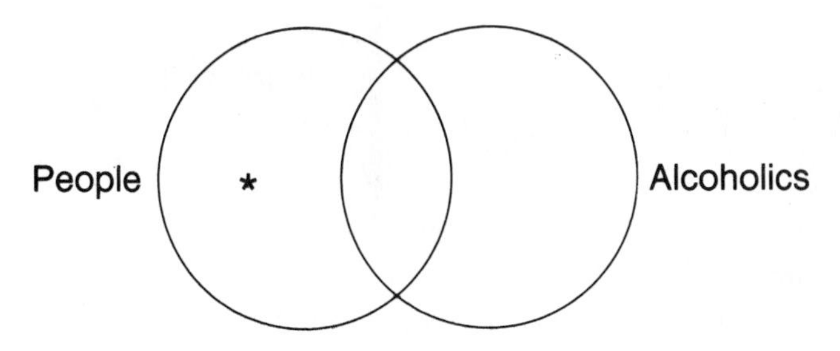

Another peculiarity is that an argument of this form is not deductively valid *on the modern interpretation:*

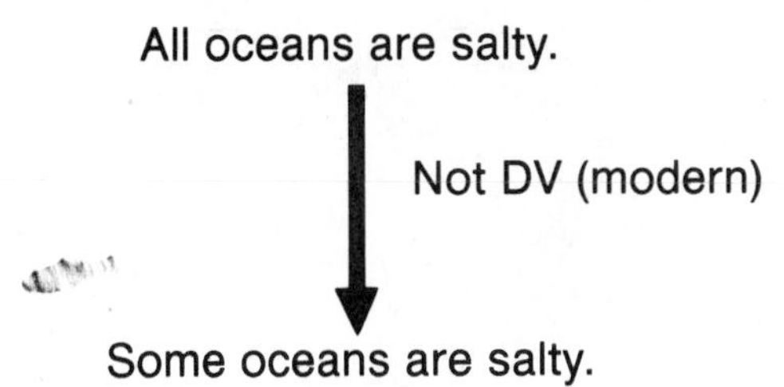

The diagram of the premise (on the modern interpretation)

All oceans are salty.

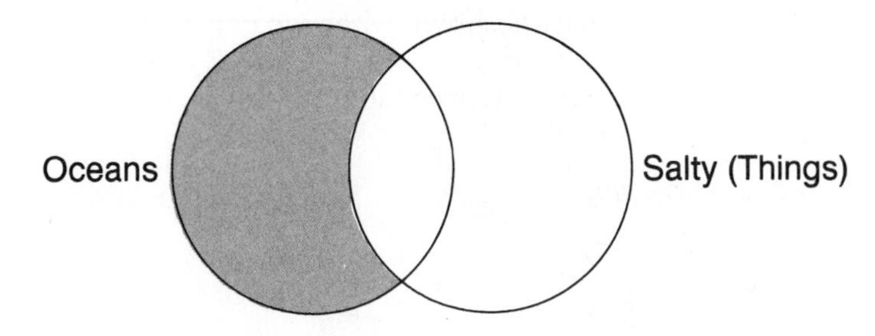

does not reveal the conclusion, which would be diagramed like this:

Some oceans are salty.

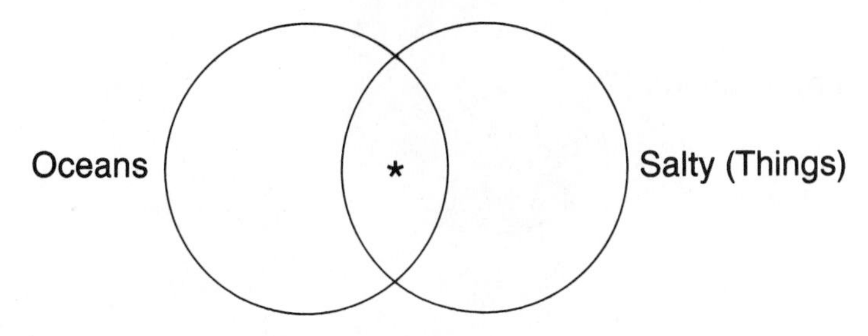

However, the classical interpretation would make the argument valid.

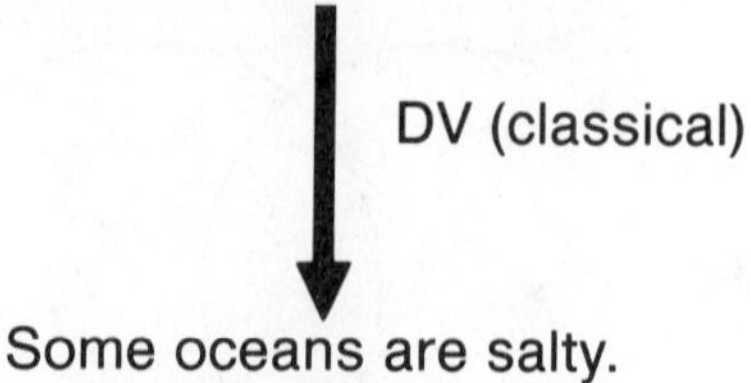

Were Aristotle to use Venn diagrams, he would diagram "All oceans are salty" as "Whatever oceans there are, and there is at least one, are all salty," that is, as:

All oceans are salty. (Classical)

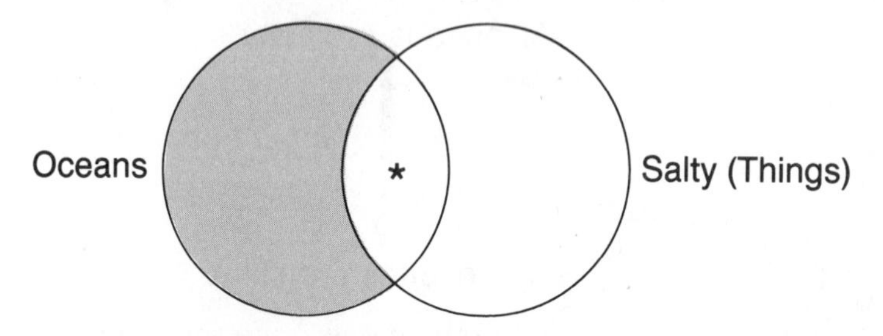

This diagram reveals the conclusion "Some oceans are salty" (because it is in effect part of the meaning the ancients assigned to "All oceans are salty").

Yet another peculiarity is shown when we consider what happens with the truthvalues of the universal statements **A** and **E** when their subject class is empty. Assume there are no leprechauns. Then the subject class of each of these statements is empty:

All leprechauns are tiny.

No leprechauns are tiny.

Diagram both statements:

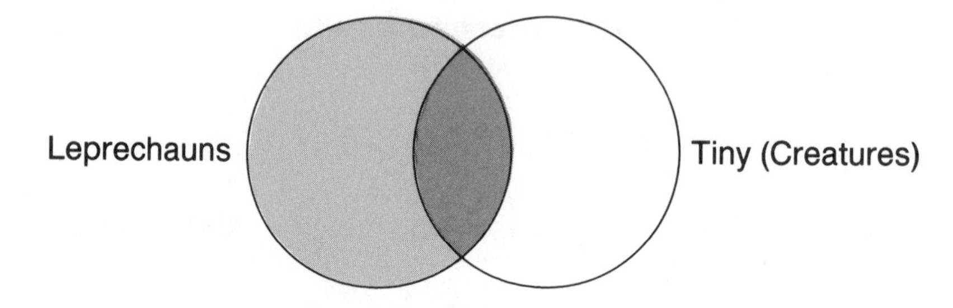

This, however, is the same as the diagram for:

There are no leprechauns.

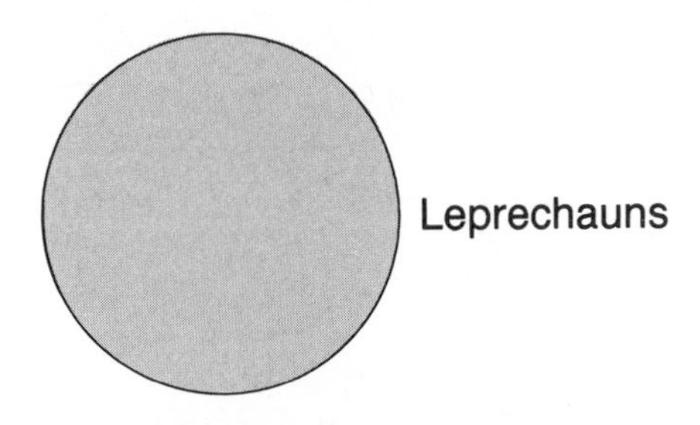

This shows that these statements are logically equivalent:

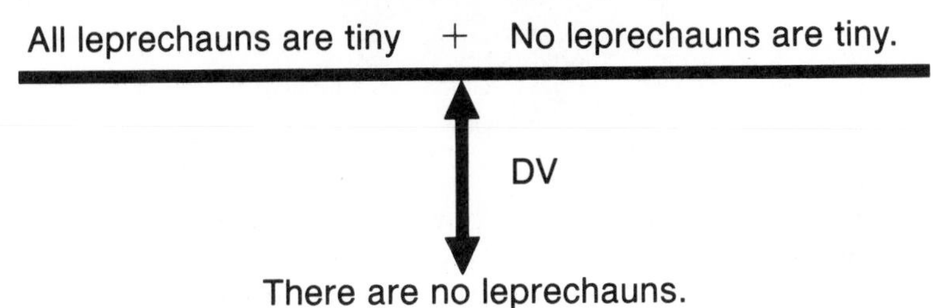

In other words, if the subject class, *X*, is empty, then both "All *X* are *Y*" and "No *X* are *Y*" are true. (This, of course, holds only for the modern interpretation of **A** and **E**, not for the classical.)

Three-Plus Premised Arguments

While the standard categorical syllogism is by definition an argument with two premises, any number of premises is possible, although three categories forms a practical limit on a workable Venn diagram. (Four-circle diagrams are possible but very hard to read and work with.) It is also possible to ask the question, "Is the argument deductively valid?" in different ways. Consider this problem:

> *Given (1) that all who read Faulkner also read Melville, (2) that there are no readers of Dickens who are not also readers of Melville, and (3) that some who read Melville also read Faulkner: Is there anyone who reads all three?*

This problem in effect asks whether this argument is deductively valid:

(1) + (2) + (3)

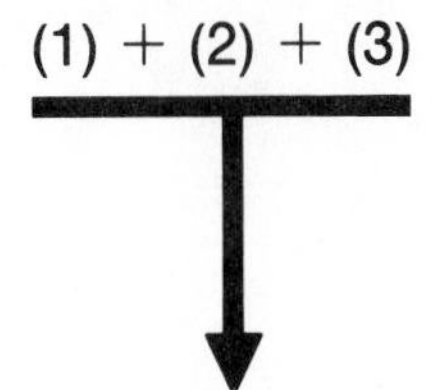

There is someone who reads all three.

We must therefore diagram *three* premises on a Venn diagram. Note that (2) put into standard categorical form reads: "All readers of Dickens are readers of Melville." The full diagram:

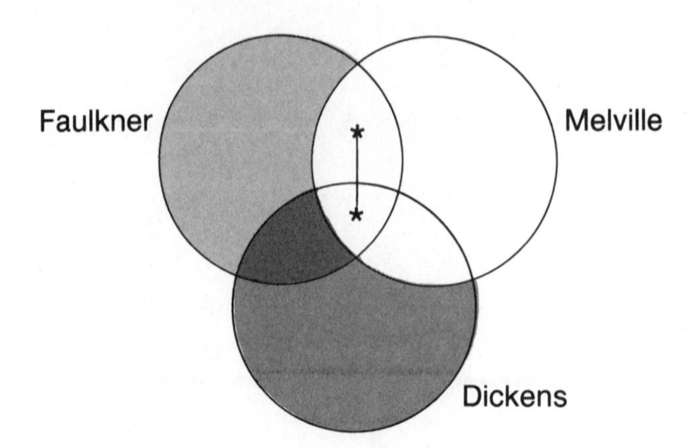

The answer to the question, "Does anyone read all three?" is "Can't tell from the information given," *not* "Yes," *not* "No." The ⁎s connected with the bar say that there may or may not be something in area #5, the class of any who read all three. (That is, from the information given, there is the possibility that the ⁎ is in area #2.) Similarly, the answer to the question, "Is the argument deductively valid?" is "No," since the conclusion doesn't necessarily follow.

Another sort of nonstandard syllogistic problem is the missing conclusion. Suppose you are given this problem:

> *No acids are alkalis, and baking soda is an alkali. What new information follows?*

This in effect asks you to supply any deductive conclusion for the argument:

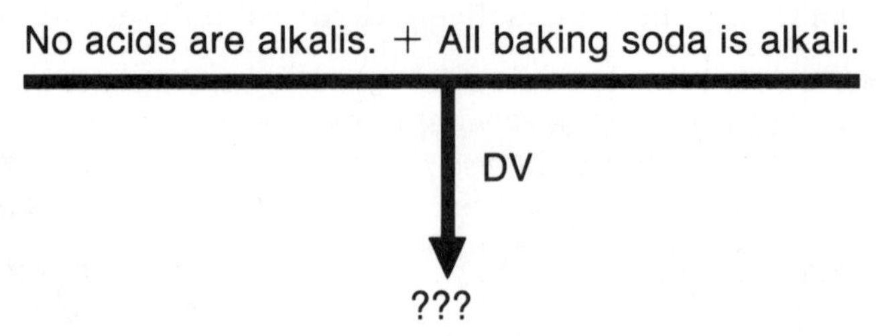

A Venn diagram of the premises

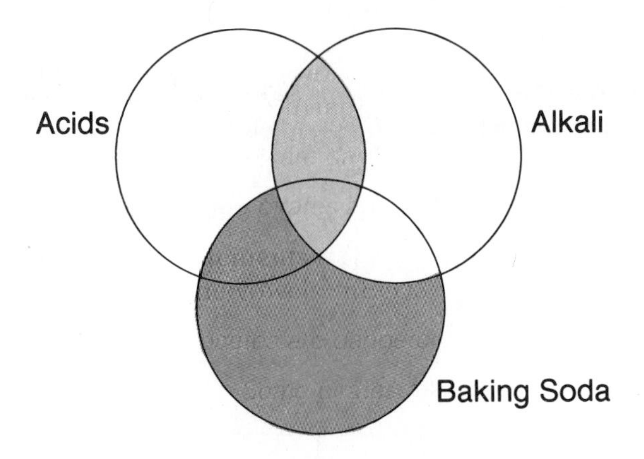

reveals that "No baking soda is an acid" is one piece of new information that follows. (The point of asking for *new* information is that any of the premises trivially follows from itself. "No acids are alkalis" deductively entails "No acids are alkalis"—but that is uninteresting.) In other words, here's the missing conclusion:

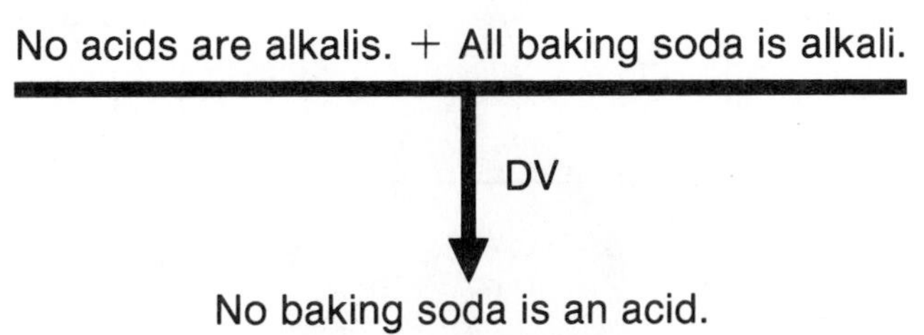

Sorites

"Sorites" (sow-RIGHT-eez) comes from the Greek for "heap." A **SORITES** (the word is the same in the singular and the plural) is a compound argument containing at least two standard categorical syllogisms as simple components where the conclusion of the first functions as the premise of the second. Schematically, a sorites looks like this:

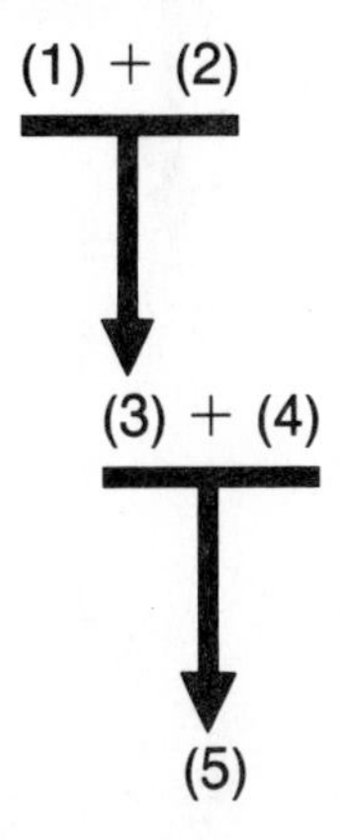

Of course, a sorites can go on: The only requirement is that it have *at least two* simple categorical syllogisms.

Here's an example:

(1) No IRA deposits are taxable income. (2) All wages are taxable income. So (3) no IRA deposits are wages. (4) Some wages are tips. So (5) some IRA deposits are not tips.

This sorites breaks down into two simple arguments. First, this:

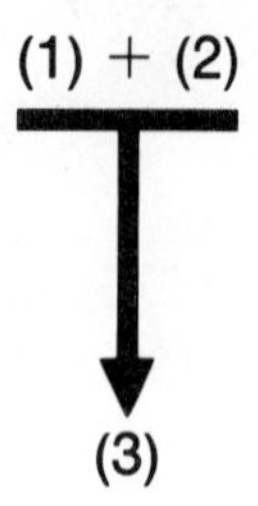

A Venn diagram shows this valid:

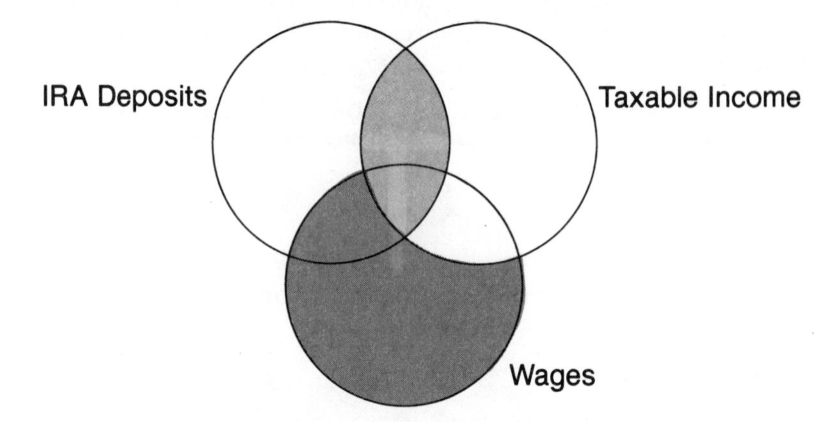

The second part of the sorites is this:

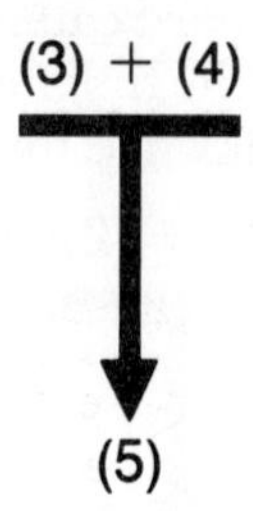

A Venn diagram shows this *invalid:*

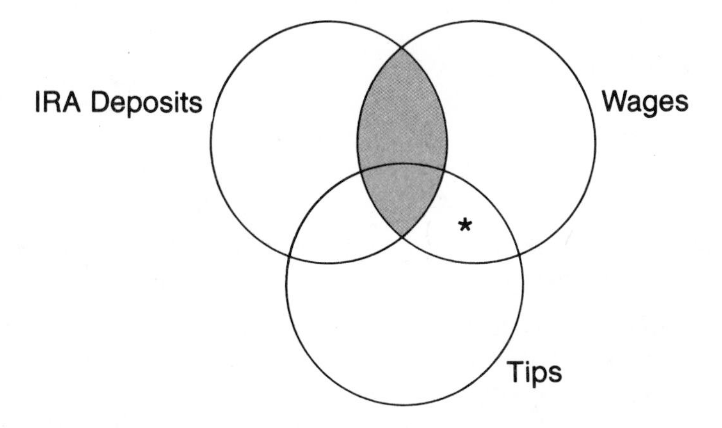

The diagram does *not* reveal the conclusion. It does *not* show that there is something that is an IRA deposit but not a tip. So the sorites *as a whole* is invalid (although its first simple syllogism is valid):

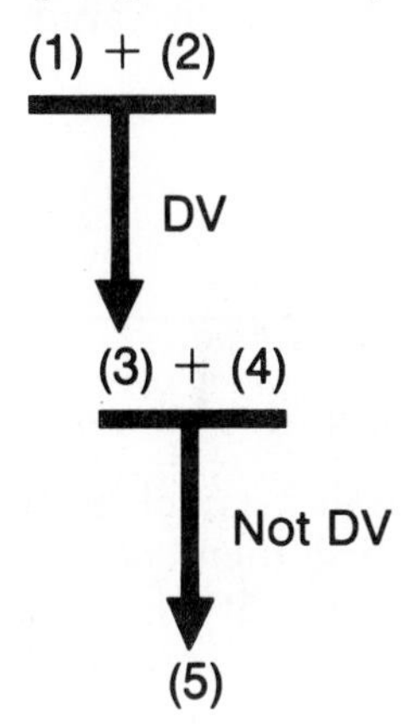

Singular Terms

Singular terms are either proper names, e.g., "Socrates," or definite descriptions, e.g., "The man in the gray flannel suit." The ever-popular syllogism

All men are mortal, and Socrates is a man. Therefore, Socrates is mortal.

is nonstandard, for it contains a premise, "Socrates is a man," that is not exactly in **A**, **E**, **I**, or **O** form. However, we can treat "Socrates" as a name of a particular, and represent him by a *. Thus, the argument can be diagramed:

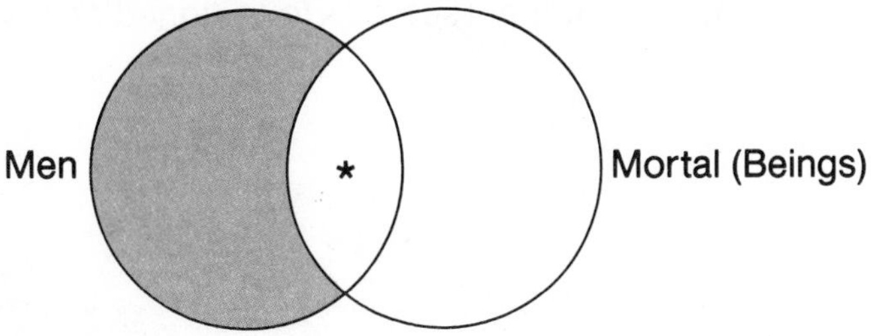

And it will be seen that the argument is valid. Socrates, appearing on the diagram as ✲, is clearly in the area of mortal men.

Too Many Terms

It is important to keep the categories straight when considering any syllogism. Some syllogisms might *appear* to have three categories, when in fact they have more. Consider this argument:

> *All universities admit bright students. All bright students tend to do well at school. So, all universities admit students who tend to do well at school.*

A casual glance may suggest that it is deductively valid. However, if we recast its statements so that each is in strict standard categorical form, we find that there are actually *five* categories, not three:

> *All universities are admitters of bright students. All bright students are students who tend to do well at school. So, all universities are admitters of students who tend to do well at school.*

The categories contained in the above argument are:

universities

admitters of bright students

bright students

students who tend to do well at school

admitters of students who tend to do well at school

The argument as it stands is deductively invalid. There are too many categories. (However, a *different* argument, one that replaces "All bright students are students who tend to do well at school" with "All admitters of bright students are admitters of students who tend to do well at school" would be DV.) The emphasis on "translating" from ordinary English into standard categorical form was made precisely to catch arguments like this one.

There is a defect in the logic of categories. It is not fine-grained enough to show some arguments to be DV. The medieval logicians were aware that this argument

All horses are four-legged animals.

All who ride horses ride four-legged animals.

was deductively valid—you cannot imagine the premise true and the conclusion false—yet it cannot be treated as a categorical argument. The premise contains two categories, "horses" and "four-legged animals," while the conclusion contains two more, different, categories, "those who ride horses" and "those who ride four-legged animals." A Venn diagram is obviously useless.

KEY POINTS

Categorical statements assert or deny membership in classes or categories. They:

- Assert that a particular is a member of a class ("John is a friend of mine" or "Some friends of mine are rich").
- Deny that a particular is a member of a class ("Jane is not a friend of mine" or "Some friends of mine are not rich").
- Assert that one class is contained by another class ("Bases are alkalis" or "All cats are mammals").
- Deny that one class is contained in another class ("Acids are not alkalis" or "No Republicans are liberals").

The asserting-denying aspect of categorical statements was codified by the medievals into abbreviations for the four standard statements:

- **A** = All *X* are *Y*.
- **E** = No *X* are *Y*.
- **I** = Some *X* are *Y*.
- **O** = Some *X* are not *Y*.

A standard categorical syllogism contains two premises, one conclusion, and three categories.

- You must be able to translate (or at least see) which form (**A**, **E**, **I**, or **O**) a statement is in and which categories it is speaking about.
- Be especially aware of "Only" and "All. . . are not."
- Be sensitive to missing quantifiers. Is "Some" or "All" or "No" the intended sense of the statement?

Venn diagrams give logical pictures of categorical statements. Remember that:

- Even a one-circle diagram, for example, one labeled "Ghosts," has two areas: "Ghosts" and "Non-Ghosts."
- Two-circle diagrams have four areas.
- Three-circle diagrams have eight areas.

You should also be able to identify the sectors. For example, a three-circle diagram for the categories "Novels," "Fictions," and "Bestsellers"

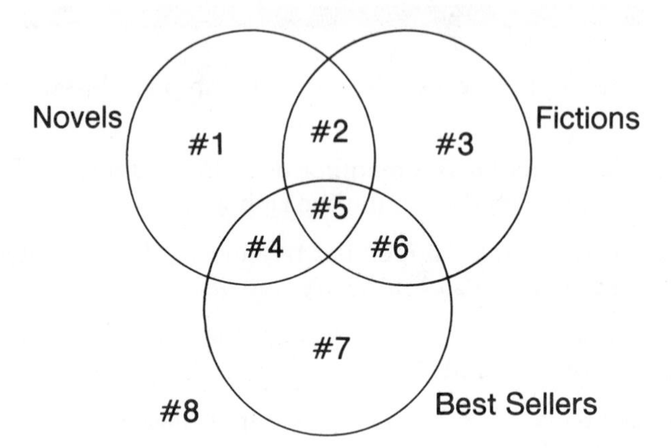

contains sectors that represent these classes:

#1 = Novels that are neither fiction nor bestsellers

#2 = Fiction novels that are not bestsellers

#3 = Fictions that is neither a novel nor a bestseller

#4 = Bestseller novels that are not fiction

#5 = Novels that are fictions and bestsellers

#6 = Bestseller fictions that is not a novel

#7 = Bestsellers that are neither fictions nor novels

#8 = Things that are neither novels, fictions, nor bestsellers

The principle behind Venn diagrams is the principle of deductive validity. The reason any argument is deductively valid is that its conclusion is somehow contained within the premises. That's why the conclusion follows with necessity in a deductively valid argument. So in proving a categorical argument deductively valid or invalid:

- Diagram only the premise(s). Do not also diagram the conclusion.
- See if the conclusion definitely appears on the diagram when only the premises are diagramed. If so, the argument is deductively valid. If not, it is deductively invalid.

Keep in mind the representational rules of Venn diagrams:

A CIRCLE represents a CLASS or CATEGORY.

A LABEL by the circle tells WHICH CATEGORY.

OVERLAPPING CIRCLES represent COMBINATIONS OF CLASSES.

SHADING IN represents DEFINITELY NOTHING THERE.

The ★ represents AN INDIVIDUAL.

The BAR represents EITHER HERE OR THERE, CAN'T TELL WHICH.

WHITE SPACE (no shading, no ★) represents NO INFORMATION ABOUT THAT AREA.

The most basic skill in using Venn diagrams is the ability to represent the four standard categorical statements. Make sure you understand how to do this.

- Under the "modern" interpretation, the universal statements, **A** and **E** have no existential import. (No ★s are used in diagraming them.)
- The **A** statement seems to confuse logic students. Remember that "All *X* are *Y*" means "There is nothing that is *X* but not *Y*."

The four standard categorical propositions and their diagrams:

A — All *X* are *Y*.

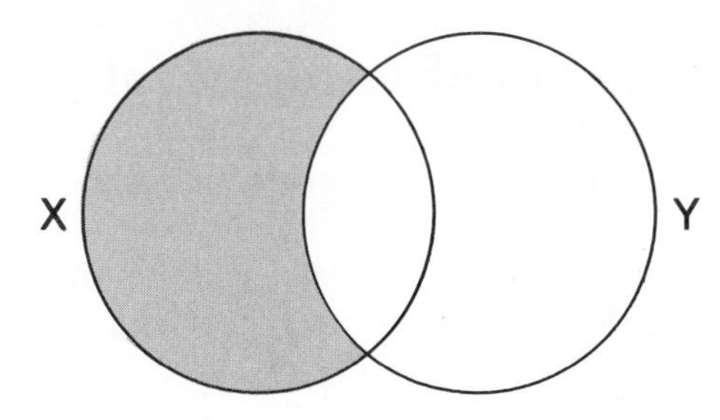

E — No *X* are *Y*.

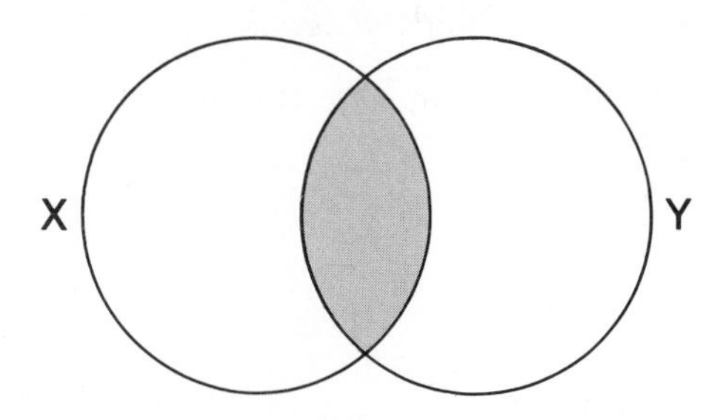

I — Some *X* are *Y*.

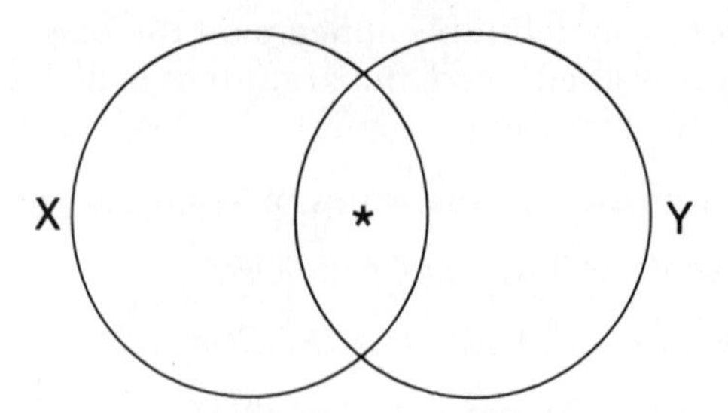

O — Some *X* are not *Y*.

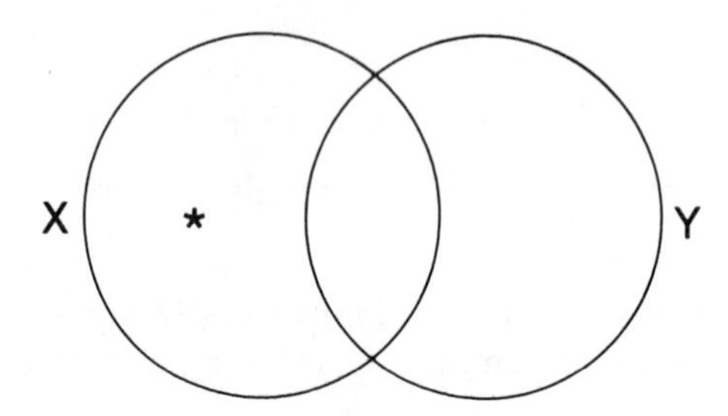

Two hints about the validity of categorical syllogisms:

- An argument with only two negative premises (**E** or **O**) cannot be deductively valid.
- An argument with only two particular premises (**I** or **O**) cannot be deductively valid.

A categorical syllogism is DV or not DV by virtue of its logical form.

Appendix: The Form of Categorical Syllogisms

Terminology has been introduced to describe the parts of a categorical syllogism. The predicate of the conclusion is the *major term* of the syllogism; the subject of the conclusion is the *minor term;* and the term that appears only in the premises is the *middle term*. In the syllogism,

1. *All thieves are immoral people.*

   Some lawyers are thieves.

   Therefore some lawyers are immoral people.

the major term is "immoral people," the minor term is "lawyers," and the middle term is "thieves."

Since exactly one premise must contain the major term, it is called the *major premise*. The major premise in the above example is "All thieves are immoral people." Also, exactly one premise must contain the minor term, and it is called the *minor premise*. The minor premise in the example is "Some lawyers are thieves."

A categorical syllogism is in *standard form* when it is arranged precisely thus:

Major premise

Minor premise

Conclusion

We can *partially* describe the form of a categorical syllogism by its *mood*, which is given by the names of the kinds of categorical statements that make it up. The mood of syllogism I is **AII**, because the syllogism is in standard form (major premise, minor premise, conclusion) and the major premise is **A**, the minor premise is **I**, and the conclusion is **I**.

Mood is only a partial description of a syllogism, however, since the middle term can appear in different places. The following is also an **AII** syllogism, but it is different from I:

II. *All immoral people are thieves.*

Some thieves are lawyers.

Therefore, some lawyers are immoral people.

I and II differ from each other in *figure*, which is determined by the position of the middle term (the term that appears twice in the premises, never in the conclusion). Since the middle term can appear in any one of four positions, there are four figures:

1st Figure	*2nd Figure*	*3rd Figure*	*4th Figure*
Middle — Major	*Major — Middle*	*Middle — Major*	*Major — Middle*
Minor — Middle	*Minor — Middle*	*Middle — Minor*	*Middle — Minor*
Minor — Major	*Minor — Major*	*Minor — Major*	*Minor — Major*

The middle terms can be visualized as outlining a shirt collar:

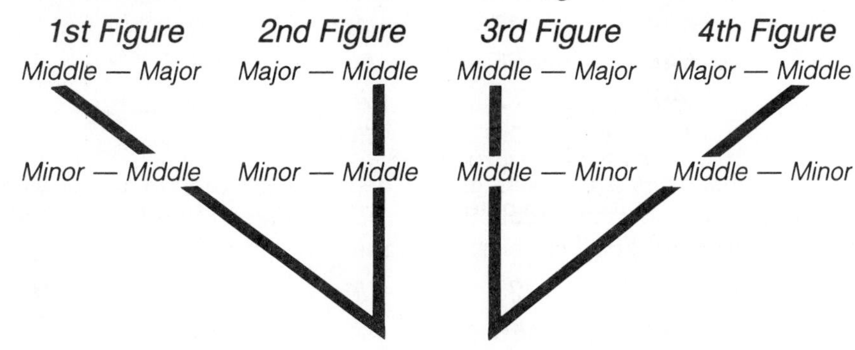

To determine the mood and figure of a syllogism:

- Find its conclusion. The subject of the conclusion will determine the minor term; the predicate will determine the major term.
- Arrange the premises, major premise first, then minor premise. This, plus the conclusion, will give the mood of the syllogism.
- The position of the middle term of the premises will show the figure of the syllogism.

Returning to our examples, syllogism I is **AII-1** (mood **AII**, 1st figure) and syllogism II is **AII-4** (mood **AII**, 4th figure).

If you are asked to construct a syllogism of a certain mood and figure—say **EIO-4**—proceed as follows. First, write three blank categorical statements of the mood **EIO**:

No ________________ *are* ________________.
Some ________________ *are* ________________.
Thus, some ________________ *are not* ________________.

Next, position the middle term:

No ____________ *are* middle.
Some middle *are* ____________.
Thus, some ________ *are not* ____________.

Finally, enter the major and minor terms:

No major *are* middle.

Some middle *are* minor.

Thus, some minor *are not* major.

There are sixty-four moods: **AAA, AAE, AAI, AAO, AEA**, . . . **OOO**. Each mood has four figures. Thus there are 256 possible categorical syllogisms. Only a small number of them are valid, however. Those *valid under both the modern and classical interpretations* of **A** and **E** are these fifteen syllogisms:

1	2	3	4
AAA	EAE	IAI	AEE
EAE	AEE	AII	IAI
AII	EIO	OAO	EIO
EIO	AOO	EIO	

This means that *every* **AAA-1** syllogism is deductively valid, no matter what terms are major, minor, or middle. Those *valid only under the classical interpretation* of **A** and **E** are these additional nine syllogisms:

1	2	3	4
AAI	AEO	AAI	AEO
EAO	EAO	EAO	EAO
			AAI

Medieval logic teachers created a sort of poem to help students remember the valid syllogistic forms. (It is a mnemonic device, like "Thirty days hath September. . . ") The capitalized words are nonsense-Latin, and their vowels name the mood of a syllogism. "Barbara" names **AAA**, "Celarent" names **EAE**, and so on. ("Barbara" is the only mnemonic in use today.) "Prioris," "secundae," "tertia," and "quarta" name the figures 1–4. Here it is:

Barbara, Celarent, Darii, Ferioque prioris;
Cesare, Camestres, Festino, Baroco secundae;
Tertia, Darapti, Disamis, Datisi, Felapton, Bocardo, Ferison habet:
Quarta insuper addit Bramantip, Camenes, Dimaris, Fesapo, Fresison.

The medievals were using the classical interpretation, of course, so they included **AII-4** (*Bramantip quarta*), for example. But the poem only names twenty syllogisms. Sixteen are valid on both interpretations, and another nine are valid on the classical interpretation, which makes twenty-five valid syllogisms the medievals would have recognized. Why does the poem omit five (classically) valid syllogisms? The answer is that logicians of the time considered them weak. For example, **AAI-1** draws a particular conclusion validly (according to the classical interpretation), but it could have drawn the stronger universal conclusion.

EXERCISES

A. Rewrite these so that they are in standard categorical form. Some may be untranslatable into standard categorical form. If this happens point it out.

***A1.** Bachelors are unmarried males.

All bachelors are unmarried males.

A2. Baking soda is not acidic.

A3. Only priests say mass.

A4. Kittens are cute.

A5. Not all income is taxable.

A6. Taxable wages decreased in 1985.

A7. Most Americans are Christian.

A8. Kangaroos are not mammals.

A9. Shortcake contains baking soda.

A10. Tourists visit Niagara Falls annually. (Hard. Think.)

B. Name the areas of this diagram:

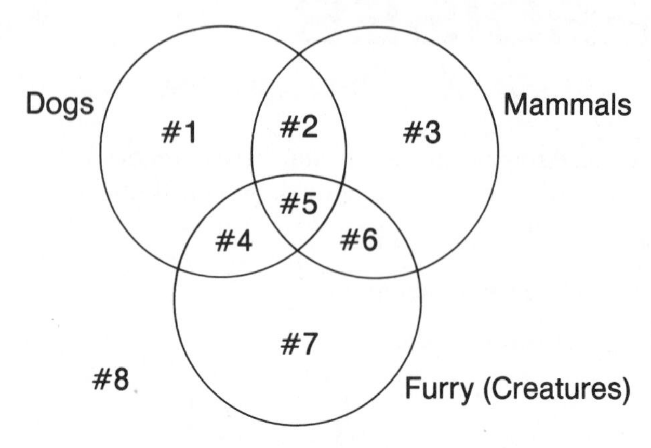

***B1.** Area #1: *Dogs that are not mammals and not furry.*

B2. Area #2:

B3. Area #3:

B4. Area #4:

B5. Area #5:

B6. Area #6:

B7. Area #7:

B8. Area #8:

C. Draw Venn diagrams for each of these statements. You must label your circles, but you need not number the areas. The categories (i.e., circles) you must use are given in parentheses.

C1. There are no ghosts. (Ghosts)

C2. Topper is a ghost. (Ghosts. Hint: Call Topper *.)

C3. All dogs are mammals. (Dogs, Mammals)

C4. All mammals are dogs. (Dogs, Mammals)

C5. Some mammals are not dogs. (Dogs, Mammals)

C6. Rover is a dog. (Dogs, Mammals. Hint: Call Rover *.)

C7. Something is a mammal. (Dogs, Mammals)

C8. All oranges are sweet. (Things From Florida, Oranges, Sweet Things. Yes, there are three circles asked for. Yes, the statement only mentions two categories.)

C9. All Florida oranges are sweet. (Things From Florida, Oranges, Sweet Things)

C10. Some oranges are sweet. (Things From Florida, Oranges, Sweet Things)

C11. There are sour Florida oranges. (Things From Florida, Oranges, Sweet Things. Assume if something isn't sweet, it's sour.)

***C12.** There are things in Florida besides oranges. (Things From Florida, Oranges, Sweet Things)

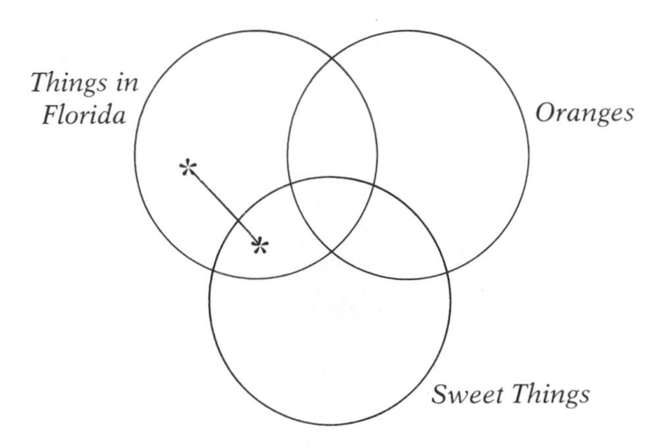

D. Say what these mean in simple English sentences.

W = Women
S = Spanish
L = Logic Students

***D1.**

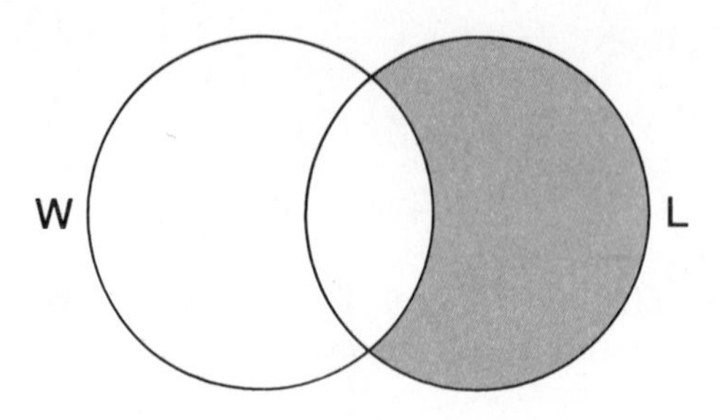

All logic students are women.

D2.

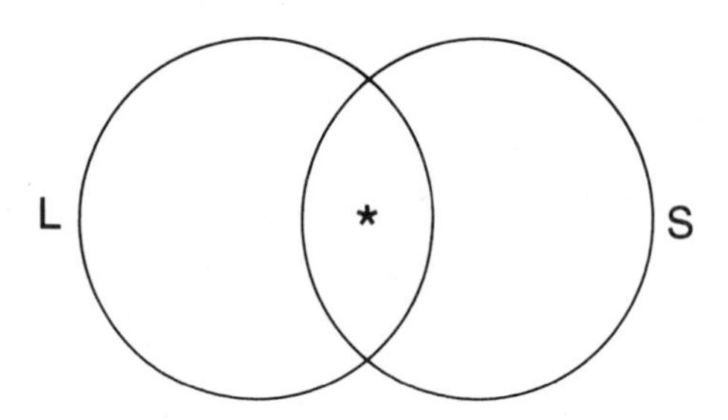

D3.

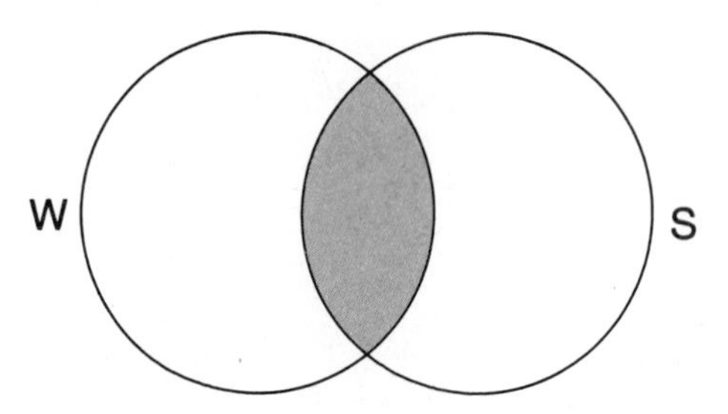

D4.

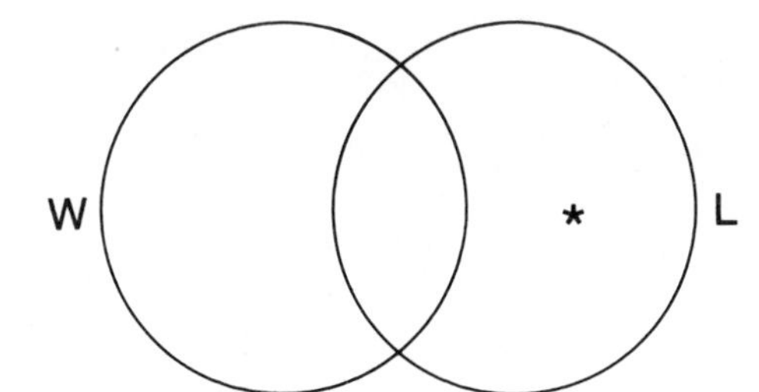

D5.

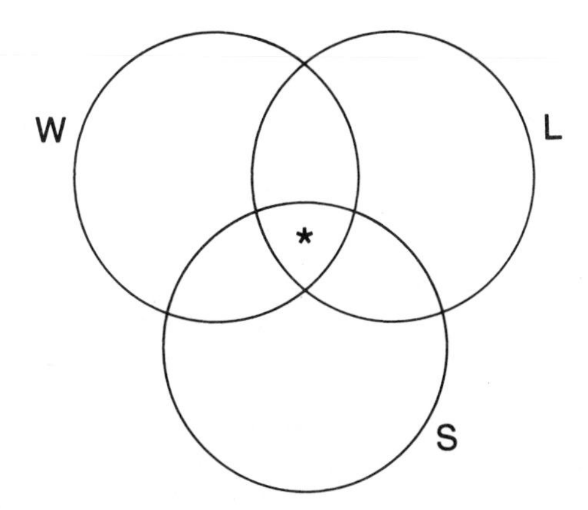

D6.

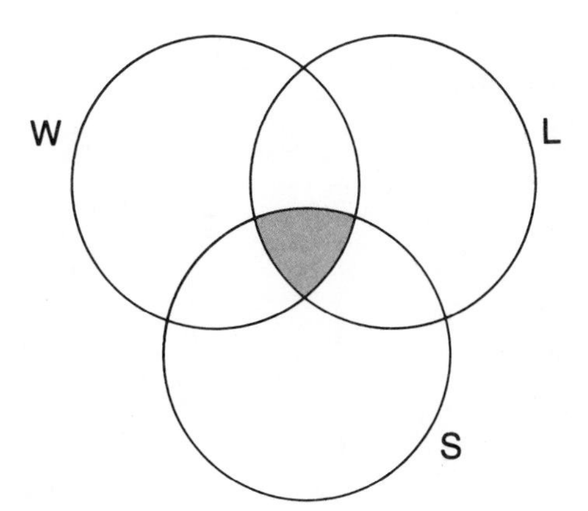

D7.

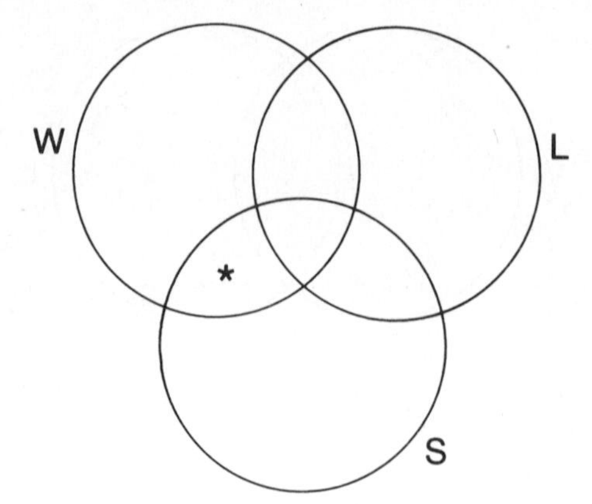

D8.

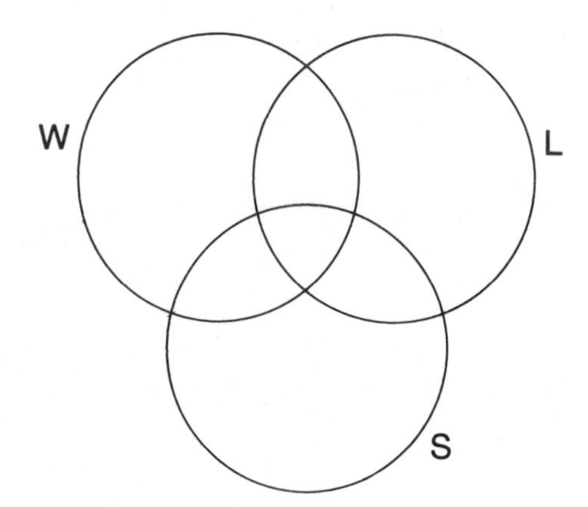

E. Use the Venn diagram below to answer the four questions that follow it.

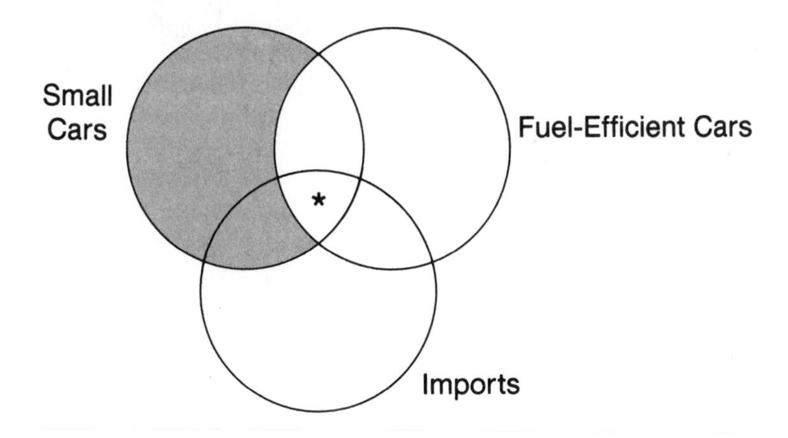

E1. Are any imports fuel-efficient?

a. Yes.
b. No.
c. Can't tell from the information given.

E2. Are any small cars fuel-*in*efficient?

a. Yes.
b. No.
c. Can't tell from the information given.

E3. Are there any imports that are not fuel-efficient?

a. Yes.
b. No.
c. Can't tell from the information given.

E4. Are some fuel-efficient cars imports?

a. Yes.
b. No.
c. Can't tell from the information given.

F. Solve these problems using Venn diagrams. You must clearly label your circles. You need not number your areas.

F1. All income is taxable. Nothing taxable can be left off Form 1040. So, no income can be left off Form 1040. Deductively valid?

F2. Some holidays do not fall on a Wednesday, because no holidays are Wednesdays, and some class days are holidays. Deductively valid?

F3. All cats are mammals and no cats are dogs. Therefore no dogs are mammals. Deductively valid? Sound?

F4. All mammals are warm-blooded. Therefore all warm-blooded animals are mammals. Deductively valid? Sound?

F5. Some computer science majors study hard, and some people who study hard get rich. So some computer science majors get rich. Deductively valid?

F6. Given that everyone who listens to Brahms also listens to Schubert and that some people who listen to Schubert also listen to Wagner, does anyone definitely listen to all three?

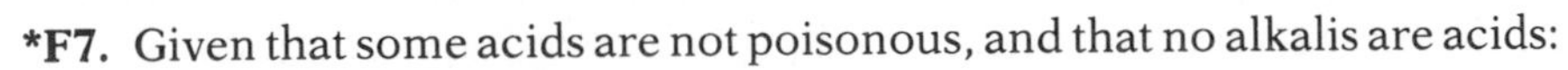

***F7.** Given that some acids are not poisonous, and that no alkalis are acids:

a. Are any acids alkalis? *No*
b. Are any poisons acids? *Can't tell from information given*
c. Are any alkalis poisonous? *Can't tell from information given*

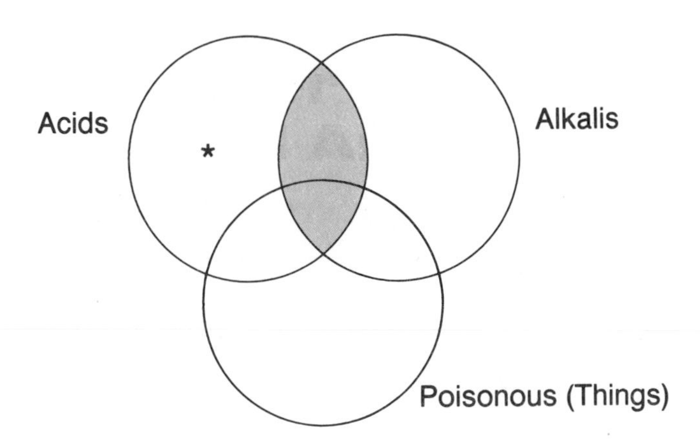

F8. Given that all who make more than $20,000 a year spend an average of $15 per month on long-distance calls, and that some residents of Detroit make more than $20,000 a year, what new information follows?

F9. Given that no corporations are charitable organizations, and that no charitable organizations make a profit, what new information follows?

F10. No baking soda is an acid, and all shortcakes contain baking soda. So no shortcakes contain acid. Deductively valid? (Hint: There is a complication in this problem.)

F11. (1) The insane are innocent, and (2) all innocent people have full civil rights. (3) Anyone with full civil rights should not be forcibly incarcerated. So (4) the insane should not be forcibly incarcerated. Deductively valid? (Hints: This is a sorites. It has a missing conclusion that depends on (1) and (2).)

G. This section is only for those who have worked through the Appendix to Chapter 6.

G1. Name the mood and figure of each of these syllogisms:

a. All seagulls are scavengers.
No scavengers are edible animals.
Therefore, no edible animals are seagulls.

b. Some parakeets are pets.
Some pets are expensive to buy
Therefore, some parakeets are expensive to buy.

G2. Using "Novels" for the major term
"Fictions" for the minor term
"Bestsellers" for the middle term
give an example of each of these forms:

a. **OAE-3**

b. **AII-2**

G3. Show why **AEO-2** is valid on the classical interpretation but invalid on the modern interpretation. (Do two three-circle Venn diagrams.)

CHAPTER 7

FALSEHOODS

The previous three chapters on deductive logic concentrated on whether the argument was deductively valid or not. An argument can be deductively valid even if its premises are false, but such an argument is unsound. It is sometimes said that the truth or falsity of the premises is not the business of "logic proper," but since so many arguments fail on soundness, it is important to take a close look at certain ways in which premises can be false. In addition, we will look at incomplete arguments: arguments with a missing premise. For such arguments can sometimes be convincing precisely because they do not state their crucial premise—which often happens to be false. Important concepts to learn include:

STEREOTYPE and PREJUDICE

LAW OF THE EXCLUDED MIDDLE

FALSE ALTERNATIVES

ENTHYMEME
— how to reconstruct and evaluate one

DILEMMAS
— and how to escape from one:

GRASPING A HORN

GOING BETWEEN THE HORNS

7.1 Review of Validity and Soundness

Chapter 3 taught you that there were two parameters of argument evaluation. The parameter of *validity* determined the degree of logical support the premise or premises offered to the conclusion. We distinguished four degrees of validity: **Deductively Valid**, **Strong**, **Medium**, and **Weak**. Chapters 4 through 6 concentrated on determining whether an argument was deductively valid or not.

However, we must not forget the second parameter of argument evaluation, *soundness*. An argument is sound just in case it is at least Strong *and* each of its premises is true. For example, this argument

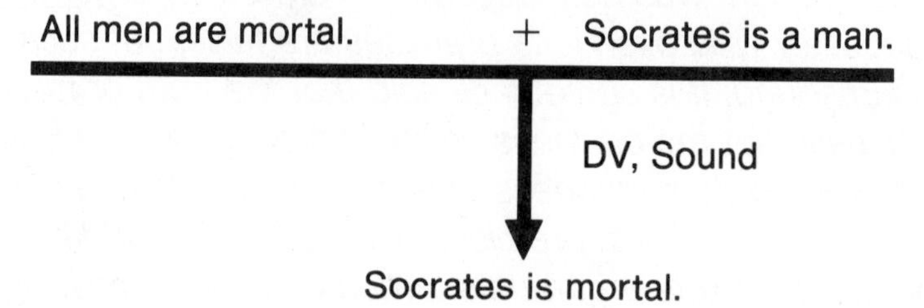

is Deductively Valid because if all the premises are true the conclusion must be true as well. A Venn diagram will prove its deductive validity:

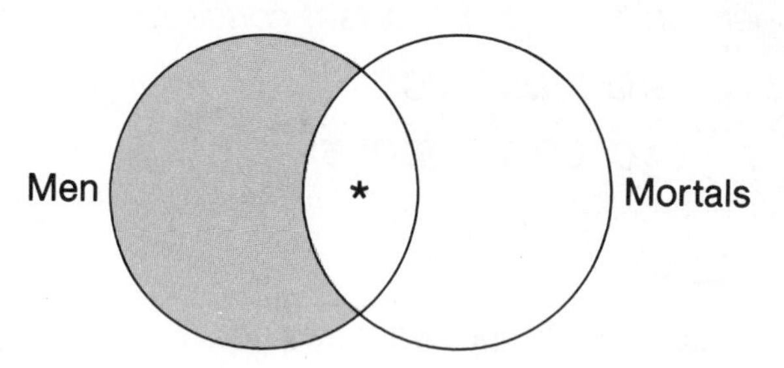

Socrates, denoted by *, turns up in the category of mortals. That is, the conclusion, "Socrates is mortal," follows deductively from the premises. In addition, the argument is Sound because the premises are all true.

This argument,

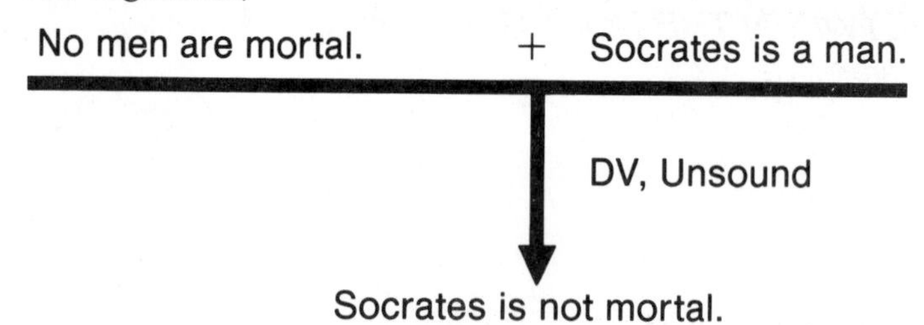

is also Deductively Valid, because *if* all the premises are true the conclusion must be true as well. A Venn diagram will establish its deductive validity:

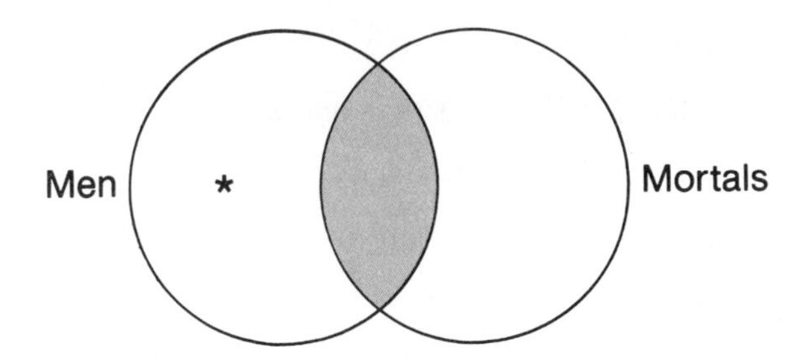

Socrates, again denoted by *, turns up *outside* the category of mortals. Hence, the conclusion, "Socrates is not mortal," follows deductively. But we know that it is *false* that no men are mortal. So the argument is Unsound, because the premises are not all true.

The only acceptable arguments—the only arguments that you should allow yourself to be convinced by—are Sound arguments. Even if a conclusion follows deductively, it might have followed from false premises, and so you have no reason to believe in its truth. And surely, just because the second argument is DV you should not suddenly decide that all the history books that say that Socrates was put to death in 399 B.C. are wrong, and that Socrates is alive somewhere today. You are right to reject the conclusion because of a false premise in the argument—or, in other words, to reject the conclusion because the argument is Unsound.

7.2 False Universals, Prejudices, and Stereotypes

A universal statement is an "All" or "No" statement. Remember that a categorical syllogism with two *particular* statements cannot be DV. So any valid categorical syllogism will need at least one universal statement.

But true universals are not easy to come by. Certain basic facts about things in the world are known, for example:

All persons are mortal.

All dogs are mortal.

All dogs are mammals.

All acids have a ph factor of less than 7.

All bodies fall at 32.2 feet/second/second.

No cats hunt in packs.

No computers fall in love.

No emeralds are colorless.

No material objects are outside space and time.

There are, of course, *false* universals, for example:

All dogs bark.

All acids turn litmus paper red.

All swans are white.

All mushrooms are safe to eat.

No students flunk calculus.

No Stephen King novels are bestsellers.

No oceans are salty.

No marsupials live in North America.

The falsity of some of these may be more obvious than others.

A big problem with false universals comes with statements dealing with human behavior. Humans are complex entities, and there are few, if any, laws of psychology of an "All" or "No" form that are *known* to be true. The reason this is a big problem is that much of our reasoning concerns humans; yet we rarely have knowledge of true universals with which to begin our arguments.

Let us define a **STEREOTYPE** as a false universal about human behavior. Examples of stereotypes might be:

All Jews are rich.

All homosexual men are effeminate.

All blacks are Democrats.

All southerners are Baptists.

No women are good at mathematics.

No professional athletes are intelligent.

No college professors are good at business.

No Catholics approve of abortion.

Let us define a **PREJUDICE** as the conviction that a false stereotype is true. Many arguments are made that use stereotypes and appear convincing because they appeal to prejudice:

He's a Catholic, and no Catholics approve of abortion. So he won't approve of abortion.

She must be rich, because she's Jewish and all Jews are rich.

Of course he'll vote Democratic. He black, and all blacks are Democrats.

And so on. Each of the above arguments is DV. Each is Unsound because each contains at least one false premise: a false stereotype.

7.3 False Alternatives

First, let us review the disjunctive syllogism:

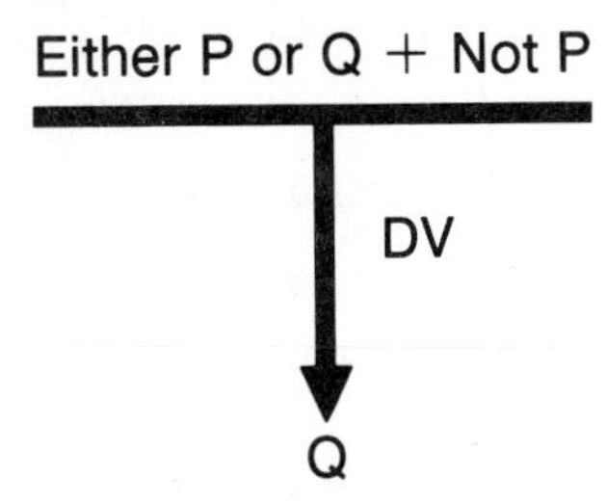

There are many instances of Sound disjunctive syllogisms. Suppose you *know* that either she's at home or in the library, and she's not at home (you just checked). You can conclude that she's in the library. That is, you make this argument:

Either she's at home or in the library. + She's not at home.

DV by DS, Sound

She's in the library.

However, there are some cases of disjunctive syllogisms that use disjunctions that are false. For example,

> *Either you're my friend or my enemy. You're not my friend. So you must be my enemy.*

This argument is DV by the rule DS. But it employs a disjunction that is false: "Either you're my friend or my enemy." This is an example of a false alternative, also known as black and white thinking (because it recognizes no other shades).

To see what a false alternative is and why some are convincing, let us look at the logical truth the false alternative tries to mimic. This is the **LAW OF THE EXCLUDED MIDDLE**:

> *Either* P *or Not* P.

The law of the excluded middle is a logical truth because it cannot be false, regardless of whether the statement *P* in question is true or false. Look at its truthtable:

P	Either P or Not P	
T	T	(F)
F	T	(T)

There is always at least one disjunct that is true. Hence the entire disjunction is always true. That's what a logical truth is.

There are many perfectly correct instances of the law of the excluded middle. Each correctly states that either alternative *has* to be true. Any "middle"—any other alternative—is "excluded." Examples:

That animal is either a dog or it isn't a dog.

When I read a poem, I either cry or I don't.

You can fit this box in your trunk or you can't.

And so on. (None of these is especially interesting, but that's the drawback in logical truth.)

False alternatives mimic the law of the excluded middle by presenting disjunctions that *appear* to exclude any other alternative, but that in all likelihood allow for more than the two alternatives presented. Examples:

You're either my friend or my enemy.

She's either conservative or liberal.

His book will be a bestseller or a flop.

He's either bald or has a full head of hair.

There are positions between being your friend or your enemy: I could be indifferent to you. She could be either conservative or liberal—or socialist, or Marxist, or libertarian, or an anarchist. His book can sell a moderate number of copies, which is between bestseller and flop. And he can be thinning on top, which is between being bald and having a full head of hair.

A statement expressing what are in fact false alternatives might appear to be true because such a statement appears to be an instance of the law of the excluded middle. It is wise to ask yourself of such disjunctions whether they present all the alternatives there could be.

Arguments employing false alternatives are Unsound, even if DV. Examples:

You're either my friend or my enemy, and you're not my friend. So you must be my enemy.

She's either liberal or conservative, and she isn't liberal. So she's conservative.

Each of these arguments is deductively valid according to the valid rule, DS. Yet each is Unsound, because each contains at least one false premise, namely the false alternatives stated by the disjunction.

It is worth emphasizing two further points. First, not every disjunction that is not an instance of the law of the excluded middle is false. For example, it might upon occasion be true and known to be true that either Sally is reading or sleeping, even though this is not an instance of the law of the excluded middle. (Maybe Sally told us she'll either be reading or sleeping and Sally is a truthful person). Second, there could be peculiar circumstances under which some alternatives that are usually false are in fact true. For example, it is generally a false alternative to say of someone that he must either be your friend or your enemy. Still, there could be a person of whom this is true (such a person perhaps has a few friends and hates everyone else, even people he hasn't met). The point about false alternatives is not that they *must* be false, but that they are false in most circumstances and hence something to watch out for in evaluating arguments.

7.4 Enthymemes

It is apparently part of human nature for us to make things quicker and easier for ourselves. Early humans domesticated sheep, goats, cattle, and pigs so they wouldn't have to spend as much time hunting or following migrating herds. Then they domesticated dogs to guard their domesticated flocks. Much later, we've come to prefer telephoning to the trouble of writing letters, the speed of microwave ovens to the time required by conventional cooking, and automatic banking machines to the time spent waiting in line for a teller. Our language has similarly undergone a kind of quickening and shortening. We prefer "don't" for "do not," use "NATO" instead of "North Atlantic Treaty Organization," and call our friend "Bill" instead of "William."

This tendency to abbreviate influences the way we express arguments in ordinary speech and writing. In particular, we are apt to leave premises unexpressed. For example, we would more readily say,

You smoke, so you're more likely to get cancer than a nonsmoker.

than

You smoke, and [all who smoke are more likely to get cancer than nonsmokers]; so you're more likely to get cancer than a nonsmoker.

The bracketed premise would probably be left unsaid (or unwritten) in casual, ordinary discourse. But technically it is needed to make the argument valid.

Without the unexpressed premise, we have an argument that looks like this:

You smoke.

Weak

You're more likely to get cancer than a nonsmoker.

As it stands, the argument doesn't look very strong, let alone DV. After all, the premise mentions nothing about cancer, but the conclusion does. In fact, as it stands, the argument is not unlike this Weak example from Chapter 3:

President Reagan supports a strong defense.

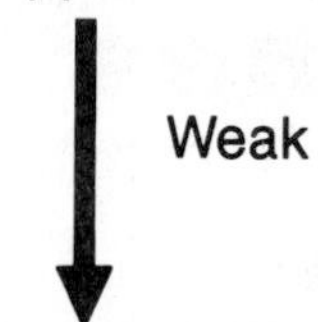

Traffic fatalities will decrease in the U.S.

Of course, we tend to read in the unexpressed premise. That is, we tend to reconstruct the argument as:

You smoke. + [All who smoke are more likely to get cancer than nonsmokers.]

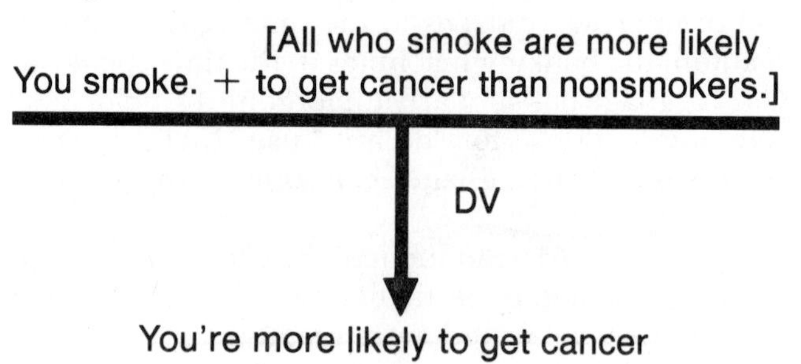

You're more likely to get cancer than a nonsmoker.

That the argument is DV can be proven by a Venn diagram (letting * represent you):

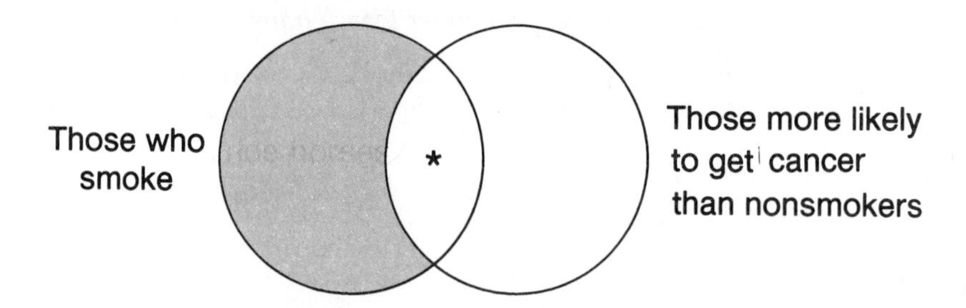

An argument with an unexpressed premise (or premises) is an **ENTHYMEME** (pronounced "EN-the-meem"). You can reasonably conclude that you're faced with an enthymeme if the argument exactly as given is Weak, but could be DV with the addition of another premise. To evaluate an enthymeme:

- State the unexpressed premise so that the argument is DV.
- Evaluate the resulting argument for soundness.

Deductive validity is easy to come by. Soundness is another matter. For the unexpressed premise is often a false stereotype (false universal) or a false alternative. (It may be that there is more than convenience that leads us to abbreviate arguments. We may sometimes not want to state out loud the *weakest* part of the argument.)

Someone says,

You're a male chauvinist, aren't you? After all, you're a man.

This is an enthymeme. There must be an unexpressed premise, for otherwise the argument would be the very Weak:

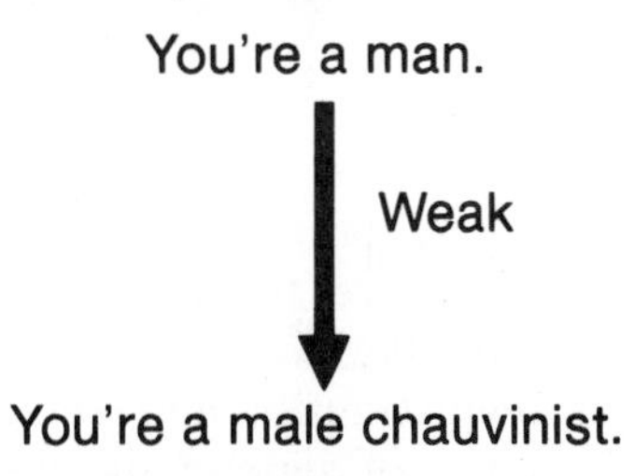

The argument read that way is Weak because its premise mentions nothing about male chauvinism but its conclusion does. So we reconstruct the unexpressed premise so as to make the argument DV:

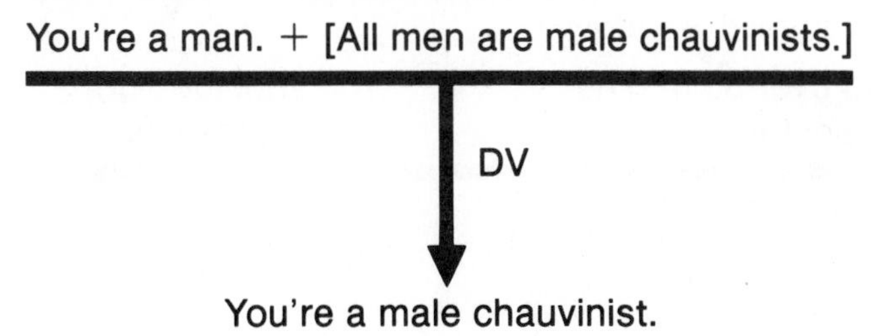

However, we now see that the argument contains a false universal: a stereotype about men that is convincing only if backed by prejudice.

Someone says,

You don't love opera. You must hate it!

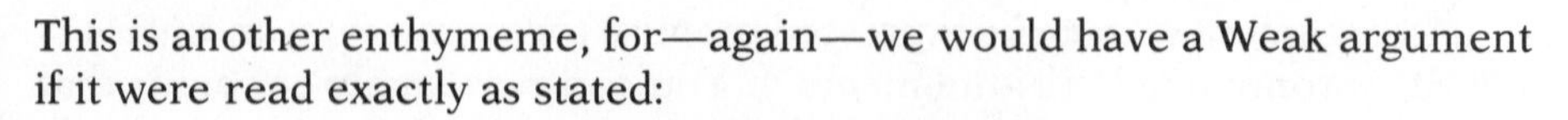

This is another enthymeme, for—again—we would have a Weak argument if it were read exactly as stated:

You don't love opera.

Weak

You hate opera.

The premise mentions nothing about hating opera. The argument cries out for a disjunction:

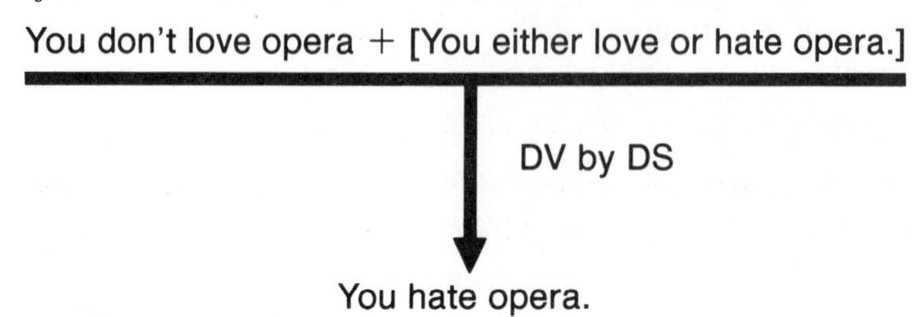

Having made the argument DV, we now examine it for soundness. And we can see that it is Unsound, for it contains a false alternative. Even if you don't *love* opera, there are other alternatives to *hating* it: you can mildly like opera, be indifferent to it, or mildly dislike it.

Recall from Chapter 2 the distinction between dependent and independent reasons. The example given of dependent reasons was:

> *Going over 55 m.p.h. is against the law and you shouldn't go against the law. So you shouldn't go over 55 m.p.h.*

This was diagramed as follows:

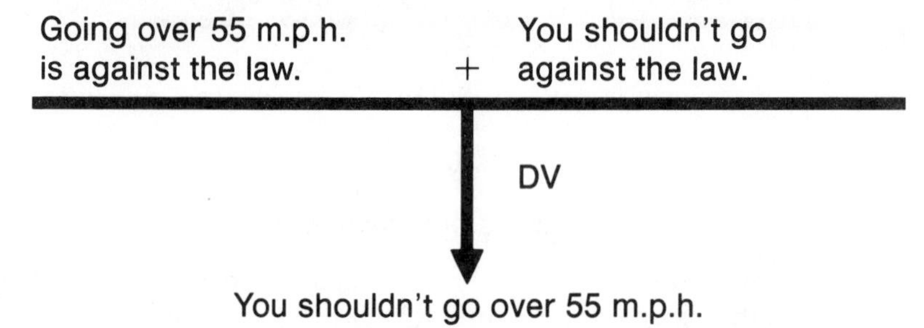

That this argument is DV can be proven by a Venn diagram, after rewriting the argument in standard categorical form:

> *All cases of going over 55 m.p.h. are cases of going against the law. No thing you should do is a case of going against the law. Therefore, no thing you should do is a case of going over 55 m.p.h.*

The Venn diagram:

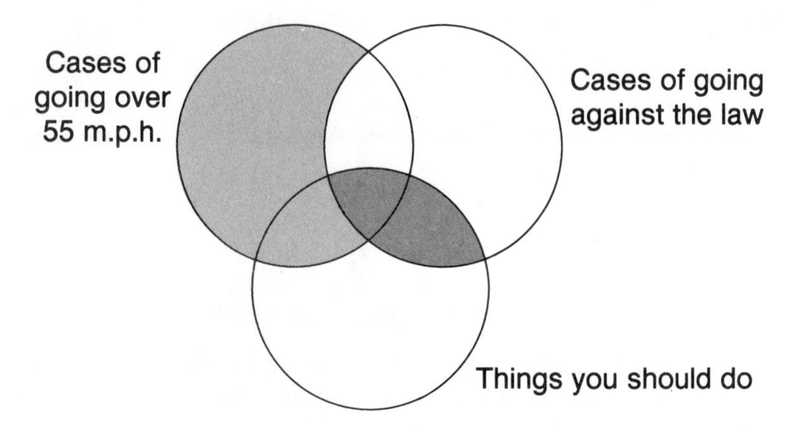

The example given for independent reasons was:

Going over 55 m.p.h. is against the law. Besides, it's unsafe. So you shouldn't go over 55 m.p.h.

The argument diagram for this argument is:

You shouldn't go over 55 m.p.h.

Recall that this produces two independent arguments:

Going over 55 m.p.h. is against the law.

You shouldn't go over 55 m.p.h.

and

[Going over 55 m.p.h.] is unsafe.

↓

You shouldn't go over 55 m.p.h.

Each of these independent arguments is an enthymeme. This is characteristic of independent reasons. The first independent argument requires the additional premise, "You shouldn't go against the law" to be DV:

Going over 55 m.p.h. is against the law. + [You shouldn't go against the law.]

You shouldn't go over 55.

The second independent argument is also an enthymeme. It requires the premise, "You should never do what's unsafe," to be DV:

Going over 55 m.p.h. is unsafe. + [You shouldn't do what's unsafe.]

You shouldn't go over 55 m.p.h.

Arguments with divergent conclusions and chain arguments are often enthymemes. This example of divergent conclusions comes from Chapter 2:

He's drunk again. This means he won't be at work. Moreover, he won't be fit to talk to.

It is diagramed like this:

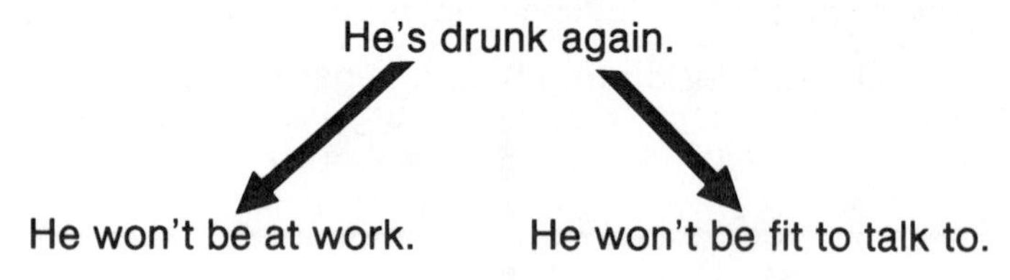

Remember that there are two independent arguments here. Each one is an enthymeme. The argument diagrams with the missing premises look like this:

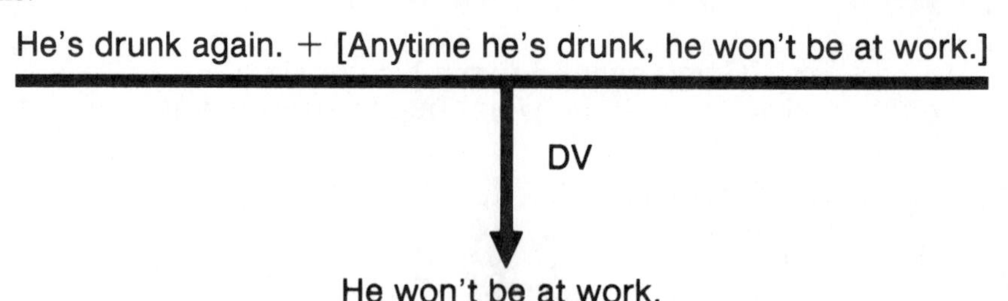

He's drunk again. + [Anytime he's drunk, he won't be fit to talk to.]

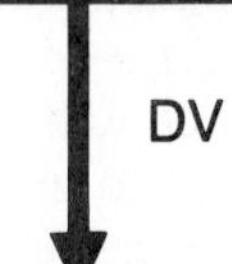

He won't be fit to talk to.

Whether each of the above arguments is Sound depends on the truth of the premises (for we have made each DV).

This chain argument,

He's drunk again. This means he won't be at work, and therefore won't be able to pay his bills.

is diagramed as follows:

He's drunk again.

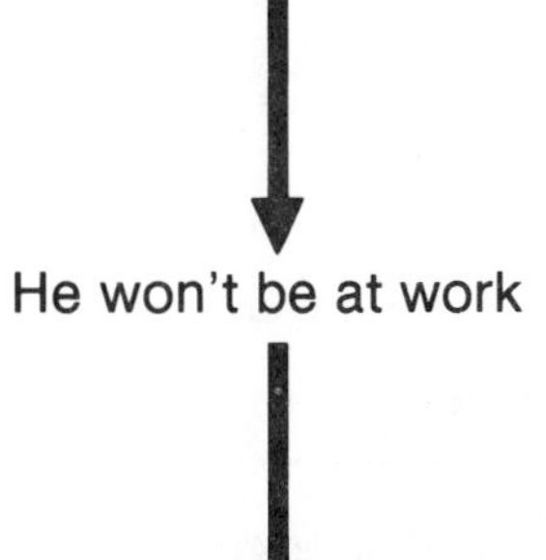

He won't be able to pay his bills.

Again, we have two independent arguments, each of which is an enthymeme that requires an additional premise to be DV. One argument is:

He's drunk again. + [Anytime he's drunk, he won't be at work.]

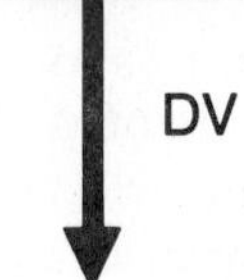

He won't be at work.

The other argument is:

He won't be at work. + [If he won't be at work, he won't be able to pay his bills.]

DV, by MP

He won't be able to pay his bills.

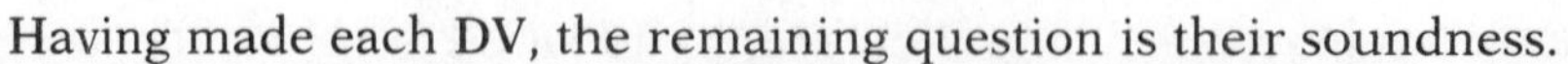

Having made each DV, the remaining question is their soundness.

The moral is: When you have an argument with independent reasons, divergent conclusions, or a chain argument, you will often have several enthymemes to evaluate. Complete each with the premise that will make each independent argument DV, and try to evaluate that premise for truth (and, accordingly, the argument for soundness).

7.5 Dilemmas

A dilemma employs a deductively valid argument form:

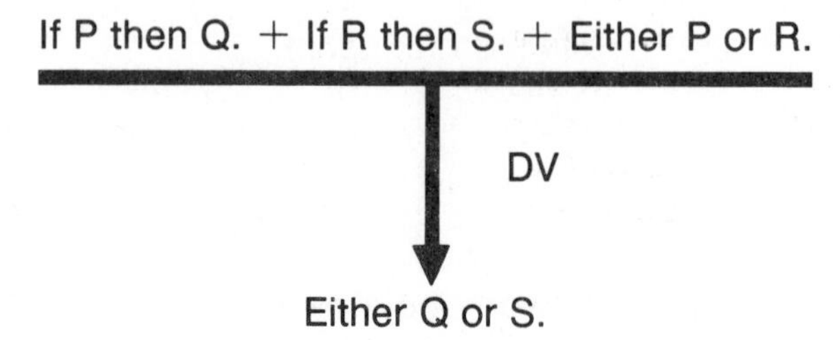

That is one version. Another version—really the same form, substituting *Not P* for *R*—goes:

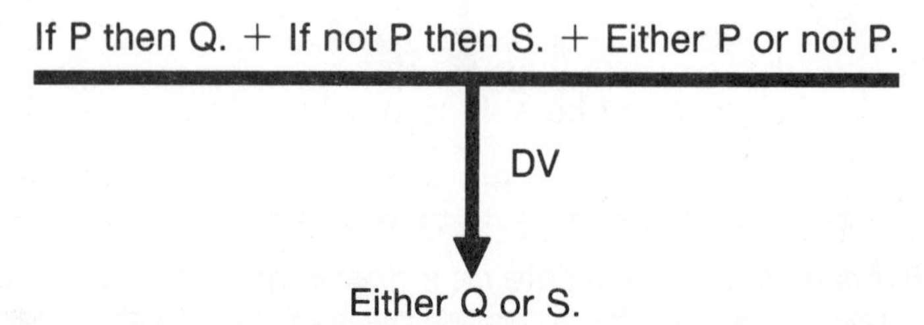

Notice that there are three premises to a dilemma: two conditionals and a disjunction. The dilemma is a kind of Modus Ponens. The disjunction states that either one of the antecedents will be true ("Either *P* or *R*"), so (by MP) either one of the consequents will be true ("Either *Q* or *S*"). In the second version, it does the same: It states that either one of the antecedents will be true (Either *P* or not *P*), so (by MP) either one of the consequents will be true (Either *Q* or *S*).

A dilemma is at heart a deductively valid argument form. As such, a dilemma is not specified as having any particular content. In practice, however, a dilemma usually attempts to portray us as trapped in one of two disagreeable alternatives. For example,

If you use salt you will get high blood pressure. If you don't use salt your food will taste bland. Either you use salt or you don't. So, either you will get high blood pressure or your food will taste bland.

Another example:

If you go to Europe this summer, you have to face the threat of terrorism. If you go to South America instead, you will have to weather their winter. Either you go to Europe or to South America. So, either you face the threat of terrorism or weather winter.

Each of these dilemmas is DV. Their soundness is another issue. Merely because a deductively valid dilemma is made does not mean that it is sound. One or more of its premises might be false. Some colorful jargon has grown up to describe various ways of attacking a dilemma. To be faced with a deductively valid dilemma is to be **CAUGHT ON THE HORNS OF A DILEMMA.** To **ESCAPE A DILEMMA** is to **ATTACK** one or more of its premises. One attacks a premise by showing it to be false. Recall that a dilemma has two conditionals. To attack one of the conditionals is to **GRASP ONE OF THE HORNS**. Also recall that a dilemma has a disjunction. To attack the disjunction is to **GO BETWEEN THE HORNS**.

Take the first example dilemma, the one about using or not using salt. At least one of the conditionals is false, namely "If you don't use salt your food will taste bland." This is false because there are many ways to liven up food besides salting it: You can add lemon juice, Worcestershire sauce, pepper, herbs, onions, etc. Thus, we have escaped the dilemma by grasping one of its horns.

The second example dilemma, regarding travel this summer, can be attacked by showing its disjunction to present false alternatives. Surely there are other travel alternatives to: "Either you go to Europe or to South America this summer." You can, for example, go to North Dakota or Australia. We have escaped this dilemma by going through it horns.

Not all dilemmas are quite so easy to escape. This dilemma is still a subject of philosophical controversy:

If the will is free then human behavior is intrinsically unpredictable and psychology as a science is impossible. If the will is not free then there is no possibility of freely chosen moral action. Either the will is free or it isn't. So either human behavior is intrinsically unpredictable and psychology as a science is impossible or there is no possibility of freely chosen moral action.

This dilemma in effect says: You can have psychology or morality but you can't have both. Whether this dilemma can be escaped is left as an exercise for the reader.

KEY POINTS

Always remember that there are two parameters of argument evaluation:

- The degree of validity: How much support do the premises lend to their conclusion if they are true?
- The question of soundness: Even if the argument is Strong or Deductively Valid, one or more of its premises might be false.

Premises can be false in many ways. We've discussed two:

- False universals: "All" or "No" statements can be false simply because there are exceptions. Be especially aware of generalizations about human behavior, for these often express stereotypes and are backed up by mere prejudice.
- False alternatives: Be aware of disjunctions that *appear* to express exhaustive alternatives but that don't, for example, "You're either my friend or my enemy."

An enthymeme is an argument with one (or more) missing premises.

- You can spot an enthymeme by seeing that the argument as it stands, *without any added premises*, is Weak but could be much stronger if a premise is added.
- To complete an enthymeme, add a premise that will make the argument DV. Often the premise to add will be either a universal or a disjunction.
- To evaluate a completed enthymeme, think about the truth or falsity of all the premises. Be especially on the lookout for false universals and false alternatives.
- Arguments whose reasons are independent, whose conclusions are divergent, or chain arguments are often enthymemes. In such cases, you will have several independent enthymemes for which you will have to supply the missing premise and evaluate the soundness of the overall argument.

A dilemma is a deductively valid argument form that typically attempts to portray us as trapped in one of two disagreeable alternatives.

- To be faced with a dilemma is to be caught on its horns.
- To escape a dilemma is to attack one or more of its premises, that is to show one or more of its premises false.

- A dilemma contains two conditionals. To attack one of the conditionals is to grasp one of the horns of the dilemma.
- A dilemma contains a disjunction. To attack the disjunction is to go between the horns of the dilemma. This is often done by showing that the disjunction presents false alternatives.
- Not all dilemmas are escapable.

EXERCISES

A. Each of the following is an enthymeme. Diagram the argument, adding the premise that is needed to make the argument deductively valid by putting it in brackets "[ ]." Then assess the result for soundness.

***A1.** Evelyn is a minority candidate. Therefore Evelyn is black.

Evelyn is a minority candidate. + *[All minority candidates are black.]*

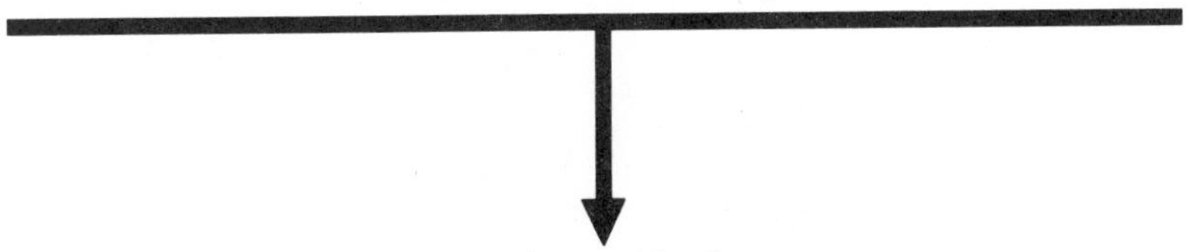

↓

Evelyn is black.

The added premise is false. Evelyn could be Hispanic, Eskimo, etc. So the argument is unsound.

A2. Woody Allen's films are comedies. Therefore, nothing serious happens in them.

A3. He's homosexual. So he must be infected with AIDS.

A4. She must be a feminist. After all, she's a woman, isn't she?

A5. Your pet isn't a dog? Well, then it must be a cat!

A6. You say it wasn't an accident that you showed up here. That means you must have planned it.

A7. She must have gone to law school. After all, Jill is a lawyer.

A8. You just deliberately kicked that dog! You must hate animals.

A9. Of course he's guilty. Didn't he admit that he threatened to kill her? (Example due to Monroe Beardsley)

A10. He got an A+, so he must have cheated.

A11. Since they want Creationism taught in public schools, contemporary Creationists cannot present their view as based on religious faith. (Philip Kitcher, *Abusing Science: The Case Against Creationism.* Cambridge, MA: The MIT Press, 1982, p. 26.)

A12. In 1957, among the thirty-three nations that chose not to exercise the death penalty, the number of murders never increased. Thus, capital punishment simply does not appear to serve as a deterrent. (Norman Mailer)

A13. On the whole, for as much as certain of the lower animals also dream, it may be concluded that dreams are not sent by God. (Aristotle, "On Prophesying by Dreams.")

A14. No two snowflakes are alike because no two snowflakes form under absolutely identical conditions. (*Nova,* "The Shape of Things.")

A15. Since IQ is related to occupation and education, it should cause no surprise that there is a relationship between IQ and socioeconomic status. (Paul R. Ehrlich and S. Shirley Feldman, *The Race Bomb*. New York: Quadrangle/The New York Times Book Co., 1977, p. 22.)

A16. But it's even difficult for investment professionals to consistently pick market peaks and bottoms, so individual investors will probably have even more difficulty in getting the market timing just right. (Merrill Lynch, *Quarterly Report of Capital Fund, Inc.*, Dec. 31, 1984.)

B. Is there any way to escape from the following dilemmas (that is, are they Unsound)? Discuss each.

***B1.** If a student is fond of learning, grades are unnecessary. If a student dislikes learning, grades will be useless. Either a student is fond of learning or dislikes it. So grades are either unnecessary or useless. (Example due to Irving M. Copi.)

The second conditional ("If a student dislikes learning, grades will be useless") is probably false. A student may dislike learning, but may desire good grades (to get a good job, to get into law school, etc.). For such a student, grades will not be useless.

B2. If we use oil there won't be enough left for future generations. If we don't use oil our economy will collapse. Either we use oil or we don't. So, either there won't be enough left for future generations or our economy will collapse.

B3. If you know the answer, you don't have to search for it. If you don't know the answer, you won't recognize it if you chance upon it. Either you know the answer or you don't. So either you don't have to search for it or you won't recognize it if you chance upon it.

B4. Some cities find themselves in this dilemma: If the city raises taxes, it will drive business and residents to the suburbs. If the city doesn't raise taxes, it will be unable to provide such necessary services as public safety that will induce business and residents to stay. Either the city raises taxes or it doesn't. So, either it will drive business and residents to the suburbs or it will be unable to provide such necessary services as public safety that will induce business and residents to stay.

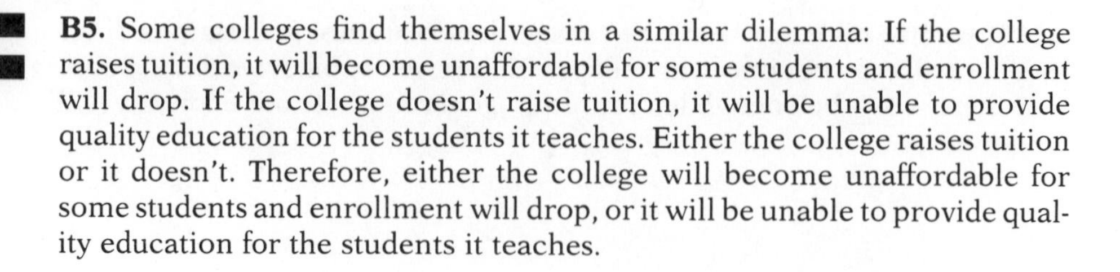

B5. Some colleges find themselves in a similar dilemma: If the college raises tuition, it will become unaffordable for some students and enrollment will drop. If the college doesn't raise tuition, it will be unable to provide quality education for the students it teaches. Either the college raises tuition or it doesn't. Therefore, either the college will become unaffordable for some students and enrollment will drop, or it will be unable to provide quality education for the students it teaches.

B6. If we apply the exclusionary rule,* some genuinely guilty people will go unpunished. If we don't apply the exclusionary rule, we will be going against the Constitution of the United States as interpreted by the Supreme Court. Either we apply the exclusionary rule or we don't. Thus, either some genuinely guilty people will go unpunished, or we will be going against the Constitution of the United States as interpreted by the Supreme Court.

*The exclusionary rule specifies that evidence gathered "without probable cause" violates the protection against "unreasonable searches and seizures" as specified in Amendment IV of the Constitution. Such evidence, according to the exclusionary rule, is to be excluded (i.e., is inadmissible) in a criminal trial. For example, if a police officer without cause opens the trunk of the car of a person stopped for going through a stop sign and discovers illegal narcotics, those narcotics cannot be used as evidence in a criminal trial for drug possession.

C. Construct a deductively valid dilemma that describes a dilemma that you once found yourself in. Discuss if there is (was) a way out of it.

CHAPTER 8

MEANING AND CIRCULARITY

An argument can be deductively valid because of the meanings of the terms in the premises and conclusion. However, we must be careful to avoid changing the meanings of the terms between premises and conclusion. This is known as "the fallacy of equivocation." Problems with meaning are also often involved with what is called "circular reasoning." This chapter will look at deductively valid arguments revolving around meaning, as well as some ways such arguments can go wrong. Important concepts in this chapter include:

DEDUCTIVE VALIDITY BY VIRTUE OF MEANING

AMBIGUITY

FALLACY OF EQUIVOCATION

RELATIVE TERMS (and equivocation)

CIRCULAR REASONING or BEGGING THE QUESTION

8.1 Deductive Validity and Meaning

Chapters 4, 5, and 6 examined cases of deductive validity that depended on the form of arguments. For example, any argument that has this form,

All X *are* Y.

All Y *are* Z.

Therefore, all X *are* Z.

is Deductively Valid. This means that each of these arguments is Deductively Valid:

All dogs are mammals.

All mammals are warm-blooded.

Therefore, all dogs are warm-blooded.

All acids taste bitter.

All things that taste bitter are unpleasant to ingest.

Therefore, all acids are unpleasant to ingest.

And so on. Another example: The rule DS (Disjunctive Syllogism) is a Deductively Valid rule:

Either P *or* Q.

Not P.

Therefore, Q.

This means that any argument that fits this form is Deductively Valid. Each of these arguments fit this form, and each is DV by the rule DS:

Either you pass or fail.

You haven't passed.

So you've failed.

Either you pay me now or I'll sue you.

You can't pay me now.

So I'll sue you.

And so on for any argument of the form DS.

However, some arguments are deductively valid because of the meanings of the terms involved, not because of their form. This straightforward example is a deductively valid argument:

Larry is a bachelor.

DV

Larry is an unmarried male.

If it's true that Larry is a bachelor, then it must be true that he is an unmarried male. Hence, the argument is DV. Note that its deductive validity is not sanctioned by any of the rules in Chapters 4 or 5. Its logical form is,

But this is not a valid rule of logic. That is, not just any argument that fits that form is DV. The argument about Larry happens to be DV because of the meaning of "bachelor."

Note also that there is no Venn diagram way of showing the Larry argument deductively valid. To go through an exercise doomed to failure, try doing one:

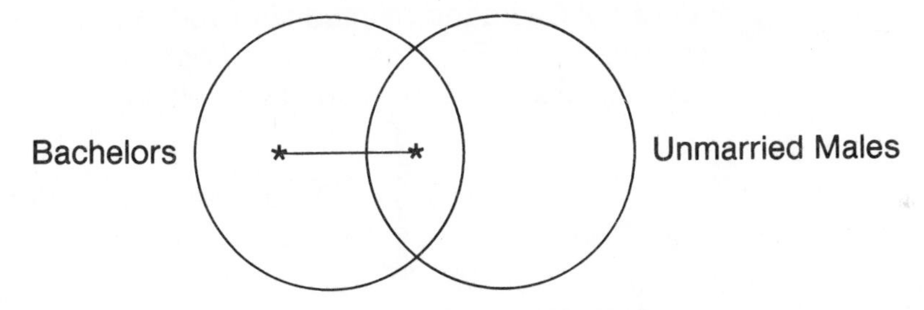

Larry, denoted on the diagram by *, is in the bachelor circle but not *definitely* in the unmarried male circle.

The fact that the Larry argument is not DV on any of the methods or rules discussed in Chapters 4 through 6 does not mean that the argument is not DV. It means that those methods and rules are inadequate for handling arguments that are DV by meaning. The only method for determining the validity of such arguments is attention to the meanings of the terms involved, and the only rules governing such arguments are the entries in a good dictionary.

We are on safest ground with scientific and technical terminology, for their meanings are the most firmly fixed. These arguments are clearly Deductively Valid:

This is water.

↓ DV, by meaning of "water"

This is H_2O.

You've caught a lobster in your trap.

↓ DV, by meaning of "lobster"

You've caught a crustacean.

John and Mary got divorced.

↓ DV, by meaning of "divorce"

John and Mary were legally married.

Andrea del Castagno painted his *Crucifixion, Deposition, and Resurrection of Christ* using watercolor applied to fresh, damp plaster.

↓ DV, by meaning of "fresco"

Andrea del Castagno painted a fresco.

Other terms, while not exactly scientific or technical, also have firmly fixed meanings. These arguments, too, are Deductively Valid:

Box *A* is heavier than Box *B*.

↓ DV, by meaning of "heavier than"

Box *B* is lighter than Box *A*.

Stephen King's latest novel sold more copies than any other work of fiction last week.

↓ DV, by meaning of "bestseller"

Stephen King's latest novel was a national fiction bestseller last week.

She's his maternal aunt.

↓ DV, by meaning of "maternal aunt"

She's his mother's sister.

8.2 Problems with Meaning

It was said earlier that the only method for determining the validity of arguments purporting to be Deductively Valid by the meanings of the terms involved is attention to the meanings of the terms involved, and that the only rules governing such arguments are the entries in a good dictionary. While this is true, such rules are not as hard and fast as, say, the rules DS or MP.

For one thing, a spoken language like English is fluid. The meanings of terms shift over time. For example, until approximately 1500 A.D. the term "knave" in English meant, "a male child, a boy." Thus, until approximately 1500 this argument would have been DV:

Your wife just gave birth to a boy.

↓ DV by meaning of "knave" (c. 1500)

Your wife just gave birth to a knave.

However, a meaning shift occurred. Today the term "knave" means "an unprincipled man given to dishonorable and deceitful practices." So, this argument,

He lies and cheats constantly.

↓ DV by meaning of "knave" (contemporary)

He's a knave.

is DV today, but could not have been DV in 1500 since this meaning of "knave" didn't exist in 1500.

There is another problem with meaning that is deeper and more perplexing. It is often difficult, if not impossible, to separate *close associations* from *meaning*. For example, it would seem that this argument is clearly DV by virtue of the *meaning* of "lemon":

This is a lemon.

↓ DV, by meaning of "lemon"

This is a citrus fruit.

But what of this argument?

This is a lemon.

↓ ???

This will taste sour.

Is it DV because of the meaning of "lemon," that is,

This is a lemon.

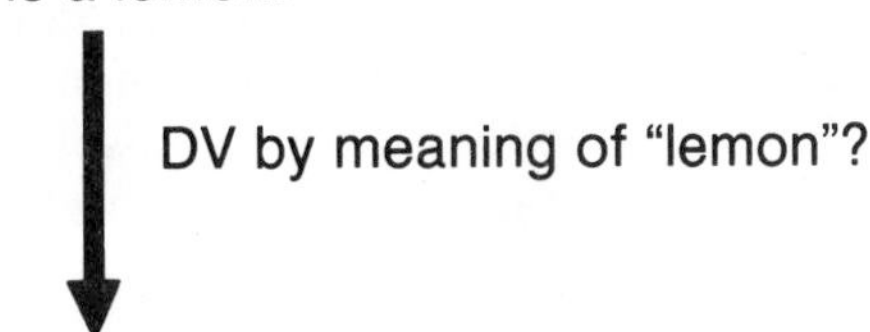

This will taste sour.

Or, is it just Strong because of the fact that all lemons in the past have tasted sour, that is,

This is a lemon.

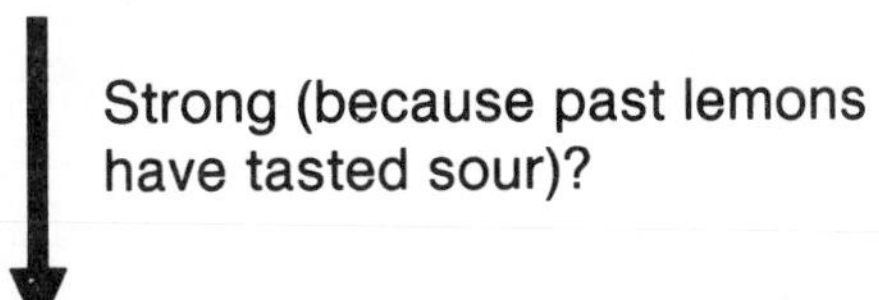

This will taste sour.

Is "being sour" part of the *meaning* of "lemon," or just a close association in the sense that lemons encountered until now are sour? Suppose you have in your hand what appears to be a lemon, but upon cutting into it and tasting it you discover it is sweet or tasteless, in any event not sour. Would you say that *by definition* you do not have a lemon? Or would you say that, contrary to experience and expectations, you have chanced across a sweet (or tasteless) lemon? The fact that there is no clearly correct answer suggests that we are not entirely sure where the meaning of a term ends and close association takes over.

This means that there is bound to be controversy over such an argument as this:

Charlotte is a feminist.

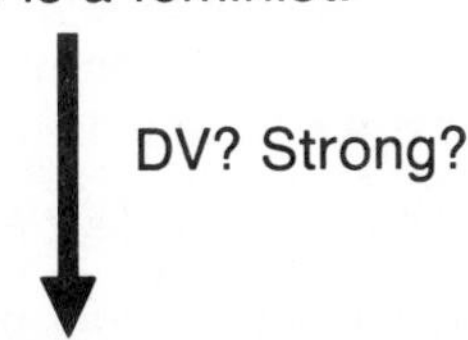

Charlotte is in favor of abortion.

Some would claim that one cannot *by definition* be a feminist and still be opposed to abortion. They would hold the above argument to be DV. Others would claim that "feminist" means merely "one in favor of equal rights for women," but not *necessarily* "one in favor of abortion." True, it would be an *uncommon* position to claim to be a feminist but to be opposed to abortion, but not a contradiction in terms.

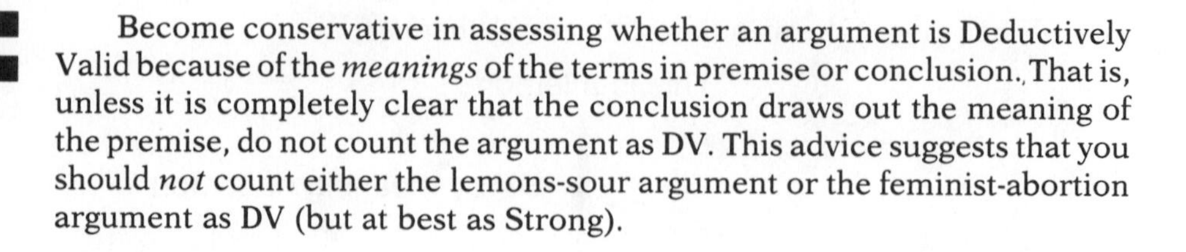

Become conservative in assessing whether an argument is Deductively Valid because of the *meanings* of the terms in premise or conclusion. That is, unless it is completely clear that the conclusion draws out the meaning of the premise, do not count the argument as DV. This advice suggests that you should *not* count either the lemons-sour argument or the feminist-abortion argument as DV (but at best as Strong).

8.3 Equivocation

In languages such as English one term often has two or more different meanings. (You might want to express this another way: It is a fact about natural languages that two different terms often have the same spelling.) For example, "bank" can mean "business establishment that will hold your money on deposit" or "side of a river"; and "duck" can mean "small swimming fowl of the family Anatidae" or "to bend suddenly to hide or avoid a blow." Therefore, each of these statements can have one of two meanings:

Jerry went to the bank.

Deborah saw her duck.

Typically, which meaning a statement is supposed to convey is prompted by context. For example, in

Saying he needed cash, Jerry went to the bank.

"bank" must mean "a place that will hold money on deposit"; and in

The escaped prisoner turned and shot at the woman. Deborah saw her duck.

"duck" must mean "to bend suddenly."

But context doesn't always prompt a meaning. Sometimes we have no context or what context we have is insufficient. For example,

Storming out of the house, Jerry went to the bank.

while providing a kind of context, does not tell us what sense of "bank" is intended—the money place or the river side. We now have a case of ambiguity. A statement is **AMBIGUOUS** if it can mean either one of two (or more) things, but we can't tell which, given the context we have.

Ambiguity plays a crucial role in a certain kind of fallacy. Suppose a statement is true in one sense but not in another. For example, suppose it's true that Jerry went to the bank (a money place) but not true that Jerry went to the bank (a riverside). Now, to equivocate is, in general, to be deliberately ambiguous. In reasoning, a **FALLACY OF EQUIVOCATION** is committed when a term in the premise(s) has more than one meaning; there is no other premise that states which meaning is at work; but the conclusion draws out just one of its meanings. The underlying form of the fallacy of equivocation is:

THE FALLACY OF EQUIVOCATION

. . . term *T* (meaning *A* or *B*) . . .

Not DV

. . . term *T* (meaning *A*) . . .

If the premise contains a term *T* that can mean *either A or B*, it is invalid to draw the conclusion that *T* means *A*—and equally invalid to deduce that it means *B*. The fallacy of equivocation thus is an instance of the (deductively invalid) disjunctive simplification discussed in Chapter 4:

P or *Q*

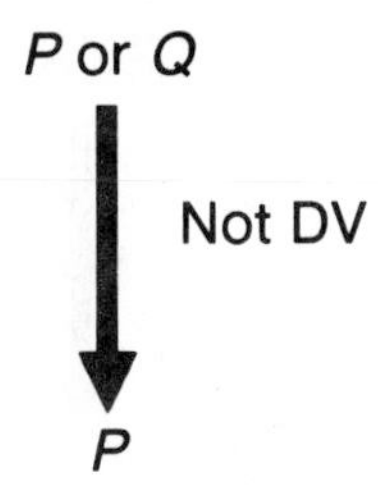

P

Equivocations give the appearance of correctness when the premise is true (or accepted) in *one* of the meanings of its terms but false in another of its meanings, while the conclusion deduces something from the false meaning. For example,

Sweden is socialistic.

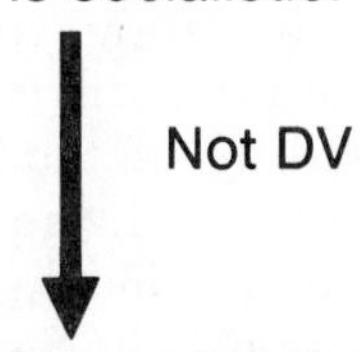

Society owns and operates the means of production and distribution in Sweden.

"Socialistic" *can* mean "the ownership and operation of the means of production and distribution by society." But the sense in which Sweden is socialistic is not that sense. Sweden is socialistic in the sense that many human services—health care, pensions, public transportation, etc.—are government-run. But there is still private ownership of the means of production in Sweden. The premise is true (in one sense of "socialistic"), but the conclusion is false. The argument commits the fallacy of equivocation.

Another fallacy of equivocation:

> *(1) Karl Marx despised his Jewish heritage. (2) He treated his wife and children shabbily. (3) He lived off his friends. (4) He had no sense of value. (5) So what could such a man know of economic value?*

Here is a diagram of the first simple argument:

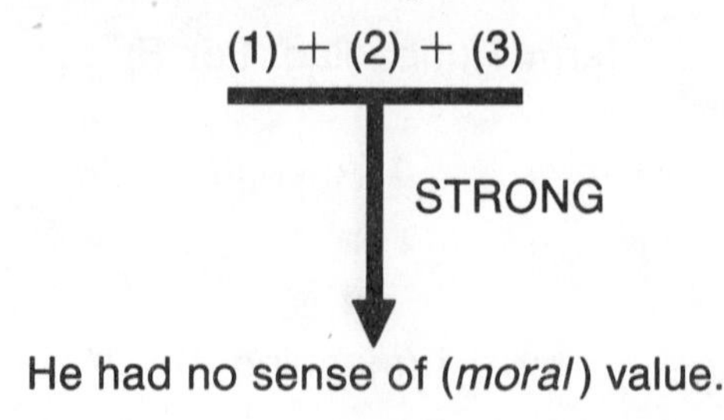

Note that this simple argument is a Strong argument for the conclusion that Karl Marx had no sense of *moral* value. This is hidden in the original formulation. Because of this, the second simple argument commits the fallacy of equivocation:

He had no sense of (*moral*) value.

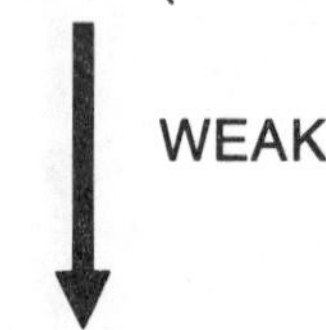

He couldn't know anything about *economic* value.

The term "value" is ambiguous. It can mean moral value, economic value, aesthetic value, sentimental value, and so on. Even if there is support for the claim that Karl Marx had no sense of *moral* value, this claim does not give us good reason to believe that he knew nothing about *economic* value. (The devil himself may be good at economics.)

In pointing out an equivocation, you must (1) show which term is ambiguous, and (2) say that the argument is fallacious because it equivocates on that term. The term "socialistic" in the Sweden argument is ambiguous between "a political system in which the government provides most human services" and "a political system in which the government owns the means of production and distribution." The Sweden argument equivocates on "socialistic." The term "value" in the Karl Marx argument is ambiguous between "moral value" and "economic value," and the argument equivocates on "value."

Relative Terms

Some terms in English are relative. These include "small," "large," "heavy," and "light." A term is **RELATIVE** if it requires some point of reference to be meaningful. For example, a small whale is small for a whale, while a large Chihuahua is large for a Chihuahua. So in saying something like

Shamu is a small whale.

we imply that Shamu is small for a whale. The point of reference for "small" is whales.

Suppose we were to ignore this point of reference. We would therefore treat "small" as a term that could be shifted from context to context without change of meaning. But such a shift cannot be done with relative terms, and to try it is to invite the fallacy of equivocation.

For example, each of the following arguments commits a fallacy of equivocation. (You can tell they go wrong somewhere, for each begins with what can be true premises and ends with what is certainly a false conclusion.)

I saw a small whale.

A whale is a mammal.

Therefore, I saw a small mammal.

There's a large Chihuahua in the back yard.

A Chihuahua is a dog.

Therefore, there's a large dog in the back yard.

Each of the above arguments commits a special kind of equivocation. Relative terms have different meanings depending on what point of reference is used to define them. "Small" as in "small whale" does not mean the same as "small" when it occurs in "small mammal." Similarly, "large" as in "large Chihuahua" does not mean the same as "large" when it occurs in "large dog." A squirrel is a small mammal; a small whale isn't. A Great Dane is a large dog; a large Chihuahua isn't. Therefore, in the first argument there is an equivocation on "small" and in the second an equivocation on "large."

8.4 Circular Reasoning, or Begging the Question

Circular reasoning in itself does not necessarily turn on the meanings of the terms of premise and conclusion. The simplest form of circular reasoning is this:

This diagram simply points out that any statement deductively entails itself. However, such arguments are clearly unconvincing. If what you want to prove is that *A* is true, it is illicit to *assume A* to begin with.

CIRCULAR REASONING means what the name suggests: arguing in a

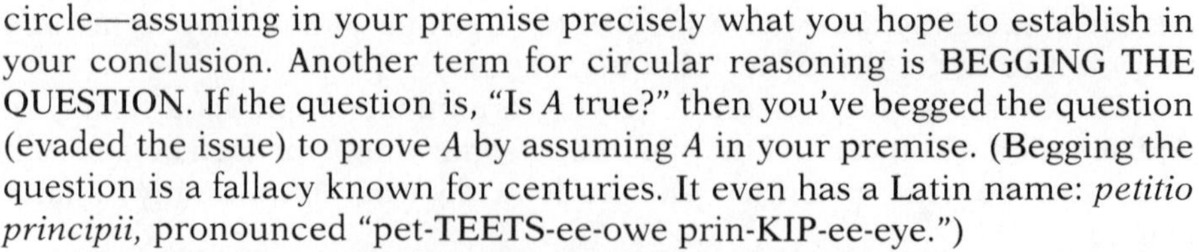

circle—assuming in your premise precisely what you hope to establish in your conclusion. Another term for circular reasoning is BEGGING THE QUESTION. If the question is, "Is *A* true?" then you've begged the question (evaded the issue) to prove *A* by assuming *A* in your premise. (Begging the question is a fallacy known for centuries. It even has a Latin name: *petitio principii,* pronounced "pet-TEETS-ee-owe prin-KIP-ee-eye.")

The prosecutor asks the witness whether the defendant was drunk on the night of January 16. The witness answers, "Yes." The prosecutor asks, "How do you know?" This is the question. The witness may give this perfectly good argument:

He drank an entire fifth of Scotch that night.

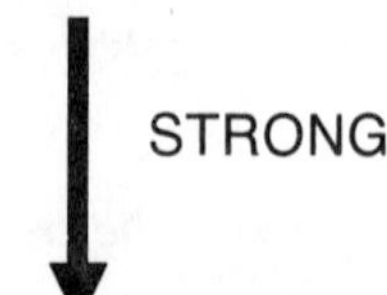

He was drunk on the night of January 16.

But suppose the witness says this instead:

He was intoxicated that night.

He was drunk on the night of January 16.

While this latter argument is DV, it begs the question (engages in circular reasoning). If the very question at issue is whether the defendant was drunk that night, it begs that question to assume the conclusion in the premise—for "intoxicated" is just a more polite term for "drunk."

You can never give evidence that a statement *P* is true by merely asserting it. You can never give evidence for *P* by asserting it twice (*P*, therefore *P*). And you can never give evidence for *P* by asserting it twice in disguise (*Q* [which just means *P*], therefore *P*).

A more subtle form of begging the question is to define a term so as to settle the issue. A husband decides to quit work to stay at home and take care of the children while his wife works. The husband's friend argues:

That isn't being a man. Being a man means to earn the household money. Being a man means leaving the children with their mother.

There is no definition of "being a man" that deductively entails either earning the household money or leaving the children with their mother. In addition, the husband's friend has begged the question. He assumes that *as a matter of meaning* a "real" man will go to work and not stay home with the children. But this is precisely what was at issue. (Presumably, there is little to the meaning of "man" outside of belonging to *homo sapiens* and having the appropriate genitalia.)

KEY POINTS

Some arguments may be Deductively Valid because the conclusion is merely a restatement of the meaning (or part of the meaning) of the premise(s).

- Before you judge the argument to be DV, make sure that the argument is deducing *meaning,* not just close association.
- In controversial cases, that is, in cases in which it is not crystal clear that the conclusion is merely a restatement of the meaning (or part of the meaning) of the premise(s), it is best to say that the argument is not DV.

Many terms in English are ambiguous: they may mean one of two (or more) different things. This can cause problems for arguments.

- The fallacy of equivocation occurs when a term in the premise can mean either *A* or *B* (or *C* or *D* or . . .), while the conclusion concludes that it means *A*.
- The fallacy of equivocation is convincing when the premise is true (or accepted) in one sense, but the conclusion draws out another (false or unaccepted) sense.
- There is a special case of the fallacy of equivocation that involves relative terms, such as "small" or "heavy." A small elephant is small for an elephant. It is an equivocation on "small" to deduce that a small elephant is a small mammal.
- To point out a fallacy of equivocation, say which term in the premise is ambiguous, and what meanings it is ambiguous between. That will be the term the argument equivocates on.

Another fallacy, called "circular reasoning" or "begging the question" (or, in Latin, "petitio principii") assumes in the premise what was to be proven in the conclusion.

- "Begging the question" is a way of evading the issue, and arguments that beg the question do just that. They assume what they were supposed to prove.
- Sometimes the question is begged by defining a term so that it covers the case, although the term does not really have that definition in ordinary usage.

EXERCISES

A. Evaluate each of the following arguments:

1. Diagram it.
2. Say whether it is Deductively Valid by meaning. If there is any controversy or uncertainty, point this out.
3. If there is an equivocation on a term between premise and conclusion, say which term is ambiguous and what the equivocation is.
4. If there is circular reasoning (begging the question), point this out.

The first four problems are done for you. Use them as illustrations of how to do the rest.

***A1.** Because Kim has a computer, she has a machine capable of rapid calculation.

Kim has a computer.

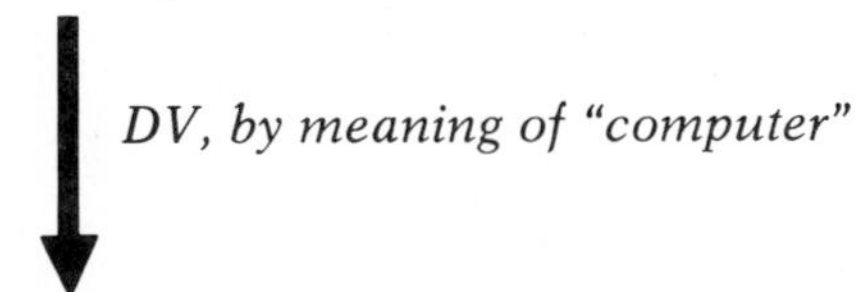

She has a machine capable of rapid calculation.

***A2.** Because Kim has a computer, she has a machine capable of thought.

Kim has a computer.

↓ *Not DV. Controversial whether computers by definition are capable of thought*

Kim has a machine capable of thought.

***A3.** Jeff sits to the right of Bill. So Jeff is more conservative on social and political issues that Bill.

Jeff sits to the right of Bill.

↓ *WEAK because commits fallacy of equivocation*

Jeff is more conservative on social and political issues than Bill.

"Right" is ambiguous between spatial and political orientation. The argument equivocates on "right."

***A4.** Good art is art that gives those with good taste pleasure. This is proven by the fact that those with good taste take pleasure only from good art.

Those with good taste take pleasure only from good art.

↓ *Circular Reasoning*

Good art is art that gives those with good taste pleasure.

A5. John is a Catholic. Therefore John believes the Pope in all matters of faith and morals.

A6. Angels are immaterial beings. Therefore nothing can physically touch them, and they cannot physically touch anything. Therefore they can't "dance on the head of a pin."

A7. She is ruminating in the pasture. Therefore she is thinking in the pasture.

A8. Jones is a poor man. He often loses at poker. Therefore he is a poor loser.

A9. He will, I'm sure, be reasonable about the matter. He is, after all, a reasonable man.

A10. Death is the end of life. But happiness is also the end of life. So, happiness must be death.

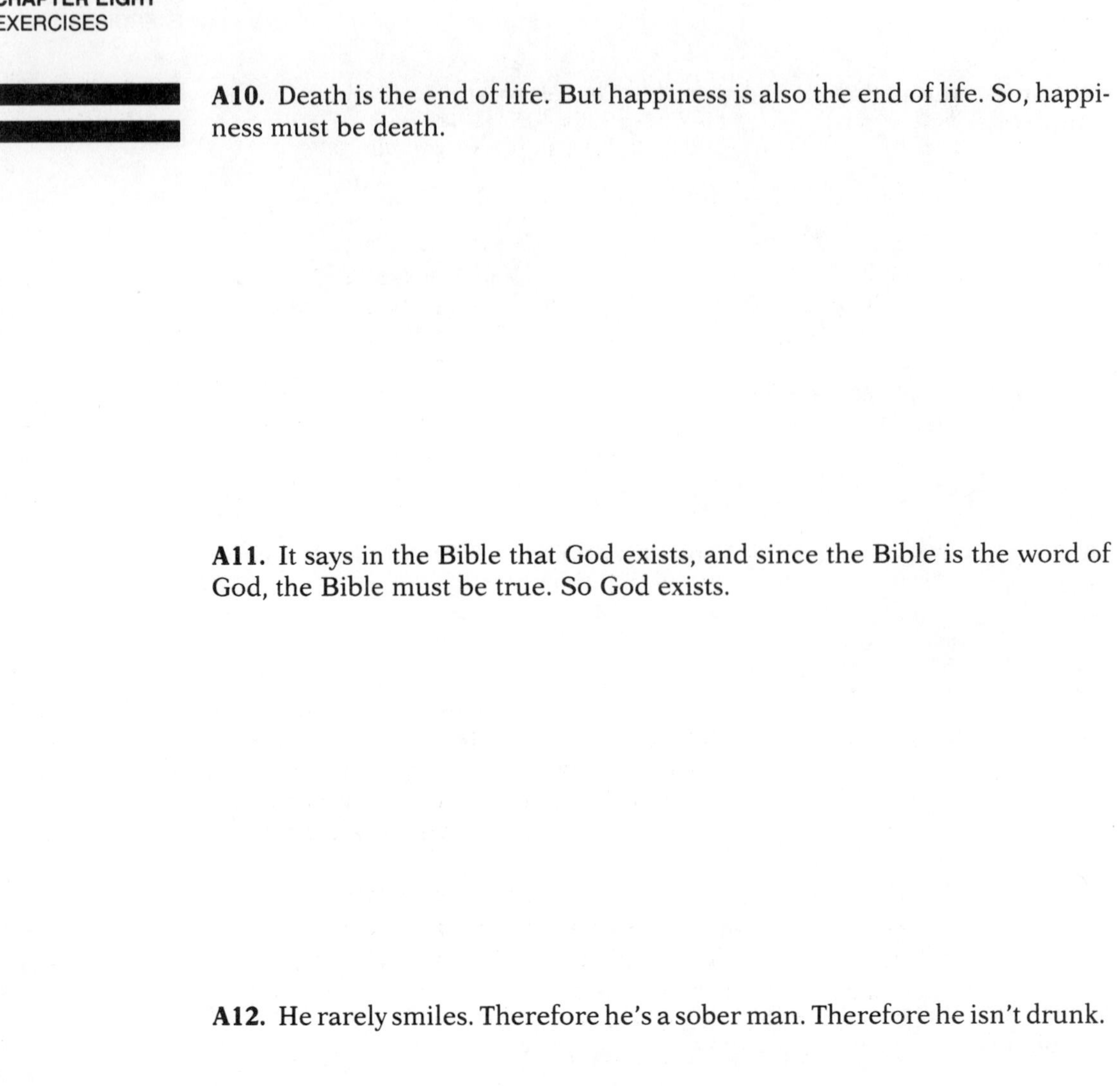

A11. It says in the Bible that God exists, and since the Bible is the word of God, the Bible must be true. So God exists.

A12. He rarely smiles. Therefore he's a sober man. Therefore he isn't drunk.

A13. It isn't legally wrong to put murderers to death. We have every legal right to do it.

A14. The law gives you the right to sue him. Therefore it's right to do so, and so you need have no moral qualms about it.

A15. Morphine is a narcotic. Therefore morphine is addictive.

A16. Cocaine is habit-forming because it is addictive.

A17. "Who did you pass on the road?" the King went on, holding his hand out to the messenger for some hay.

"Nobody," said the messenger.

"Quite right," said the King: "this young lady saw him too. So of course Nobody walks slower than you." (Lewis Carroll, *Through the Looking Glass.*)

A18. There is no such thing as "pure knowledge," for knowledge that has no practical application is not really knowledge at all.

A19. This is a diamond. Therefore it will scratch glass.

A20. Everyone ought to be accorded equality of opportunity. If so, then Wayne State University ought not to refuse admission to anyone.

A21. Your violin is out of tune. A violin is a musical instrument. So, your musical instrument is out of tune.

A22. Your piano is quite small for a piano. A piano is a music instrument. Your piano is a small musical instrument.

A23. Wheaten Terriers are seldom found in America, so if yours runs away you're unlikely to find him.

A24. Since abortion is murder, abortion even during the first trimester of pregnancy ought to be outlawed.

B. Compose arguments of the following types:

B1. An argument that is Deductively Valid by meaning.

B2. An argument that is not Deductively Valid by meaning, but that has a "close association" between premise and conclusion.

B3. An argument that commits the fallacy of equivocation, but not by equivocating on a relative term.

B4. An argument that commits the fallacy of equivocation by equivocating on a relative term.

B5. An argument that begs the question (engages in circular reasoning).

PART THREE

INDUCTIVE LOGIC

CHAPTER 9

INDUCTIVE GENERALIZATIONS

We begin our study of inductive logic with an examination of two typical sorts of inductive argument: inductive generalizations and inductive syllogisms. Chapters 4 through 8 concentrated on deductive validity. There, the primary question was whether a given argument was Deductively Valid. Beginning with this chapter, our focus will be on whether a given argument is Strong. Important concepts introduced in this chapter include:

INDUCTIVE GENERALIZATIONS:
UNIVERSAL GENERALIZATIONS
STATISTICAL GENERALIZATIONS

THE ASPECTS OF INDUCTIVE GENERALIZATIONS:
THE POPULATION
THE PROJECTED PROPERTY
THE SAMPLE

THE RULES FOR EVALUATING INDUCTIVE GENERALIZATIONS:
CONSISTENCY
UNIFORMITY
QUANTITY
VARIETY

FALLACIES YIELDING WEAK INDUCTIVE GENERALIZATIONS:
FALLACY OF HASTY GENERALIZATION
FALLACY OF BIASED SAMPLING

INDUCTIVE SYLLOGISMS:
MOST and FEW
STATISTICAL SYLLOGISMS

9.1 Induction and Deduction

Deduction is the attempt to draw out a conclusion that is already contained in the premises. Take Modus Ponens (MP) for example:

If Blue Moon came in first, you've won $1,000.

Blue Moon came in first.

Therefore, you've won $1,000.

The conclusion "You've won $1,000" is already contained in the premises. This is why MP is a Deductively Valid argument form. The conclusion is *necessarily* true, if the premises are true, for the premises already have stated the conclusion (though not explicitly).

Induction, on the other hand, attempts to go beyond the information contained in the premises. The conclusion of an inductive argument says more than is said in the premises. Take this inductive generalization for example:

Blue Moon has come in first in each of the dozen races he has run in the past year.

Therefore, Blue Moon will come in first in today's race.

The premise speaks of Blue Moon's performance in the past, but the conclusion speaks of his performance in the future (i.e., today's race, which hasn't been run yet). Such an argument cannot be Deductively Valid, for it is always possible for the premise ("Blue Moon has come in first in each of the dozen races he has run in the past year") to be true but the conclusion ("Blue Moon will come in first in today's race") to be false.

While inductive arguments cannot in general be Deductively Valid—although see the discussion of "probably" below—they can be Strong. Recall (from Chapter 3) that what we would call in ordinary English a "good" argument is called by logicians a "sound" argument. A sound argument has two features: (1) All of its premises are true; and (2) It is either Deductively Valid or Strong. Our primary concern in inductive logic is whether an argument is Strong.

The definition of "Strong" given in Chapter 3 was this:

STRONG. A simple justification is Strong just in case while supposing its premises to be true, its conclusion is *very likely* to be true as well. The premises of a Strong justification, if true, give you a very good reason to believe that the conclusion is true. If the premises of a Strong argument are true, the truth of the conclusion is a good bet.

The dividing line we will be most concerned with is that between Strong arguments and Medium arguments. The definition of "Medium" from Chapter 3 was:

> **MEDIUM.** A simple justification is Medium just in case while supposing its premises to be true, *its conclusion has about as much chance of being true as it has of being false.* The premises of a Medium justification, even if true, do not give you a compelling reason to believe that the conclusion is true. It would be unwise to bet that the conclusion of a Medium argument is true, even if its premises are true.

Medium arguments cannot be good (i.e., sound) arguments, for an argument whose premises only give Medium support to its conclusion does not give us very good reason to believe in the truth of that conclusion. The whole point of logic is to get us from truths (true premises) to other truths (true conclusions) without leading us astray. If the premises of a Deductively Valid argument are true, the conclusion has to be true. We can't be led astray there. If the premises of a Strong argument are true, then the conclusion *is very likely to be true.* We can be led astray in a Strong argument, but the strong likelihood is that we won't be. The problem with Medium arguments—it is even worse with Weak arguments—is that the likelihood of being led astray is greater than in Strong arguments.

There is a habit of expressing the conclusions of inductive arguments using the terms "probably," "in all likelihood," etc. For example,

> *For the past 38 years, I have sneezed throughout the month of September. Therefore, I'll* probably *sneeze through this September as well.*

When a term like "probably" appears in a conclusion, it strengthens the argument. For example, this argument is DV if we take the conclusion literally:

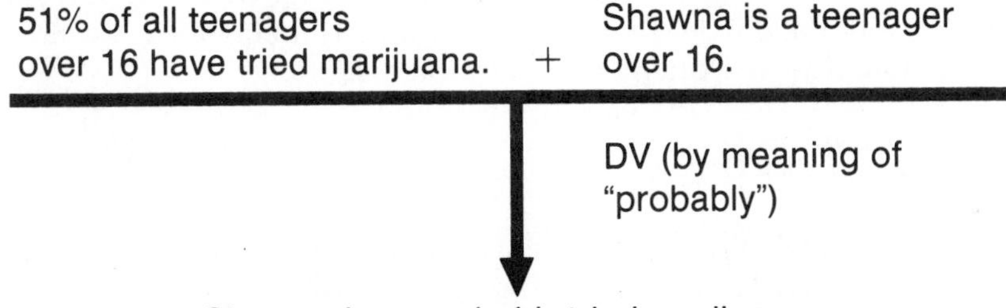

Shawna has *probably* tried marijuana.

But the argument is only Medium if we ignore the "probably" in the conclusion:

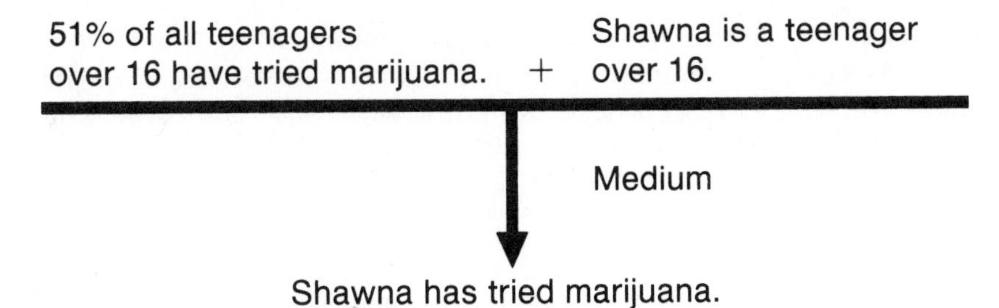

It is more informative to ignore the "probablys" that turn up in conclusions, for it is misleading to upgrade what is really a Weak or Medium argument to a DV one merely because a "probably" turns up in the conclusion.

Inductive logic, as we study it here, frames rules for assessing when an argument is Strong. There are different sorts of inductive arguments, and therefore different rules for assessing each. However, there are two differences between the rules of inductive logic and the rules of deductive logic.

First Difference

In deductive logic you were told that this argument is Deductively Valid (it follows the rule MP):

If Blue Moon came in first, you've won $1,000.

Blue Moon came in first.

Therefore, you've won $1,000.

You were also told that this next argument is not Deductively Valid (it commits the fallacy of affirming the consequent):

If Blue Moon came in first, you've won $1,000.

You've won $1,000.

Therefore, Blue Moon came in first.

Note that for the rules of deductive logic there is a yes-or-no answer to the question, Is a certain argument Deductively Valid?

The rules of inductive logic are less clear cut. You will be told what factors make an argument Strong*er* or Weak*er*, but there will be no hard-and-fast rules for determining when an argument is Strong. We can rigidly separate Deductively Valid from Deductively Invalid arguments, but we cannot always separate Strong from Medium arguments.

Second Difference

In order to assess whether an argument is Deductively Valid according to the rules of deductive logic, you need no information outside the argument. For example, this argument:

She is in either the kitchen or the bedroom, and she's not in the kitchen. So, she's in the bedroom.

is Deductively Valid. You know this because you know that the argument obeys the Deductively Valid rule, disjunctive syllogism (DS). You need not know anything else: You need not know who "she" is or even what a kitchen is.

However, many inductive arguments require information outside the argument to assess their degree of validity. Contrast these two inductive arguments:

For 52 Tuesdays, "Moonlighting" has been on TV at 9 P.M.

↓

"Moonlighting" will always be on Tuesday at 9 P.M.

I've seen 52 emeralds, and each one was green.

↓

All emeralds are green.

These arguments have a very similar form: Each contains a premise with 52 pieces of data (or 52 premises, if you like); each draws a universal conclusion from those data. Yet we know that TV shows are not eternal, and so we know that it is highly unlikely that "Moonlighting" will *always* be on TV on Tuesdays at 9 P.M. We also know that emeralds are different: with substances like precious stones there is a strong uniformity. The greenness of emeralds will not get "cancelled" like a TV show. In other words, we know that the emerald-argument is stronger than the TV-argument even though they are similar in form. And we know this because of facts *outside the argument.*

9.2 The Need for Induction

If deductive validity gives you certainty—if in a Deductively Valid argument you know that when the premises are true, the conclusion has to be true—why settle for less than deductive validity? Why even bother with induction? For four reasons:

Incomplete Evidence

We are often presented with only partial or incomplete data. For example, we have not seen *every* raven, especially ravens yet unborn (future ravens). We must therefore have recourse to an inductive argument from ravens we have observed to ravens unobserved:

All ravens observed until now have been black.

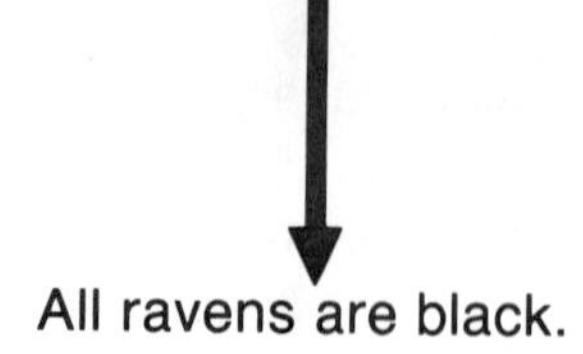

All ravens are black.

Convenience

It is often extremely inconvenient—time-consuming and costly—to observe *all* cases of a certain phenomenon. For example, suppose we want to know how many American Catholics approve of abortion. There are millions of American Catholics, and while it would be barely possible to ask each of them, it would be too costly and time-consuming to even try. However, we could interview a representative group of American Catholics. Perhaps we might come up with these data and make this induction:

27% of American Catholics interviewed approve of abortion if the mother chooses it.

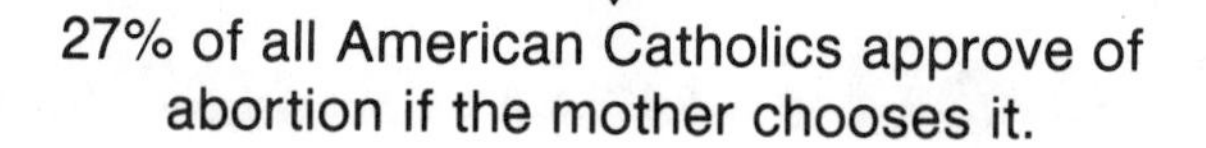

27% of all American Catholics approve of abortion if the mother chooses it.

Exceptions

The categorical syllogism needs at least one universal premise to be Deductively Valid. (A categorical syllogism with only particular premises cannot be DV.) So, if we know a universal, say "All humans dream," we can construct a Sound categorical syllogism: "All humans dream, Sam is human, so Sam dreams." But often we know that some universals are false. For example, we know that it is false that all tenured professors in American universities have doctorates and that it is false that no tenured professors in American universities have doctorates. Does this mean that we cannot make any arguments on this subject? No, for we know that *most* tenured professors in American universities have doctorates. We could construct this inductive argument:

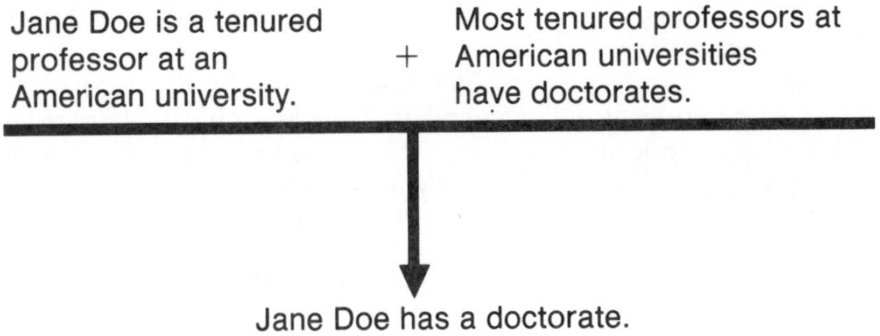

Jane Doe is a tenured professor at an American university. + Most tenured professors at American universities have doctorates.

Jane Doe has a doctorate.

Uncertainty

Do we know, for example, whether *no* liberals support aid for the contras in Nicaragua or whether *all* feminists support legal abortion? An argument that used either of these universals as a premise would be unconvincing. Therefore we have recourse to inductive arguments that use premises that are not universals. For example, we are unsure whether *no* liberals support aid for the contras, but we are sure that *few* do:

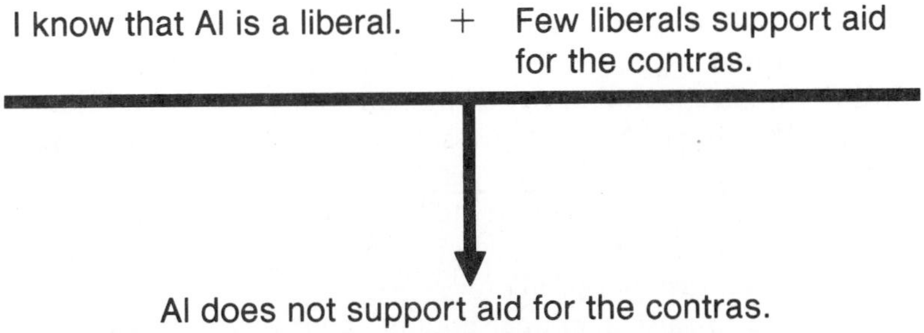

I know that Al is a liberal. + Few liberals support aid for the contras.

Al does not support aid for the contras.

Our knowledge of the world is incomplete and imperfect, but at least induction enables us to use the knowledge that we have.

9.3 How Induction Works

We sometimes make wild guesses and sometimes we turn out to be right. You might bet on 2-4-8 to win in tonight's lottery, and turn out to be right. (Congratulations!) But this was a wild guess. You didn't *know* that 2-4-8 would turn up tonight. However, when I predict that this September I'll start sneezing, *on the basis of past Septembers*, I am not making a wild guess. I am using a Strong inductive argument. What's the difference between a good inductive argument and a wild guess?

Induction relies on the truth of certain assumptions about regularity in the world. Among these assumptions are:

The future will be like the past. We expect that events that have occurred in the past with regularity will occur again. It became cold in Michigan every November; it will do so again this year. I have never hit a tennis ball and have it explode; therefore I can hit this one safely. My pocket calculator has been unerringly right in the past; it will give me the right answer this time too. And so on.

A representative part reflects the whole. We expect that if we have a representative part of something, what is true of it will be true of what it is a part of. I liked my taste of this pot of soup; therefore, I'll like a whole bowl of it. Every time I've driven with Fast Eddie he's been a speed demon; therefore, Fast Eddie is a speed demon even when I'm not with him. Twenty-seven percent of these 1,000 Catholics I've polled approve of abortion on demand; so 27% of all Catholics approve of abortion on demand. And so on.

Similar things will have similar qualities. We do not expect extreme diversity among similar things. Baseballs, ping pong balls, beach balls, and tennis balls will roll down an inclined plane; therefore golf balls will too. I know that it is expensive to insure Corvettes, Mazda RX7s, and Jaguars, so it is expensive to insure Ferraris. Although I don't know her, I know that her four sisters are tall; so she is too. And so on.

I have said that we rely on such assumptions in making inductions. If they weren't true, we would have no basis for induction. Every inductive argument would in effect be a wild guess. However, it is not easy to show that such assumptions are true. The best justification of these assumptions is that they constantly continue to work. It did become cold again in Michigan this November; I did like the whole bowl of soup; the golf ball did roll down the inclined plane—all just as I predicted.

It is possible to raise skeptical doubts about this justification, not the least of which is that it sounds circular: Induction will work because it has worked—itself an inductive argument! This, in fact, is one of the classic problems of philosophy, known as "the problem of induction." Luckily, we need not pursue it further here.

9.4 Inductive Generalization

INDUCTIVE GENERALIZATIONS are the paradigm of inductive arguments. Indeed, some dictionaries incorrectly define "induction" to mean "inductive generalization"—"incorrectly" because there are other kinds of induction. There are two kinds of inductive generalization.

A **UNIVERSAL GENERALIZATION** begins with a number of particular observations or instances, and generalizes to a universal conclusion from these. This is a universal generalization with 100 (dependent) premises:

Example 1

Raven #1 is observed to be black. +
Raven #2 is observed to be black. +
Raven #3 is observed to be black. +
.
.
.
Raven #100 is observed to be black.

↓

All ravens are black.

Universal generalizations can have negative conclusions, as in this example:

Example 2

I've seen hundreds of cats, and not a one has been naturally pink.

↓

No cats are naturally pink.

A **STATISTICAL GENERALIZATION** also begins with a number of particular observations, but generalizes to a less than universal conclusion. The conclusion of a statistical generalization can be, literally, a statistic:

Example 3

Person #1 plays Serious Pursuit and is under 30. +
Person #2 plays Serious Pursuit and is under 30. +
Person #3 plays Serious Pursuit and is under 30. +
Person #4 plays Serious Pursuit and is under 30. +
Person #5 plays Serious Pursuit and is under 30. +
Person #6 plays Serious Pursuit and is under 30. +
Person #7 plays Serious Pursuit and is under 30. +
Person #8 plays Serious Pursuit and is under 30. +
Person #9 plays Serious Pursuit and is *over* 30. +
Person #10 plays Serious Pursuit and is *over* 30.

↓

80% of people who play Serious Pursuit are under 30.

In addition, the conclusion of a statistical generalization can be informally stated, using "most" or "few," for example:

Example 4

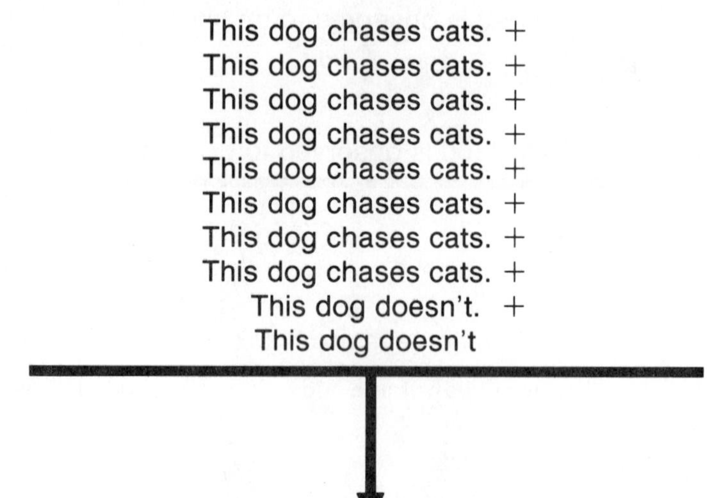

Either argument is called a statistical generalization, for each generalizes to a less-than-universal conclusion.

We have four example inductions: two universal generalizations, one about the color of ravens (Example 1), another about the color of cats (Example 2); and two statistical generalizations, one about the age of people who play Serious Pursuit (Example 3), another about dogs chasing cats (Example 4). Is any Strong? Which ones? Why? We need rules to judge their degree of validity.

9.5 Consistency, Uniformity, Quantity, Variety

We'll begin with a few definitions.

A **POPULATION** is the group we want to discover something about. The population in each of the four example arguments in the previous section was:

Example 1: Ravens

Example 2: Cats

Example 3: People who play Serious Pursuit

Example 4: Dogs

The population in an inductive generalization is the subject of the conclusion.

The **PROJECTED PROPERTY** is the property the frequency of which we wish to investigate in the population. The projected property in the four example arguments was:

Example 1: Being black

Example 2: Being pink

Example 3: Being under 30

Example 4: Chasing cats

The projected property is the predicate of the conclusion of an inductive generalization.

A SAMPLE is the set of observations made of the population. In our previous cases:

Example 1: Sample is 100 ravens

Example 2: Sample is "hundreds" of cats

Example 3: Sample is 10 people who play Serious Pursuit

Example 4: Sample is 10 dogs

The sample is the set of premises in an inductive generalization.

Go back to the examples to make sure you understand what the population, the projected property, and the sample is in each.

Now for some rules.

The first rule is perhaps the most obvious of all. Suppose a teenager observes his friends, and makes this induction:

All my friends, and I have many, have
acne (except for Joanne—I hate her).

All teenagers have acne.

This is clearly a Weak argument. The facts—the premises—don't support the conclusion. The first rule of inductive logic is:

> **CONSISTENCY.** The conclusion must not contradict the evidence given in the premise(s). If it does, the argument is Weak.

While consistency might appear to be obvious, there is a tendency to ignore "inconvenient" facts. We might say that "everyone" cheats on his or her income tax or that "all" used cars are unreliable, even though we know of exceptions.

There is another use for the CONSISTENCY rule, other than ignoring "inconvenient" facts. An inductive argument proceeds on the evidence available. New evidence can strengthen or weaken a conclusion. Let us

focus on how evidence weakens a conclusion. Suppose this argument contains the evidence you have at hand:

Almost all small grocery store owners in Detroit are Chaldean.

Mr. X owns a small grocery store in Detroit.

Therefore, Mr. X is Chaldean.

We can certainly consider this a Strong argument. However, suppose a new piece of evidence becomes available: Mr. *X* is Greek.

Almost all small grocery store owners in Detroit are Chaldean.

Mr. X owns a small grocery store in Detroit.

Mr. X is Greek.

Therefore, Mr. X is Chaldean.

This argument is certainly Weak, for it violates CONSISTENCY.

A Strong argument can be significantly weakened by new evidence. It must have appeared to people before Columbus that the earth was flat. The everyday evidence of the senses confirmed this: The earth *looks* flat (more or less). The common conclusion was that the earth was like a flat plate or tray somehow floating in space. Yet when explorers were able to circumnavigate the world without falling off its edge, the conclusion of the argument was inconsistent with this newly discovered fact. An old Strong argument was now Weak, for its conclusion, that the earth was flat, was inconsistent with new evidence. (It should be mentioned that not everyone before Columbus believed that the earth was flat. Aristotle (384–322 B.C.), for example, argued that the earth was a sphere from the fact that the earth casts a round shadow on the moon during an eclipse.)

The next rule of inductive logic has to do with the likelihood of *future* exceptions. Suppose twelve-year-old Jimmy makes this inductive generalization:

I've taken many math tests, and have always done well on the ones I've taken. Therefore, I'll always do well on any math test I'll take in the future.

This argument is Medium to Weak, for the kind of math tests a twelve-year-old child has taken will be different from the kind of math tests that same child may take in high school or college. Jimmy might do well in arithmetic, but will he do just as well in trigonometry or calculus? Here's the rule:

> **UNIFORMITY.** The greater the likelihood that future or unobserved occurrences of a projected property in a population will be *significantly different* from present or observed instances, the *weaker* the argument. The greater the likelihood that future or unobserved instances of a projected property in a population will be *very similar* to present or observed instances, the *stronger* the argument.

The UNIFORMITY rule essentially states that if we have good reason to believe that the future will be *unlike* the past (with respect to some population and projected property), then an inductive generalization about that population and property will be Weak. Little Jimmy's argument violates UNIFORMITY, for the sorts of math tests he is likely to take in the future will be very different from the sorts of math tests he has taken in the past.

The application of the UNIFORMITY rule requires outside knowledge. It is precisely UNIFORMITY that shows that this earlier example:

For 52 Tuesdays, "Moonlighting" has been on TV at 9 P.M.

Weak

"Moonlighting" will always be on Tuesday at 9 P.M.

is weaker than this argument:

I've seen 52 emeralds, and each one was green.

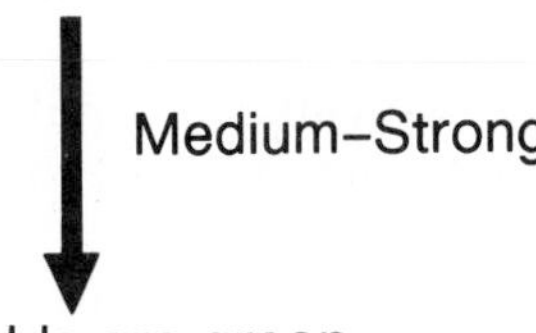

Medium–Strong

All emeralds are green.

We know that the continuity of TV shows is less uniform than the continuity of color in precious stones.

The third rule of inductive logic has to do with sample size. It should be fairly obvious that the more observations you make—that is, the larger the sample—the better your argument. More explicitly stated, the rule is:

> **QUANTITY.** The *larger* the sample, the *stronger* the argument. The *smaller* the sample, the *weaker* the argument. A Strong argument has a sufficiently large sample.

Note that the QUANTITY rule does not say how large a sample must be before an argument is counted as Strong. (It is beyond the scope of this book—if not inductive logic itself—to formulate a more precise account of quantity.) There are, however, clear cases in which the QUANTITY rule is violated. Such arguments commit the:

> **FALLACY OF HASTY GENERALIZATION.** If the size of the sample is too small, the argument is said to commit the fallacy of hasty generalization, and is therefore Weak.

For example, this argument is Weak:

My wife is insanely jealous.

↓ Weak–Fallacy of Hasty Generalization

All women are insanely jealous.

Bad logic—in particular, hasty generalization—is sometimes behind prejudice. For example,

A Lithuanian used-car dealer once cheated me.

↓ Weak–Fallacy of Hasty Generalization

All Lithuanians are cheats.

There is a reciprocity between the UNIFORMITY rule and the QUANTITY rule. Suppose you do not know the color of ravens, although you know that they are birds. Suppose also that you know that animals in general, and birds in particular, do not vary too much in color. In other words, you know that a population of birds is likely to be uniform with respect to color. Under such circumstances, your argument can be stronger with fewer observations.

But if you are investigating a population about which you know little or about which you know there is likely to be variation with respect to the projected property, then you need more observations for a Strong argument. For example, suppose you want to discover the average retail price of a certain prescription drug, but you know little about it. You don't know whether the price tends to vary very much or very little, or whether it varies from store to store or from geographic area to geographic area. Under such conditions of relative ignorance, you would need more observations (price checks at more stores) to get a Strong argument for the average retail price of the drug than you would need if you knew that retail prices for drugs tended to be as uniform as the color of ravens or emeralds.

Mere quantity is not sufficient. Suppose you wonder how many Americans like opera. (The population is *Americans* and the projected property is *liking opera*.) You next proceed to ask your friends, and since you have many friends, you end up with a sample of 100. Your inductive generalization looks like this:

Bob dislikes opera. +
Carol dislikes opera. +
Ted dislikes opera. +
Alice dislikes opera. +
Bernice likes opera. +
.
.
and so on, finding that 1 out of 5 likes opera.
.
.

↓

Only 1 out of 5 Americans likes opera.

Even though you have a sample size of 100 (so you are not doing a Hasty Generalization), there is still something wrong with this argument. It does not include sufficient variety.

The rule is this:

VARIETY. The more variety in the sample, the stronger the argument. The less variety in the sample, the weaker the argument. A Strong argument has sufficient variety.

What kind of variety is called for depends on the nature of the population and the projected property. Some examples:

- We know that voting behavior is strongly tied to such factors as socioeconomic status, race, religion, ethnicity, gender, and age. A wealthy white Episcopalian male physician is likely to have different electoral preferences than a poor black Baptist female practical nurse. Variety is introduced into a sample of voters when the pollster ensures that the sample includes those relevant factors.
- We know that the color of animals is often influenced by such factors as gender, season, age, and geographic location. Some animals are one color as babies, another as adults; some change coloration with the season; there is occasionally color variation even among the same species from locale to locale. A sample of the population of some animal that is intended to show what color(s) that animal is should include those factors.
- We know that the properties of substances are strongly influenced by temperature. Water, for example, is a solid below 32° Fahrenheit, a liquid above 32° but below 212° Fahrenheit, and a gas above 212° Fahrenheit. So if you came across an unknown liquid it would be rash to conclude that it is *always* a liquid until you examine it under a variety of temperatures.

You can see that what kind of variety needs to be introduced into the sample depends strongly on our prior knowledge of the population. We may not know what color ravens are, but if we know that they are birds, and therefore animals, we should make observations that include gender, season, age, and locale. With respect to the opera argument, perhaps college-educated people are more likely to like opera than others, or perhaps rural people are less likely to like opera than urban people. The argument as given simply polled your friends. This is insufficient variety. Your friends may all like rock or be under the age of twenty. This is hardly representative of the American population as a whole. Violations of VARIETY are said to commit the:

FALLACY OF BIASED SAMPLING. If the sample has too little of the variety appropriate for that population and projected property, then the argument commits the Fallacy of Biased Sampling and is therefore Weak.

The opera-argument did not account for the variety of taste that we would expect to occur in a population. By favoring your friends, you commit the fallacy of biased sampling.

One common instance of biased sampling occurs in the informal polls sometimes conducted by the media. For example, the *Detroit Free Press* has a daily feature called "Soundoff." Every day, a question is asked. On July 10, 1986, the question was, "Should police athletic teams practice on department time?" (This followed a news story in which it was reported that the Detroit Police Department's tug-of-war team practices and plays at least half its season on the department payroll.) Readers are invited to call one phone number to vote "Yes," another number to vote "No." The results are reported the next day. On July 11, accordingly, it was reported that of 671 calls, 76% voted "No," while 24% voted "Yes." Now 671 is not too small a sample, but consider this argument:

Of 671 callers, 76% of those who called think the Detroit police department should not practice on department time.

↓ Weak–Fallacy of biased sampling

76% of Detroiters think the Detroit police department should not practice on department time.

The sample does not ensure variety. For all we know, only those who buy the *Free Press* called (thereby excluding those who read the *Detroit News* or who read no newspaper), or only those who have telephones called (thereby excluding many of the poor), or only those who had time called (thereby excluding the busy), or perhaps many members of the Detroit Police Department called (thereby weighting the results more strongly in their favor). For all we know, the sample excludes nonreaders of the *Free Press*, the poor, the busy, and includes too many police officers. (It should be mentioned that the *Free Press* publishes a disclaimer every day: "Soundoff is a non-scientific, reader-opinion feature.")

The four rules, CONSISTENCY, UNIFORMITY, QUANTITY, and VARIETY together serve to locate Strong inductive generalizations. Of the four, only CONSISTENCY is an all-or-nothing rule. The conclusion of an induction is either consistent with its premises (the data) or it isn't, and if it isn't the argument cannot be Strong. The other three rules are expressed in terms of gradation (e.g., the more observations, the stronger the argument). These do not precisely specify when an argument becomes Strong. Such specification is beyond the scope of this book, if not of inductive logic itself. This, however, does not mean we cannot make judgments about the strength of arguments. In particular, we will often know when one argument is stronger (or weaker) than another.

For example, consider these two arguments:

Argument A

Adult raven #1 is observed in Michigan to be black. +
Adult raven #2 is observed in Michigan to be black. +
Adult raven #3 is observed in Michigan to be black. +

.
.
.

Adult raven #100 is observed in Michigan to be black.

Medium–Weak

All ravens are black.

Argument *A* is Medium to Weak because it lacks VARIETY: Only adult ravens are observed, and only ravens in one locale are observed.

Argument B

Raven	Age	Where Observed	When Observed	Color
#1	Adult	Michigan	Winter 1985	Black
#2	Baby	Ontario	Spring 1986	Black
#3	Adult	Texas	Spring 1986	Black
#4	Baby	Italy	Summer 1986	Black
		And so on, making a variety of observations		
#50	Adult	Australia	Fall 1986	Black

Stronger than
Argument A

All ravens are black.

Argument *B* contains more VARIETY (though less QUANTITY) than Argument *A*. Argument *B* avoids some of the biases of Argument *A*: *B* observes both adults and baby ravens, and observes them in a variety of locales.

Note that there is a trade-off between QUANTITY and VARIETY. In general, the more VARIETY introduced into an argument, the less QUANTITY is necessary. Argument *B* has only fifty premises (observations), half the quantity of Argument *A*. Yet *B* is stronger, for it contains greater VARIETY than *A*. You might, for example, make thousands of observations of your child's behavior. Yet to generalize to the conclusion, say, that *all* children suck their thumbs on the basis of your child's behavior is not as strong an ar-

gument as one containing fewer observations but a greater variety of children.

This fact is of special importance in polling techniques. The Gallup Poll (and other similar polls) uses a relatively small sample—about 1,500—to predict such national trends as who will win an election. This is because the Gallup Poll introduces considerable VARIETY into its observations. This proves to be convenient, since it is very time-consuming and expensive to interview people and if time and cost can be reduced, as they can by VARIETY, so much the better.

9.6 Inductive Syllogisms

If you have a Strong universal generalization, its conclusion can function as the premise of a deductive syllogism:

Observed hundreds of
crows during different
times of the year and
in different locales,
and each was black.

Strong

All crows are black. + There is a crow outside.

Deductively Valid

It will be black.

But suppose you have a statistical generalization to a conclusion that is of the form "Most, or few, or N% of *X* are *Y*." You can construct an inductive syllogism using such a conclusion as a premise.

Most and Few. Suppose you reach a conclusion such as "Most dogs chase cats" or "Few students are philosophy majors." Now what? You can construct an inductive syllogism of either form:

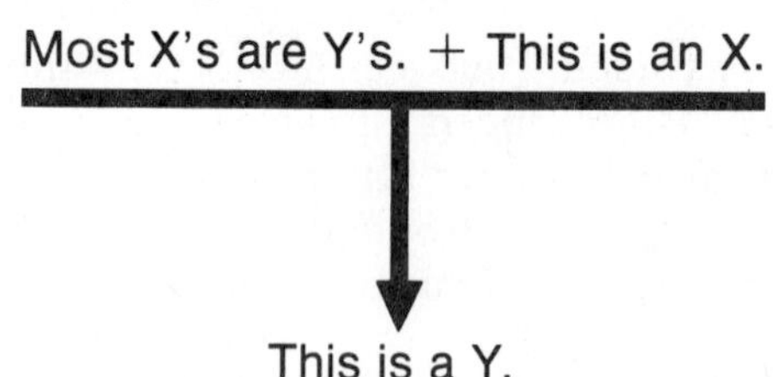

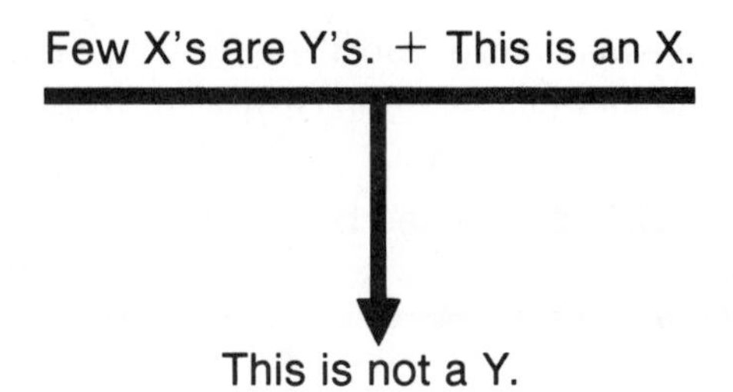

Some specific examples:

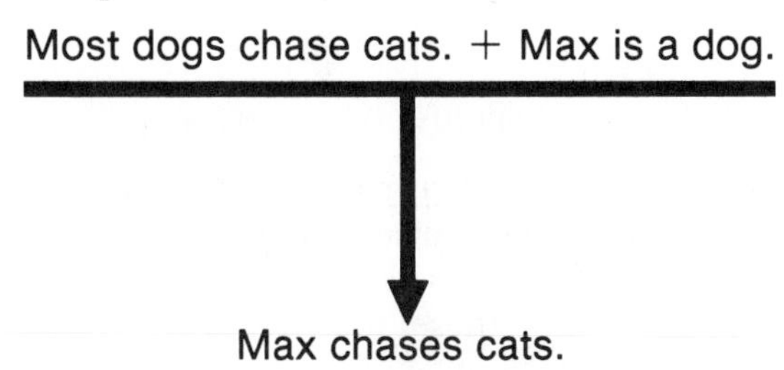

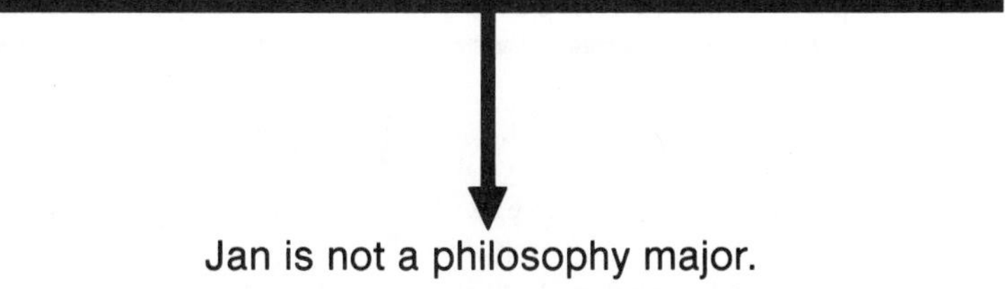

Although we will discuss this kind of inductive syllogism in its most typical form, i.e., using "most" and "few," it should be remembered that just as there were several ways to express the universal ("all" or "no") premise there are several ways to express the less-than-universal premise. These statements mean roughly the same thing:

Most Studebakers are reliable.

Studebakers are generally reliable.

It is likely that a Studebaker will be reliable.

These statements, too, mean roughly the same thing:

Few Edsels are reliable.

Edsels are in general unreliable.

It is unlikely that a Edsel will be reliable.

The problem in evaluating inductive syllogisms using "most" or "few" is that in English "most" and "few" are ambiguous. Sometimes people use "most" to mean "more than 50%" and "few" to mean "less than 50%." However, inductive syllogisms where "most" or "few" have these meanings are not Strong. (These same ambiguities carry over to "in general" and "likely.") For example,

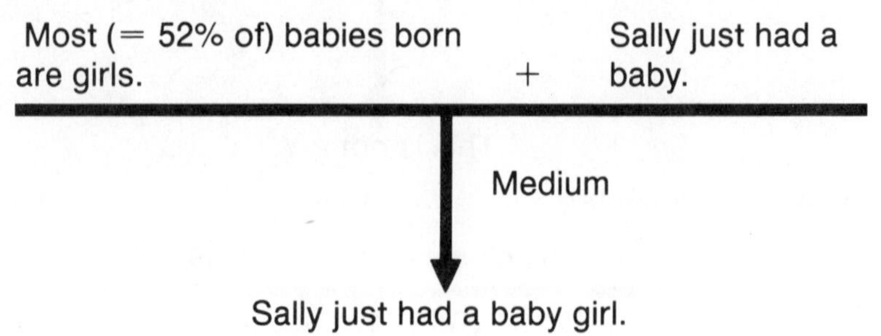

The truth of this conclusion is not very likely—not likely enough to call the argument Strong—even if the premises are true.

Of course, sometimes "most" is used to mean "almost all" and "few" to mean "almost none." Under these meanings we can generate Strong inductions:

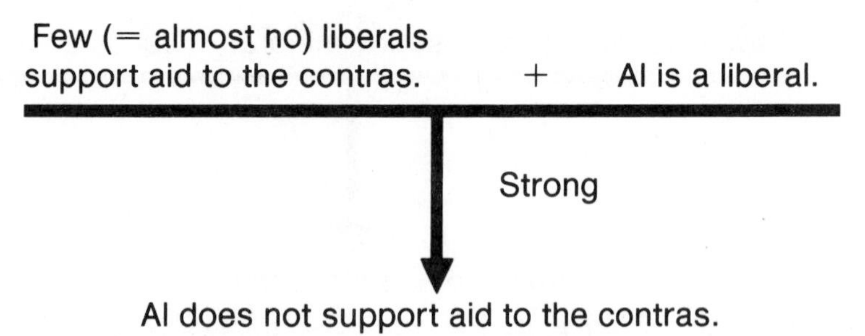

But of course the baby-argument earlier would be Unsound if we took "most" there to mean "almost all." (Its first premise, "Most babies born are girls," would be false.)

I would suppose that most (= almost all) people mean "almost all" by "most" and "almost no" by "few." The problem is that someone might occasionally sneak in a meaning of "most" as "more than 50%" and of "few" as "less than 50%." Not knowing which meaning is meant, we cannot be sure of the degree of validity of the argument. For example, what degree of validity does this argument have?

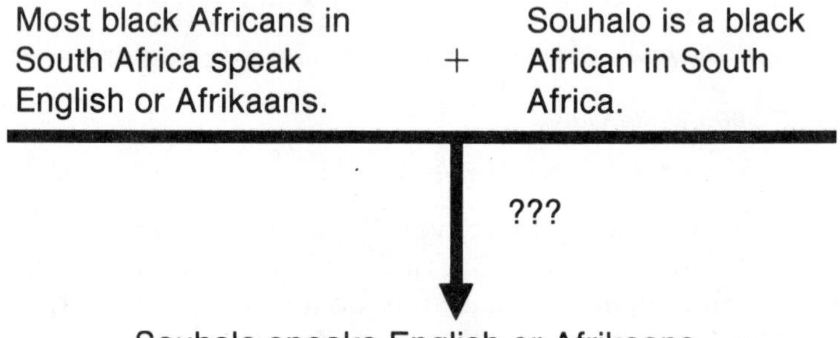

Answer: We can't tell its degree of validity until we know which sense of "most" is employed.

There are two ways of discovering this. You can ask the speaker, if available. Or you can look at the argument, if any, that leads to the "most" or "few" premise. If, for example, there were an inductive generalization that led to the conclusion, "Most (= a very large majority) of black Africans in South America speak English or Afrikaans," then you could evaluate the inductive syllogism above as Strong. If neither method is available (the maker of the argument is not around; the argument that leads to the "most" or "few" statement is nowhere in evidence), then the strength of the argument is ambiguous between Medium and Strong: In other words, you can't tell if the argument is Strong.

The Statistical Syllogism

The statistical syllogism is more precise than the syllogism using "most" or "few." It is of the form:

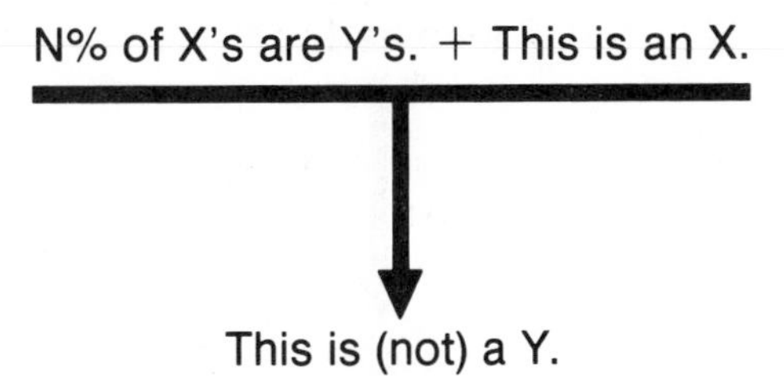

For example:

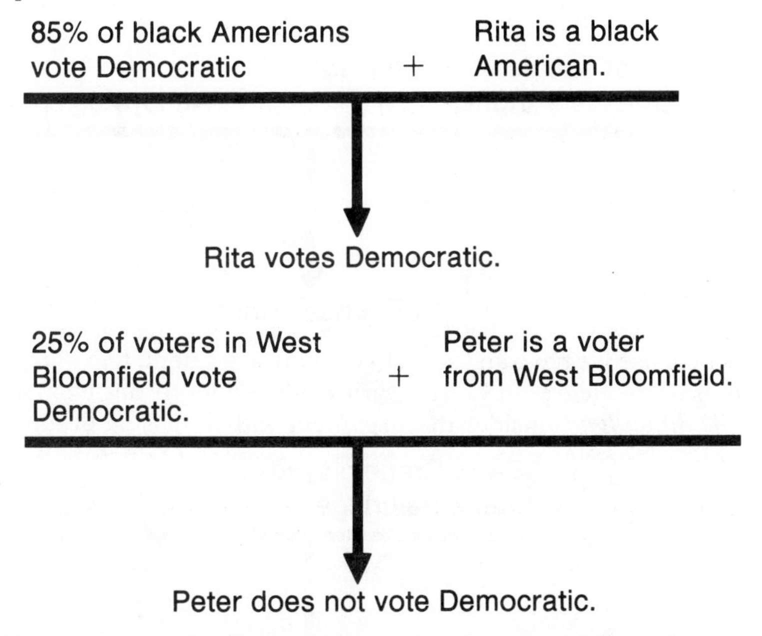

Whether a statistical syllogism is Strong or less depends on the percent. A Strong argument is defined as one in which the premises, if true, make the truth of the conclusion very likely. The two example arguments above are Strong. Things are not always so clear, however. Here is a caution and a difficulty.

The caution: The support for the statistical premise of a statistical syllogism may be great or terrible. This has no bearing on the degree of validity of the statistical syllogism itself. For example, here are two arguments (the "facts" are made up) for the same statistical conclusion, one Weak–Medium, the other Strong:

Out of 10 people suffering from psoriasis studied, 9 also had arthritis.

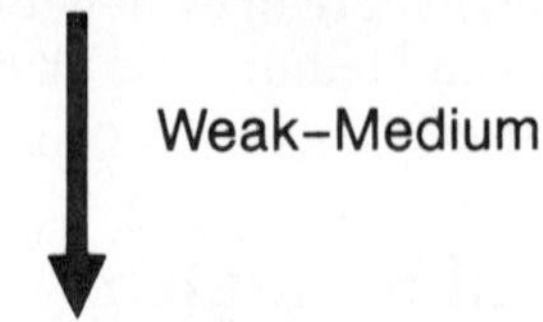

90% of people with psoriasis also have arthritis.

Out of 10,000 people suffering from psoriasis studied, 9,000 also had arthritis.

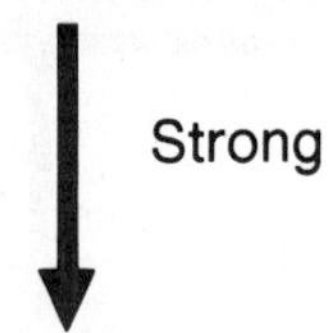

90% of people with psoriasis also have arthritis.

It doesn't matter which argument supports the statistical premise in this syllogism, for the syllogism is still Strong:

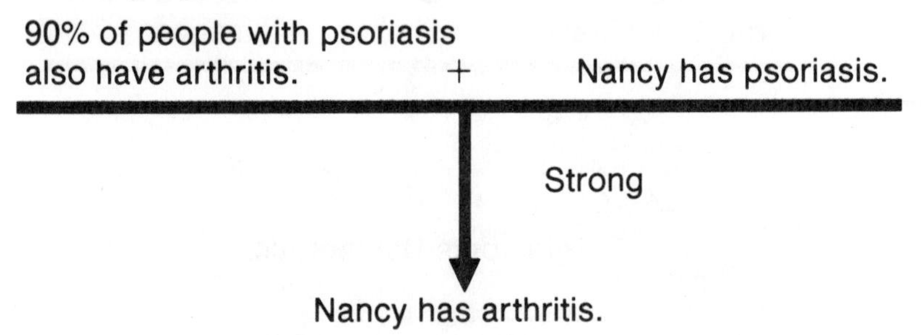

This is because we have an (inductive) chain argument: two *independent* arguments whose degree of validity varies independently one from the other.

The difficulty: Consider this argument with a missing premise:

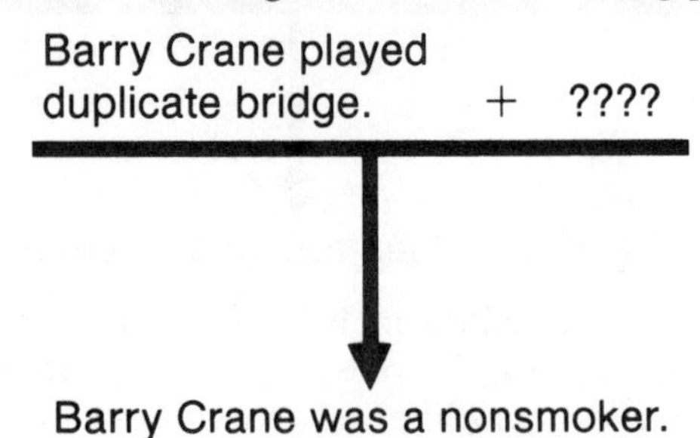

Suppose we have a number of premises we could add to the argument:

99% of duplicate bridge players are nonsmokers.

90% of duplicate bridge players are nonsmokers.

85% of duplicate bridge players are nonsmokers.

75% of duplicate bridge players are nonsmokers.

72% of duplicate bridge players are nonsmokers.

68% of duplicate bridge players are nonsmokers.

60% of duplicate bridge players are nonsmokers.

28% of duplicate bridge players are nonsmokers.

Which makes the argument Strong? It is clear that 99% makes the argument Strong, while 60% would make it Medium and 28% would make it Weak. But where will we draw the line between Strong and Medium? 85% still makes it a good bet that Barry Crane was a nonsmoker. So presumably does 75%. What of 72%? Is this a Medium or a Strong argument?

You might ask yourself, Would I bet on the truth of the conclusion if I knew the premises were true? However, not everyone would bet the same way. Some might bet on 72%, some not. We might stipulate that a minimum of 75% is needed for a Strong argument, but it is unlikely that we could justify such a stipulation. After all, precisely why would 75% make the truth of the conclusion very likely but 72% not? The problem is that we are trying to translate from words, "very likely," to a number, and we should expect some disagreement, just as we might if we were to try to say when precisely in degrees Fahrenheit it becomes "very cold": 30°? 25°? 20°? 10°?

Given that we cannot expect universal agreement on the strength of a statistical syllogism with a premise somewhat below 75%, we should say that such arguments are borderline between Strong and Medium (or Medium–Strong), hence not clearly Strong.

KEY POINTS

An inductive argument attempts to go beyond the information contained in its premises.

- Inductive arguments cannot in general be Deductively Valid. The maker of an inductive argument aims at a Strong argument.
- Only Deductively Valid or Strong arguments can be Sound. Arguments below Strong cannot be Sound.
- A Strong argument is one in which if the premises are true, the conclusion is very likely to be true.

- Inductive arguments that use the term "probably" (or "likely") in their conclusion can be Deductively Valid. It is however best when assessing the strength of such arguments to ignore such hedging terms.

There are two differences between the rules of deductive logic and the rules of inductive logic:

- The rules of deductive logic tell us definitely whether an argument is Deductively Valid. There is a clear yes-or-no answer. Many of the rules of inductive logic tell us what makes an inductive argument strong*er* or weak*er*, but do not tell us absolutely when an argument is Strong.

- In order to assess a deductive argument as Deductively Valid, we need to know only the rules of deductive logic. But sometimes, in order to assess the strength of an inductive argument, we need to know facts other than the rules of inductive logic.

There are some facts of life that make inductive arguments necessary.

- We are often presented with incomplete evidence. We have not seen every raven, especially unborn (future) ravens. Yet we often must come to some conclusion about ravens, such as what color they are.

- We are often not in a position to observe *all* cases of a phenomenon. It would be extremely costly and time-consuming to interview every voter in order to predict election results.

- We cannot always have universal ("all" or "no") premises. Some pieces of knowledge, e.g., that most tenured professors in American universities have doctorates, are not universal. Yet such pieces of knowledge can still be made to function in arguments, although only in inductive arguments.

- We are occasionally uncertain as to whether, for example, *all* feminists support abortion but we are quite certain that *most* feminists support abortion. An argument employing the universal is likely to be unconvincing.

Induction is not a matter of wild guessing. There are assumptions we make about how the world behaves, and these assumptions underlie induction. Among such assumptions are:

- The future will be like the past.

- A representative part reflects the whole.

- Similar things will have similar qualities.

There are two kinds of inductive generalization. In each, an inductive argument is made that goes beyond the information contained in the premises—from something observed to something unobserved.

- A universal generalization begins with a number of particular observations and generalizes to a universal ("all" or "no") conclusion.

- A statistical generalization begins with a number of particular observations and generalizes to a less-than-universal conclusion ("most" or "few" or "N%").

Definitions:

- A population is the group we want to discover something about.
- The projected property is the property the frequency of which we wish to investigate in the population.
- The sample is the set of observations made of the population.

There are four rules for judging the strength of an inductive generalizations:

- CONSISTENCY. The conclusion must not contradict the evidence given in the premise(s). If it does, the argument is Weak.
- UNIFORMITY. The greater the likelihood that future or unobserved occurrences of a projected property in a population will be significantly different from present or observed instances, the weaker the argument. The greater the likelihood that future or unobserved instances of a projected property in a population will be very similar to present or observed instances, the stronger the argument.
- QUANTITY. The larger the sample, the stronger the argument. The smaller the sample, the weaker the argument. A Strong argument has a sufficiently large sample.
- VARIETY. The more variety in the sample, the stronger the argument. The less variety in the sample, the weaker the argument. A Strong argument has sufficient variety.

There are two fallacies traditionally associated with inductive generalization.

- FALLACY OF HASTY GENERALIZATION. If the size of the sample is too small, the argument is said to commit the fallacy of hasty generalization, and is therefore Weak.
- FALLACY OF BIASED SAMPLING. If the sample has too little of the variety appropriate for that population and projected property, then the argument commits the fallacy of biased sampling, and is therefore Weak.

There are some reciprocities (tradeoffs) among the rules.

- There is a reciprocity between UNIFORMITY and QUANTITY. If you know (in advance) that a population is likely to be uniform with respect to the projected property (e.g., that a species of bird is likely to be uniform in color), then you need fewer observations than if you have no idea about uniformity.

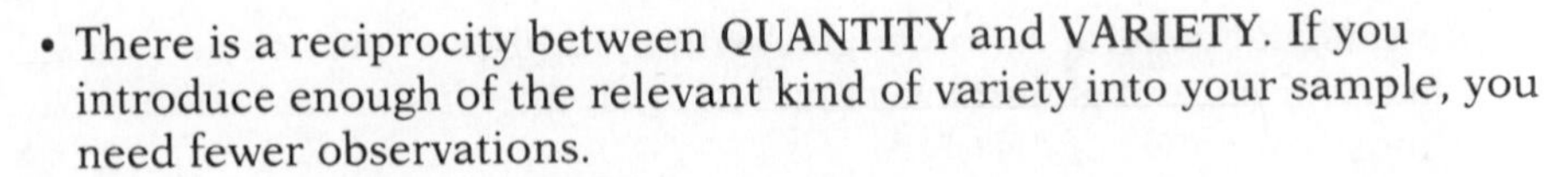

- There is a reciprocity between QUANTITY and VARIETY. If you introduce enough of the relevant kind of variety into your sample, you need fewer observations.

If you've come, in an inductive generalization, to a universal conclusion ("all" or "no"), then you can proceed to construct deductive arguments. But if you come to a less-than-universal conclusion, you can proceed only via inductive syllogisms. We studied two:

- Most and Few. "Most dogs chase cats, and Max is a dog. Therefore Max chases cats." These inductive syllogisms can be Strong only when we know that "most" means "almost all" and "few" means "almost no."
- Statistical Syllogisms. "82% of students from Wealthy High go to college, and Peggy is a student from Wealthy High. Therefore Peggy goes to college." These inductive syllogisms can be Strong only when the percent is high enough to make the truth of the conclusion very likely. Some arguments (e.g., suppose only 72% of students from Wealthy High go to college) are borderline between Strong and Medium.

EXERCISES

A. Keeping in mind the rules for inductive generalization—CONSISTENCY, UNIFORMITY, QUANTITY, and VARIETY—and the two fallacies—HASTY GENERALIZATION and BIASED SAMPLING:

1. Decide the degree of validity—DEDUCTIVELY VALID, STRONG, MEDIUM, or WEAK—of these arguments.
2. You must justify your answer, e.g., "This argument is WEAK because it violates CONSISTENCY."
3. You may "split" your answer, e.g., MEDIUM–STRONG, if you believe the case to be borderline or controversial, but you must justify the splitting.
4. If there is some reason you cannot decide the strength of the argument, point this out (e.g., you have to know what "most" means).

(The "facts" in these arguments are by-and-large fictitious.)

***A1.** Dog #1 in the animal shelter is stray or abandoned. +
Dog #2 in the animal shelter is stray or abandoned. +
Dog #3 in the animal shelter is stray or abandoned. +
.
.
.
Dog #100 in the animal shelter is stray or abandoned.

Weak–Fallacy of Biased Sampling

All dogs are stray or abandoned.

Sample is only of dogs in animal shelters—which, of course, are either stray or abandoned.

A2. A pollster stops people on the corner of Broadway and 57th in New York City between noon and 2 P.M., and asks each, "Are you a resident of New York City?" If the person answers, "No," he or she is not asked anything further. If the person answers, "Yes," he or she is asked, "Do you approve of capital punishment for convicted child molesters?" 100 New York City residents respond to the second question, at which point the pollster goes home to tabulate his results. The pollster is surprised to find that all New York City residents polled gave the same response. He constructs this induction:

Every one of 100 New York City residents polled approve of capital punishment for convicted child molesters.

↓

All New York City residents approve of capital punishment for convicted child molesters.

A3. We've spent five evenings together and have gotten along splendidly.

↓

Our marriage will no doubt work very well.

A4. 90% of pizzeria owners are native-born Italians.

Mr. *X* is a pizzeria owner.

Therefore Mr. *X* is a native-born Italian.

A5. 90% of pizzeria owners are native-born Italians.

Mr. McMurphy is a pizzeria owner.

Therefore Mr. McMurphy is a native-born Italian.

A6.

I've cheated on exams quite frequently and have never gotten caught.

↓

I'll always get away with any cheating I may do.

A7. Japanese male #1, a Sumo wrestler, weighs over 200 lbs. +
Japanese male #2, a Sumo wrestler, weighs over 200 lbs. +
Japanese male #3, a Sumo wrestler, weighs over 200 lbs. +

.
.
.

Japanese male #100, a Sumo wrestler, weighs over 200 lbs.

↓

All Japanese males weigh over 200 lbs.

A8. No person has ever lived forever.

↓

No person will live forever.

A9.

Every economic depression in the past has occurred at the same time as large sunspots.

↓

The next economic depression will occur at the same time as large sunspots.

A10. Every person who has taken Drug *X* has exhibited no adverse side reactions.

Drug *X* has been administered to thousands of males in good condition between 20 and 29 years of age.

Therefore, Drug *X* causes no adverse side reactions.

A11. Most people who have blond hair also have blue eyes.

Larry has blond hair.

Therefore Larry has blue eyes.

A12. Three runners, A, B, and C, race against each other frequently. A has won 60% of the races, B has won 30%, and C 10%. Therefore A will win the next race she runs against B and C.

A13. Suppose a fundamentalist religious organization reports the following: 99% of all letters we receive, and we receive thousands, support prayer in public schools and are against abortion. It is clear, then, that the overwhelming majority of Americans support prayer and are against abortion.

A14. For hundreds of years, no one has ever been able to grow citrus trees in northern Canada.

↓

There's little probability that anyone will ever be able to grow citrus trees there.

A15. The following is not (I assume) fictitious. It comes from *The Detroit Free Press*, June 21, 1987, p. 17A:

Detroit had one of its warmest springs ever. . . The National Weather Service notes that this is the 12th year on record to have above-normal temperatures in April, May and June. The other 11 all were followed by hot summers.

a. What conclusion should be drawn?

b. How strongly is this conclusion supported (i.e., what degree of validity does the argument have)?

A16. Diagram this argument and assess its degree of validity:

My dog has fleas, so all dogs have fleas, and so your dog has fleas too.

B. With reference to the following three arguments in A above, state the population, the projected property, and the sample for:

Argument A1:

*POPULATION: *Dogs*

*PROJECTED PROPERTY: *Being stray or abandoned*

*SAMPLE: *100 dogs in animal shelters*

Argument A2:

POPULATION:

PROJECTED PROPERTY:

SAMPLE:

Argument A3:

POPULATION:

PROJECTED PROPERTY:

SAMPLE:

C. Below are three arguments with a similar form. Which is strongest and why? Which is weakest and why? (Hint: consider UNIFORMITY.)

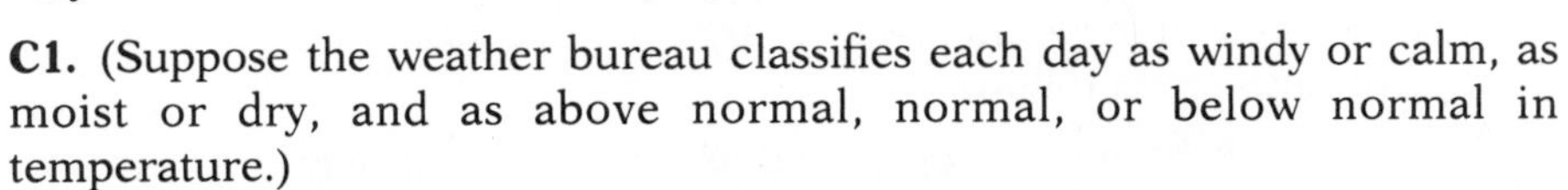

C1. (Suppose the weather bureau classifies each day as windy or calm, as moist or dry, and as above normal, normal, or below normal in temperature.)

90% of July Fourths in Michigan for the last 100 years were calm, dry, and normal in temperature.

↓

The next July Fourth in Michigan will be calm, dry, and normal in temperature.

C2. A certain typist, who has typed 100 pages of material, makes an average of two errors per page.

↓

The next page she types will contain two errors.

C3. 100 emeralds have been observed, and each was green.

↓

The next emerald will be green.

In each of parts D, E, and F below you are given an argument or situation. You are then given a number of different suppositions. Your problem is to decide what each supposition would do to the argument or situation if actually true. Mark your answers as follows:

S = A supposition that would tend to make the argument Stronger.

W = A supposition that would tend to make the argument Weaker.

N = A supposition that would have no effect on the degree of validity of the argument.

D. Here's an argument. The facts are made up (except that the names of real American colleges and universities are used).

University of Michigan: 75% of women asked approve of government-funded day-care centers.

University of California, Berkeley: 82% of women asked approve of government-funded day-care centers.

Bates College: 65% of women asked approve of government-funded day-care centers.

Notre Dame University: 45% of women asked approve of government-funded day-care centers.

Smith College: 92% of women asked approve of government-funded day-care centers.

Florida State University: 70% of women asked approve of government-funded day-care centers.

Harvard University: 94% of women asked approve of government-funded day-care centers.

University of Pittsburgh: 80% of women asked approved of government-funded day-care centers.

University of Iowa: 52% of women asked approve of government-funded day-care centers.

Arizona State University: 65% of women asked approve of government-funded day-care centers.

Therefore, 72% of women at American colleges or universities approve of government-funded day-care centers.

Mark each of the following "S," "W," or "N" (see instructions for parts D, E, and F).

___W___ *D1. Suppose at each college or university, only women who lived on campus were polled.

___W___ *D2. Suppose at each college or university, women were polled only in classes dealing with some aspect of Women's Studies.

___N___ *D3. Suppose one of the premises happens to be false.

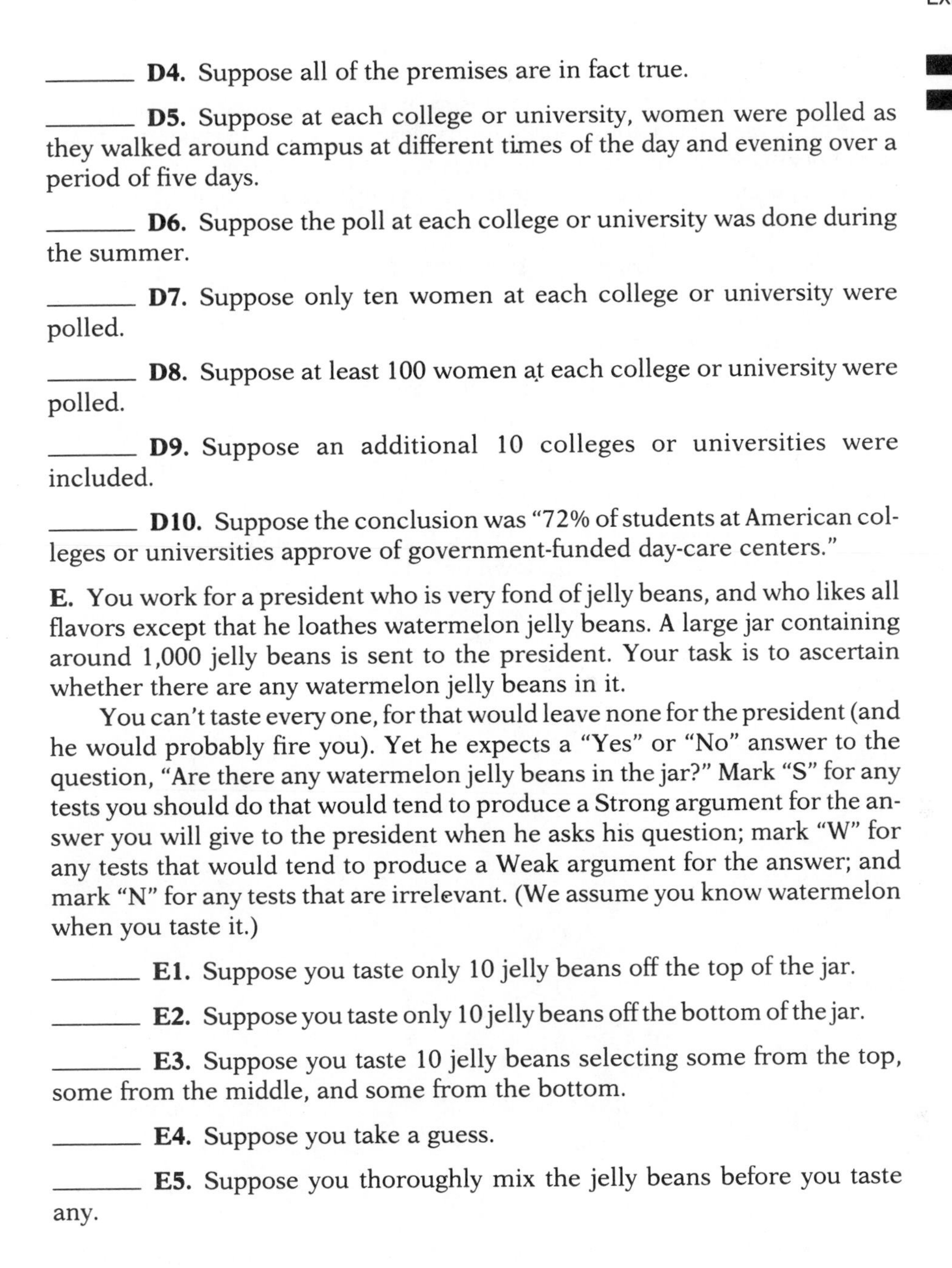

_______ **D4.** Suppose all of the premises are in fact true.

_______ **D5.** Suppose at each college or university, women were polled as they walked around campus at different times of the day and evening over a period of five days.

_______ **D6.** Suppose the poll at each college or university was done during the summer.

_______ **D7.** Suppose only ten women at each college or university were polled.

_______ **D8.** Suppose at least 100 women at each college or university were polled.

_______ **D9.** Suppose an additional 10 colleges or universities were included.

_______ **D10.** Suppose the conclusion was "72% of students at American colleges or universities approve of government-funded day-care centers."

E. You work for a president who is very fond of jelly beans, and who likes all flavors except that he loathes watermelon jelly beans. A large jar containing around 1,000 jelly beans is sent to the president. Your task is to ascertain whether there are any watermelon jelly beans in it.

You can't taste every one, for that would leave none for the president (and he would probably fire you). Yet he expects a "Yes" or "No" answer to the question, "Are there any watermelon jelly beans in the jar?" Mark "S" for any tests you should do that would tend to produce a Strong argument for the answer you will give to the president when he asks his question; mark "W" for any tests that would tend to produce a Weak argument for the answer; and mark "N" for any tests that are irrelevant. (We assume you know watermelon when you taste it.)

_______ **E1.** Suppose you taste only 10 jelly beans off the top of the jar.

_______ **E2.** Suppose you taste only 10 jelly beans off the bottom of the jar.

_______ **E3.** Suppose you taste 10 jelly beans selecting some from the top, some from the middle, and some from the bottom.

_______ **E4.** Suppose you take a guess.

_______ **E5.** Suppose you thoroughly mix the jelly beans before you taste any.

F. The Traffic Research Council (TRC) says that the national lowering of highway speed limits to 55 m.p.h. will save lives. Its argument is that in each of the three years when lower speed limits were in effect in 35 states, the number of deaths from automobile accidents was reduced at least 20% from the previous annual rate. This was true in every year in every one of the 35 states surveyed.

Mark each of the following "S," "W," or "N" (see instructions for parts D, E, and F).

_______ **F1.** Suppose the TRC had looked at 20 states.

_______ **F2.** Suppose the TRC looked at those 35 states for only one year during lowered speed limits.

_______ **F3.** Suppose the TRC had looked at the other 15 states and discovered that the number of deaths was not reduced.

_______ **F4.** Suppose the TRC looked at the other 15 states and discovered that the number of deaths went down only 15%.

CHAPTER 10

ANALOGICAL ARGUMENTS

Another kind of inductive argument, the analogical argument, is perhaps more common in day-to-day reasoning than inductive generalizations or inductive syllogisms. This chapter shows you what an analogical argument is and how to evaluate one. The important concepts in this chapter are:

ANALOGY

ANALOGICAL ARGUMENT
— and these aspects of one:
UNKNOWN INSTANCE
UNKNOWN PROPERTY
KNOWN INSTANCE
KNOWN PROPERTIES

THE RULES FOR ASSESSING ANALOGICAL ARGUMENTS:
SIMILARITY
RELEVANCE

TWO FALLACIES YIELDING WEAK ANALOGICAL ARGUMENTS:
FALLACIOUS DISANALOGY
IRRELEVANT ANALOGY

10.1 Analogies and Analogical Arguments

An **ANALOGY** is a statement of similarity. Two (sometimes more) things are compared and said to have some feature(s) in common. Usually an analogy is intended to get someone to understand something unfamiliar by pointing out some similarity with something familiar. For example, if you don't know what a mango tastes like I can give you some idea by pointing out a similarity between the taste of a mango (something unfamiliar) and the taste of a peach (something familiar). I say,

A mango tastes like a peach.

This is a simple analogy—a statement, not an argument. It says merely that this is like that. More complex analogies say not only that this is like that, but are more specific in what respects this is like that:

The structure of any major gramophone company is like an iceberg: the part which shows, at least to the public, is only a fraction of the whole. (John Culshaw, Ring Resounding. *The Viking Press, 1967, pp. 16–17.)*

Here John Culshaw points out that the recording—what the public sees (hears)—is only a small part of any record company. He points this out by drawing an analogy between a gramophone company and an iceberg. Again, we have only a statement, not an argument.

Analogies may be dull or interesting; they may induce understanding or leave the reader in the dark; they may be true or false. However, the important point is that an analogy in itself is not an argument. An analogy is a statement of similarity. It says "This is like that" or "This is like that in this respect." But a mere statement cannot be an argument. An argument requires two or more statements, one of which must present evidence for the truth of the other.

However, analogies can function in arguments, and when they do we have an analogical argument. An **ANALOGICAL ARGUMENT** draws a conclusion about something unknown or unfamiliar on the basis of a similarity with something known or familiar. Suppose you are browsing in the bookstore for something to read. Suppose you know that you have enjoyed Stephen King novels in the past, and here before you is a new Stephen King novel. You may by analogy conclude that you will enjoy this new novel as well. Your analogical argument will look something like this:

Each of Carrie, 'Salem's Lot, The Shining, *and* Christine *is a novel, is by Stephen King, and is in the horror genre.*

I have read and enjoyed Carrie, 'Salem's Lot, *and* The Shining.

Therefore, I will also enjoy Christine.

Analogical arguments, like the one above, are inductive arguments. They purport to provide Strong reasons to believe the conclusion. But they differ from inductive generalizations in that analogical arguments essentially and explicitly contain an analogy. The basic structure of an analogical argument is this:

The analogy: A, B, C, *and* D *each have features* W, X, *and* Y.

What is known: *In addition* A, B, *and* C *each have feature* Z.

Concluding something about what was unknown: *Therefore,* D *also has feature* Z.

You know that several works (*A, B, C,* and *D*) are similar: They each have features *W, X,* and *Y* (are novels, are by Stephen King, and are in the horror genre). You further know something about *A, B,* and *C* (that you enjoyed each). You conclude something about what was unknown: that *D* will also have that feature (you will enjoy it, too).

Do not be misled by the fact that in giving the form of an analogical argument above I used four things (*A, B, C,* and *D*) and four features (*W, X, Y,* and *Z*). This was merely for convenience. An analogical argument can compare two things with respect to two features:

Philosophy of Art and Philosophy of Religion are each philosophy courses.

I did very well in Philosophy of Art.

Therefore, I'll do very well in Philosophy of Religion.

Or an analogical argument can compare a hundred things with respect to many features:

Hydrochloric acid, sulphuric acid, . . . , and citric acid (you mention a hundred substances) are each proton donors, each turns litmus red, each dissociates in water to yield hydrogen ions, each reacts with zinc to yield hydrogen gas, . . . (you mention a few more similarities).

Hydrochloric acid, sulphuric acid, . . . (you mention ninety-nine of the hundred substances, all except citric acid) each tastes sour.

Therefore, citric acid tastes sour.

Each is an analogical argument, because each attempts to predict that the unknown will be similar to the known.

The task for inductive logic is to frame rules for judging the strength of an analogical argument. Just as inductive generalizations can be Strong, Medium, or Weak, so too can analogical arguments.

10.2 Similarity and Relevance

The reason we need analogical arguments is that we often know that two (or more) things are similar in some respects, but we do not (yet) know that they are similar in other respects. In the first sample analogical argument, we knew that *Carrie, 'Salem's Lot, The Shining,* and *Christine* were similar in some respects (novels, by Stephen King, in the horror genre); but we did not (yet) know that they were similar in other respects (i.e., whether *Christine* would be enjoyed by me).

If we *knew* that two things—two apples, for example—were similar in *all* respects, except for the fact that they are separate objects (and so one may be in the refrigerator and the other on the counter), then we would know that if the first apple tastes sour then the second apple will also taste sour. That is, we would have a Deductively Valid argument:

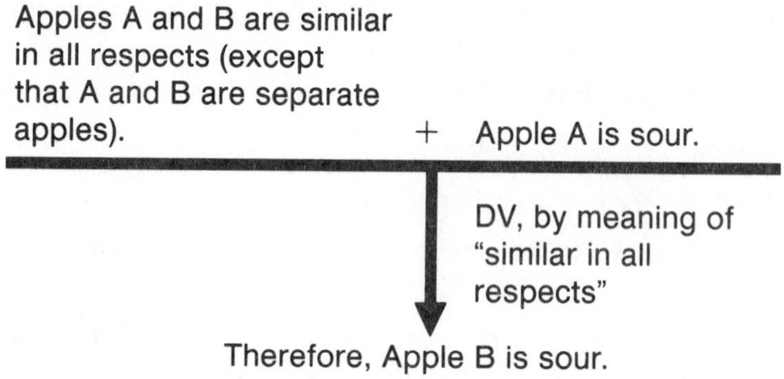

Apples A and B are similar in all respects (except that A and B are separate apples). + Apple A is sour.

DV, by meaning of "similar in all respects"

Therefore, Apple B is sour.

However, often we do not know that two things are similar in all respects. The usual case is this: We have two apples, *A* and *B*. We bite into *A*, and discover that apple *A* is sour. We then make an analogical argument (i.e., an inductive argument) that apple *B* will be sour too:

Apples A *and* B *are similar: Each came from the same tree, each is about the same size, each was picked at the same time, and each has the same color.*

Apple A *is sour. (You just tasted it.)*

Therefore, apple B *will be sour too*

The basis for our trust in analogical arguments is the assumption (discussed in 9.3), "Similar things will have similar qualities." That is, we assume that when we know that two or more things are similar in a number of respects, they are likely to be similar in other respects. And that is just what an analogical argument purports to establish.

A few definitions will make the rules for evaluating analogical arguments easier to state.

The **UNKNOWN INSTANCE** in an analogical argument is the item (or items) our efforts at discovery are aimed at. In the Stephen King–argument the unknown instance was *Christine*; in the philosophy-argument the unknown instance was *Philosophy of Religion*; and in the acid-argument the unknown instance was *citric acid.*

The **UNKNOWN PROPERTY** in an analogical argument is the feature (or features) we are investigating in the unknown instance(s). In the Stephen King–argument the unknown property was *will be enjoyed by me*; in the philosophy-argument the unknown property was *will do well in*; and in the acid-argument the unknown property was *tastes sour.*

The **KNOWN INSTANCE(S)** in an analogical argument is the set of items less the unknown instance some of whose features we already know. In the Stephen King–argument the known instances were *Carrie, 'Salem's Lot,* and *The Shining*; in the philosophy-argument the known instance was *Philosophy of Art*; and in the acid-argument the known instances were hydrochloric acid, sulphuric acid, and 97 other substances.

The **KNOWN PROPERTIES** in an analogical argument is the set of features you already know are had by both the known and unknown instances. In the Stephen King–argument, the known properties were *being a novel, by Stephen King,* and *in the horror genre.* In the philosophy course-argument, there was only one known property: *being a philosophy course.* In the acid-argument, there were a number of known properties: *being a proton donor, turning litmus red, dissociating in water to yield hydrogen ions, reacting with zinc to yield hydrogen gas,* and more.

Since it's important for you to understand these terms and how they pick out the parts of analogical arguments, here is a brief schematic review. Consider an analogical argument of this form:

I know that A, B, C, *and* D *each have features* W, X, *and* Y.

I know that in addition A, B, *and* C *each have feature* Z.

Therefore, D *also has feature* Z.

The unknown instance is *D*: This is the item under investigation. The unknown property is feature *Z*: You're wondering whether *D* has *Z*. The known instances are *A, B,* and *C*: You already know a few things about them. The known properties are features *W, X,* and *Y*: You already know that the known instances (*A, B,* and *C*) and the unknown instance (*D*) share these.

The first rule for assessing an analogical argument is:

SIMILARITY. The more known features shared between the known instances and the unknown instance, the stronger the argument. The fewer known features shared between the known instances and the unknown instance, the weaker the argument.

Take the philosophy-argument. This version of it:

Philosophy of Art and Philosophy of Religion are each philosophy courses.

I did very well in Philosophy of Art.

Therefore, I'll do very well in Philosophy of Religion.

is surely weaker than this version of it:

Philosophy of Art and Philosophy of Religion are each philosophy courses, each is taught by the same professor, each has multiple choice exams, neither has a term paper.

I did very well in Philosophy of Art.

Therefore, I'll do very well in Philosophy of Religion.

The second version contains more similarities—shares more known features—between the known instances and the unknown instance.

The SIMILARITY rule for analogical arguments is like the QUANTITY rule for inductive generalizations. The QUANTITY rule told us that the more instances (observations) in an inductive generalization, the stronger that argument will be. The SIMILARITY rule tells us that the more features shared among the known and unknown instances in an analogical argument, the stronger that argument will be.

Corresponding to the SIMILARITY rule, there is a fallacy that renders any analogical argument Weak:

FALLACIOUS DISANALOGY. Any striking dissimilarity (disanalogy) between the known and unknown instances makes the analogical argument Weak.

The striking dissimilarity need not be explicitly stated in the analogical argument; but if you know such a disanalogy exists, you must pronounce the argument Weak. For example, suppose an astronomer in the eighteenth century were to make this analogical argument:

We know that all the planets revolve around the sun and receive its light and heat, each is spherical, and each is a solid mass.

We know that the Earth has organic life forms.

Therefore, the other planets must also have organic life forms.

But you know that there are striking disanalogies between the Earth and the other planets: The Earth has an atmosphere, water, and moderate temperatures capable of supporting organic life forms. The other planets lack one or the other of these features. Since there are disanalogies that make the astronomer's argument fallacious, the argument commits the fallacy of FALLACIOUS DISANALOGY, and is therefore Weak.

The SIMILARITY rule is not sufficient for evaluating analogical arguments, as this example will show:

I know that Adam, Bob, Cal, Dave, and Ed are each six feet tall, each has a mustache, each is a black male, and each goes to the same church.

I know that Adam, Bob, Cal and Dave are highly intelligent.

Therefore, Ed is highly intelligent too.

Something is wrong with this argument. True, there are a number of similarities between the known instances (Adam, Bob, Cal, and Dave) and the unknown instance (Ed). Each is the same height, has a mustache, is black, and attends the same church. But these similarities are irrelevant to intelligence. In other words, even though the known and unknown instances have much else in common, we cannot infer much about intelligence. We need another rule to sort this out:

RELEVANCE. The known properties must be relevant to the unknown property.

If the RELEVANCE rule is violated, we have a fallacious argument:

IRRELEVANT ANALOGY. If the known properties are irrelevant to the unknown property, the argument contains irrelevant analogies and is therefore Weak.

The RELEVANCE rule for analogical arguments is like the UNIFORMITY rule for inductive generalizations. The UNIFORMITY rule told us that inductive generalizations about populations where there is little expectation of uniform behavior are likely to be Weak. The RELEVANCE rule tells us that analogical arguments where there is only a "surface" similarity are also likely to be Weak. In effect, both RELEVANCE and UNIFORMITY say: Beware of merely accidental or coincidental uniform behavior or similar features.

The SIMILARITY and RELEVANCE rules along with their corresponding errors, FALLACIOUS DISANALOGY and IRRELEVANT ANALOGY, allow us to evaluate analogical arguments. Since analogical arguments are common and of somewhat different kinds, we'll examine some instances in the following sections.

10.3 Everyday Analogical Arguments

In everyday circumstances we often attempt to gain knowledge of the unknown by analogy with our knowledge of the known. A number of everyday analogical arguments are discussed below. Because some of these arguments are to some extent made-up, we can only point out considerations that would be raised in assessing their strength. We cannot always say that the argument is (or is not) Strong.

Shopping:

I owned a pair of Portrock shoes, and they were comfortable and lasted a long time.

Here is another pair of Portrock shoes in the shoe store.

They too will be comfortable and last a long time.

Is this a Strong argument? The only similarity mentioned in the argument is that both pairs of shoes are the same brand. This is not an irrelevant analogy, as it would be if the only similarity mentioned was that both pairs of shoes were brown (which is irrelevant to comfort and wear). But you must consider whether there are any striking dissimilarities. Perhaps the pair you owned were loafers and had thick rubber soles; perhaps the new pair you are considering buying are tie shoes with thin leather soles. These dissimilarities would tend to weaken the analogical argument.

Dating:

I've dated Arlene, Beth, and Cindy. Each was a lawyer, and although they were intelligent and pretty, I never had a good time with any one of them on a date.

I've just been introduced to Darlene, who's also a lawyer and seems intelligent. She's certainly pretty.

But I conclude that I wouldn't have a good time on a date with Darlene.

Is this a Strong argument? You must consider whether the analogies are relevant. Is there something about lawyers that makes for a bad date (for you)? Something about intelligent women? Something about pretty women? Or is it just a coincidence that Arlene, Beth, and Cindy happened to be intelligent, pretty lawyers with whom you never had a good time? (The answer here cannot be given absolutely for everyone. Maybe there's some quirk about you such that *you* would have a bad time on a date with any lawyer. If so, as the argument pertains to *you* there might not be any striking disanalogies. But as the argument pertains to someone else, it might contain irrelevant analogies.)

Voting:

Representative Jones has in her twenty-four years in Congress been a strong supporter of unions.

She's up for reelection this year.

If reelected, she'll continue to be a strong supporter of unions.

This is a somewhat unusual analogical argument. The known instances are Representative Jones's twenty-four years of strong support of unions. The unknown instance is her continued strong support of unions if reelected. (In effect, the argument concludes that Representative Jones's future politics will be similar to her past politics.) The similarities are certainly relevant. It's not as if the argument said that for twenty-four years Representative Jones wore a hat and took the bus to Capitol Hill, and therefore could be expected to support unions. The issue in assessing the strength of this argument is whether there are any striking disanalogies. If Representative Jones, for example, avoided reaffirming her strong commitment to unions during her election campaign, say by side-stepping questions on the issue, you might conclude that the argument is not Strong—or is even Weak by virtue of a FALLACIOUS DISANALOGY.

Everyday science:

I've painted my house with Flemish Boy exterior latex paint five times, and each time it lasted five years before beginning to chip and flake.

I'm going to paint my house again with Flemish Boy exterior latex paint again.

Therefore, it will last five years before beginning to chip and flake.

Science is not the monopoly of the physicist or chemist working in the laboratory. Each of us does science, as the above analogical argument shows: We make predictions about the future based on similarities with the past.

Is the paint-argument Strong? The analogies would appear to be relevant: the new paint is the same brand and kind as the old. Could there be striking disanalogies? Consider the color and condition of the house. Suppose the previous colors were in the light brown family, and the new color was dark blue. You should consider the possibility that dark colors do not last as long as light colors. Or perhaps the wood of the house has deteriorated over time, and consequently will not hold a coat of paint as well as it did twenty-five years ago.

These remarks are put forth as considerations for the evaluation of the argument, not as definite objections to it. If any of them are true, then there would be disanalogies between the previous behavior of the paint and the present, disanalogies that would lead us to call the argument less than Strong.

Miscellaneous analogical arguments:

The current campaign in China to discourage couples from having more than one child seems to Americans totalitarian and an unacceptable invasion of privacy. However we must realize that China has undertaken this policy because they perceive a steadily growing population as a serious threat to their already strained agricultural resources. We in America grant that serious threats often justify force on the part of the government. Many think drafting citizens to face a serious threat is justified; many think it is acceptable for the government to require inoculations of school children; many find nothing wrong with quarantining victims of highly infectious and deadly diseases. Since these things are not perceived as totalitarian or unjustified invasions of privacy by many Americans, perhaps we should change our attitude towards China's birth control policy.

This analogical argument claims that China's policy is strongly discouraging more than one child per couple is practiced, not because the Chinese merely want to intrude into family affairs, but because they perceive a steadily expanding population as a serious national threat. The argument further claims that we Americans, who think of ourselves as freedom-loving and democratic, are also willing to curtail freedoms in the face of serious threats to the general well-being. It concludes that we Americans ought to rethink our attitudes towards China.

This is a difficult analogical argument to evaluate. The analogies drawn do not seem to be irrelevant: There are real similarities between China's childbearing policy and certain policies pursued by America's democratic government. The question, then, appears to be: Are there any FALLACIOUS

DISANALOGIES between China's childbearing policy and American acceptance of the draft, inoculating children, and quarantining victims of highly infectious, deadly diseases? Perhaps the decision to have children is significantly more private and personal. Perhaps it can be argued that there is a natural right to bear children, with which no government can interfere, but that there is no natural right to ignore a clear danger to national security (e.g., no right to avoid the draft), or to go to school, or to endanger others with some disease. This latter course of reasoning would show some weakness in the argument, though it itself turns on the controversial premise that there is a natural right to bear children that cannot be interfered with. (In a time of famine, can it be morally permissible to bear as many children as one chooses?)

Logic can tell you to look for irrelevant analogies or fallacious disanalogies. But logic cannot incontrovertibly show you which analogies are irrelevant or fallacious.

Often, analogical arguments are expressed as enthymemes:

> *We do not punish people for being left-handed or forbid the use of sign language by the deaf. So why should we punish or forbid homosexual acts between consenting adults?*

An enthymeme (see section 7.4) is an argument in which a premise is not explicitly stated. Inductive, as well as deductive, arguments can be enthymemes. The argument above is an analogical argument that is an enthymeme: It needs a premise that is not explicitly stated. The premise it needs is one that points out the similarities between being left-handed or being deaf on the one side, and being homosexual on the other side:

> *Homosexuality is like being left-handed or deaf: It is, in general, a condition that is not chosen by a person.*

This analogy—the analogy stated in the missing premise—does not seem to be irrelevant. The evaluation of the complete argument turns on whether there are any FALLACIOUS DISANALOGIES between homosexuality and left-handedness or deafness. Homosexuality involves sex, but left-handedness or deafness in themselves do not. Many people disapprove of homosexuality, but few if any disapprove of left-handedness or deafness. Are these disanalogies striking enough to render the argument less than Strong?

That homosexuality involves sex is not in itself a striking disanalogy, for the argument trades on whether something is or is not freely chosen by someone. True, homosexuals *could* refrain from homosexual acts; but left-handed people *could*, however inconveniently, use their right hands to write and the deaf *could* refrain from signing. That many people disapprove of homosexuality (but not of left-handedness or deafness) might seem to be a striking disanalogy, although it must be remembered that the argument is intended to point out that there may be no reason for such disapproval, given that homosexuality is in general a condition that is not chosen. (Resolution left to the reader.)

10.4 Analogical Arguments in the Law

Analogical arguments are an important tool in legal reasoning. There is a basic principle of fairness in Anglo-American law: *Like cases must be treated alike*. Just as it would be unfair for the parent to punish Jack for lying but not Jill for the same offense, it would be unfair for the judge to fine Corporation A for pollution but not Corporation B.

However, what is sometimes unclear in particular cases is whether they are "like" other cases. Suppose there is a law that says, "Vehicles are not permitted in the park," and establishes a $50 fine for any violations. If the judge fines Bob for driving his car in the park, it would be unfair of him not to fine Carol for driving her car in the park. But suppose Carol drove through the park, not in a car but in a truck. Is this case like Bob's? Suppose she drove through the park on a bicycle? Is this case like Bob's?

Judges are often faced with hard cases, and one way a case can be hard is that it brings forth an instance in which it is unclear whether the new instance is or is not like old instances. Carol's driving through the park in the truck or bicycle is a simple example of a hard case. The judge, in such hard cases, must construct analogical arguments, perhaps arguing:

Cars and bicycles have wheels and are used as transportation.

I've fined the driver of a car for violating the law.

Therefore, I must fine the driver of a bicycle for violating the law.

However, Carol's lawyer might attempt to point out that the judge's analogical argument is not Strong because there are disanalogies between cars and bicycles that make the argument fallacious. Her lawyer might point out that cars are noisier than bicycles, that cars spew forth exhaust fumes but bicycles don't, and that cars are more dangerous to pedestrians than bicycles. In effect, Carol's lawyer is trying to establish that Carol's case is *un*like Bob's.

New inventions, processes, and the like often make for hard cases. It had been established for a long time that the First Amendment right of free speech applied not only to verbal utterances but also to written material. But around the turn of the century the motion picture was invented. Should the First Amendment right of free speech also apply to the movies? Like cases must be treated alike, but are movies like speeches and books? It was eventually decided that they were, on these grounds:

Speeches, written material, and movies are public expressions of personal opinion or outlook.

It is long established that speeches and written material are protected by the First Amendment.

Therefore, movies too are protected by the First Amendment.

This seems to be a Strong argument, but perhaps the reader can discover fallacious disanalogies. (Keep in mind that to be protected by the First Amendment means that the state cannot by law interfere with public speech, e.g., by seizing movies it disagrees with.)

10.5 Analogical Arguments in Metaphysics

Philosophy has occasional recourse to analogical arguments. A well-known case is the so-called problem of other minds.

I have access to my own mental states. I know that I think, doubt, feel pain, am sometimes happy, am sometimes tired, and so on. Do other people think, doubt, feel pain, and so on as well? Or are they automatons—complex, organic robots? If you think you know that other people think, doubt, feel pain, and the rest, how do you know this?

It is crucial to recognize that the philosophical problem of other minds concerns essentially private, interior states. There is no doubt that people have bodies, that they say things like, "I thought I saw a pussy cat" or "I feel exhausted," or that their faces curl up and their eyes shed tears when they bang their bare toe against the radiator. The question is: Do they have *interior* mental states, like I do, that correspond to these outward behavioral displays?

One prominent solution to the problem of other minds is an analogical argument, which could be stated like this:

> *It is certain at least to me that I have thoughts, doubts, feelings of pain and of fatigue, and many other mental states.*
>
> *Other people are like me: Their bodies are similar, they speak, they sometimes say "Ow! That really hurt" or "Boy, I'm exhausted."*
>
> *Therefore, other people have minds just as I do: They experience internal states such as thinkings, doubtings, and feelings of pain and fatigue.*

One noteworthy feature of analogical arguments in metaphysics is that their conclusions are generally not verifiable in any other way. If you make this everyday argument,

> *Wines* A, B, C, *and* D *are each burgundies, each made from California grapes, and each three years old.*
>
> *Wines* A, B, *and* C *were full-bodied and went well with steak au poivre.*
>
> *Therefore wine* D *will be full-bodied and will go well with steak au poivre.*

you can verify the conclusion. Even if you count the argument as Strong, you can always uncork wine *D* and test if the conclusion is true. But you can't "uncork" people's heads to see if they have minds. (You will see that they have brains, but this is not the same thing.) So the analogical solution to the problem of other minds completely depends on whether we count the analogical argument as Strong.

The question as to whether the analogical argument about the existence of other minds is Strong is not easy to resolve.

For. Other people are so much externally like me. Their bodies are shaped very much like mine. Other people look more like me than they do like, say, a cheese or a dog. They seem to speak a language, and in speaking often and clearly seem to express thoughts or feelings. They flinch if they touch the hot end of a cigarette, collapse on the couch after a long hike. These similarities are sufficient in number and sufficiently relevant to make a Strong argument.

Against. The shape of other people's bodies is not a particularly relevant similarity. We could imagine (even if we couldn't prove) other beings—from outer space, for example—whose bodies were as different from ours as ours is from a wheel of cheese, and could imagine (even if we couldn't prove) that such beings had thoughts, pains, and the rest. In addition, a computer could be taught to say "Ouch" if you banged on it, or "I'm really bushed" at the end of a long day. But it is hard to believe that this amounts to good evidence that the computer *feels* pain or *feels* tired. In short, the analogical argument about other minds suffers from probable IRRELEVANT ANALOGY, and if not Weak, is not clearly Strong.

The resolution is left as an exercise to the reader.

KEY POINTS

An analogy is a statement of similarity.

- In an analogy, two (or more) things are said to be alike, or alike in certain respects.
- An analogy by itself is not an argument, for it is merely a statement. But analogies can be premises of arguments.

An analogical argument is an inductive argument that employs an analogy as a premise.

- An analogical argument begins by stating that some things (*A*, *B*, and *C*) are alike in certain respects (*X* and *Y*).
- It proceeds by next stating that it is further known that some of these things (*A* and *B*) are also alike in another respect (*Z*).
- It concludes by inferring that the other thing (C) also has this feature (*Z*).

The basis for our trust in analogical arguments is the assumption that similar things will have similar qualities. Hence, the degree of similarity is important in evaluating analogical arguments.

Some definitions of the parts of an analogical argument:

- The unknown instance in an analogical argument is the item (or items) our efforts at discovery are aimed at.
- The unknown property in an analogical argument is the feature (or features) we are investigating in the unknown instance(s).
- The known instance(s) in an analogical argument are the items (other than the unknown instance) some of whose features we already know.
- The known properties in an analogical argument are the features you already know are had by both the known and unknown instances.

The rules for evaluating analogical arguments, and their attendant fallacies, are:

- SIMILARITY. The more known features shared between the known and the unknown instance, the stronger the argument. The fewer known features shared between the known instances and the unknown instance, the weaker the argument.
- FALLACIOUS DISANALOGY. Any striking dissimilarity (disanalogy) between the known and the unknown instances makes the analogical argument Weak.
- RELEVANCE. The known properties must be relevant to the unknown property.
- IRRELEVANT ANALOGY. If the known properties are irrelevant to the unknown property, the argument contains irrelevant analogies and is therefore Weak.

The SIMILARITY rule for analogical arguments is like the QUANTITY rule for inductive generalizations. The RELEVANCE rule is like the UNIFORMITY rule for inductive generalizations.

A number of different kinds of analogical argument were discussed. Two points should be kept in mind:

- The rules and fallacies for analogical arguments must be attended to conscientiously. Be especially alert for striking disanalogies and for irrelevant analogies between the known and unknown instances.
- It is sometimes difficult to come to a definite conclusion about the degree of validity of an analogical argument—especially when the argument is made up for textbook purposes and we are accordingly not in possession of all the facts.

EXERCISES

A. Some of the following are analogical arguments, some are just analogies. For each:

1. Decide whether it is an argument or not. If it is not an argument, say so and go on to the next problem.
2. If it is an argument, evaluate its degree of validity: Deductively Valid, Strong, Medium, or Weak. You may "split" your answer, e.g., Strong-Medium.
3. Justify your evaluation. Why did you say the argument was, for example, Weak? Why did you say the argument was Strong-Medium, rather than Strong or Medium?
4. If it is an argument that is missing a premise (i.e., if it's an enthymeme), supply the missing premise before evaluating the argument.

A1. A few months ago, when Sidney Harris's column was reduced from five times to three times per week, Bob Talbert remarked that it looked like columnist Lewis Grizzard would be a fine replacement for Harris.

After reading Grizzard's column for the past few months, I consider Talbert's comment to be roughly equivalent to saying that the Sistine Chapel could adequately be repainted with a Wagner power roller. (L.Q., Letter, *Detroit Free Press,* July 8, 1985.)

***A2.** James is six years old. His sister Joan is twelve years old. James says to his mother, "You let Joan stay up until eleven. We're both your children. You should let me stay up until eleven too."

It is an argument. In particular, it is an enthymeme, and requires the missing premise, "What you let Joan do you should let me do." But it is a Weak argument, for there is a disanalogy strong enough to render the argument fallacious: twelve-year-olds and six-year-olds need not have the same bedtimes, for six-year-olds need more sleep (and in general have fewer privileges).

A3. After a number of people had been attacked by pit bulls in Florida, there was a proposal to ban all pit bulls from urban areas. Someone, objecting, said, "It's like arguing: We should imprison everyone because this will keep the bad people from hurting anyone." (Reported on "All Things Considered," August 7, 1985.)

A4. The porpoise has lungs, warm blood, hair, and nurses its young with milk. Human beings, too, have lungs, warm blood, hair, and nurse their young with milk. Therefore the porpoise has bones, a four-chambered heart, nerves, and blood vessels.

a. In this argument (yes, it's an argument), name its parts.

The unknown instance:

The unknown properties:

The known instances:

The known properties:

b. Evaluate its degree of validity and justify your evaluation.

A5. Just as we need more police to deal with traffic problems than we did 75 years ago, so we need more [Supreme] courts to deal with cases. (Former Justice Warren Burger.)

A6. Interracial marriage is unnatural. Canaries do not mate with sparrows, goldfish do not mate with trout, and cats do not mate with dogs.

A7. It is essential for parents to provide guidance for their children. A vine needs a pole to grow on, and so children need a firm hand from their parents.

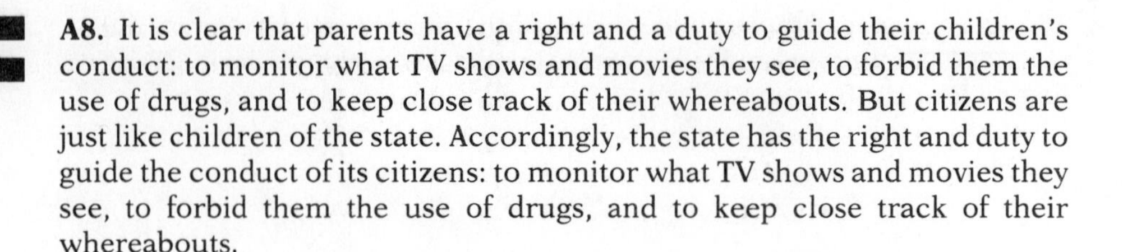

A8. It is clear that parents have a right and a duty to guide their children's conduct: to monitor what TV shows and movies they see, to forbid them the use of drugs, and to keep close track of their whereabouts. But citizens are just like children of the state. Accordingly, the state has the right and duty to guide the conduct of its citizens: to monitor what TV shows and movies they see, to forbid them the use of drugs, and to keep close track of their whereabouts.

A9. Saying that fermentation causes bacteria (rather than the other way around) is like saying that the waterwheel makes the river flow (rather than the other way around).

A10. Any invasion of privacy (e.g., reading a private letter, eavesdropping on a private conversation, peeking through a keyhole) is like theft: It takes something without permission. And since theft is wrong and forbidden by law, so too are invasions of privacy. They too are wrong and ought to be forbidden by law.

A11. Surgeons have X-rays to guide them during an operation. Carpenters have blueprints to guide them when they build a house. Lawyers have briefs to guide them during a trial. So students should be allowed to look at their textbooks during examinations.

A12. I know that I sometimes feel sad, sometimes feel pain, sometimes feel anxious, sometimes feel joy. My dog is very much like me: He's a mammal, warm-blooded, has a brain. He even looks sad or anxious or happy sometimes. He yelps if I step on his paw. Therefore, my dog has feelings just like me.

A13. We know that when a large, heavy object impacts on the earth it makes a hole proportionate to the size of the object. The craters on the moon look like these holes on earth. Therefore, the craters on the moon were made when large, heavy objects struck the surface of the moon.

A14. The universe as a whole resembles an ordinary watch: Each has parts that coordinate and operate with other parts; all of the parts of each seem to be needed, for there seems to be, both in the universe and in the watch, nothing extraneous; and in each there is order, continuity, and harmony, not chaos. We know that an intelligence designed the watch. Must we not conclude that an intelligence designed the universe?

In each of the following, you are first given an analogical argument. You are then given a variety of further statements. You are to assume the statement to be true, and decide what effect, if any, it would have on the degree of validity of the argument. Write:

S = The statement, if true, would tend to make the argument Stronger.

W = The statement, if true, would tend to make the argument Weaker.

N = The statement, if true, would have no effect on the degree of validity of the argument.

Note: Do not evaluate the initial argument. Just say whether each supposition would tend to make the initial argument strong*er* or weak*er* (or neither).

B. Books, magazines, and newspapers are forms of expression protected by the First Amendment's right to free speech. Movies are just like books, magazines, and newspapers: forms of expression. Therefore movies, too, are protected by the First Amendment's right to free speech.

___*N*___ ***B1.** Suppose movies are largely mere fictions (made-up stories).

___*N*___ ***B2.** Suppose movies are made for private profit.

_______ **B3.** Suppose movies are mostly pictures, while books, magazines, and newspapers are mostly words.

_______ **B4.** Suppose movies *show* (picture) violent or sexual acts, while books, magazines, and newspapers merely *describe* such things.

_______ **B5.** Suppose movies need special equipment to view (projectors, screens) but books, magazines, and newspapers do not need special equipment to read (apart from eyes).

Note: B1 and B2 are marked "N" because these suppositions even if true would not distinguish movies from books, magazines, and newspapers, for some of these are also mere fictions or written for private profit, yet are still under the protection of the First Amendment.

C. I've had half a dozen shirts. Each came out of the dryer with hardly a wrinkle in it. Therefore this new shirt I've just bought will come out of the dryer almost wrinkle-free.

_______ **C1.** Suppose the half-dozen shirts were permanent press but the new shirt is all cotton.

_______ **C2.** Suppose the half-dozen shirts were white and the new shirt is blue.

_______ **C3.** Suppose the half-dozen shirts and the new shirt were made by the same manufacturer.

_______ **C4.** Suppose the half-dozen shirts were made in Korea but the new shirt was made in Taiwan.

_______ **C5.** Suppose the half-dozen shirts and the new shirt are made from the same kind of fabric.

D. A motel owner predicts that her business will be very good this coming summer, given that the three previous summers' business was very good. Which supposition would strengthen (S), which would weaken (W), which would have no effect (N) towards drawing this conclusion?

_______ **D1.** Suppose that the three previous summers occurred during economic prosperity, but that an economic recession is now under way.

_______ **D2.** Suppose that an amusement park near her motel, which had operated during the three previous summers, just closed up.

_______ **D3.** Suppose that the motel owner has decided not to make any repairs or do any repainting for the coming summer.

_______ **D4.** Suppose that the price of gas will go up drastically before the coming summer.

_______ **D5.** Suppose that the motel owner turns out to be right: During the coming summer her business is very good indeed.

E. Harold decides to go out for pizza to Aldo's, his favorite pizzeria, but when he gets there he discovers that it is closed for remodeling. But Benno's pizzeria is open. Harold argues: Aldo's and Benno's are pizzerias. Aldo's serves great pizza. So, I conclude, will Benno's. Which supposition would strengthen (S), which would weaken (W), which would have no effect (N) toward drawing this conclusion?

_______ **E1.** Suppose that Aldo's and Benno's are owned by the same person.

_______ **E2.** Suppose that Aldo's and Benno's are in the same city.

_______ **E3.** Suppose that Aldo's and Benno's use the same pizza recipe.

_______ **E4.** Suppose that Harold turns out to be wrong: The pizza at Benno's is not as good as the pizza at Aldo's.

_______ **E5.** Suppose that Harold loves anchovies on his pizza.

F. Judge Solomon hears two cases: Each involves robbery at gunpoint. The defendants Harley and Davidson are each convicted by a jury. Judge Solomon argues: Since I sentenced Harley to five years in prison, I must—to be fair—sentence Davidson to five years in prison.

_______ **F1.** Suppose that Harley has committed this very crime in the past, but this is Davidson's first offense.

_______ **F2.** Suppose that Davidson is married but that Harley is single.

_______ **F3.** Suppose that Harley was unemployed but that Davidson has a job.

_______ **F4.** Suppose that Harley used a more powerful gun than Davidson.

_______ **F5.** Suppose that Harley is black and Davidson is white.

CHAPTER 11

CAUSAL ARGUMENTS

Another kind of inductive argument attempts to determine the cause of some event. This is the causal argument. We will learn what "the cause of an event" means, what a causal argument is, Mill's Methods for establishing causal arguments, and two fallacies that make any causal argument weak. The key concepts of this chapter include:

CAUSAL STATEMENT

CAUSAL ARGUMENT and fallacies such an argument can commit:
POST HOC FALLACY
CONFUSING CAUSE AND EFFECT

MILL'S METHODS for assessing causal arguments:
METHOD OF AGREEMENT
METHOD OF DIFFERENCE
JOINT METHOD
METHOD OF CONCOMITANT VARIATION

CAUSAL HYPOTHESIS

MASS and SINGULAR PHENOMENA

11.1 "The" Cause of an Event

The lights in the house flicker and go off completely. What caused them to do this? Medical science wonders about the cause of leukemia. The insurance company wonders what caused the damage to the building. The jury has to decide whether the cause of someone's death was suicide or murder. Although it might seem that we understand the question perfectly well and it is only the answer we don't (yet) know, in fact the concept of *cause* is not well understood and is the topic is philosophical controversy.

To cite the cause of something is to make a causal statement. A causal statement is of the form,

A *(or* A *and* B *and . . .) caused* X.

where the capital letters stand for events. An event is, simply, something that happened. A **CAUSAL STATEMENT** claims that one or more circumstances, *A* (or *A* and *B* and . . .) stand in a certain relation, which we call "causal," to another event or events, *X*.

Suppose a certain barn burned down. This is an event, and it is the event we wish to seek the cause of. We want to know what other event or events that preceded the barn's burning down is the cause of the barn's burning down. Maybe "we" are an insurance company, or arson investigators, or the distraught but curious owners of the barn. It doesn't matter. What is it we are looking for in looking for the cause of the barn's burning down?

Suppose we discover that a horse kicked over a kerosene lantern. That is, we know that a certain event, which we'll label (A), occurred:

(A) The horses' kicking over a kerosene lantern.

We then put forth the following causal statement:

(S1) (A) caused the barn to burn down.

This answer, if justified, would be enough to satisfy the insurance company or arson investigator or barn owner.

But from another viewpoint, the horse's kicking over the kerosene lantern cannot *in itself* be "the" cause of the barn's burning down. After all, fire cannot start or continue without oxygen; the lantern wouldn't have fallen over without gravity; and the straw wouldn't have ignited unless the lantern gave off sufficient heat. Let's list these:

(B) The presence of oxygen.

(C) The presence of gravity.

(D) The presence of sufficient heat.

Perhaps what we should have said is:

(S2) (A), (B), (C), and (D) caused the barn to burn down.

But even (S2) is not the "whole" story, for the horse couldn't have kicked the lantern over unless he was born; the lantern had to have been placed where the horse could reach it; the horse had to have sufficient strength (e.g., not be too ill) to kick the lantern over. Let's also list these:

(E) The horse's having been born.

(F) The lantern's having been placed where the horse could reach it.

(G) The horse's having sufficient strength to kick the lantern over.

Now we might feel we have to make this causal statement:

(S3) (A), (B), (C), (D), (E), (F), and (G) caused the barn to burn down.

Well, why stop here? The horse's mother had to have been born, the lantern had to be manufactured, the builder of the barn had to build it, the builder had to have been born, and so on. But the "and so on" is so overwhelming here, for it suggests that to state the cause of the barn's burning down we have to tell the entire story of the world!

This, however, is crazy. (S1) is a perfectly acceptable causal statement. It's not that (S2) and (S3) are false exactly; it's just that they tell more than we wanted to hear. In speaking of "the" cause of something, we speak somewhat loosely. When we are told that the horse kicked over the lantern and this was the cause of the barn's burning down, we assume that certain other facts are also true. While the fire in the barn could not have started unless (B) through (G)—and much more!—were facts, we relegate these to the background. Hence conditions like those expressed in (B) through (G) are sometimes called **BACKGROUND CONDITIONS**. Background conditions are assumed to be true and to play some role in the causal process; but are not properly speaking part of what we mean by "the cause of an event."

What do we mean by "the cause of an event" if not "*everything* that had to have been true in order for the event to have occurred"? It seems that in looking for the cause of an event we are looking for some prior event that is out of the ordinary or unusual or novel. We tend to take for granted the presence of oxygen, gravity, sufficient heat, and the rest (as background conditions), and to look for the unusual. Here, then, is a definition:

"A caused X" means that A is among the set of events that played a role in making X happen, but A is out of the ordinary, novel, unusual, or otherwise of interest.

For example, someone might wonder how Anne Boleyn died. I say that she was beheaded or, to make a proper causal statement, "The beheading of Anne Boleyn caused her death." Now this is a true and satisfactory causal statement, although it disregards a huge number of background conditions. For example, it fails to mention that Anne Boleyn lost huge quantities of blood, that her heart stopped, that she was unable to breathe, that the executioner had to have been born, etc. My causal statement disregards these background conditions because it wants to get to what was unusual, novel, out of the ordinary about Anne Boleyn's death. It in effect says that it was Anne Boleyn's being beheaded that caused her death, and not her falling

from the Tower of London, having a heart attack, eating a poisoned mushroom, or any of the numberless other ways someone could die.

What we next have to investigate is how to discover the cause of an event—how to know whether some causal statement is true.

11.2 Causal Arguments and Their Fallacies

Sometimes we know well what the cause of an event was. If I hit my thumb with a hammer and feel pain, I know that the cause of my pain is having hit my thumb. But sometimes we don't know what the cause of an event was. Then we need a Strong argument justifying any causal statement we might put forth. An argument purporting to justify a causal statement is a **CAUSAL ARGUMENT**. The form of a causal argument is:

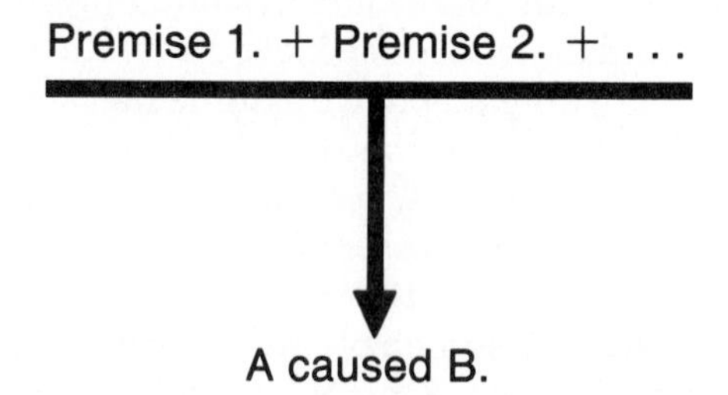

This does not tell you very much, except that you need some sort of premises to establish the conclusion. The problem is what sort of premises will make a causal argument Strong. We will look at one solution, Mill's Methods (although Mill's Methods are fallible and limited). But before proceeding to these, we should examine the pitfalls—or fallacies—causal arguments can fall into. There are at least two.

Post Hoc ergo Propter Hoc

This Latin phrase means, "After this, therefore because of this." For short, this is called the post hoc fallacy. It is a fundamental fact about causes that a cause must come before its effect. The **POST HOC FALLACY** points out that if we know *merely* that event *A* came before event *B*, we are not entitled to conclude that *A* causes *B* (in any sense of "cause"). The form of any Post Hoc Fallacy is this:

A occurred prior to B.

↓ Weak–Post Hoc Fallacy

A causes B.

Arguments of this sort are fallacious because we don't yet have evidence to believe that the earlier event, *A*, *made* the later event, *B*, happen. It may be mere coincidence that *A* happened and then *B* happened.

Suppose you observe that Joan broke a mirror and then lost her job (which was bad luck). Suppose you reason that breaking the mirror caused her to lose her job. In effect, you've made the argument that commits the post hoc fallacy:

Joan broke a mirror and then lost her job.

↓ Weak–Post Hoc Fallacy

Joan's breaking the mirror caused her to lose her job.

Confusing Cause with Effect

As with the post hoc fallacy, this fallacy trades on the fact that causes and effects are close together in time. A child viewing the waterwheel turning and the river flowing may conclude that the waterwheel causes the river to flow. The child has confused cause with the effect, for it is the river's flowing that causes the waterwheel to turn. The child's reasoning can be set out this way:

For many hours I have sat here, watching the waterwheel turning and the river flowing.

↓ Weak–Confusing Cause with Effect

The waterwheel's turning causes the river to flow.

Such an error in reasoning is not made only by children. For many years it was observed that there were bacteria present in fermenting liquids, e.g., in beer or sour milk. And for many years it was assumed that fermentation was some sort of decomposition of the liquid, a decomposition which caused the growth of bacteria. The reasoning was:

Over and over again, we have observed the presence of bacteria in fermenting liquids.

Weak–Confusing Cause with Effect

Fermentation causes bacteria.

Today we know that the presence of bacteria causes fermentation, not the other way around.

The Alleged Fallacy of Common Cause

Sometimes another fallacy is mentioned in connection with causal arguments, the fallacy of common cause. Suppose it is believed that

A *is the cause of* B.

But in fact there is another event, *C*, that is the cause of *A* and the cause of *B*, i.e.,

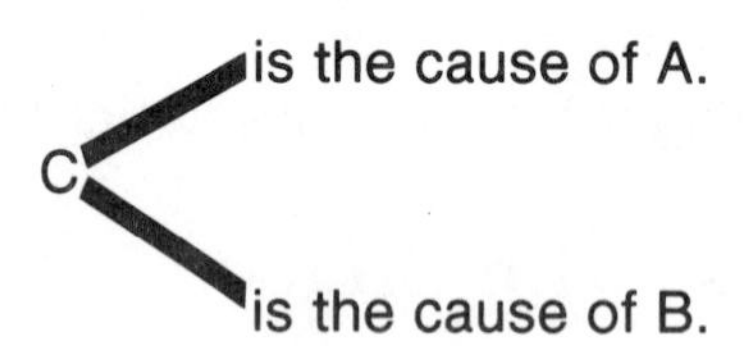

Then, to hold that *A* is the cause of *B* is said to commit the fallacy of common cause.

To be sure, if it is false that *A* is the cause of *B*, then it is a kind of fallacy (a fallacy of soundness) to believe so. And if it is true that it is really C that causes *A and* causes *B*, then it is natural to say that *A* and *B*, rather than themselves being in a causal relation, are in fact products of a common cause.

But is the fallacy of a common cause different from the post hoc fallacy? No, because it seems that the only reason for asserting "*A* causes *B*" in the first place is that *A* always comes before *B*.

We can see this if we look over a hypothetical example. A psychologist has a patient with the following case history: At age thirteen the patient became obese and then depressed. The psychologist might insist that the patient's becoming obese caused the patient to become depressed. The psychologist would be said to be in error if in fact there is a third factor—for example, having been rejected by his peers—that caused the patient's obesity *and* that caused his depression. The psychologist's error is just the post hoc fallacy.

11.3 Mill's Methods

Mill's Methods are designed to avoid the post hoc fallacy and confusing cause with effect. They are named after their propounder, the English philosopher John Stuart Mill (1806–1873), who described them in his *System of Logic* (1843). Mill formulated five of these methods. We will study four here: the method of agreement, the method of difference, the joint method of agreement and difference, and the method of concomitant variation.

The Method of Agreement

The method of agreement establishes one kind of causal argument. Suppose we are wondering what caused a certain event, *X*. We hypothesize (see 11.4 below for more on hypotheses) that another event, *A*, is the cause of *X*. The method of agreement tells us that if *A always* occurs before *X* in the instances we know of, then *A* can reasonably be said to be the cause of *X*. Schematically, the method of agreement can be put this way:

The Method of Agreement

Case	*Did A occur?*	*Did X then occur?*
#1	*Yes*	*Yes*
#2	*Yes*	*Yes*
#3	*Yes*	*Yes*
.	.	.
.	.	.
.	.	.
#n	*Yes*	*Yes*

Therefore, A is the cause of X.

For example, suppose that six students who have eaten in a cafeteria become ill. Each suffers from stomach pain and nausea. The method of agreement tells us: Look to see what circumstance (event) is *common* to all six students.

On the cafeteria menu, let us suppose, there were the following items: chicken soup (C), salad (S), turkey (T), gravy (G), mashed potatoes (P), and rice pudding (R). We interview each of the six students to determine what each ate at the cafeteria. We chart our results:

Student	What Was Eaten						Ill?
1	C	S	T		P	R	Yes
2		S	T	G		R	Yes
3	C		T	G	P	R	Yes
4	C	S		G	P	R	Yes
5	C	S	T			R	Yes
6		S	T	G	P	R	Yes

The method of agreement tells us that the event or circumstance in common is likely to be the cause. The only thing that is in common here is R: rice pudding. Thus we can conclude with some likelihood that eating rice pudding is the cause of the students' illness. Our causal argument is:

Student	What Was Eaten						Ill?
1	C	S	T		P	R	Yes
2		S	T	G		R	Yes
3	C		T	G	P	R	Yes
4	C	S		G	P	R	Yes
5	C	S	T			R	Yes
6		S	T	G	P	R	Yes

Therefore, rice pudding caused the students' illness.

The Method of Difference

The method of difference establishes another kind of causal argument. We are again wondering what caused a certain event, *X*, and hypothesize that event *A* caused *X*. The method of difference tells us that if the absences of *A* is constantly accompanied by the absence of *X*, then *A* can reasonably be said to be the cause of *A*. The method of difference, put simply, looks like this:

The Method of Difference

Case	Did A occur?	Did X then occur?
#1	No	No
#2	No	No
#3	No	No
.	.	.
.	.	.
.	.	.
#n	No	No

Therefore, A is the cause of X.

Suppose, again, that six students became ill (stomach pain, nausea) after eating in the cafeteria. Also suppose the ill students are too ill to be interviewed. We can interview the students who ate in the cafeteria but who did *not* become ill. The method of difference tells us to look to see if anything is different among students who did *not* get ill. Our interview results with the students who did not become ill are charted below:

Student	*What Was Eaten*					*Ill?*
7	*C*	*S*	*T*	*G*	*P*	*No*
8		*S*	*T*	*G*	*P*	*No*
9			*T*	*G.*	*P*	*No*
10	*C*		*T*		*P*	*No*
11		*S*		*G*	*P*	*No*
12	*C*	*S*	*T*		*P*	*No*

Examining the chart, we see that none of the students who did not become ill ate the rice pudding. We are entitled to conclude with some likelihood that it was the rice pudding that caused the illness of the students who became ill. Our causal argument is:

Student	*What Was Eaten*					*Ill?*
7	*C*	*S*	*T*	*G*	*P*	*No*
8		*S*	*T*	*G*	*P*	*No*
9			*T*	*G*	*P*	*No*
10	*C*		*T*		*P*	*No*
11		*S*		*G*	*P*	*No*
12	*C*	*S*	*T*		*P*	*No*

Therefore, the rice pudding caused the students' illness.

The Joint Method of Agreement and Difference

The joint method is not a new method, but simply a combination of the method of agreement and the method of difference:

The Joint Method

Case	*Did A occur?*	*Did X then occur?*
#1	*Yes*	*Yes*
#2	*No*	*No*
#3	*Yes*	*Yes*
.	.	.
.	.	.
.	.	.
#n	*No*	*No*

Therefore, A is the cause of X.

Using the same example, to apply the joint method we interview the students who became ill and the students who did not. Our results are tabulated below, as a causal argument with our conclusion:

Student	*What Was Eaten*						*Ill?*
1	*C*	*S*	*T*		*P*	*R*	*Yes*
2		*S*	*T*	*G*		*R*	*Yes*
3	*C*		*T*	*G*	*P*	*R*	*Yes*
4	*C*	*S*		*G*	*P*	*R*	*Yes*
5	*C*	*S*	*T*			*R*	*Yes*
6		*S*	*T*	*G*	*P*	*R*	*Yes*
7	*C*	*S*	*T*	*G*	*P*		*No*
8		*S*	*T*	*G*	*P*		*No*
9			*T*	*G*	*P*		*No*
10	*C*		*T*		*P*		*No*
11		*S*		*G*	*P*		*No*
12	*C*	*S*	*T*		*P*		*No*

Therefore, the rice pudding caused the student's illness.

The joint method shows both that rice pudding (R) was eaten by all who became ill (the method of agreement) and that rice pudding was not eaten by some who did not become ill (the method of difference).

The joint method is not, as you can see, a new method, but a combination of the other two methods. However, the joint method gives us a stronger argument than either the method of agreement or the method of difference used in isolation. The joint method not only tells us that eating rice pudding was the factor present in all the ill students, but that it was also the factor absent in six students who did not become ill.

The Method of Concomitant Variation

In the illness example above, we had a yes-or-no situation: A student either became ill or did not. Some events are not quite of this yes-or-no variety. We have events consisting of something increasing or something decreasing. The method of concomitant variation establishes a causal argument for such events. If *X* is the event we want to find the cause of, and if *X* is not a yes-or-no type of event, then the method of concomitant variation tells us to see if another event, *A*, always varies along (concomitantly) with *X*. The chart below gives us a simple form of the method of concomitant variation:

The Method of Concomitant Variation

Case	*State of A*	*State of X*
#1	*Increasing*	*Increasing*
#2	*Increasing*	*Increasing*
#3	*Decreasing*	*Decreasing*
.	.	.
.	.	.
.	.	.
#n	*Increasing*	*Increasing*

Therefore, A is the cause of X.

In effect, the method of concomitant variation is the joint method of agreement and difference applied to increasings and decreasings.

Let us take as our example rental rates in a certain motel in a resort area. Rental rates may hold steady (there is always a 75% occupancy rate). But rental rates may also vary. Sometimes they go down to a 50% occupancy rate; sometimes they increase to a 100% occupancy rate.

A certain motel owner notices that her motel rates, which for years have been at a steady 75% occupancy rate, have for the past eight years gone up and down. She decides to try to discover the cause of the variation. Since the event in question is not a "Did it occur? Yes or no" type, she uses the method of concomitant variation. She hypothesizes that it is the fluctuations in gasoline prices that cause the variations in her rental rates. She charts the two:

Year	*Average Occupancy Rate*	*Gas Price Per Gal.*
1979	*75%*	*$1.29*
1980	*70*	*1.34*
1981	*68*	*1.38*
1982	*65*	*1.41*
1983	*60*	*1.45*
1984	*55*	*1.51*
1985	*65*	*1.42*
1986	*80*	*1.12*

The chart shows that the average occupancy rate and the gasoline price vary together (concomitantly): The higher the price of gas, the lower the occupancy rate, and the lower the price of gas, the higher the occupancy rate. The method of concomitant variation says that this makes it likely that the price of gas causes the occupancy rate of the motel to increase and decrease. Thus the motel owner can conclude:

> *Therefore, fluctuations in the price of gas cause fluctuations in the rental rates in my motel.*

Any one of Mill's Methods must be supplemented by another rule, the QUANTITY rule discussed in Chapter 9:

QUANTITY. The larger the sample, the stronger the argument. The smaller the sample the weaker the argument. A Strong argument has a sufficiently large sample.

The sample in the case of causal arguments is simply the cases looked at. In our example of the ill students, we presented a sample of six in illustrating each of the methods of agreement and difference, and a sample of twelve in illustrating the joint method. In our example of the fluctuating motel occupancy rates, we had a sample size of eight. The QUANTITY rule simply says the larger the sample the stronger the argument and, vice-versa, the smaller the sample the weaker the argument. This argument

Student	*What Was Eaten*						*Ill?*
1	*C*	*S*	*T*		*P*	*R*	*Yes*
2	*C*	*S*	*T*	*G*	*P*		*No*

Therefore, the rice pudding caused the students' illness.

is certainly weaker—is at best Weak-Medium—than the full argument with a sample size of twelve.

The reason the QUANTITY rule is needed is that we want to distinguish genuine causal relations from mere coincidence. In the argument just above (with two students) it might be mere coincidence that one student who became ill ate the rice pudding while another who did not become ill did not eat the pudding. But when we have twelve students where this is true, the argument is Stronger since we have less probability of coincidence.

11.4 Hypotheses and Mill's Methods

Mill's Methods are designed to test a causal hypothesis. A **CAUSAL HYPOTHESIS** is a good guess as to the cause of some event. In the case of the ill students we in effect had to launch a hypothesis about the cause of their illness. We hypothesized that it was something each ate in the cafeteria. This was not unreasonable. After all, they became ill after eating in the cafeteria. But without some sort of hypothesis about the cause of their illness, Mill's Methods cannot begin to work.

Suppose we had no hypothesis, that is, we simply had no idea what caused the students' illness. Mill's Methods would be useless. We would have a chart something like this:

Student	*???*	*Ill?*
1		*Yes*
2		*Yes*
3		*Yes*
4		*Yes*
5		*Yes*
6		*Yes*
7		*No*
8		*No*
9		*No*
10		*No*
11		*No*
12		*No*

Such a chart tells us only that at least six students became ill, and at least six students did not, which we already knew. Such a chart tells us nothing whatsoever about the cause of the illness. Unless we have a hypothesis—something to put under the "???" of the chart above—we cannot begin to use Mill's Methods to test whether that hypothesis is the cause of the illness.

We know that the cause must precede its effect. However, there are innumerable events that preceded the students' illness. One event was that they ate certain things in the cafeteria. But they also studied, sat in chairs, took showers, spoke to one another, and so on. Their illness was also preceded by even more remote events (from a causal point of view): The Pope said Mass in Rome that morning; a famous poet died in New York City that day; an industrial accident that released methane gas occurred in Munich just hours before the students got ill in Chicago; a bee stung a young girl in Des Moines moments before the students became ill; and so on and on. In effect, we have numberless events that preceded the students' illness and we have to pick one (or some small number) to test by Mill's Methods. Schematically, the situation is like this:

Possible Causes	*Effect*
Cafeteria food?	
Studying?	
Chair sitting?	
Talking with each other?	*Six students becoming ill in Chicago*
Pope saying Mass in Rome?	
Famous poet dying in New York?	
Industrial accident in Munich?	
Bee stinging a young girl?	
Etc.	

With infinite time and patience we could theoretically test all these events to see which was the cause of the students' illness. But we have neither infinite time nor patience. We have to select some small number of events to test. Our causal hypothesis (or hypotheses) must build on past

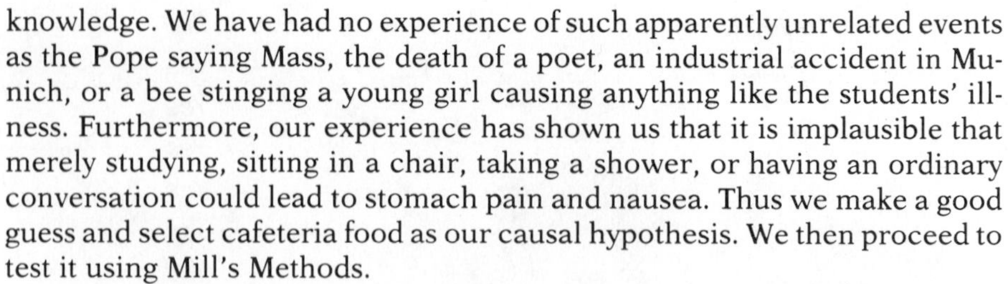

knowledge. We have had no experience of such apparently unrelated events as the Pope saying Mass, the death of a poet, an industrial accident in Munich, or a bee stinging a young girl causing anything like the students' illness. Furthermore, our experience has shown us that it is implausible that merely studying, sitting in a chair, taking a shower, or having an ordinary conversation could lead to stomach pain and nausea. Thus we make a good guess and select cafeteria food as our causal hypothesis. We then proceed to test it using Mill's Methods.

Recall that there were six food items available to the students to eat. Our hypothesis was that one (perhaps more) of these food items caused the students' illness. We had to have something to go on, something to see if it was always present in the ill students (the method of agreement), something to see if it was always absent in the non-ill students (the method of difference), or both (the joint method).

Mill's Methods in themselves cannot suggest a hypothesis; they can only test a hypothesis once one is formed. The problem here is that there are no simple rules for forming hypotheses. In the case of the ill students, we know from past experience that "bad" food often causes stomach pain and nausea. This suggests the hypothesis that it was something the students ate in the cafeteria that caused their illness.

11.5 Two Limitations of Mill's Methods

Available Hypotheses

Mill's Methods are limited to testing the causal hypothesis (or hypotheses) at hand. They cannot test causal hypotheses that were never propounded. This is an inherent limitation in Mill's Methods.

To return yet again to the "mystery" of the students' illness: We hypothesized that it was something about the cafeteria food that made the students ill. We discovered, through Mill's Methods, that it was the rice pudding. How secure can we be in this belief?

It is, for example, quite possible that some altogether different event caused the students' illness, and that it is a sheer accident that all the ill students and only the ill students ate rice pudding. In other words, it is quite possible that the data presented in this chart are absolutely correct:

Student	*What Was Eaten*						*Ill?*
1	*C*	*S*	*T*		*P*	*R*	*Yes*
2		*S*	*T*	*G*		*R*	*Yes*
3	*C*		*T*	*G*	*P*	*R*	*Yes*
4	*C*	*S*		*G*	*P*	*R*	*Yes*
5	*C*	*S*	*T*			*R*	*Yes*
6		*S*	*T*	*G*	*P*	*R*	*Yes*
7	*C*	*S*	*T*	*G*	*P*		*No*
8		*S*	*T*	*G*	*P*		*No*
9			*T*	*G*	*P*		*No*
10	*C*		*T*		*P*		*No*
11		*S*		*G*	*P*		*No*
12	*C*	*S*	*T*		*P*		*No*

Yet it is still possible that some altogether different event caused their illness.

Suppose each of the students had dental X-rays taken the day before, and either because of a malfunction in the X-ray machine or because of error or negligence by the X-ray technician each of the students had received too high a dose of X-rays. Suppose further that the rice pudding was just fine: It was not the cause of the students' illness; the overdose of X-rays was. Mill's Methods cannot show this because an overdose of X-rays was not a hypothesis we tested. It just didn't occur to us to test it.

This means that Mill's Methods in themselves cannot infallibly avoid a post hoc fallacy. In the supposition above, it was just a coincidence that all the ill students and only the ill students ate rice pudding before becoming ill. The true cause was an overdose of X-rays.

Schematically, the problem with Mill's Methods can be put this way. Suppose you are looking for the cause of event *X*. You hypothesize that it is *A* that is the cause of *X*. This is borne out by the joint method as follows:

Case	*Was* A *Present?*	*Did* X *Occur?*
#1	*Yes*	*Yes*
#2	*Yes*	*Yes*
#3	*No*	*No*
#4	*No*	*No*

And so on. . .

Therefore, A *caused* X.

Yet *A* has only an accidental relation with *X*. It is really *B* that is the cause of *X*—although you haven't tested for *B*, because *B* as a causal hypothesis didn't occur to you.

This general possibility does not mean that Mill's Methods are useless.

First, causal arguments are inductive arguments, and there is always the possibility that the conclusion of any inductive argument is false. The conclusion could be false in this inductive argument:

99.9% of all feminists oppose beauty pageants, and Gerald is a feminist. Therefore Gerald opposes beauty pageants.

But the possibility that its conclusion is false does not prevent this argument from being Strong. So, too, we could have a Strong argument that indicated that the cause of the students' illness was the rice pudding, even if in fact (unbeknownst to us) the cause was an overdose of X-rays.

Second, the more data that are gathered using Mill's Methods, the stronger the argument. If, for example, we had only these facts in the case of the ill students:

Student	*What Was Eaten*						*Ill?*
1	*C*	*S*	*T*		*P*	*R*	*Yes*
7	*C*	*S*	*T*	*G*	*P*		*No*

we would hardly have a Strong argument that it was something about the rice pudding that caused the students' illness.

The QUANTITY rule states that the larger the sample, the stronger the argument. Consider this inductive generalization:

Crow #1 is black.
Crow #2 is black.
Crow #3 is black.
.
.
.
Crow #10,000 is black.

Therefore, all crows are black.

We should count this as a Strong argument. This doesn't mean we can't be absolutely sure that somewhere or other there isn't a pink crow hopping around. The argument as it stands gives us very good reason to believe that all crows are black.

So, too, in considering a causal argument that uses Mill's Methods we ought to take into account the QUANTITY of the evidence. The larger the sample showing event *A* to be the cause of event *X* the less the probability that *A* is only accidentally (i.e., not causally) related to *X*. In our illustration of the joint method (applied to the ill students case), we had a simple size of twelve. True, something else—an overdose of X-rays—could have caused their illness. But a large sample size that consistently points to the rice pudding gives us good reason to believe that it was the rice pudding that caused the illness.

Third, any inductive argument—and in particular, any causal argument—can become stronger or weaker when new information is added. This argument is Weak not Strong any longer, for we have a new piece of information:

> *99.9% of all feminists oppose beauty pageants, and Gerald is a feminist. But Gerald has just told us that he does* not *oppose beauty pageants. Therefore Gerald opposes beauty pageants.*

Thus, the following facts might justify us in our causal claim that it was the rice pudding that caused the students' illness:

Student			*What Was Eaten*			*Ill?*
1	*C*	*S*	*T*		*P*	*R*	*Yes*
2		*S*	*T*	*G*		*R*	*Yes*
3	*C*		*T*	*G*	*P*	*R*	*Yes*
4	*C*	*S*		*G*	*P*	*R*	*Yes*
5	*C*	*S*	*T*			*R*	*Yes*
6		*S*	*T*	*G*	*P*	*R*	*Yes*
7	*C*	*S*	*T*	*G*	*P*		*No*
8		*S*	*T*	*G*	*P*		*No*
9			*T*	*G*	*P*		*No*
10	*C*		*T*		*P*		*No*
11		*S*		*G*	*P*		*No*
12	*C*	*S*	*T*		*P*		*No*

But suppose we interview two more students, and come up with these further data:

Student			*What Was Eaten*			*Ill?*
13	*C*	*S*	*T*		*P*	*R*	*No*
14		*S*	*T*	*G*		*R*	*No*

Now we no longer have a Strong argument that it was the rice pudding alone that caused the students' illness, for two students who ate rice pudding did *not* become ill.

Singular and Mass Phenomena

There is another kind of limitation in Mill's Methods. Mill's Methods require a mass phenomenon, that is, several similar cases, to yield results. In the case of the students' illness, we had a number of students who became ill and a number who did not: a mass phenomenon. In the case of the motel owner, we had a number of years with fluctuating rental rates to examine: again, a mass phenomenon.

Not all causal events are part of a mass phenomenon. Some are singular. The example of a barn's burning down, which introduced this chapter, is a singular phenomenon. Could we use Mill's Methods to justify our causal claim that it was the horse's kicking over the lantern that caused the barn to burn down? Call the barn that burned down Cal's barn. Mill's Methods would tell us to look not only at Cal's barn, but also at other cases (at Ann's

barn, at Bob's barn, at Dan's barn, etc.) in order to see any agreement or difference (or both):

Barn	*Burned down?*	*Horse kicked over lantern?*
Ann's	*No*	*No*
Bob's	*No*	*No*
Cal's	*Yes*	*Yes*
Dan's	*No*	*No*

Therefore, the horse's kicking over the lantern caused Cal's barn to burn down.

First, this is an odd argument. Certainly, it does not represent the way anyone—an arson investigator, for example—would have reasoned that it was the horse's kicking over the lantern that caused Cal's barn to burn down.

In addition, since there are many ways barns could burn down (besides horses kicking over lanterns, barns could be struck by lightning, be set aflame by arsonists, etc.), Mill's Methods will not prove that the cause was the horse's kicking over the lantern. Suppose two other barns, Ed's and Fred's, burned down. Suppose Ed's was struck by lightning, while Fred's was set aflame by an arsonist:

Barn	*Burned down?*	*Horse kicked over lantern?*
Ann's	*No*	*No*
Bob's	*No*	*No*
Cal's	*Yes*	*Yes*
Dan's	*No*	*No*
Ed's	*Yes*	*No*
Fred's	*Yes*	*No*

Therefore, the horse's kicking over the lantern caused Cal's barn to burn down.

But now this argument is Weak. This evidence as presented by Mill's Methods suggests that something other than the horse caused Cal's barn to burn down. True, there is agreement and difference among Ann's, Bob's, Cal's, and Dan's barns suggesting the horse, but this is contradicted by the evidence of Ed's and Fred's barns. Someone using Mill's Methods to determine the cause of Cal's barn's burning down should probably give up on the horse, just as we should give up on the rice pudding were we to discover that some students who ate rice pudding did not become ill.

But it might well be wrong to give up on the horse hypothesis! We might have all sorts of evidence—a horse in the barn, a broken lantern near the where the horse was—that point to the horse as the cause of the fire. In this case, it is Mill's Methods together with the QUANTITY rule that are at fault.

Mill's Methods taken together with the QUANTITY rule, therefore, make sense only when we are dealing with a mass phenomenon. A **MASS PHENOMENON** is a number of events that we have good reason to believe have causes of the same type. Such mass phenomenon cases include the students who got ill and the different rental rates over time at the motel. It *seems* these have the same cause, and so it makes sense to compare them to one another. A **SINGULAR PHENOMENON** is an event we have no good reason to believe has a cause of the same type as another, similar, event. In the case of such a singular phenomenon as a barn's burning down, we have no good reason (usually) to think that if Cal's barn burned down yesterday, then the cause is likely to be the same for Ed's barn and Fred's barn. So it would not make sense to apply Mill's Methods and QUANTITY to determine the cause of the singular event, Cal's barn's burning down.

There is a limited sense in which we can use Mill's Methods to assess the cause of a singular phenomenon. The limited sense is to not employ the QUANTITY rule. The joint method says, in effect: Look to see what's the same (agreement) and what's different (difference) about the situation. To take the burned barn case, if everything is the same except that there is an overturned lantern, then there is some reason to believe that the overturned lantern caused the barn to burn down. If my computer stops working, and everything is the same except that it is now 95° in the room, then there is some reason to believe that the heat caused my computer to stop. But these arguments are Weak to Medium in themselves. Giving up the QUANTITY rule impairs Mill's Methods. They have to be supplemented by correct causal laws to yield Strong arguments, such as the law that heat impairs the workings of computers. If we do not supplement Mills' Methods with such causal laws, we risk a post hoc fallacy.

11.6 Mill's Methods in Science

Not all scientific research is concerned with discovering the cause of some event. Robert Boyle's experiments (mid seventeenth century) with compressing air in a closed tube were designed to measure the "springiness" of the air. These led to Boyle's Law, which states that the pressure and volume of a gas are inversely proportional to one another (or $PV=k$, where P is pressure, V is volume, and k is a constant of proportionality). Nowhere does Boyle treat the cause of anything. His results describe the behavior of gases on a very general level. However, many scientific experiments are concerned with the cause of something. We will look at three cases.

Semmelweis and Puerperal Fever

Ignaz Semmelweis (1818–1865) was a Hungarian physician who was on the staff of the Vienna General Hospital, a teaching institution. There were two obstetrical wards, the First Obstetrical Clinic, which was a teaching service for medical students and of which Semmelweis was house officer, and the Second Obstetrical Clinic, which was a teaching service for midwives. It could not help but be noticed that the maternal neonatal mortality rates for

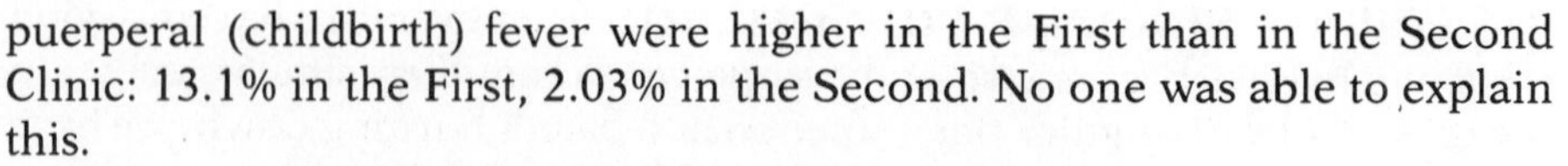

puerperal (childbirth) fever were higher in the First than in the Second Clinic: 13.1% in the First, 2.03% in the Second. No one was able to explain this.

A friend of Semmelweis and a professor at the hospital, Jakob Kolletschka, died after his finger was punctured during a post mortem (an autopsy). An autopsy on him revealed a condition similar to women who had died of puerperal fever. This apparently suggested to Semmelweis the causal hypothesis that it was "cadaveric matter" carried on the hands of physicians and medical students from the post mortem room to the First Obstetrical Clinic that caused puerperal fever.

Semmelweis demanded that all attending physicians and students wash their hands in a solution of chlorinated lime before examining a patient. Despite opposition from his staff, his order was complied with, and the mortality rate from puerperal fever in the First Clinic declined to 2.38%. Subsequently, there was a temporary reversal of this decline, which Semmelweis eventually traced to contamination from two patients in the First Clinic, one of whom had uterine cancer, the other a knee infection.

Semmelweis's hypothesis and his experiment can be simplified to show how they followed Mill's Method of Concomitant Variation:

"Cadaveric matter"	*Mortality rate?*	*Circumstance*
	First Clinic	
Present	*13.1%*	*Attending doctors and students come from autopsy room without washing hands.*
Absent	*2.38%*	*Attending doctors and students wash in solution of chlorinated lime.*
Present	*Exact rate not told but goes above 2.38%*	*Attending doctors and students pass infectious matter from infected patients.*
	Second Clinic	
Absent	*2.03%*	*Midwives did not do autopsies, hence had no contact with "cadaveric matter"*

Therefore, "cadaveric matter" causes puerperal fever.

Whenever "cadaveric matter" is present the rate increases, whenever it is absent the rate decreases. This gives good reason to believe that Semmelweis's hypothesis is true. Some of his contemporaries, however, refused to accept his results. The director of the First Obstetrical Clinic was one, and he forced Semmelweis from his post. Semmelweis returned to his native Hungary where he continued his obstetrical practices and lectured on his results—in Hungarian, since the Austrian authorities refused to allow him to lecture in German. He later suffered from mental illness and died in an asylum, ironically from an infection similar to puerperal fever.

Pasteur and Spontaneous Generation

The existence of microorganisms (bacteria, protozoa, etc.) in such liquids as sour milk and beer was known from the days of the Dutch scientist and microscope maker, Anton van Leeuwenhoek (1632–1723). Through his lens, Leeuwenhoek observed what he called "animalcules" (which we would today know as bacteria). The question then became: Where did these things come from?

One answer was the doctrine of spontaneous generation. It held that living organisms such as Leeuwenhoek's "animalcules" arise independently of any immediate parent, from some capacity of inanimate substances to produce them. The British scientist John Needham (1713–1781) performed an experiment in which he boiled mutton gravy in a hermetically sealed flask (to destroy any "animalcules" present in it). He let the flask sit, then opened it, examined the contents under a microscope, and saw "animalcules." Needham concluded that the theory of spontaneous generation must be true. Where else could the "animalcules" come from, except (somehow) from what he called the "vegetative powers" of the mutton gravy itself?

A series of experiments similar to Needham's were performed by the great Italian scientist Lazzaro Spallanzani (1729–1799). Spallanzani boiled his mutton broth longer and at higher temperatures than Needham did. Spallanzani did not observe "animalcules" in his hermetically sealed flask as Needham did. (In fact, Spallanzani explained the difference by pointing out that Needham's sterilization techniques were faulty.) But when Spallanzani opened his sealed flasks, he too eventually observed "animalcules." Where did they come from? Thus Spallanzani's experiments were inconclusive against the doctrine of spontaneous generation.

The great French chemist Louis Pasteur (1822–1895) performed a series of experiments similar to Spallanzani's. (Pasteur was an admirer of the Italian scientist, and commissioned a full-length portrait of Spallanzani that he hung in his dining room.) Pasteur tried to prove two things. First, that mutton broth (or any other liquid—milk, grape juice, etc.) could not by itself bring bacteria (as "animalcules" are now known) into existence. Second, that bacteria entered sterilized liquids through the air.

Actually Pasteur's experiments consisted of two different parts. The first part was a virtual repetition of Spallanzani's experiments. Pasteur designed a series of swan-necked flasks that looked like this:

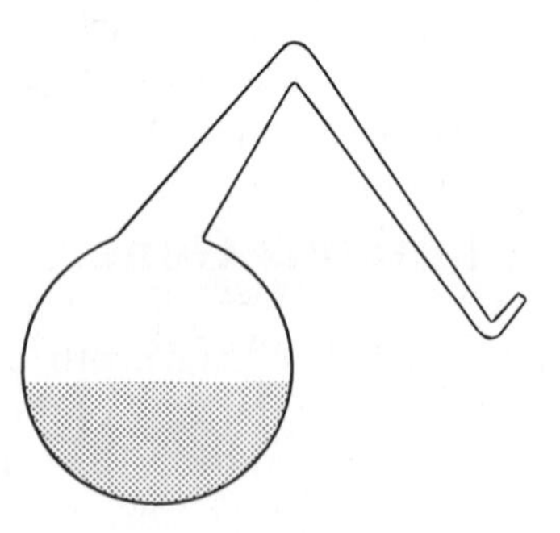

The point of the swan necks was to prevent air from entering the flasks.

Into these he introduced various liquids: infusions of meat (such as mutton broth), infusions of cereal seeds, sugared yeast water, etc. He divided his flasks into three groups. Group A flasks were not sterilized by boiling. Since they were not sterilized, Pasteur soon observed the presence of bacteria in them. Group B flasks were sterilized by boiling and left to stand in temperatures conducive for bacterial life. Group C flasks were sterilized by boiling, and later the swan neck of the flask was broken off. Pasteur's results can be put this way:

Flasks	*Boiled?*	*Broken?*	*Bacteria present?*
Group A	*No*	*No*	*Yes*
Group B	*Yes*	*No*	*No*
Group C	*Yes*	*Yes*	*Yes*

Therefore, a sterilized liquid will remain bacteria-free as long as it is not exposed to the air.

This experiment by Pasteur shows that boiling prevents the presence of bacteria. A boiled liquid such a meat broth if kept away from air will not spontaneously generate bacteria. (In fact, some of Pasteur's Group B flasks exist to this day, and to this day there is no evidence of microorganisms in any of them.) By the method of difference, Pasteur concluded that the difference between his Group B and Group C flasks was the presence of air.

The next part of the experiment was designed to show that bacteria entered sterilized liquids via the air, thus explaining why Group C flasks eventually showed evidence of microorganisms but Group B flasks did not. Pasteur used filters made up of gunpowder cotton. He heated these filters to a high enough temperature to destroy any microorganisms they might contain. Some filters—call these Group D—Pasteur kept away from any contact with the air. Other filters—call these Group E—Pasteur forced air through. He then verified that Group E filters contained microorganisms.

Thus Pasteur established that microorganisms do not spontaneously generate from the "vegetative powers" of liquids, but rather enter them when they come into contact with the air. This was the beginning of the germ theory of disease, the view that airborne microbes can attack a person and cause serious illness and even death.

The Transmission of Malaria

The nineteenth century saw progress in the discovery of the causes and prevention of malaria (yellow fever). Giovanni Grassi (1854–1925) noticed that wherever there was malaria there were mosquitos, but that wherever there were mosquitos there wasn't always malaria. He hypothesized that it was a particular species of mosquito that caused malaria, and through a relatively simple use of the joint method he proved that it was the female *Anopheles* mosquito that transmitted malaria. Volunteers who subjected themselves to being bitten by various species of mosquitos contracted malaria only when they were bitten by the female *Anopheles*.

In 1899 Grassi demonstrated that *Anopheles* was born uninfected, and transmitted malaria only after biting infected humans. This experiment can be represented this way:

Mosquito	*Fed on infected humans?*	*Transmitted malaria?*
M Anopheles	*No*	*No*
F Anopheles	*No*	*No*
M Anopheles	*Yes*	*No*
F Anopheles	*Yes*	*Yes*

Therefore, only a female Anopheles *who has fed on an infected human transmits malaria.*

According to the joint method, the only time malaria is transmitted is when a human is bitten by a female *Anopheles* who has fed on an infected human. Otherwise malaria is not present.

The United States began building the Panama Canal in 1906. The first three years were spent, among other things, in attempting to eradicate malaria, a serious and persistent problem in the region. Colonel William Gorgas directed the construction of the canal, as well as experiments designed to determine the cause of malaria. It was now known that at least the *Anopheles* mosquito transmitted the disease. But it was not yet known whether contact with persons already infected with malaria (e.g., by using their eating utensils) could also spread the disease.

The hypothesis Colonel Gorgas's researchers tried to prove (or disprove) was that contact with infected persons did not transmit the disease.

Two mosquito-proof buildings were erected. In the first, a mosquito-proof screen divided the building into two spaces. In one space, fifteen mosquitos that had fed on malaria victims were set free. A non-immune volunteer entered this space, was bitten by seven mosquitos, and four days later came down with malaria. Call this *Test A*. Two other non-immune volunteers slept for thirteen nights in the outer space, which was mosquito-free, without contracting the disease. Call this *Test B*.

Three non-immune volunteers occupied the other mosquito-proof building for twenty days. They used clothing, bedding, and eating utensils that had been soiled by malarial victims and had not been washed or otherwise treated. These volunteers were strictly quarantined and protected from mosquitos. None of them contracted malaria. The experiment was repeated twice. Call these *Tests C1, C2*, and *C3*. (The non-immunity of the volunteers was proven only when, later, they contracted malaria.)

The form of the experiment is this:

Infected mosquitos?	*Soiled articles?*	*Malaria?*	*Test*
Yes	*No*	*Yes*	*A*
No	*No*	*No*	*B*
No	*Yes*	*No*	*C1*
No	*Yes*	*No*	*C2*
No	*Yes*	*No*	*C3*

Therefore, mosquitoes and not contact with malarial victims cause malaria.

Here again we see the joint method at work. Only when mosquitos are present did someone contract malaria (the method of agreement). Without mosquitos—in particular, without mosquitos but with articles soiled by malarial victims—there was no transmission of malaria (the method of difference).

KEY POINTS

A causal statement is of the form, "*A* (or *A* and *B* and . . .) caused *X*," where each capital letter stands for an event. An event is something that happened.

What do we mean by saying that *A* caused *X*?

- We do not mean reciting the "totality" of circumstances that had to have been present in order for *X* to have happened, for this would mean virtually reciting the history of the world.
- By "*A* caused *X*" we mean that *A* is among the events that played a role in making *X* happen, and *A* is out of the ordinary, novel, unusual, or otherwise of interest.

To justify a causal statement, we need a causal argument. There are at least two fallacies that any causal argument should help us avoid.

- The post hoc fallacy. *A* occurred prior to *B*, therefore *A* caused *B*. Just because some event, *A*, happens with regularity before event *B* does not in itself prove that *A* is the cause of *B*. Claiming it does commits the post hoc fallacy.
- Confusing cause with effect. Events that regularly occur together might be causally related. This fallacy holds that causal observation might take what is in fact the effect to be the cause.

Mill's Methods are designed to avoid these causal fallacies and to establish a causal argument. We've studied four of Mill's Methods.

The Method of Agreement

Case	*Did A occur?*	*Did X then occur?*
#1	*Yes*	*Yes*
#2	*Yes*	*Yes*
#3	*Yes*	*Yes*
.	.	.
.	.	.
.	.	.
#n	*Yes*	*Yes*

Therefore, A is the cause of X.

The Method of Difference

Case	*Did A occur?*	*Did X then occur?*
#1	*No*	*No*
#2	*No*	*No*
#3	*No*	*No*
.	.	.
.	.	.
.	.	.
#n	*No*	*No*

Therefore, A is the cause of X.

The Joint Method

Case	*Did A occur?*	*Did X then occur?*
#1	*Yes*	*Yes*
#2	*No*	*No*
#3	*Yes*	*Yes*
.	.	.
.	.	.
.	.	.
#n	*No*	*No*

Therefore, A is the cause of X.

The Method of Concomitant Variation

Case	*State of* A	*State of* X
#1	*Increasing*	*Increasing*
#2	*Increasing*	*Increasing*
#3	*Decreasing*	*Decreasing*
.	.	.
.	.	.
.	.	.
#n	*Increasing*	*Increasing*

Therefore, A *is the cause of* X.

Each of Mill's Methods is also subject to this rule:

QUANTITY. The larger the sample, the stronger the argument. The smaller the sample, the weaker the argument. A Strong argument has a sufficiently large sample.

Mill's Methods are designed to test a causal hypothesis, that is, a good guess as to the cause of some event.

- Without a causal hypothesis, any one of Mill's Methods cannot even get off the ground.
- But Mill's Methods cannot in themselves suggest a causal hypothesis.
- Further, Mill's Methods may confirm the hypothesis that *A* is the cause of *X*, even though in fact *B* is the cause of *X* (because we never posited *B* as a causal hypothesis and so never tested it).
- In addition, Mill's Methods make sense only when applied to mass phenomena (a number of events that appear to have the same type of cause), not to a singular phenomenon (an event that there is no reason to believe shares the same type of cause with another apparently similar event).

EXERCISES

A. In the following (fabricated) study, use Mill's Methods to determine which drug(s) in combination or alone cure disease *X*. The drugs are named *A, B,* and *C*. Each was administered to a patient with disease *X*.

Patient	*Which drug administered?*			*Patient cured?*
	A	B	C	
#1	*Yes*	*Yes*	*No*	*Yes*
#2	*Yes*	*No*	*Yes*	*Yes*
#3	*No*	*Yes*	*No*	*No*
#4	*No*	*No*	*Yes*	*No*
#5	*No*	*No*	*No*	*No*
#6	*Yes*	*No*	*No*	*Yes*

A1. According to these test results, which drug(s) cure disease *X*?

A2. Which of Mill's Methods did you use?

B. Suppose the study continues. Two more patients with disease *X* are tested:

Patient	Which drug administered?			Patient cured?
	A	B	C	
#1	Yes	Yes	No	Yes
#2	Yes	No	Yes	Yes
#3	No	Yes	No	No
#4	No	No	Yes	No
#5	No	No	No	No
#6	Yes	No	No	Yes
#7	Yes	Yes	Yes	No
#8	No	Yes	Yes	No

B1. Now which drug(s) cure disease *X*? (Hard. Think.)

B2. Which of Mill's Methods did you use to reach your conclusion?

C. Suppose a man finds that he is ill with a headache and upset stomach each morning. He hypothesizes that this is caused by something he drank the evening before. He proceeds to test his hypothesis this way:

Day	Liquor?	Club soda?	Ill?
Sunday	Bourbon	Yes	Yes
Monday	Scotch	Yes	Yes
Tuesday	Rum	Yes	Yes
Wednesday	Tequila	Yes	Yes
Thursday	Rye	Yes	Yes
Friday	Vodka	Yes	Yes
Saturday	Gin	Yes	Yes

Therefore, club soda is the cause of his headache and upset stomach.

C1. Which of Mill's Methods is this man using?

C2. Since it is highly likely that his conclusion is false, how could he improve his argument?

D. Suppose that a certain woman's television screen flickers on and off often. (She lives in Manhattan.) She conceives the hypothesis that passing elephants cause the flickering. She decides to test her hypothesis this way:

Day	*Time*	*TV flickers?*	*Elephants passed?*
10/6	*9 P.M.*	*No*	*No*
10/8	*7 A.M.*	*No*	*No*
10/15	*4 P.M.*	*No*	*No*
10/30	*7 P.M.*	*No*	*No*
11/5	*11 P.M.*	*No*	*No*
11/8	*3 P.M.*	*No*	*No*
11/15	*4 A.M.*	*No*	*No*

Therefore, elephants passing cause her TV to flicker.

D1. Which of Mill's Methods is she using?

D2. Since her conclusion in unlikely to be true, what would improve her argument?

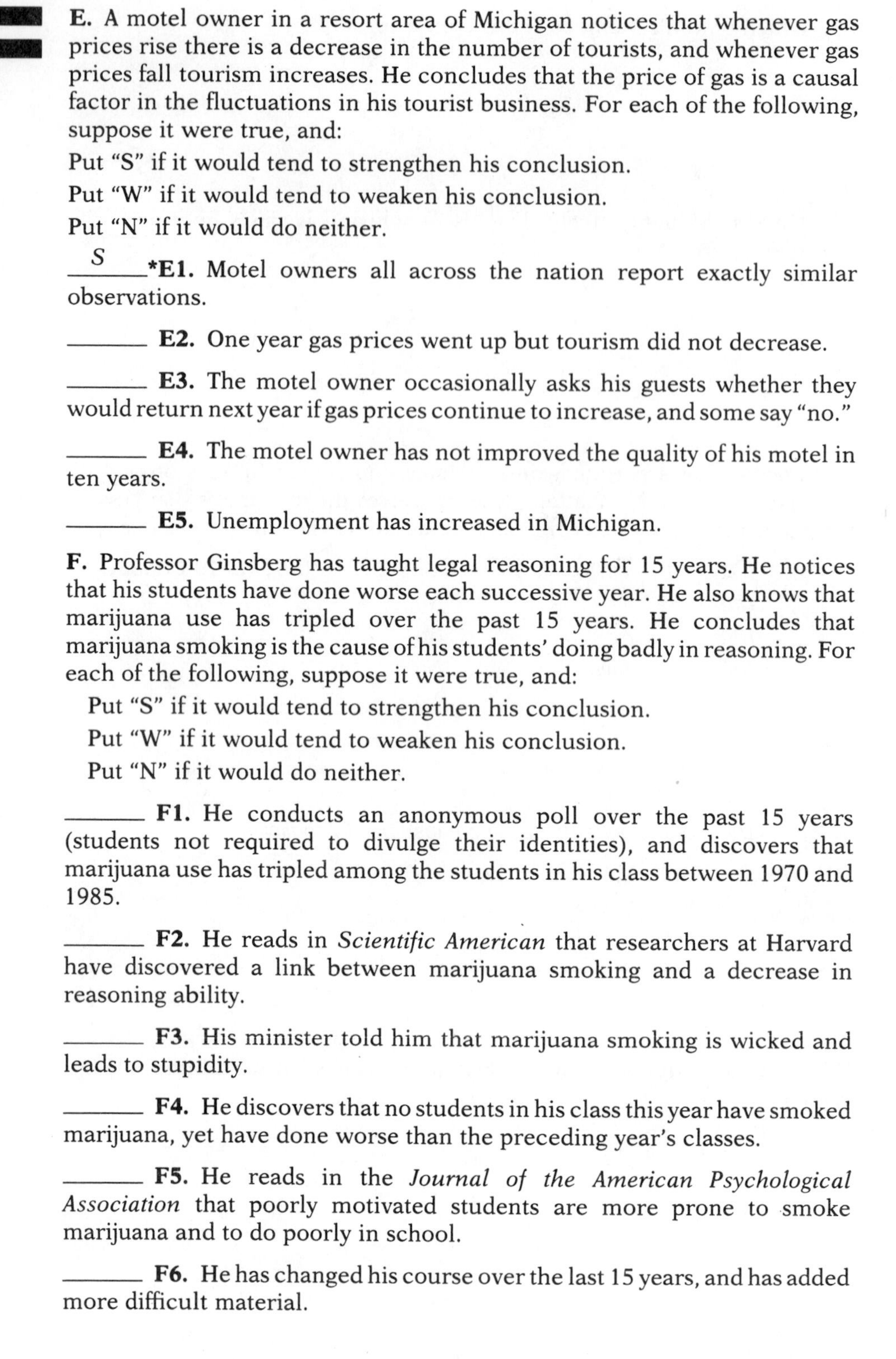

E. A motel owner in a resort area of Michigan notices that whenever gas prices rise there is a decrease in the number of tourists, and whenever gas prices fall tourism increases. He concludes that the price of gas is a causal factor in the fluctuations in his tourist business. For each of the following, suppose it were true, and:

Put "S" if it would tend to strengthen his conclusion.

Put "W" if it would tend to weaken his conclusion.

Put "N" if it would do neither.

__*S*__ ***E1.** Motel owners all across the nation report exactly similar observations.

______ **E2.** One year gas prices went up but tourism did not decrease.

______ **E3.** The motel owner occasionally asks his guests whether they would return next year if gas prices continue to increase, and some say "no."

______ **E4.** The motel owner has not improved the quality of his motel in ten years.

______ **E5.** Unemployment has increased in Michigan.

F. Professor Ginsberg has taught legal reasoning for 15 years. He notices that his students have done worse each successive year. He also knows that marijuana use has tripled over the past 15 years. He concludes that marijuana smoking is the cause of his students' doing badly in reasoning. For each of the following, suppose it were true, and:

Put "S" if it would tend to strengthen his conclusion.

Put "W" if it would tend to weaken his conclusion.

Put "N" if it would do neither.

______ **F1.** He conducts an anonymous poll over the past 15 years (students not required to divulge their identities), and discovers that marijuana use has tripled among the students in his class between 1970 and 1985.

______ **F2.** He reads in *Scientific American* that researchers at Harvard have discovered a link between marijuana smoking and a decrease in reasoning ability.

______ **F3.** His minister told him that marijuana smoking is wicked and leads to stupidity.

______ **F4.** He discovers that no students in his class this year have smoked marijuana, yet have done worse than the preceding year's classes.

______ **F5.** He reads in the *Journal of the American Psychological Association* that poorly motivated students are more prone to smoke marijuana and to do poorly in school.

______ **F6.** He has changed his course over the last 15 years, and has added more difficult material.

G. Consider this somewhat made-up example. (It is not entirely made-up, since very primitive people do not know the basic mechanics of reproduction.) A certain primitive tribe has no contact with the outside world. This tribe, let us suppose, requires a woman to bathe in a certain river that runs through its territory after sexual intercourse. This river is considered sacred because (it is believed that) a god lives in it. All women of the tribe scrupulously observe this rule, and only women who have had sexual intercourse are allowed to bathe in the river. Fairly often, women become pregnant. The people of the tribe conclude—perhaps have believed all along—that bathing in the sacred river causes pregnancy. After all, they seem to have a good reason: No one has ever gotten pregnant without bathing in the sacred river.

G1. What causal hypothesis is this tribe proving?

G2. Which of Mill's Methods are they using?

G3. Are they committing any causal fallacies?

G4. Which experiments could they perform that would disprove their conclusion?

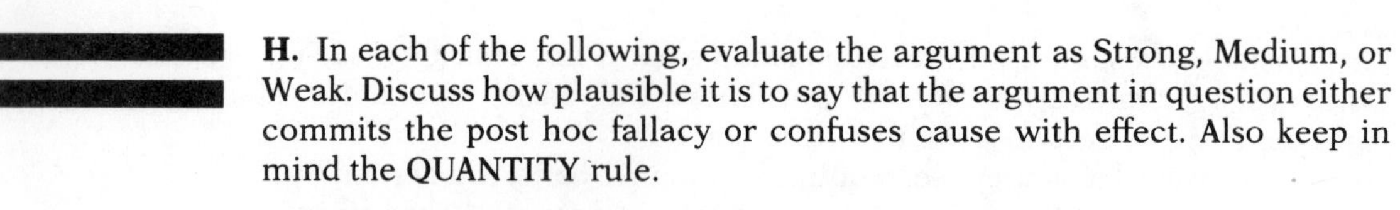

H. In each of the following, evaluate the argument as Strong, Medium, or Weak. Discuss how plausible it is to say that the argument in question either commits the post hoc fallacy or confuses cause with effect. Also keep in mind the QUANTITY rule.

H1. Marilyn Monroe committed suicide after several years of psychotherapy. Therefore, psychotherapy caused her death.

H2. Well-dressed people are often successful. Poorly dressed people are often unsuccessful. Therefore, being well-dressed is a cause of success.

H3. Patients with terminal cancer are depressed and irritable. Therefore, depression and irritability cause cancer.

H4. As a teacher for 14 years, I've observed that successful students attend class regularly. Therefore attending class regularly is a cause of success in education.

H5. Every time I say "Sit!" my dog sits. Therefore, my saying "Sit!" is the cause of my dog's sitting.

H6. I sat in a draft. Then I caught a cold. Therefore the draft caused my cold.

H7. I'm overweight. Every time I'm depressed I eat. Therefore depression is the cause of my being overweight.

CHAPTER 12

EVERYDAY INDUCTIONS

Inductive generalizations, analogical arguments, and causal arguments, the subjects of the last three chapters, form three distinct types of inductive argument. Besides these, there are a number of miscellaneous inductions that occur with some frequency in everyday discourse: hence everyday inductions. We will look at how to assess their degree of validity, with some special warnings about the fallacies associated with them. New important concepts in this chapter to learn and apply are:

GENETIC FALLACY

AD HOMINEM FALLACY

TU QUOQUE ARGUMENT

APPEALS TO AUTHORITY
—STRONG and FALLACIOUS

APPEALS TO THE PEOPLE

APPEALS TO FEELING
—LEGITIMATE and FALLACIOUS

APPEALS TO FORCE

APPEALS TO IGNORANCE
—recognize FALLACIOUS appeals

THE GAMBLER'S FALLACY

12.1 Genetic Fallacies

First let us review the distinction (from 1.2) between justification and explanation. A **JUSTIFICATION** is an argument that purports to provide reasons that some statement is true. All the arguments, both deductive and inductive, studied in this book have been justifications. An **EXPLANATION** purports to explain why some statement is true. An explanation does not try to convince you that some statement is true; it assumes the statement to be true, and tries to explain why.

An example might better elucidate the difference. Take the statement,

John is afraid of the dark.

Someone might try to *justify* this statement in the following way:

John sleeps with the lights on, and he once began to scream when the electricity went out in the evening. I conclude that he is afraid of the dark.

Alternatively, someone might try to *explain* this statement, perhaps in the following manner:

When he was a child, John's mother frequently locked him in a closet. That's why John is afraid of the dark.

The justification attempts to give a reason to believe that the statement, "John is afraid of the dark," is true. The explanation assumes the truth of this statement, and tries to explain why "John is afraid of the dark" is true. The justification is best understood in a context where someone is skeptical as to whether John really is afraid of the dark. Such a person is to be offered a justification. The explanation is best understood in a context where someone is more or less convinced that John is afraid of the dark, but has no idea why. Such a person is to be offered an explanation.

Havoc occurs if you try to mix the two—to offer a justification when an explanation was called for, or vice versa.

Suppose I know John slightly, but do not know anything one way or the other about his emotional responses to the dark. You say to me, "John is afraid of the dark." I'm skeptical, since to me John appears quite normal. In effect, I ask for a justification. Suppose you instead give me an explanation posing as a justification:

You don't believe that John is afraid of the dark? Well, this will convince you: John's mother frequently locked him in a closet when he was a child.

This is hardly a convincing *justification*. I may readily grant that John's mother frequently locked him in a closet when he was a child. But this gives me no good reason to believe that John is afraid of the dark.

Alternatively, suppose I'm quite well aware that John is afraid of the dark. I, too, know that he sleeps with the lights on and have heard him scream when the electricity went out. However, I haven't a clue as to why he is afraid of the dark. I invite you to offer an explanation. Suppose you instead give a justification posing as an explanation:

Here's why John is afraid of the dark: He sleeps with the lights on and once he screamed when the electricity went out.

This does not explain to me why John is afraid of the dark. It may justify that claim but doesn't say why it's true.

The term "genesis" means "origin" or "beginning." To describe the genesis of something is to describe how it came to be the way it is—to explain it. The **GENETIC FALLACY** is an explanation (a genesis) posing as a justification. The rule relative to the Genetic Fallacy for assessing justifications is:

GENETIC FALLACY RULE. An argument that attempts to argue that some statement is true (or false) merely on the basis of how that statement came to be made commits the genetic fallacy and is therefore Weak.

For example, the mother of a friend of mine once had a cake recipe come to her in a dream (really). Were I to say something like this,

That cake will taste awful. After all, the recipe for it came to your mother in a dream.

I would be committing the genetic fallacy. It might well be true that the origin (genesis) of the recipe is, oddly enough, a dream. But this is not a good reason to believe that it will be a failure. On the other hand, the following argument does not commit the genetic fallacy, and could well justify my claim:

That cake will taste awful. After all, the recipe for it calls for string, leaves, and canary droppings.

12.2 Arguments Ad Hominem

The Latin "ad hominem" means "directed at the person." An argument commits the **AD HOMINEM FALLACY** when it uses some fact or other about the person making a statement to prove the truth or falsity of the statement itself.

The usual case of ad hominem fallacy is abusive. One attempts to discredit a person's statement by attempting to discredit the person. The most vicious case is to cast aspersions on the ethnicity or religiosity of the person making a statement. For example, the nineteenth-century Viennese music critic, Eduard Hanslick, criticized the music of the composer Richard Wagner for lacking good musical form. Wagner responded something like this:

Eduard Hanslick's criticisms of my music can have no validity, since Hanslick is, after all, Jewish.

The fact that Hanslick was Jewish has, of course, no bearing on whether his

criticisms of Wagner's music have validity. Wagner's argument commits the ad hominem fallacy, and is accordingly Weak. Were Wagner to have made an argument like this:

> *Hanslick criticizes my music for being "formless." But my opera,* Die Meistersinger von Nürnberg, *shows a mastery of many traditional forms of music (chorale, sonata, etc.).*

he would not have committed an ad hominem fallacy, for this argument at least addresses Hanslick's criticisms, not Hanslick himself.

Ad hominem arguments need not discredit the person making the claim. An argument that attempts to get you to believe a person's statement by praising that person is just as much an ad hominem fallacy as one that attempts to get you to disbelieve a person's statement by abusing him.

For example, John and Elizabeth are on the town council of Midville. John makes this statement at a meeting:

> *A traffic light at the intersection of Jardin and Cherry Streets is badly needed.*

This statement might be challenged. "Why is that true?" some other council member might ask. Suppose Elizabeth makes this argument:

> *John has worked long and hard for the good of the town of Midville. So if he says a traffic light is badly needed, a traffic light is badly needed.*

The above argument commits the ad hominem fallacy (and is therefore Weak). It tries to justify the statement that a traffic light is needed at a certain intersection by pointing out the good qualities of the person who made that statement. What is needed is some argument like this:

> *Traffic has gotten very heavy at the intersection of Jardin and Cherry Streets. There have been several collisions already. Therefore a traffic light is badly needed at that intersection.*

This argument has at least the virtue of addressing itself to the statement, not to the person who made the statement.

Not every argument that uses facts about a person commits an ad hominem fallacy. Suppose Ann says to Barbara:

> *He says he'll show up on time, but he's not to be trusted.*

Barbara asks Ann to justify her statement. Ann makes this argument:

> *He's very often said to me in the past that he'll be at a certain place at a certain time, and very often he doesn't show up on time or doesn't show up at all. So when he says to you that he'll show up on time, he's not to be trusted.*

This is a Strong argument. In effect, it is an inductive generalization: a conclusion drawn on the basis of past experience. It does use facts about a person to justify a statement, but since the statement it justifies concerns a person, no ad hominem fallacy is committed.

A rule summing this up is needed:

AD HOMINEM RULE. An argument that uses positive or negative facts about a person to attempt to show the person's statement true or false commits the ad hominem fallacy and is accordingly Weak. An argument that relies on an inductive generalization about a person using facts about the person's past behavior does not commit the ad hominem fallacy, and may well be Strong.

Sometimes there is no real distinction between an ad hominem fallacy and a genetic fallacy. Rocky says,

A will needs two witnesses to be valid.

Preppy argues,

That's not true. You only say it because you heard it when you were in prison.

Let it be true that Rocky did hear it in prison. Let it also be true that that's why Rocky says it. However, Preppy's argument is Weak. That Rocky says it because he heard it in prison is *not* a reason against the truth of "A will needs two witnesses to be valid." Preppy's argument could be counted as an ad hominem fallacy: It points out some "negative" fact about Rocky, the person who made the statement, in order to argue against the statement itself. But Preppy's argument could also be counted as a genetic fallacy, since it tries to use the origin (genesis) of the statement in order to show the falsity of the statement. In the end, it is of little importance whether Preppy's argument is called an ad hominem fallacy or a genetic fallacy. Weak is Weak.

12.3
The Tu Quoque Argument

The Latin *tu quoque* (pronounced "TOO KWO-kway") means "you too." As an argument form, it attempts to prove something false by showing it inconsistent with other attitudes or behavior. Its general fallacious form is:

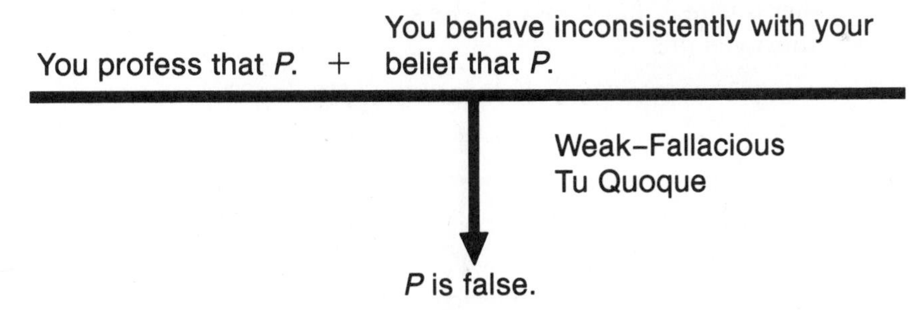

For example, a parent might condemn a child's use of drugs by saying "Drugs are really dangerous." But that child notices the parent saying this with a cigarette in one hand and a martini in the other. The child might then argue:

You say that drugs are really dangerous. But you too use drugs all the time: You smoke and drink every evening before dinner. So drugs are not *really dangerous!*

This argument is Weak. In particular, it's a fallacious tu quoque argument. The parent's behavior is simply irrelevant to the truth or falsity of the conclusion. People often act inconsistently with their beliefs. This does not show those beliefs to be false.

The fallacious tu quoque argument is thus a kind of ad hominem argument. It uses facts about a person to attempt to show that that person's statements (or beliefs) are false. What distinguishes the tu quoque argument is the kind of facts about a person it uses. It uses behavior inconsistent with the statement in order to try to show the statement false. But this is like trying to show that the law of gravity is false just because I made an attempt to float in mid air unaided!

Not every argument that looks like a tu quoque fallacy is one. Contrast, for example, this variation of the preceding argument. Suppose the child says to the parents:

You say that drugs are really dangerous. But you too use drugs all the time: You smoke and drink every evening before dinner. So you're acting contrary to your own beliefs (or have a double standard or are being hypocritical).

This is no longer a fallacious tu quoque argument. In fact, it is at least a Strong argument—perhaps even Deductively Valid (because of the meaning of "acting contrary to your own beliefs").

12.4 Appeals to Authority

Quite frequently, the only justification a person can offer that some statement or other is true is that someone else said it. The simplest form of an appeal to authority is this:

Person *X* said that *P*.

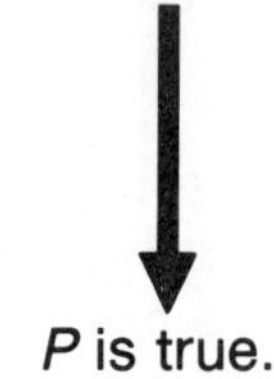

P is true.

Some appeals to authority make for Strong arguments. Others do not. Let's try to mark off the difference.

The crucial test for whether an appeal to authority is Strong or less than Strong is whether the person in question is an appropriate and reliable authority on the subject being addressed. This sort of argument counts as a Strong appeal to authority:

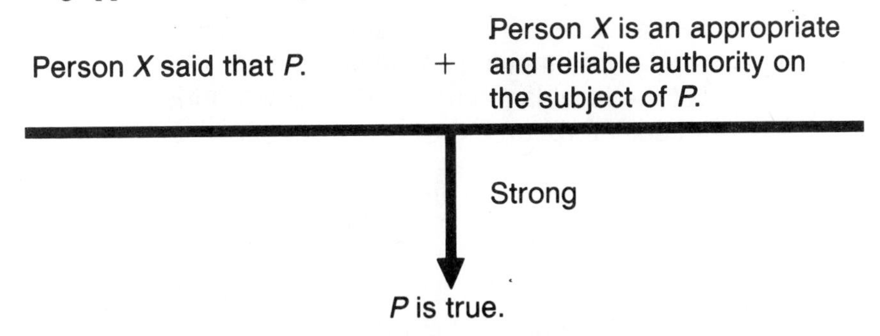

Conversely, if the person in question is either an inappropriate or unreliable authority on the subject of *P*, then the argument is Weak. This argument form is a Weak appeal to authority:

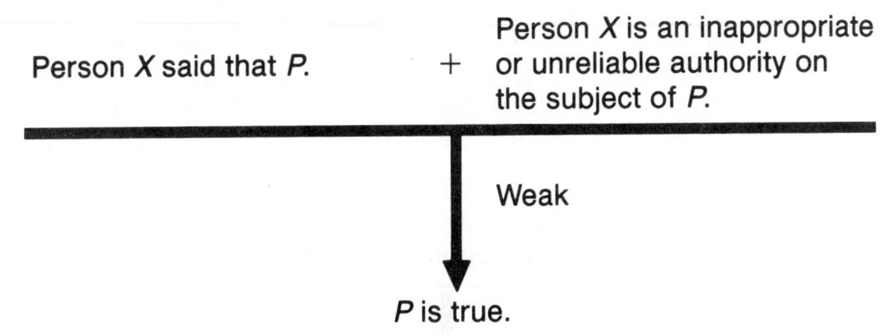

Such Weak appeals to authority are **FALLACIOUS APPEALS TO AUTHORITY**.

The reader might be tempted to raise this objection: No matter how appropriate or reliable an authority someone is, the mere fact that he or she said that *P* doesn't in itself prove "*P*" to be true. However, don't forget that an appeal to authority is an inductive argument, and the standard of proof for an inductive argument is lower than for a deductive argument. We expect only that an inductive argument be Strong. It is of course true that someone could be the best authority in the world on the subject of *P*, could say that *P*, and could still be wrong. But this is only to point out (yet again) that the conclusion of an inductive argument, even of a Strong and Sound inductive argument, could be false.

The problem confronting us is to give some account of appropriateness and relevance, and here it seems we cannot give a hard and fast set of rules. The medieval philosophers thought it appropriate and relevant to cite Aristotle on almost any subject from the cause of rain to the existence of God. "As The Philosopher [they meant Aristotle] said . . ." the medievals very frequently wrote to justify some claim or other. We today would hardly consider Aristotle an appropriate or relevant authority on the subject of rain. Perhaps who counts as an appropriate or relevant authority changes from era to era.

Still, it is possible to give fairly clear examples of contemporary Strong and Weak (fallacious) appeals to authority.

Father Jones, a noted Catholic doctrinal scholar and theologian, says that Catholic doctrine forbids the use of condoms during sexual intercourse to prevent conception.

↓ Strong

Catholic doctrine forbids the use of condoms during sexual intercourse to prevent conception.

If the premise is true—that is, if Father Jones really is a noted Catholic doctrinal scholar and theologian, and if it is true that he says that Catholic doctrine forbids the use of condoms during sexual intercourse to prevent conception—then we have very good reason to believe that the conclusion is true—that is, that Catholic doctrine really does forbid the use of condoms during sexual intercourse to prevent conception. Another argument:

Doctor Smith, a licensed physician and internist for a dozen years, says that aspirin relieves swelling but that acetaminophen does not.

↓ Strong

Aspirin relieves swelling but acetaminophen does not.

Suppose we were to reverse the two:

Father Jones, a noted Catholic doctrinal scholar and theologian, says that aspirin relieves swelling but that acetaminophen does not.

↓ Weak–Fallacious Appeal to Authority

Aspirin relieves swelling but acetaminophen does not.

Father Jones might be an appropriate and reliable authority on the subject of Catholic doctrine, but he is not—at least not in virtue of his being an authority on Catholic doctrine—an appropriate and reliable authority on the subject of pain relievers.

Doctor Smith, a licensed physician and internist for a dozen years, says that Catholic doctrine forbids the use of condoms during sexual intercourse to prevent conception.

↓ Weak–Fallacious Appeal to Authority

Catholic doctrine forbids the use of condoms during sexual intercourse to prevent conception.

Doctor Smith, as a licensed physician and internist, is not an appropriate authority on the subject of Catholic doctrine. Hence this argument appeals to the wrong sort of authority, and this argument is a fallacious appeal to authority.

At this point, the reader may again object: But couldn't Father Jones be right about pain relievers? Couldn't Doctor Smith be right about Catholic doctrine? The answer is: Of course they *could* be right. But this isn't the issue. The problem logic has to solve is how to pick out good from bad arguments—how to tell when we have a good reason to believe the conclusion of an argument and when we do not have a good reason. That Father Jones, noted Catholic doctrinal scholar and theologian that he is, tells us that Catholic doctrine is thus-and-such is a good reason for believing that Catholic doctrine *is* thus-and-such. That Doctor Smith, licensed physician and internist that she is, tells us that pain relievers work in a certain way is good reason for believing that they *do* work in that way. But when Father Jones pronounces on pain relievers or when Doctor Smith pronounces on Catholic doctrine, we no longer have good reason to believe that what they say is true—even if it turns out to be true! (Remember that the fact that the conclusion of an argument is true shows nothing about the degree of validity of that argument.)

We can give some obvious instances of good authorities: Catholic scholars are appropriate and relevant authorities on matters of Catholic doctrine; so are licensed physicians on pain relievers; so are corporate lawyers on matters of corporate law; so are butchers on the best ways to butcher a cow; so are bakers on the best way to knead dough; so are candlestick makers on how to make long-burning candles; and so on. We can also give examples of unreliable or inappropriate authorities: movie stars on the most effective pain relievers, famous athletes on the best credit cards, and so on.

The logical point is not that anything a candlestick maker says on the subject of candles must be true. Rather, it's that if a candlestick maker is an appropriate and reliable authority on the subject of candlestick making, then the fact that an appropriate and reliable authority is making certain pronouncements on the subject of candlestick making is itself a good reason to believe these pronouncements are true.

This fact supports the rationality of having expert testimony in courtrooms. If a judge or jury needs to know whether the accused is mentally ill or used proper bookkeeping procedures, attorneys (either for the defense or

prosecution) often produce expert witnesses: a psychologist on mental illness or a certified public accountant on bookkeeping procedures.

The rule for assessing appeals to authority is this:

> **APPEAL TO AUTHORITY RULE.** An argument that attempts to justify its conclusion by appeal to an authority is Strong if the authority is appropriate and reliable, fallacious (and therefore Weak) if the authority is not appropriate or not reliable.

Of course, we need some criteria for appropriateness and reliability. (1) An appropriate authority on matters of *X* is someone who has mastered the skill or knowledge of *X*. An inappropriate authority on matters of *X* is someone who has mastered neither. (2) A reliable authority on matters of *X* is someone who has a good track record, that is, someone who has been right in the past on matters of *X*. An unreliable authority on matters of *X* is someone who has a bad track record on matters of *X*. A good track record is evidence of mastery of fact and of good reasoning abilities. (3) Interested experts are less reliable than disinterested experts. Someone who has a personal interest in having others believe that something is true is less reliable than someone who has no personal stake in the matter.

Experts, as is well known, sometimes disagree. Psychologist Neiman says the accused was able to tell right from wrong at the time of the crime; psychologist Marcus disagrees. Doctor Smith says acetaminophen will not relieve swelling; Doctor Wesson disagrees.

It may often be true that of two disagreeing experts one is more appropriate or reliable than the other. In that case, the best expert gives you the strongest reason for believing that the view that expert endorses in true.

But if each expert is more or less equally reliable and appropriate we have new information that changes the degree of validity of the argument. That is, if this argument was considered Strong:

Doctor Smith says acetaminophen will not relieve swelling. +
Doctor Smith is an appropriate and reliable authority.

Strong

Acetaminophen will not relieve swelling.

New, conflicting information when incorporated into a different inductive argument yields at best a Medium argument:

Doctor Smith says acetaminophen will not relieve swelling. +
Doctor Wesson says acetaminophen will relieve swelling +
Each is an appropriate and reliable authority.

Weak–Medium

Acetaminophen will not relieve swelling.

In other words, the fact that appropriate, reliable Doctor Smith said so is no longer a convincing reason to believe it since equally appropriate, reliable Doctor Wesson said not so.

When equally appropriate and reliable experts disagree, it is irrational to simply pick one out and believe your favorite. Rather, we have to become experts in a sense ourselves. We have to look at the evidence for or against the truth of some statement. It is no longer any use to see which expert affirmed or denied that statement.

We have been speaking so far of appeals to *formal* authority, to lawyers on matters of corporate law, to psychologists on matters of criminal insanity, and the like. However, individuals can serve as *informal* authorities.

We often enough take someone's word for it. In effect, we rely on an informal appeal to authority. For example,

Gertrude says that she saw Pablo take
the wallet from Alice's purse.

Pablo did take the wallet from Alice's purse.

Gertrude may not be a formal authority on anything—on police work or criminal behavior, for example. But she counts as an informal authority. Arguments like the one above are quite common, their evaluation commonsensical.

We would like to say that informal appeals to authority are Strong when the authority is appropriate and reliable—the same criteria as we used for the assessment of formal appeals to authority. However, what we mean by an appropriate informal authority is not someone who has received special training or has special knowledge, but rather someone who was in a position to know that what he or she said is true. An inappropriate authority is someone not in such a position. Like formal experts, a reliable informal authority is also someone who has a good track record on truth, that is, someone who has shown trustworthiness and good reasoning abilities in the past. An unreliable informal authority is a person who have a bad track record on truth.

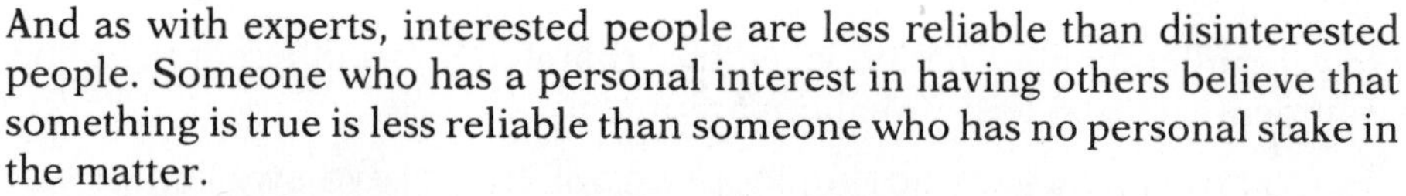

And as with experts, interested people are less reliable than disinterested people. Someone who has a personal interest in having others believe that something is true is less reliable than someone who has no personal stake in the matter.

So we must ask of the argument above: Was Gertrude in a position to have seen Pablo take the wallet from Alice's purse? Does Gertrude have a good track record with respect to the truth? Is Gertrude someone who has a gripe against Pablo?

This is pretty much what courts of law and juries try to determine when they assess direct witness testimony. What the language of the law refers to as "the credibility of a witness" we refer to in the language of inductive logic as "the degree of strength of an appeal to authority." (It might be mentioned that American law allows appeals to authority to go only so far. Gertrude is allowed to testify that she saw Pablo take the wallet from Alice's purse. But I am not allowed to testify that I heard Gertrude say that she saw Pablo take the wallet from Alice's purse, for the law would dismiss that sort of testimony as "hearsay.")

There is one controversial issue we shall briefly address on the subject of appeals to authority. This is whether there are issues on which there are no appropriate or relevant authorities. The area of value judgments is one such area. Two examples:

Andrew Porter, long-time music critic for *The New Yorker*, says that the current Metropolitan Opera's production of *Norma* is badly sung and incoherently staged.

Therefore, the current Metropolitan Opera's production of *Norma* is badly sung and incoherently staged.

Father Jones, noted Catholic doctrinal scholar and theologian, says that abortion is wrong.

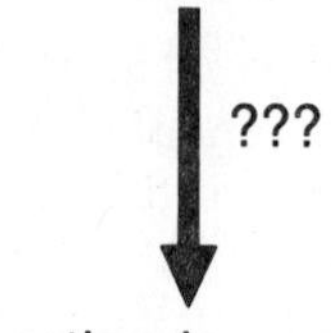

Abortion is wrong.

It is unclear how we should assess these appeals to authority. On the one hand, each cites an authority—a noted music critic in the first case, a noted expert on Catholic doctrine in the other—which *if* any authority is appropriate and relevant, the authority cited is. On the other hand, it is not obvious that there are any appropriate and relevant authorities in matters of aesthetics and ethics. Should we "trust" the film critic who says the movie is awful and not go? Should we "trust" the priest, minister, or rabbi who tells us that thus-and-such is wrong? These questions are virtual repetitions of other questions: Can there be an authority on matters of aesthetics or ethics? Can someone know more than you or I about what is beautiful or what is good, in the way that, for example, an architect knows more than you or I about what sort of foundation is required for a three-story house? (Question left to the reader.)

12.5
The Appeal to the People

Known variously as "the appeal to the mob," "the appeal to the gallery," and "the appeal to the masses," we'll call this argument the **APPEAL TO THE PEOPLE**, from its traditional Latin name, the *argumentum ad populum*. Its form is this:

Everyone says that P.

P is true.

The appeal to the people is actually a kind of appeal to authority because it treats the endorsement, not of an individual, but of a community as giving warrant for believing the truth of the conclusion.

It is rare that an appeal to the people is Strong or Sound. This is because (1) "everyone" is rarely an authority on anything and (2) "everyone" usually includes just the speaker's associates.

The list of things that "everyone" is alleged to have said at one time or the other should be enough to warn anyone away from using an appeal to the people (at least those who want to make a Strong argument). At one time or another "everyone" has said the earth is flat; if you sail far enough you'll fall off the ends of the earth; eye exercises will cure near-sightedness; masturbation will cause near-sightedness; cocaine is not addictive; oil prices will stay sky high; and so on. And each and every one of these has turned out to be false.

The desire to "fit in" and not be "different" explains some of the attraction of appeals to the people. For if a speaker says that "everyone" says this or that, it takes a certain amount of fortitude to dissent. The mind is swayed into accepting as true what "everyone" says is true. Thus,

Everyone drinks liquor.

↓ Weak–Fallacious Appeal to the People

There's nothing harmful in it.

That "everyone" drinks liquor even if true (which it isn't) would not be a good reason to believe there's nothing harmful in it, for "everyone" is not a good authority on what is and is not harmful.

An argument may have hidden within it a fallacious appeal to the people:

> *Everyone here talks about how badly Susan managed the funds. She should be removed from the position of treasurer.*

When diagramed, this argument is a chain argument with the middle conclusion suppressed:

Everyone here talks about how badly Susan managed the funds.

↓ Weak–Fallacious Appeal to the People

[Susan badly managed the funds.]

↓ Strong

She should be removed from the position of treasurer.

Remember that the second part of the chain is not weakened by the first part. However, since we have no good reason to believe the premise of the second chain, we have no good reason to believe its conclusion.

However, not every argument that appeals to the people is fallacious. In the last act of *Carmen*, a crowd of people see Don Jose stab Carmen. Suppose each testifies to that effect (in a hypothetical sequel: *Carmen Part 2*). That is, we have this argument:

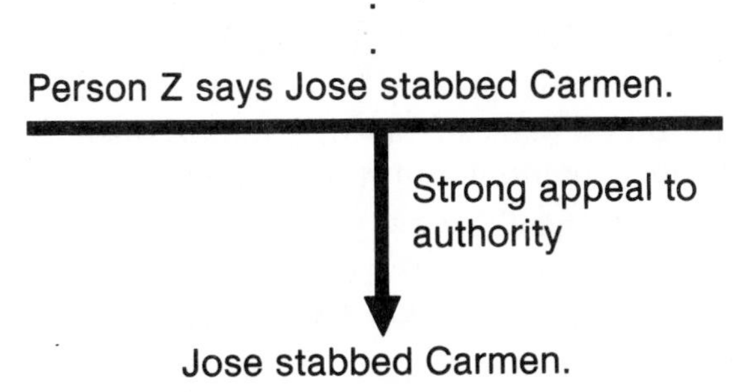

The difference here is that we have a case of an informal appeal to authority, and if we assume that each person is appropriate and reliable then we have a Strong argument. But the Susan-argument above has no such redeeming feature: It uses gossip and innuendo as the justification for the truth of a statement.

12.6 Appeals to Feeling

The philosopher Plato recognized the power feeling exerts on our behavior, and he constructed his ideal state, described in *Republic*, with an eye towards warding off aspects of life that stir strong feeling, romantic love and art being especially dangerous here (or so Plato thought). In our own time, the psychologist Sigmund Freud also acknowledged the hold feeling has over our lives. The process of psychoanalysis that Freud invented is largely a matter of bringing unconscious and repressed feeling to consciousness in order that its control over our behavior might be lessened. Throughout history, successful speakers, lawyers, and politicians have played on the feelings of their audiences. In one of Shakespeare's greatest speeches, Mark Antony turns the Roman crowd against the assassins of Julius Caesar:

If you have tears, prepare to shed them now.
You all do know this mantle. I remember
The first time ever Caesar put it on;
'Twas on a summer's evening, in his tent,
That day he overcame the Nervii.
Look! in this place ran Cassius' dagger through;
See what a rent the envious Casca made;
Through this the well-beloved Brutus stabb'd,
And as he pluck'd his cursed steel away,

Mark how the blood of Caesar follow'd it,
As rushing out of doors, to be resolv'd
If Brutus so unkindly knock'd or no;
For Brutus, as you know, was Caesar's angel.
Judge, O you gods, how dearly Caesar lov'd him!

Here is Mark Antony showing the crowd Caesar's bloody cloak, recalling Caesar in happier times, pointing out the wounds made by each assassin, calling Casca envious, pointing out how much Caesar loved Brutus. The crowd's response to Mark Antony's speech is highly emotional, as Mark Antony has calculated.

Revenge! About! Seek! Burn! Fire! Kill! Slay! Let not a traitor live!

the mob shouts.

Such is the power of feeling. Being human, we are susceptible to appeals to feeling. Being students of logic, we can try to counteract those appeals.

Not all appeals to feeling are arguments. There are no arguments in Mark Antony's speech above, although the entire speech is an appeal to the feelings of the Roman plebians. But some appeals to feelings are arguments; these we'll call **APPEALS TO FEELING**. Their form is somewhat vague. Either:

Some way of calling forth positive feelings
towards the statement that *P*.

P is true.

Or:

Some way of calling forth negative feelings
towards the statement that *P*.

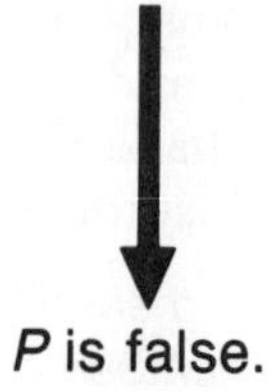

P is false.

In general, such arguments are Weak. The fact that you feel positively toward some statement is little guarantee that the statement is true. Conversely, the fact that you feel negatively toward some statement is little guarantee that the statement is false. To put it another way, our feelings in general are not very good indicators about the way the world really is. A **FALLACIOUS APPEAL TO FEELING** is an argument that in one way or another summons up positive feelings to justify the truth of a statement or negative feelings to justify the falsity of a statement.

Perhaps the most prominent cases of fallacious appeals to feeling occur in courtrooms:

My client is the greatest Cubist painter in the world. So surely he is innocent of stealing Alice's wallet.

This argument is a fallacious appeal to feeling. Let us grant that the lawyer's client is indeed the greatest Cubist painter in the world. This hardly justifies the conclusion, that he is innocent of stealing Alice's wallet. Appeals to feeling, when looked at calmly, from a distance, are atrocious arguments. That they convince at all—and they sometimes do—is testimony to the power of feeling over rational thought.

Just as not all appeals to feeling are arguments, not all appeals to feeling that are arguments are fallacious. We saw that not every case of citing facts about a person commits the ad hominem fallacy. So too there are cases in which some sort of appeal to feeling produces an acceptable argument:

There are thousands of undernourished, diseased babies in Ethiopia. So it is urgent that you donate to the Red Cross.

This is a kind of appeal to feeling. It summons up images of starving, dying children, hence feelings of pity and (the arguer hopes) the desire to help them. It makes the listener disposed to accept the conclusion. Yet the argument does provide a reason to donate to the Red Cross: There are thousands of undernourished, diseased babies in Ethiopia. In other words, this argument is not a fallacious appeal to feeling, even though feelings may well be aroused in the course of considering the argument.

12.7 Appeals to Force

A cousin of the appeal to feeling is the appeal to force. An **APPEAL TO FORCE** is the attempt to get someone to accept a statement as true (or false) through threats, bribes, intimidation, etc. Such appeals are usually fallacious. For example, the hit man tells the eye witness to a murder:

You saw nothin'—because if you did, you'll be dead too!

If this is an attempt to justify the statement "You saw nothin'" with a death threat, then it is an argument of sorts. But it is a terribly Weak argument. Threats, bribes, intimidation, and the like can't make false what's true. The hit man can threaten all he wants. This doesn't make it false that the witness saw the murder.

As with many of the other arguments in the chapter, there are justifications that resemble fallacious appeals to force but that are not Weak. Con-

sider how the eyewitness might reason after hearing the hit man's "argument":

> *He's very likely to carry out his threat. And the police can't offer me protection. So it would be safest for me to say that I didn't see anything.*

The premises of the above argument, if true, give good reason to believe the conclusion.

12.8 Arguments from Ignorance

An **ARGUMENT FROM IGNORANCE** in its fallacious form has one of two simple, basic structures. Either:

Statement *P* hasn't been proven true.

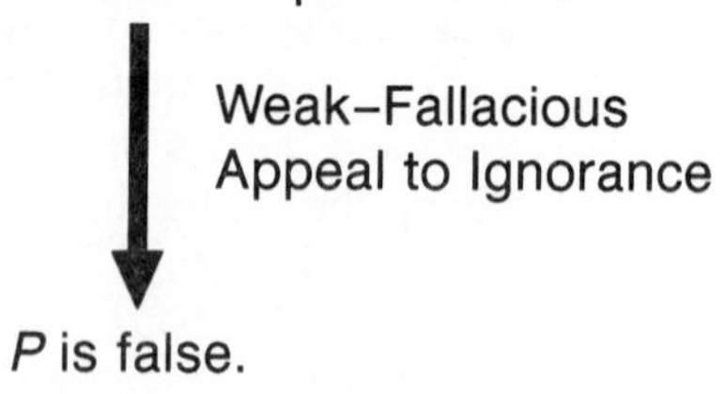

P is false.

Or:

Statement *P* hasn't been proven false.

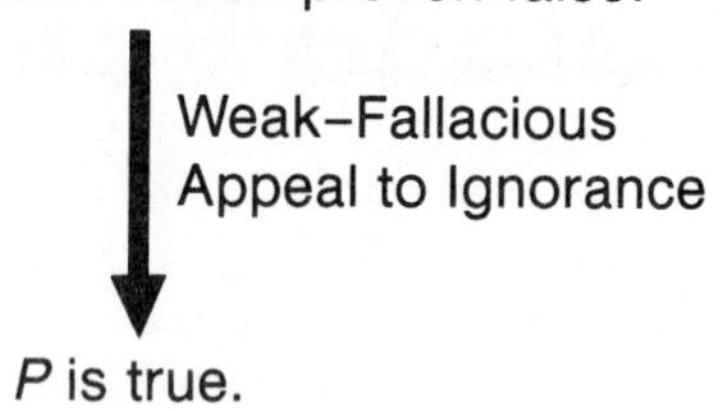

P is true.

Some simple examples:

> *It has not been conclusively proven that there are no ghosts. So I conclude that there are ghosts.*

> *It has not been conclusively proven that there are ghosts. So I conclude that there are no ghosts.*

Such arguments are fallacious (and therefore Weak) because it simply does not follow from the fact that a statement is true because it hasn't been shown to be false and, vice versa, it simply does not follow that a statement is false because it hasn't been proven true.

If such arguments were Strong, they could establish the most outrageous conclusions. You claim that every once in a while, at night, while I'm asleep, gremlins come into my home office library and rearrange the books, silently, and put them back in order every morning before I get up. I say to you that this is preposterous. If your appeal to ignorance were Strong, you would in effect have good reason to believe in gremlins:

> *You can't show me that gremlins* don't *rearrange your books occasionally at night, only to put them back in order in the morning. So, therefore, gremlins* do *just that!*

However, this is a fallacious appeal to ignorance. There is no good reason whatsoever in this argument to believe in its conclusion.

Two important warnings must be offered about arguments from ignorance.

First, there are Strong arguments that superficially resemble fallacious appeals to ignorance. For example,

Exhaustive tests have shown that it
is not true that aspartame causes cancer.

Aspartame does not cause cancer.

This argument is Strong, not fallacious, because if its premise is true—if it's true that exhaustive tests have shown that the statement "Aspartame causes cancer" is false—then we have good reason to believe that the conclusion is true. This argument is a Strong inductive generalization, not a fallacious appeal to ignorance.

Second, there is something in American law known as "legal presumption." The best-known legal presumption is "A person is innocent until proven guilty." A less well-known legal presumption is this: If a man and woman have gone through a legal wedding and have spent the night together, it is presumed that they have consummated their marriage (i.e., have had sexual intercourse). The law uses such presumptions to place the burden of proof. The prosecutor must prove the defendant in a criminal case guilty, since the defendant's innocence is presumed. Someone seeking a marriage annulment must prove that the marriage was not consummated, since the law presumes that it was (if the couple spent the night together). This makes it appear as if the law accepts some appeals to ignorance as valid, not fallacious. That is, the law accepts such arguments as these:

Brian has not been proven guilty.

Brian is not guilty (i.e., is innocent).

It has not been proven that George and Martha did not consummate their marriage.

↓

George and Martha consummated their marriage.

These appear to be appeals to ignorance. Are we to say that the law accepts what logic rejects (thereby showing the law to be in part irrational)?

No, for in fact arguments based on legal presumption are not really fallacious appeals to ignorance, despite their appearing to be so. There is an ambiguity, introduced by the law, in such terms as "guilt," "innocence," and "consummated a marriage." The ambiguity can be represented this way:

Innocent ⟨ In fact innocent / Legally determined to be innocent

Guilty ⟨ In fact guilty / Legally determined to be guilty

Consummated a marriage ⟨ In fact consummated a marriage / Legally determined to have consummated a marriage

Someone may be in fact innocent, but not have been legally determined to be innocent. Someone may have been legally determined to be guilty, but not be in fact guilty. Someone may be legally determined to have consummated a marriage, but in fact did not consummate the marriage. In other words, a simple statement such as,

He's guilty.

is ambiguous. Which is meant?

He's been legally determined to be guilty.

He's in fact guilty.

When the law speaks—e.g., when a judicial ruling is made—the law intends the legal sense of these terms. Thus, when the law presumes that a duly married couple who spent the night together have consummated their marriage, the law intends the legal sense of this term. But what is the legal sense of these terms? Part of what the law means by such terms as "legal guilt" or "legal consummation of a marriage" involves legal proof. That is, "legal guilt" means (in part) "proven guilty using valid legal procedure," and "legal consummation of a marriage" means (in part) "spent the night together after having been validly married."

The previous arguments, then, are not guilty of committing a fallacious appeal to ignorance. Rather, they are Deductively Valid by the meaning of the terms involved (see Chapter 8):

Brian has not been proven LEGALLY guilty.

↓ DV, by meaning of "LEGALLY guilty"

Brian is not LEGALLY guilty (i.e., is LEGALLY innocent).

It has not been proven that George and Martha did not LEGALLY consummate their marriage.

↓ DV, by meaning of "LEGALLY consummate"

George and Martha LEGALLY consummated their marriage.

12.9 The Gambler's Fallacy

The Gambler's Fallacy involves some misconceptions about the nature of probability, and so first we should introduce some correct conceptions. Here's one rule:

n = *the number of possibilities*

s = *some specific possibility*

t = *the number of tries*

The probability of getting s = s/n × t.

For example, take an ordinary deck of 52 playing cards. Suppose you are asked the probability of drawing the ace of spades in one try. In this case,

n = *52*

s = *1 (there's one ace of spades)*

t = *1 (one try)*

The probability of getting the ace of spades = 1/52 × 1.

For another example, take again an ordinary deck of 52 playing cards. Suppose you are this time asked the probability of drawing an ace in one try. In this case,

n = 52

s = 4 (there are 4 aces)

t = 1 (one try)

The probability of drawing an ace = 4/52 × 1 = 1/13.

Let's see how the gambler's fallacy is committed. You are gambling. The game you're playing is simple. You bet against someone that you will draw an ace. An ordinary deck of 52 cards is used. You draw a card at random. If it's an ace, you win $10. If you don't draw an ace, you lose $1. (Never mind if these are good odds.) Whatever card you draw is replaced in the deck, and you can try again. Suppose you make 6 tries, and fail to draw an ace. You might be tempted to make this argument to yourself:

I've failed to draw an ace
six times in a row.

↓ Weak–Gambler's Fallacy

I'm almost certain to draw an
ace the next time.

The reason this argument is Weak is that your odds for drawing an ace *are the same for each try (1/13)*! Just because you've failed to draw an ace for six tries does not mean that your chances on the seventh try are somehow increased. Your chances on the seventh try are exactly the same as for each of the first six: 1/13, no more, no less.

I suspect that committing the gambler's fallacy is rooted in superstitious ideas about luck. "My luck is bound to change this time," losing gamblers say to themselves, thereby convincing themselves that the odds will miraculously be changed in their favor. But the odds are mathematically determined, and have nothing to do with luck.

The gambler's fallacy, in effect, links two events together that have nothing to do with one another. More accurately, the form of the fallacy is this:

THE GAMBLER'S FALLACY. Suppose there are two events, *E1* and *E2*, which are such that

a. There is a certain probability that *E2* will occur.

b. This probably will remain unaffected whether *E1* occurs or not.

The gambler's fallacy is committed when it is assumed that because *E1* occurred, the probability of *E2* is changed (goes up or down).

In the preceding example about drawing an ace, the gambler's fallacy was committed because one event (*E1* = six tries that failed to produce an ace), does not affect the probability of another event (*E2* = drawing an ace on the seventh try). Yet the argument denied this.

The gambler's fallacy is usually associated with—as the name suggests—gambling. Yet other situations that are not strictly speaking games can give rise to the gambler's fallacy. Suppose you are going on a transatlantic flight. You are worried about being hijacked by terrorists. For the sake of argument, suppose that in the past 1 out of 10,000 airplanes on transatlantic flights gets hijacked. Therefore the probability that your plane will be hijacked is 1/10,000. Suppose you try to beat the odds by carrying a rabbit's foot in your pocket. You in effect make this argument to yourself:

I'm carrying my lucky rabbit's foot.

↓ Weak–Gambler's Fallacy

I'm less likely (i.e., my chances are
less than 1/10,000) to get hijacked.

This argument is Weak since carrying a rabbit's foot cannot change the odds of your being hijacked.

As with the case of some of the other fallacies discussed in this chapter, not every argument that looks like the gambler's fallacy *is* a gambler's fallacy. Suppose, again, that you are taking a transatlantic flight, and that 1 out of 10,000 transatlantic flights are hijacked. But now suppose that this is only an average. Suppose that some kinds of flights are hijacked more frequently than others. Suppose that flights originating from Canada have only a 1 in 12,000 chance of being hijacked. If you make this argument,

For my transatlantic crossing, I'll take
a flight out of Toronto.

↓ Strong

My odds of being hijacked are less than 1/10,000

you've made a Strong induction. You haven't committed the gambler's fallacy, and the reason is that you've done something that has actually changed your odds.

KEY POINTS

GENETIC FALLACY. An argument that attempts to argue that some statement is true (or false) merely on the basis of how that statement came to be made commits the genetic fallacy and is therefore Weak.

- "That cake will taste awful, for the recipe for it came to your mother in a dream" commits the genetic fallacy. It might explain how the recipe came about, but does not justify the conclusion that the cake will taste awful.

AD HOMINEM ARGUMENTS are arguments directed at a person.

- **AD HOMINEM RULE.** An argument that uses positive or negative facts about a person to attempt to show the person's statement true or false commits the **AD HOMINEM FALLACY** and is accordingly Weak. An argument that relies on an inductive generalization about a person using facts about the person's past behavior does not commit the ad hominem fallacy, and may well be Strong.
- Both "She's an upstanding citizen, so her claim must be true" and "He's a convicted criminal so his claim must be false" commit the ad hominem fallacy.
- Not all arguments that use facts about a person commit the ad hominem fallacy. "She's lied constantly in the past, so her word is simply not to be trusted now" is a Strong inductive generalization.

The **TU QUOQUE FALLACY** is a kind of ad hominem argument. It's form is: You profess that *P* is true, yet you behave inconsistently with the fact of *P*, so *P* is false.

- Example: "You say that drugs are really dangerous. But you too use drugs all the time: You smoke and drink every evening before dinner. So drugs are *not* really dangerous!"

APPEALS TO AUTHORITY are arguments that attempt to prove their conclusion by citing an authority that confirms it.

- **APPEAL TO AUTHORITY RULE.** An argument that attempts to justify its conclusion by appeal to an authority who supports the conclusion is Strong if the authority is appropriate and reliable, fallacious (and therefore Weak) if the authority is not appropriate or not reliable.
- Strong appeals to authority cite appropriate and reliable authorities. For example, "The cancer specialist says that chemotherapy will put your cancer into remission, so chemotherapy will put your cancer into remission" is a Strong appeal to authority.

- Fallacious appeals to authority cite either inappropriate or unreliable authorities. For example, "The cancer specialist says that you can go for 10,000 miles without an oil change, so you can go for 10,000 miles without an oil change" is a fallacious appeal to authority.

- An informal appeal to authority is made when we take someone's word for it even though that person is not a "specialist" in anything. "Gertrude says that she saw Pablo take the wallet from Alice's purse, so Pablo did take the wallet from Alice's purse" is an informal appeal to authority. Here we have to decide if Gertrude was in a position to know that what she says is true and if Gertrude is reliable.

- Some areas, notably aesthetics and ethics, may not be grounds for any kind of appeal to authority. It is controversial whether there could be authorities in such areas. Is an experienced music critic in a better position than you or I know that the symphony is good? Is a member of the clergy in a better position than you or I to know that abortion is wrong?

APPEALS TO THE PEOPLE are arguments that attempt to justify a statement on the grounds that "everybody" says that statement is so. Such appeals are a kind of appeal to authority, appealing not to the authority of some individual but rather to the authority of a community. But since "everybody" is not an authority on anything, appeals to the people are usually Weak.

Arguments that **APPEAL TO FEELINGS** attempt to succeed by arousing positive feelings toward some statement in order to get you to think the statement is true, or by arousing negative feelings toward some statement in order to get you to think the statement is false.

- Such arguments are in general fallacious. "My client is a great painter, therefore he is innocent of stealing the wallet" gives next to no good reason to believe that its conclusion is true.

- However, not every argument that arouses feelings is a fallacious appeal to feeling. "There are thousands of undernourished, diseased babies in Ethiopia; so you ought to donate to the Red Cross" is an argument that might well arouse strong feelings, but actually gives a good reason to donate to the Red Cross.

An **APPEAL TO FORCE** is the attempt to get someone to accept a statement as true (or false) through threats, bribes, intimidation, etc. Such appeals are usually fallacious, for threats, bribes, intimidation, and the like cannot make what is true false.

ARGUMENTS FROM IGNORANCE are fallacious. They have one of two forms: (1) "*P* hasn't been proved true, so *P* is false." (2) "*P* hasn't been proved false, so *P* is true."

- Example of a fallacious appeal to ignorance: "It hasn't been shown that there are no ghosts, so there are ghosts."

- But there are arguments that superficially resemble fallacious appeals to ignorance, but that are not fallacious at all.

- "Exhaustive tests have shown that *P* is false, so *P* is false" is a Strong inductive generalization, not a fallacious appeal to ignorance.
- Legal presumptions like "He's not been proven guilty, so he's innocent," appear to be appeals to ignorance but are actually Deductively Valid by virtue of the legal meanings of "guilty" and "innocent."

The **GAMBLER'S FALLACY** assumes that doing something that has nothing to do with the odds will somehow change the odds.

- "I've lost every hand at poker so far this evening. So I'm bound to win the next hand" is an example of the gambler's fallacy.
- However, sometimes you can change the odds. This argument does not commit the gambler's fallacy: "I've lost every hand so far tonight, but I've just put four aces up my sleeve, so I'm bound to win the next poker hand."

EXERCISES

For each of the following:

1. Decide whether it is or contains a justification. If there is no justification (but instead an explanation or just a series of statements) say so, and go on to the next problem.

2. If there is a justification in the problem, diagram it. Use the shorthand method (numbering the statements) where possible. If needed, rewrite the argument.

3. Assess its degree of validity: Deductively Valid, Strong, Medium, or Weak.

4. Justify your assessment. In particular, if a justification commits a fallacy, point out which fallacy it commits.

***1.** In Shakespeare's *Julius Caesar*, Brutus (one of Caesar's assassins) says to the Roman crowd:

> *Believe me for mine honour, and have respect to mine honour, that you may believe. (III.ii)*

This is a justification. The argument restated is:

I am honorable. + You should respect my honor.

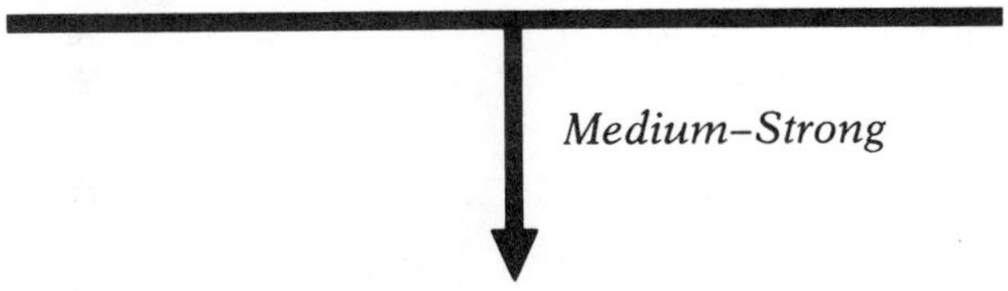

Medium–Strong

You should believe me.

This is not, appearances aside, an ad hominem fallacy. If the premises are true—in particular, if Brutus really is honorable—then it will make for a Medium to Strong inference to the conclusion that you should believe him. After all, doesn't being honorable imply being worthy of being believed?

2. There is a God, for if you don't believe in Him He'll damn you to Hell.

3. He: "It ain't no good because it's broke."
She: "Your argument must be bad because it uses bad grammar."
How good is *her* argument?

***4.** The seventeenth-century French mathematician Pierre de Fermat presented without proof a certain theorem, which has become known as "Fermat's Last Theorem."* (1) ⟨No mathematician has ever been able to prove it true, even though prizes have been offered for a proof,⟩ so (2) ⟨it must be false.⟩

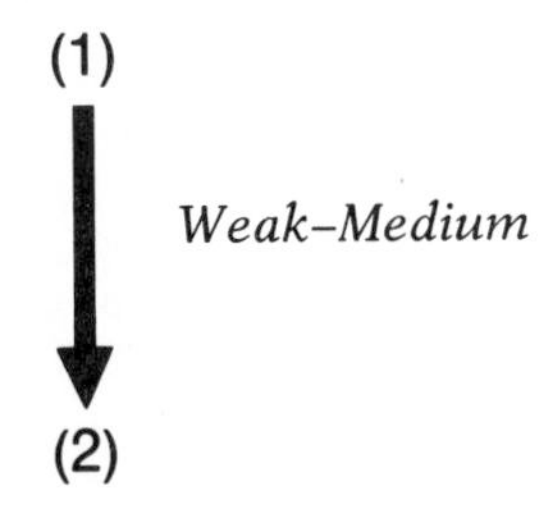

Although this looks like a fallacious appeal to ignorance (and hence a Weak argument), it isn't clearly a fallacy for the fact that no mathematician since the seventeenth century has been able to prove Fermat's Last Theorem true is some *reason to believe that it's false.*

5. A person's belief in God is the result of an infantile wish for fatherly protection against the misfortunes of life. So there really is no God.

*Fermat's Last Theorem states that the equation,

$$X^n + Y^n = Z^n$$

where X, Y, and Z are non-zero integers, has no solutions for n greater than 2.

6. Oh, Officer, I don't deserve a ticket for speeding. I'm out of work, out of money, and out of luck.

7. Oh, Officer, I don't deserve a ticket for speeding. The speed limit on this road is 40 m.p.h., and I was careful not to go over 35.

8. Former President Richard Nixon has given several speeches on foreign policy. But the man is a known liar—as proved by the Watergate scandal. So how can you accept anything he says on foreign policy?

9. I never noticed any static on the phone. So there isn't any.

10. You say *my* tie doesn't go with my jacket. But look at you. Your hair is pink and you're wearing black lipstick, a leather shirt, and a kilt! Your taste is not to be trusted.

11. The Ayatollah says that wearing makeup is wrong. So wearing makeup *is* wrong.

12. The Book of Genesis of the Old Testament contradicts the theory of evolution, and therefore that theory is wrong.

13. John is a ruthless businessman, so he must be trying to trick you when he says that the check is in the mail.

14. Quincy told you that the prime minister didn't lie. But how can you believe him? Quincy's the minister's brother!

15. He maintains that labor unions generally promote better working conditions. But he's only saying this because his father is active in the labor movement.

16. There is no listing for "Alfred E. Newman" in the phone directory. Therefore he doesn't have a phone.

17. Tails will show on the next toss of the coin, for the past six tosses have been heads.

18. Tails will not show on the next toss of the coin, for the past six tosses have been heads.

19. Tails will not show on the next toss of the coin, for the past one million tosses have been heads.

20. No one thinks a woman must have a baby she doesn't want. So abortion on demand is a humanitarian requirement.

21. You often claim to be in favor of improving the lot of the less fortunate. Yet you always vote Republican and are stingy in your contributions to charity. So I think that you're insincere.

22. You Americans have no right to condemn our racial policies, for you Americans have your own history of segregation. (Remark by P. W. Botha, Prime Minister of South Africa)

23. Perhaps there may be some one who is offended at me, when he calls to mind how he himself on a similar, or even a less serious occasion, prayed and entreated the judges with many tears, and how he produced his children in court, which was a moving spectacle, together with a host of relations and friends; whereas I, who am probably in danger of my life, will do none of these things. The contrast may occur to his mind, and he may be set against me, and vote in anger because he is displeased at me on this account. Now if there be such a person among you—mind, I do not say that there is—to him I may fairly reply: My friend, I am a man, and like other men, a creature of flesh and blood, and not 'of wood or stone,' as Homer says; and I have a family, yes, and sons, O Athenians, three in number, one almost a man, and two others who are still young; and yet I will not bring any of them hither in order to petition you for acquittal. (Socrates' defense of himself during his trial for "impiety" and "corrupting the young" as reported by Plato in the *Apology*.)

24. Many investors think that if they try to 'time' their purchases and sales with market lows and highs that they will win at the investment game. But it's even difficult for investment professionals to consistently pick market peaks and bottoms, so individual investors will probably have even more difficulty in getting the market timing just right. (Merrill Lynch, Quarterly Report of Capital Fund, December 21, 1984)

25. For, if the distinction of degrees is infinite, so that there is among them no degree, than which no higher can be found, our course of reasoning reaches this conclusion: that the multitude of natures themselves is not limited by any bounds. But only an absurdly foolish man can fail to regard such a conclusion as absurdly foolish. There is, then, necessarily some nature which is so superior to some nature of natures, that there is none in comparison with which it is ranked as inferior. (St. Anselm, *Monologium*.)

GLOSSARY

AD HOMINEM FALLACY Ad hominem is Latin for "at the person." An argument commits the ad hominem FALLACY when it uses some fact or other about the person making a statement to prove the truth or falsity of the statement itself. "Freud's theory of infantile sexuality is nonsense, for Freud only propounded it because he was a dirty old man" commits the ad hominem fallacy.

AMBIGUITY A statement is ambiguous if it can mean either one of two (or more) things, but we can't tell which, given the context we have. "Jerry went to the bank." Did Jerry go to the side of a river or to a place where money is kept? See FALLACY OF EQUIVOCATION and RELATIVE TERMS.

ANALOGICAL ARGUMENT An INDUCTIVE ARGUMENT that draws a conclusion about something unknown or unfamiliar on the basis of a similarity with something known or familiar. For example, "I've enjoyed reading novels *A*, *B*, and *C*. Each of these was by the same author. Novel *D* is by that author too, and so I conclude I'll enjoy reading it too." The rules for evaluating analogical arguments are SIMILARITY and RELEVANCE. See also UNKNOWN INSTANCE, UNKNOWN PROPERTY, KNOWN INSTANCE, and KNOWN PROPERTIES. The FALLACIES associated with analogical arguments are FALLACIOUS ANALOGY and IRRELEVANT ANALOGY. Compare ANALOGY.

ANALOGY An analogy is a statement of similarity, e.g., "A mango tastes like a peach." In itself, an analogy is not an ANALOGICAL ARGUMENT.

ANTECEDENT The antecedent of a CONDITIONAL is the statement that follows "if" or precedes "only if." The antecedent of "If it rains, we'll go to the movies" is "It rains." See SUFFICIENT CONDITION. Compare CONSEQUENT and NECESSARY CONDITION.

APPEAL TO AUTHORITY

An appeal to authority is an INDUCTIVE ARGUMENT. "Doctor Jones says your appendix has to come out, so your appendix has to come out" is an appeal to authority. Appeals to authority are STRONG when the authority is appropriate and reliable. Compare FALLACIOUS APPEAL TO AUTHORITY.

ARGUMENT

Discourse in which evidence in the form of statements, called PREMISES, is given to establish the truth of another statement, called the CONCLUSION. See JUSTIFICATION, LOGIC, VALIDITY, and SOUNDNESS.

ARGUMENT DIAGRAM

A graphic method of illustrating the structure of an ARGUMENT. The most basic structure is an arrow pointing from the PREMISE to the CONCLUSION:

For example, "He's a heroin addict, and therefore unreliable." See DEPENDENT REASONS, INDEPENDENT REASONS, DIVERGENT CONCLUSION, and CHAIN ARGUMENT.

ARISTOTELEAN INTERPRETATION

An interpretation of the (A) and (E) categorical statements according to which these statements are taken to imply the existence of members of the subject class. For example, the Aristotelean interpretation claims that both "All pirates are dangerous" and "No pirates are dangerous" imply the existence of pirates. On this interpretation, "All *A* are *B*" means "There are *A*'s and all of them are *B*," while "No *A* are *B*" means "There are *A*'s but none of them are *B*." See CATEGORICAL STATEMENT and EXISTENTIAL IMPORT. Compare MODERN INTERPRETATION.

BACKGROUND CONDITIONS

Background conditions are assumed to be true and to play some role in the causal process, but are not, properly speaking, part of what we mean by "the CAUSE of an event."

BEGGING THE QUESTION

Another term for CIRCULAR REASONING.

BICONDITIONAL

A biconditional asserts a LOGICAL EQUIVALENCE. The biconditional is expressed in English as "P if and only if Q," which asserts both "If P then Q" and "If Q then P." The truthtable for the biconditional is:

P,	Q	P if and only if Q
T	T	T
T	F	F
F	T	F
F	F	T

The biconditional "*P* if and only if *Q*" asserts that *P* is a NECESSARY CONDITION and a SUFFICIENT CONDITION for *Q*. Compare CONDITIONAL.

CATEGORICAL STATEMENT

A categorical statement is a statement that describes some relation between two CATEGORIES. The four standard categorical statements, with their standard abbreviations, are: (A) All *X* are *Y*. (E) No *X* are *Y*. (I) Some *X* are *Y*. (O) Some *X* are not *Y*. (A) and (E) are UNIVERSAL STATEMENTS. (I) and (O) are particular statements. (A) and (I) are affirmative because they assert that two categories are related. (E) and (O) are negative because they deny membership in some category. See EXISTENTIAL IMPORT, ARISTOTELEAN INTERPRETATION, MODERN INTERPRETATION, QUANTIFIER, and ONLY.

CATEGORICAL SYLLOGISM

A categorical syllogism is a deductive argument with two premises and a conclusion, all of which must be CATEGORICAL STATEMENTS and that contain exactly three CATEGORIES. Compare SYLLOGISM. (See also MAJOR TERM, MINOR TERM, MIDDLE TERM, MAJOR PREMISE, MINOR PREMISE, MOOD, and FIGURE.)

CATEGORY

A category is simply a group or set of things. Examples of categories are *pirates, pirates who sail the Caribbean,* and *dangerous pirates.* Each of these names a different category. See CLASS.

CAUSAL ARGUMENT

A causal argument is an INDUCTIVE ARGUMENT that a CAUSAL STATEMENT is true. See MILL'S METHODS, POST HOC FALLACY, and CONFUSING CAUSE AND EFFECT.

CAUSAL HYPOTHESIS

A causal hypothesis is a good guess as to the cause of some event. A causal hypothesis is testable by MILL'S METHODS.

CAUSAL STATEMENT

A causal statement is of the form, "*A* (or *A* and *B* and . . .) caused *X*." Compare CAUSAL ARGUMENT. "*A* caused *B*" means that *A* is among the set of events that played a role in making *B* happen, but *A* is out of the ordinary, novel, unusual, or otherwise of interest. Compare BACKGROUND CONDITIONS.

CHAIN ARGUMENT

An argument that has two or more conclusions is a chain argument when one conclusion is advanced on the basis of some premise(s), and that conclusion is then used as the reason for yet another conclusion. Compare DIVERGENT CONCLUSIONS. The basic structure of a chain argument is:

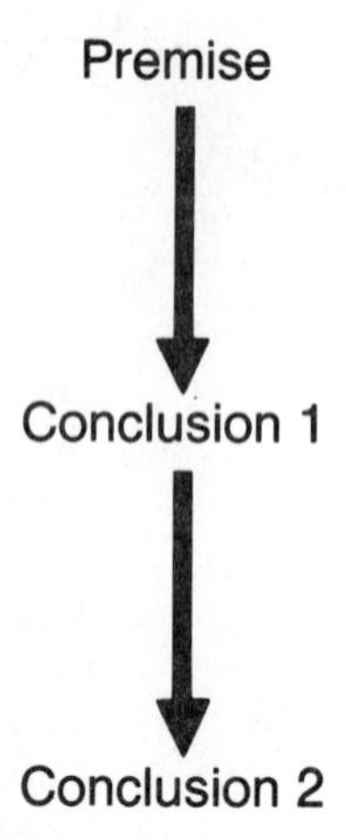

For example, "He's a heroin addict, and so he's unreliable; and because he's unreliable, he'll be a poor employee."

CIRCULAR REASONING

Circular reasoning is arguing in a circle: assuming in your premise precisely what you hope to establish in your conclusion. Another term for circular reasoning is BEGGING THE QUESTION. If the question is "Is *X* true?" you've begged the question by assuming *X* in your premise, only to "prove" it in the conclusion. For example, "God exists because it says so in the Bible, and the Bible is true because it is God's word." The Latin term for this fallacy is PETITIO PRINCIPII.

CLASS

The more modern name for CATEGORY.

CLASSICAL INTERPRETATION

See ARISTOTELEAN INTERPRETATION.

COMPOUND JUSTIFICATION

A compound justification is a complex argument consisting of at least two SIMPLE JUSTIFICATIONS. A compound justification, when diagrammed, would have more than one "arrow." For example,

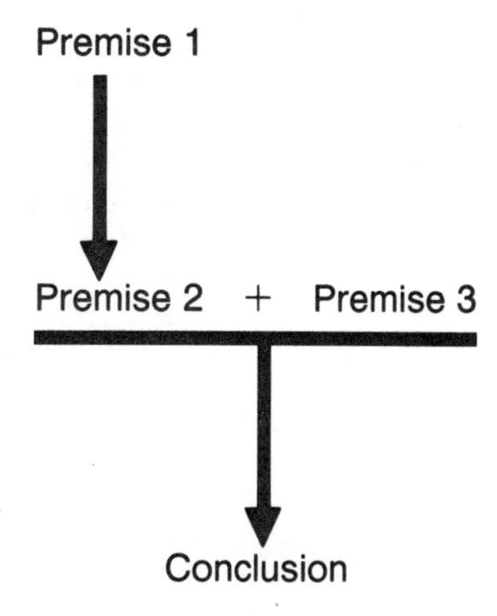

COMPOUND STATEMENT

A compound statement is a statement that contains one or more positive statements as meaningful parts. "He's at home or he's at the office" is a compound statement. Compare SIMPLE STATEMENT.

CONCLUSION

The statement or statements in an argument that is supposedly proved by other statements, called PREMISES. See ARGUMENT.

CONCLUSION INDICATOR

A term or terms that often comes before the CONCLUSION of an ARGUMENT. Examples of conclusion indicators are "therefore," "thus," and "it follows that." Arguments need not have conclusion indicators.

CONDITIONAL

A conditional is a COMPOUND STATEMENT. It can be expressed in a number of ways: "If *P* then *Q*," If *P*, *Q*," "*Q*, if *P*," "*P* only if *Q*," and so on. The truthtable for the conditional is:

P, Q	If P then Q
T T	T
T F	F
F T	T
F F	T

See ANTECEDENT, CONSEQUENT, SUFFICIENT CONDITION, NECESSARY CONDITION, BICONDITIONAL, CONTRAPOSITION, MODUS PONENS, MODUS TOLLENS, FALLACY OF AFFIRMING THE CONSEQUENT, FALLACY OF DENYING THE ANTECEDENT, HYPOTHETICAL SYLLOGISM, and UNLESS EQUIVALENCE.

CONFUSING CAUSE AND EFFECT

A FALLACY associated with CAUSAL ARGUMENTS, which as its name suggests asserts that A caused B when in fact it is B that caused A. For example, believing that the water wheel causes the river to flow confuses cause and effect.

CONJUNCT

Any statement that is part of a CONJUNCTION. For example, "He's eaten" is one conjunct of the conjunction "He's eaten and is satisfied."

CONJUNCTION

A conjunction is a COMPOUND STATEMENT that asserts that each CONJUNCT is true. The terms "and," "but," "although," "while," and "(even) though" are used to assert conjunction. The truthtable for conjunction is:

P, Q	P and Q
T T	T
T F	F
F T	F
F F	F

This truthtable in effect says that a conjunction is true only when all its CONJUNCTS are true. See CONJUNCTION ORDER, SIMPLIFICATION, and NEITHER. Compare DISJUNCTION.

CONJUNCTION ORDER

A rule that asserts that the order of CONJUNCTS in a CONJUNCTION is irrelevant to the truthvale of the conjunction:

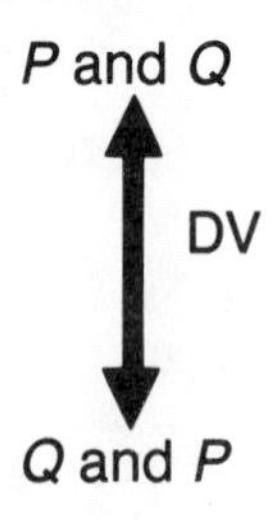

See LOGICAL EQUIVALENCE.

CONNECTIVE

A term that creates a COMPOUND STATEMENT out of one or more SIMPLE STATEMENTS. The connectives studied in *Basic Logic* are TRUTHFUNCTIONAL CONNECTIVES.

CONSEQUENT

The consequent of a CONDITIONAL is the statement that follows "then" (if there is a "then") or that follows "only if" (when there is an "only if"). For example, the consequent of "If it rains, we'll go to the movies" is "We'll go to the movies." See NECESSARY CONDITION. Compare ANTECEDENT and SUFFICIENT CONDITION.

CONSISTENCY

As used in this book, consistency is a rule for evaluating INDUCTIVE GENERALIZATIONS: The conclusion of an inductive generalization must not contradict the evidence given in the premises. If it does, the argument is WEAK. See UNIFORMITY, QUANTITY, and VARIETY.

CONTRADICTION

A contradiction is a necessarily false statement, typically of the form "*P* and not *P*." See LOGICAL IMPOSSIBILITY.

CONTRAPOSITION

A valid rule of deductive logic for CONDITIONALS:

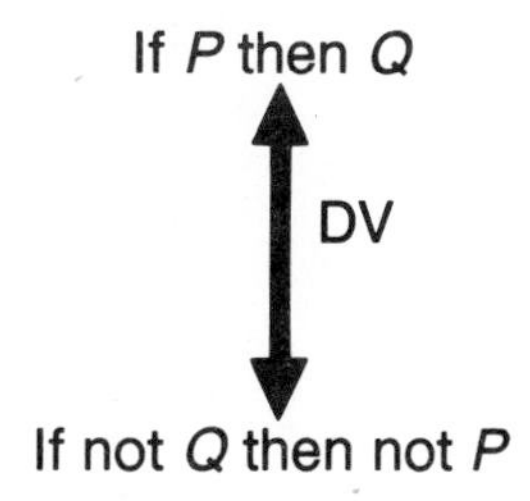

Take care not to confuse contraposition with this invalid rule:

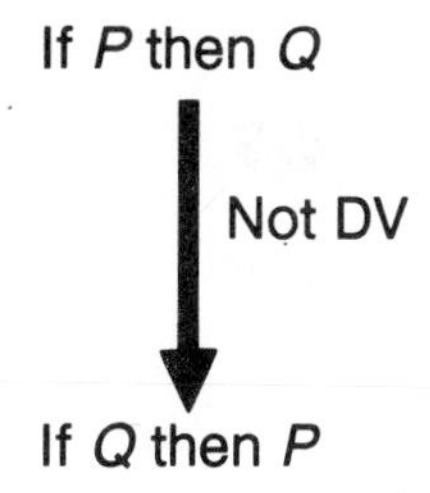

See DEDUCTIVE VALIDITY and LOGICAL EQUIVALENCE.

DEDUCTION

Deduction is the attempt to draw out a conclusion that is supposedly already contained in the premises. Verbally, deduction is expressed in a DEDUCTIVE ARGUMENT. The maker of a deductive argument aspires to a DEDUCTIVELY VALID argument. "All crows are black; this is a crow; therefore it is black" is a deductive argument. Compare INDUCTION.

DEDUCTIVE ARGUMENT

See DEDUCTION.

DEDUCTIVE LOGIC

Rules for determining when an argument is DEDUCTIVELY VALID. In *Basic Logic*, deductive logic is studied in Part Two.

DEDUCTIVE VALIDITY

A SIMPLE JUSTIFICATION is deductively valid just in case while supposing its premises to be true, its conclusion must be true as well. Deductive Validity is the highest degree of support premises can lend their conclusions. An argument that is Deductively Valid and has all true premises is SOUND. See DEDUCTION. In this book DEDUCTIVE VALIDITY is often abbreviated DV.

DEGREES OF VALIDITY

The amount of support the premises lend the conclusion of an argument. An argument can be DEDUCTIVELY VALID, STRONG, MEDIUM, or WEAK.

DE MORGAN'S LAWS

Valid rules of deductive logic asserting a LOGICAL EQUIVALENCE between CONJUNCTION and DISJUNCTION:

See SCOPE and DEDUCTIVE VALIDITY.

DEPENDENT REASONS

An argument that has two or more premises or reasons contains dependent reasons when the reasons together make the overall strength of the argument much higher than they would considered separately. Compare INDEPENDENT REASONS. The basic structure of an argument with dependent reasons is:

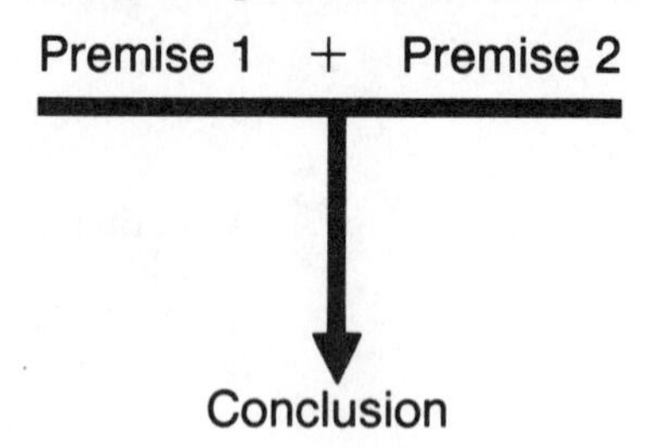

For example, "Going over 55 m.p.h. violates the law and you shouldn't violate the law; so you shouldn't go over 55 m.p.h."

DILEMMA

A dilemma employs a DEDUCTIVELY VALID argument form:

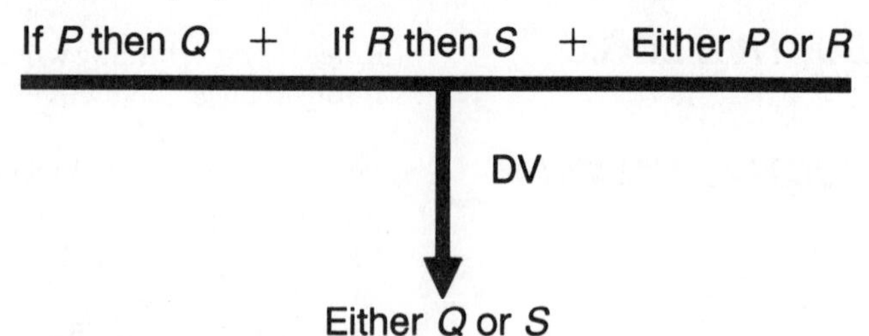

The main issue about any dilemma is whether its premises are true. To be faced with a DV dilemma is to be caught on its horns. To escape a dilemma is to show one or more of the premises to be false. To disprove one of the CONDITIONALS is to grasp one of the horns of the dilemma. To attack the DISJUNCTION is to go between the horns. See FALSE ALTERNATIVES.

DISJUNCT

A statement that is part of a DISJUNCTION. For example, "She's at home" is one disjunct of the disjunction, "She's either at the library or at home."

DISJUNCTION

A COMPOUND STATEMENT that joins two (or more) SIMPLE STATEMENTS with "Either. . . or" or simply "Or." The TRUTH-TABLE for disjunction is:

P,	Q	P or Q
T	T	T
T	F	T
F	T	T
F	F	F

This truthtable in effect says that a disjunction is true when any one of its DISJUNCTS is true. See DISJUNCTIVE ORDER and DISJUNCTIVE SYLLOGISM. Compare CONJUNCTION and NEITHER.

DISJUNCTIVE ORDER

A rule that says that the order of DISJUNCTS in a DISJUNCTION is irrelevant to the truthvalue of the disjunction:

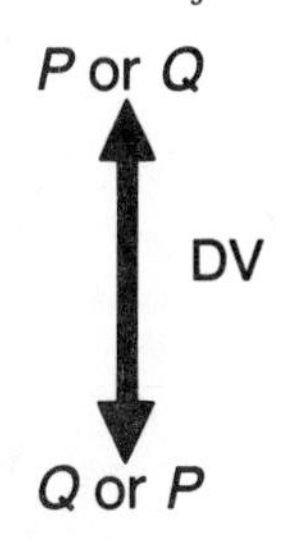

See LOGICAL EQUIVALENCE.

DISJUNCTIVE SYLLOGISM

A valid rule of deductive logic:

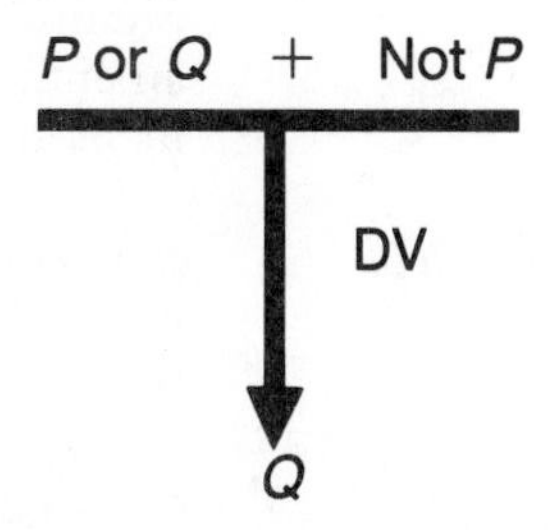

See DEDUCTIVE VALIDITY and DISJUNCTION.

DIVERGENT CONCLUSIONS

An argument that has two or more conclusions has divergent conclusions when each is inferred separately from the same premise(s). Compare CHAIN ARGUMENT. The basic structure of an argument with divergent conclusions is:

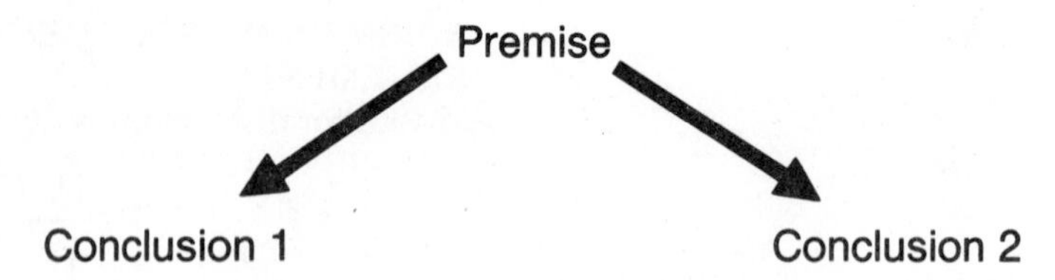

For example, "Because he's a heroin addict, he'll be unreliable, and besides, he'll also be desperate for cash."

DOUBLE NEGATION

A valid rule of deductive logic:

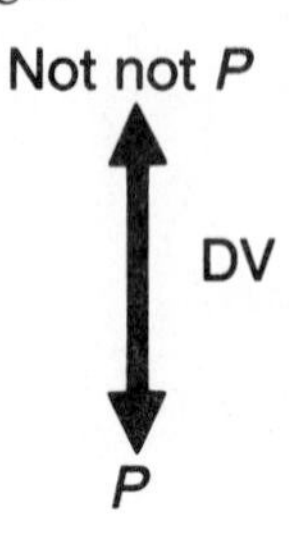

See LOGICAL EQUIVALENCE.

DV

Abbreviation for DEDUCTIVELY VALID.

ENTAILMENT

When an argument is DEDUCTIVELY VALID, its premises are said to entail their conclusion. "Entails" and implies" are synonyms. See IMPLICATION.

ENTHYMEME

An enthymeme is an argument with an unexpressed premise (or premises). For example, "Socrates is mortal because he's human" is an enthymeme because it leaves unexpressed the premise "All humans are mortal."

EXISTENTIAL IMPORT

A statement is said to have existential import when it implies the existence of members of the subject class. In any standard interpretation, the PARTICULAR STATEMENTS, (I) and (O), each have existential import. That is, the (I) statement, for example "Some pirates are dangerous," implies the existence of pirates. The (O) statement, for example "Some pirates are not dangerous," also implies the existence of pirates. However, interpretations of the UNIVERSAL STATEMENTS, (A) and (E), differ as to whether they assign existential import. The ARISTOTELEAN INTERPRETATION claims that (A) and (E) statements have existential import. The MODERN INTERPRETATION denies that (A) and (E) have existential import. See CATEGORICAL STATEMENT.

EXPLANATION
An explanation usually accepts some statement as true, and tries to provide an account of why that statement is true. "John's mother locked him in the closet when he was a child, and that's why he's afraid of the dark" is an example of an explanation. Compare JUSTIFICATION. See also GENETIC FALLACY.

FALLACIES OF SOUNDNESS
A secondary sense of "fallacy" that refers to special ways the premises of an argument can be false. See FALSE ALTERNATIVES, FALSE UNIVERSALS, STEREOTYPE, and PREJUDICE.

FALLACIOUS APPEAL TO AUTHORITY
An APPEAL TO AUTHORITY is fallacious when the authority appealed to is either inappropriate or unreliable.

FALLACIOUS APPEAL TO FEELING
A fallacious appeal to feeling is an argument that in one way or another summons up positive feelings to justify the truth of a statement or negative feelings to justify the falsity of a statement.

FALLACIOUS APPEAL TO FORCE
A kind of argument that attempts to show the truth of some statement by appealing to threats, bribes, intimidation, etc. Always a WEAK argument.

FALLACIOUS APPEAL TO IGNORANCE
A fallacious appeal to ignorance moves from the premise that some statement hasn't been proven true (false) to the conclusion that that statement is therefore false (true).

FALLACIOUS APPEAL TO THE PEOPLE
An argument that attempts to prove the truth or falsity of some statement by claiming (as its premise) that "everyone" says that statement is true (or false).

FALLACIOUS DISANALOGY
A FALLACY committed by an ANALOGICAL ARGUMENT that strongly violates the SIMILARITY rule: Any striking dissimilarity (disanalogy) between the known and unknown instances makes the analogical argument WEAK. Compare IRRELEVANT ANALOGY.

FALLACY
A fallacy in its primary sense is a LOGICAL FALLACY, which is an error in reasoning resulting in a WEAK argument. See FALLACY OF AFFIRMING THE CONSEQUENT, FALLACY OF DENYING THE ANTECEDENT, FALLACY OF EQUIVOCATION, CIRCULAR REASONING, BEGGING THE QUESTION, FALLACY OF HASTY GENERALIZATION, FALLACY OF BIASED SAMPLING, FALLACIOUS DISANALOGY, IRRELEVANT ANALOGY, POST HOC FALLACY, CONFUSING CAUSE AND EFFECT, GENETIC FALLACY, AD HOMINEM FALLACY, TU QUOQUE FALLACY, FALLACIOUS APPEAL TO AUTHORITY, FALLACIOUS APPEALS TO THE PEOPLE, FALLACIOUS APPEAL TO FEELING, FALLACIOUS APPEAL TO FORCE, FALLACIOUS APPEAL TO IGNORANCE, and GAMBLER'S FALLACY. A secondary sense of "fallacy" is described under FALLACIES OF SOUNDNESS.

FALLACY OF AFFIRMING THE CONSEQUENT

A FALLACY that yields a WEAK argument. It is of the form:

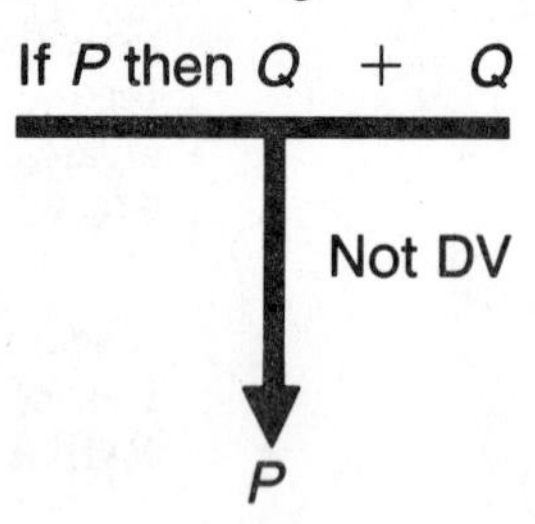

See CONDITIONAL and CONSEQUENT. Compare MODUS PONENS, MODUS TOLLENS, and FALLACY OF DENYING THE ANTECEDENT.

FALLACY OF BIASED SAMPLING

A FALLACY that should be avoided in INDUCTIVE GENERALIZATIONS: If the SAMPLE has too little of the VARIETY appropriate for that POPULATION and PROJECTED PROPERTY, then the argument commits the fallacy of biased sampling and is therefore WEAK. "Each of my friends hates opera; therefore everybody hates opera" commits the fallacy of biased sampling.

FALLACY OF DENYING THE ANTECEDENT

A FALLACY that yields a WEAK argument. It is of the form:

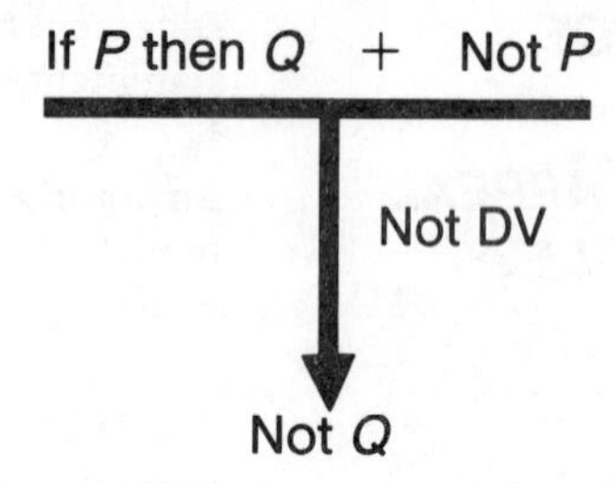

See CONDITIONAL and ANTECEDENT. Compare MODUS PONENS, MODUS TOLLENS, and FALLACY OF AFFIRMING THE CONSEQUENT.

FALLACY OF EQUIVOCATION

The fallacy of equivocation is committed when a term in the premise(s) has more than one meaning; there is no other premise that states which meaning is at work; but the conclusion draws out just one of its meanings. See RELATIVE TERMS and AMBIGUITY.

FALLACY OF HASTY GENERALIZATION

A FALLACY that should be avoided in INDUCTIVE GENERALIZATIONS. If the size of the SAMPLE is too small, the argument is said to commit the fallacy of hasty generalization, and is therefore WEAK. For example, "My wife is insanely jealous, therefore all women are insanely jealous" commits the fallacy of hasty generalization. See QUANTITY.

FALSE ALTERNATIVES

A false alternative is, in general, a DISJUNCTION that is false. In particular, a false alternative is a disjunction that appears to obey the LAW OF THE EXCLUDED MIDDLE, but in reality does not. "You're either my friend or my enemy" is a false alternative, for this disjunction does not exhaust the possibilities (I may be indifferent to you). See DILEMMA.

FIGURE

A description of the CATEGORICAL SYLLOGISM according to the position occupied by its MIDDLE TERM. There are four figures.

GAMBLER'S FALLACY

The gambler's fallacy takes some event (E1) that cannot in fact influence the probability of another event (E2), but nevertheless assumes that if E1 happens, E2 becomes more (or less) likely to happen. "I've not thrown a six for several turns now, so I'm bound to throw one this time," the crap shooter fallaciously argues.

GENETIC FALLACY

A genetic fallacy is an EXPLANATION posing as a JUSTIFICATION. "That cake will taste awful. After all, the recipe for it came in a dream" commits the genetic fallacy. That the recipe for it came in a dream might explain the origin (genesis) of the recipe, but it cannot justify the conclusion that the cake will taste awful.

HYPOTHETICAL SYLLOGISM

A valid rule of deductive logic that chains together CONDITIONALS:

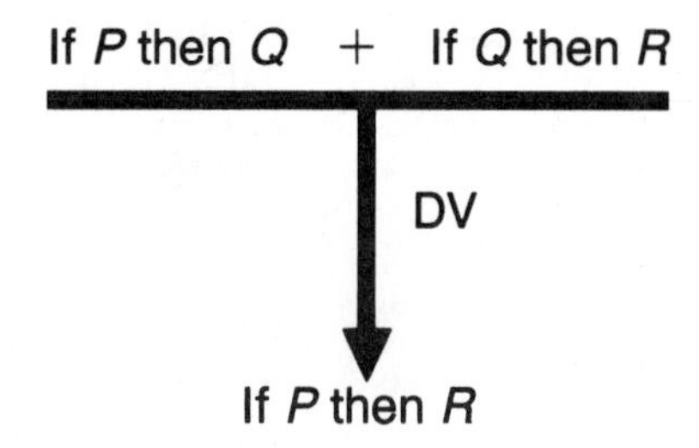

See DEDUCTIVE VALIDITY.

IMPLICATION

In an argument that is DEDUCTIVELY VALID, the premises are said to imply their conclusion. "Implies" and "entails" are synonyms. See ENTAILMENT.

INDEPENDENT REASONS

An argument that has two or more premises or reasons has independent reasons when together they do not make the overall strength of the argument much higher than they would considered separately. Compare DEPENDENT REASONS. The basic structure of an argument with independent reasons is:

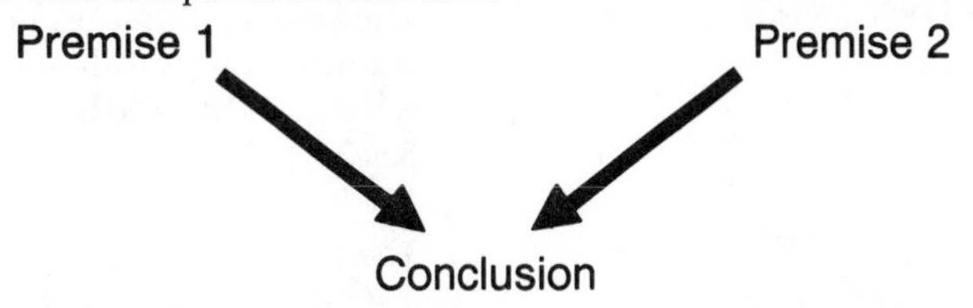

For example, "Going over 55 m.p.h. violates the law. Besides it's unsafe. So you shouldn't do it."

INDUCTION

Induction attempts to go beyond the information contained in the premises. Verbally, induction is expressed in an INDUCTIVE ARGUMENT. The maker of an inductive argument aspires to a STRONG argument. "Most emeralds are green; this is an emerald; therefore it is green" is an inductive argument. Compare DEDUCTION.

INDUCTIVE ARGUMENT

See INDUCTION.

INDUCTIVE GENERALIZATION

Inductive generalizations are INDUCTIVE ARGUMENTS. There are two types: UNIVERSAL GENERALIZATIONS and STATISTICAL GENERALIZATIONS. The rules for evaluating inductive generalizations are CONSISTENCY, UNIFORMITY, QUANTITY, and VARIETY. The FALLACIES associated with inductive generalizations are FALLACY OF HASTY GENERALIZATION and FALLACY OF BIASED SAMPLING.

INDUCTIVE LOGIC

The rules for determining when an argument is STRONG. In *Basic Logic* inductive logic is studied in Part Three.

INDUCTIVE SYLLOGISM

An INDUCTIVE ARGUMENT that can take several forms: "Most *X*'s are *Y*'s, this is an *X*, so this is a *Y*." "Few *X*'s are *Y*'s, this is an *X*, so this is not a *Y*." "90% of *X*'s are *Y*'s, this is an *X*, so this is a *Y*."

IRRELEVANT ANALOGY

A FALLACY that is committed by ANALOGICAL ARGUMENTS that strongly violates the RELEVANCE rule: If the KNOWN PROPERTIES are irrelevant to the UNKNOWN PROPERTY, the argument contains irrelevant analogies and is therefore WEAK. Compare FALLACIOUS DISANALOGY.

JOINT METHOD

A combination of the METHOD OF AGREEMENT and the METHOD OF DIFFERENCE. If *B* always occurs when *A* is present and never occurs when *A* is absent, then we have very good reason to believe that *A* is the cause of *B*. See MILL'S METHODS.

JUSTIFICATION

A justification is an argument proper. A justification seeks to provide reasons that a statement is true. A justification seeks to convince or persuade. Compare EXPLANATION.

KNOWN INSTANCE

The known instance(s) in an ANALOGICAL ARGUMENT is the set of items less the UNKNOWN INSTANCES some of whose features we already know. See KNOWN PROPERTIES, UNKNOWN PROPERTY, SIMILARITY, and RELEVANCE.

KNOWN PROPERTIES

The known properties in an ANALOGICAL ARGUMENT is the set of features you already know are had by both the KNOWN and UNKNOWN INSTANCES. See SIMILARITY, RELEVANCE, and UNKNOWN PROPERTY.

LAW OF THE EXCLUDED MIDDLE

The law of the excluded middle is "Either *P* or not *P*," that is, either a statement is true or it's false. Some statements, called FALSE ALTERNATIVES, seem to obey the law of the excluded middle, but in reality do not.

LOGIC

Logic is the study of ARGUMENTS. In particular, logic seeks to determine the DEGREE OF VALIDITY of arguments. Deductive logic attempts to provide rules for DEDUCTIVE VALIDITY. Inductive logic attempts to provide rules to determine when an induction is STRONG. See also DEDUCTION and INDUCTION.

LOGICAL EQUIVALENCE

Two (or more) statements are logically equivalent when they are true and false under exactly the same circumstances. In ARGUMENT DIAGRAMS we represent logically equivalent statements with a double-headed arrow. This diagram says that *P* and *Q* are logically equivalent:

When two statements are logically equivalent, each implies the other. That is, if *P* and *Q* are logically equivalent then the argument from *P* to *Q* and from *Q* to *P* are each DEDUCTIVELY VALID. An example of logical equivalence is DOUBLE NEGATION.

LOGICAL FALLACY

The primary meaning of FALLACY. A logical fallacy is an error in reasoning that results in a WEAK argument. Compare FALLACIES OF SOUNDNESS.

LOGICAL IMPOSSIBILITY

A state of affairs is logically impossible when it implies a CONTRADICTION. It is logically impossible, for example, that the premises of a DEDUCTIVELY VALID argument be true and its conclusion false. Compare LOGICAL POSSIBILITY.

LOGICAL POSSIBILITY

A state of affairs is logically possible just in case it does not imply a CONTRADICTION. It is logically possible, for example, that the premises of a STRONG argument be true and its conclusion false. Compare LOGICAL IMPOSSIBILITY.

MAJOR TERM

The predicate of the conclusion of a CATEGORICAL SYLLOGISM in STANDARD CATEGORICAL FORM. See MIDDLE TERM and MINOR TERM.

MASS PHENOMENON

A mass phenomenon is a number of events that we have good reason to believe have causes of the same type. See MILL'S METHODS. Compare SINGULAR PHENOMENON.

MEDIUM

A SIMPLE JUSTIFICATION is Medium just in case while supposing its premises to be true, its conclusion has about as much chance of being true as it has of being false. Medium arguments cannot be good, i.e., SOUND arguments.

METHOD OF AGREEMENT If *B* always occurs in the presence of *A*, then we have reason to believe that *A* is the cause of *B*. See MILL'S METHODS.

METHOD OF CONCOMITANT VARIATION If *A* and *B* change together, e.g., whenever *A* increases so does *B*, then we have reason to believe that *A* is the cause of *B*. See MILL'S METHODS.

METHOD OF DIFFERENCE If *B* never occurs when *A* is absent, then we have reason to believe that *A* is the cause of *B*. See MILL'S METHODS.

MIDDLE TERM The term in a CATEGORICAL SYLLOGISM that appears only in its premises, not in the conclusion. See MAJOR TERM and MINOR TERM.

MILL'S METHODS Methods for avoiding the POST HOC FALLACY and CONFUSING CAUSE AND EFFECT, and for establishing STRONG arguments for CAUSAL STATEMENTS. The Methods studied in this book are the METHOD OF AGREEMENT, the METHOD OF DIFFERENCE, the JOINT METHOD, and the METHOD OF CONCOMITANT VARIATION. See CAUSAL ARGUMENT, MASS PHENOMENON, and SINGULAR PHENOMENON.

MINOR TERM The subject of the conclusion of CATEGORICAL SYLLOGISM. See MAJOR TERM and MIDDLE TERM.

MODERN INTERPRETATION An interpretation of the (A) and (E) categorical statements according to which these statements do not imply the existence of members of the subject class. On the modern interpretation, neither "All pirates are dangerous" nor "No pirates are dangerous" implies the existence of pirates. Thus, "All *A* are *B*" means "If anything is an *A*, it is also a *B*," and "No *A* are *B*" means "If anything is an *A*, it is not also a *B*." See CATEGORICAL STATEMENT and EXISTENTIAL IMPORT. Compare ARISTOTELEAN INTERPRETATION.

MODUS PONENS A valid rule of deductive logic for CONDITIONALS:

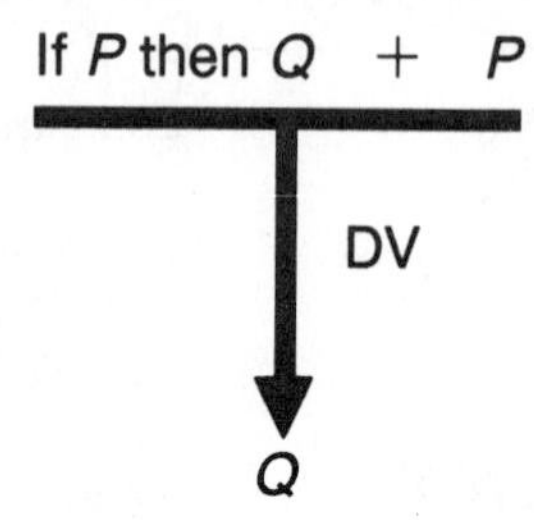

See DEDUCTIVE VALIDITY. Compare MODUS TOLLENS, FALLACY OF AFFIRMING THE CONSEQUENT, and FALLACY OF AFFIRMING THE ANTECEDENT.

MODUS TOLLENS

A valid rule of deductive logic for conditionals:

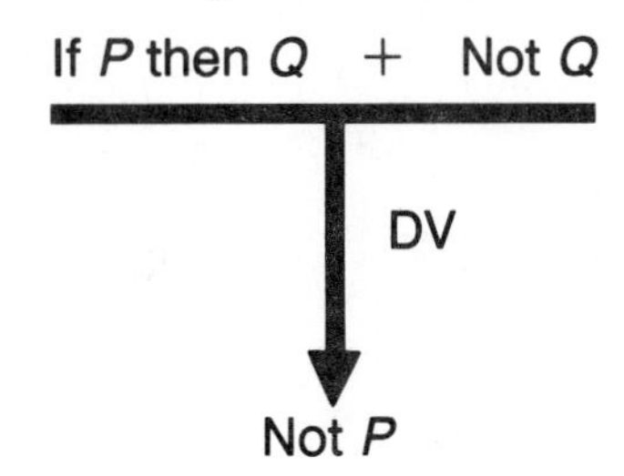

See DEDUCTIVE VALIDITY. Compare MODUS PONENS, FALLACY OF AFFIRMING THE CONSEQUENT, and FALLACY OF AFFIRMING THE ANTECEDENT.

MOOD

A description of the form of a CATEGORICAL SYLLOGISM when it is in STANDARD CATEGORICAL FORM, according to the names of the kinds of CATEGORICAL STATEMENTS that make it up, for example AAA. See FIGURE.

NECESSARY CONDITION

The CONSEQUENT of a CONDITIONAL. For example, "It's an insect" is a necessary condition of "It's an ant" for it occurs as the consequent of the true conditional. "If it's an ant, then it's an insect." More simply, a necessary condition is a circumstance for something, *X*, such that *X* won't happen unless that circumstance first happens.

NEGATION

If "*P*" is the SIMPLE STATEMENT, then "Not *P*" is the negation of this simple statement. For example, "He will come" has as its negation "He won't come." The TRUTHTABLE for negation is:

P	Not P
T	F
F	T

See also DOUBLE NEGATION.

NEITHER

A way of expressing the CONJUNCTION of two CONJUNCTS, each of which are NEGATIONS. "Neither *P* nor *Q*" means "Not *P* and not *Q*."

ONLY

A nonstandard QUANTIFIER. "Only *P* are *Q*" means "All *Q* are *P*." See CATEGORICAL STATEMENT.

PARTICULAR STATEMENT

Mainly the (I) and (O) CATEGORICAL STATEMENTS. "Some *A* are *B*" means "There is at least one *A* and it is a *B*," and "Some *A* are not *B*" means "There is at least one *A* but it is not a *B*. See EXISTENTIAL IMPORT. Other statements such as "Socrates is wise" are also particular, since they speak of the particular, Socrates. Compare UNIVERSAL STATEMENT.

PETITIO PRINCIPII

Another name for CIRCULAR REASONING.

POPULATION

In an INDUCTIVE GENERALIZATION, the population is the group we want to discover something about. In "I've observed 100 crows, and each was black; therefore all crows are black" the population is crows. See PROJECTED PROPERTY and SAMPLE.

POST HOC FALLACY

A FALLACY associated with CAUSAL ARGUMENTS. It moves from the premise that *A* occurred before *B* to the conclusion that *A* caused *B*. Such arguments are WEAK. The full name of the fallacious argument is "Post hoc, ergo propter hoc," which means, "After this, therefore because of this."

PREJUDICE

As used in this book prejudice is the conviction that a STEREOTYPE is true. See FALLACIES OF SOUNDNESS.

PREMISE

The statement or statements in an argument that provide the reason(s) or evidence for another statement. See ARGUMENT and CONCLUSION.

PREMISE INDICATOR

A term or terms in an ARGUMENT that often come before the PREMISE. Examples of premise indicators are "because," "since," and "for." An argument need not have premise indicators.

PROJECTED PROPERTY

In INDUCTIVE GENERALIZATION, the projected property is the property the frequency of which we wish to investigate in the POPULATION. In "I've observed 100 crows, and each was black; therefore all crows are black," the projected property is *being black*. See SAMPLE.

QUANTIFIER

A term that basically tells how much of a CATEGORY is being spoken of. The standard categorical quantifiers are "All," "No," and "Some." "Only" is a nonstandard quantifier in categorical logic. Induction uses such quantifiers as "Most," "Few," and "90%."

QUANTITY

A rule for evaluating INDUCTIVE GENERALIZATIONS: The larger the SAMPLE, the STRONGER the argument. The smaller the sample, the WEAKER the argument. A STRONG argument has a sufficiently large sample. Violations of the quantity rule lead to the FALLACY OF HASTY GENERALIZATION. See CONSISTENCY, UNIFORMITY, and VARIETY.

REASONING

Reasoning is discourse in which evidence in the form of statements is given for the truth of other statements. See ARGUMENT.

REASONING INDICATOR

A reasoning indicator is a term that sometimes appears in arguments to show which statements are premises or which are conclusions. For example, "since," "because," and "for" come before PREMISES; "thus," "therefore," and "so" come before CONCLUSIONS.

RELATIVE TERMS

A term is relative if it requires some point of reference to be meaningful. For example, the term "small" is a relative term. "Small" describes very different sizes in "small dog" and "small whale." See FALLACY OF EQUIVOCATION and AMBIGUITY.

RELEVANCE A rule for evaluating ANALOGICAL ARGUMENTS: The KNOWN PROPERTIES must be relevant to the UNKNOWN PROPERTY. Violations of the relevance rule yield the FALLACY of IRRELEVANT ANALOGY.

SAMPLE A sample is the set of observations made of the POPULATION in an INDUCTIVE GENERALIZATION. In "I've observed 100 crows, and each was black; therefore all crows are black" the sample is *100 crows*. See PROJECTED PROPERTY.

SCOPE As used in this book, scope refers to what a NEGATION like "not" negates. There is a difference between "It is not both raining and sunny" and "It is not raining and not sunny." See DE MORGAN'S LAWS and NEITHER.

SIMILARITY A rule for evaluating ANALOGICAL ARGUMENTS: The more KNOWN PROPERTIES shared between the KNOWN INSTANCES and the UNKNOWN INSTANCES, the STRONGER the argument. The fewer known properties shared between the known instances and the unknown instance, the WEAKER the argument. Violations of the similarity rule yield a fallacy, FALLACIOUS DISANALOGY.

SIMPLE JUSTIFICATION A simple justification is a justification that has one "arrow" on an argument diagram. Compare COMPOUND JUSTIFICATION.

SIMPLE STATEMENT A simple statement is a positive statement that contains no other statements as parts. "He's at home" is a simple statement. Compare COMPOUND STATEMENT.

SIMPLIFICATION A rule that asserts that any CONJUNCTION implies any one of its CONJUNCTS:

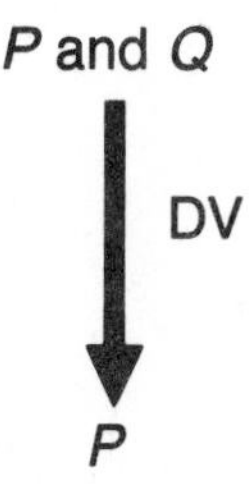

SINGULAR PHENOMENON A singular phenomenon is an event we have no good reason to believe has a cause of the same type as another, similar, event. See MILL'S METHODS. Compare MASS PHENOMENON.

SOUND Soundness is the technical logical term for what may be called in ordinary English a good argument. An argument is sound when it is either DEDUCTIVELY VALID or STRONG, and all of its premises are true. Its opposite is UNSOUND.

STANDARD CATEGORICAL FORM A CATEGORICAL SYLLOGISM is in standard categorical form when it is ordered: premise containing MAJOR TERM, premise containing MINOR TERM, conclusion.

STATEMENT

A statement is what is expressed by language only when what is expressed can be either true or false. "It's raining" is a statement. "Please, let it stop raining" is not.

STATISTICAL GENERALIZATION

A statistical generalization is an INDUCTIVE GENERALIZATION that begins with a number of particular observations or instances, and generalizes to less than UNIVERSAL conclusion. For example, "I've observed 100 diamonds and 90 were clear; therefore 90% of all diamonds are clear." Compare UNIVERSAL GENERALIZATION.

STEREOTYPE

As used in this book, a stereotype is a false universal about human behavior. See PREJUDICE, FALLACIES OF SOUNDNESS, and UNIVERSAL STATEMENT.

STRONG

A SIMPLE JUSTIFICATION is Strong just in case while supposing its premises to be true, its conclusion is very likely to be true as well. The maker of an inductive argument aims at a Strong argument. A Strong argument that has all true premises is SOUND. See INDUCTION.

SUFFICIENT CONDITION

The ANTECEDENT of a CONDITIONAL. For example, "It's an ant" is a sufficient condition for "It's an insect" since it occurs as the antecedent of the true conditional, "If it's an ant then it's an insect." More simply, a sufficient condition for something, *X*, is a circumstance such that if that circumstance happened, so would *X*. Compare NECESSARY CONDITION.

SYLLOGISM

A syllogism is any argument with two premises and one conclusion. See CATEGORICAL SYLLOGISM, DISJUNCTIVE SYLLOGISM, HYPOTHETICAL SYLLOGISM, and INDUCTIVE SYLLOGISM.

TRUTHFUNCTIONAL CONNECTIVE

A truthfunctional connective is a term that is defined by a TRUTHTABLE, and that determines the truthvalue of a COMPOUND STATEMENT given the truthvalues of its SIMPLE STATEMENTS. The truthfunctional connectives studied in *Basic Logic* are "and," "or," "not," "if. . . then," and their synonyms.

TRUTHTABLE

A truthtable assumes that any statement is either True or False, and defines "or," "not," "and," and "if. . . then" in terms of the truthvalue of the COMPOUND STATEMENT given the truthvalues of the SIMPLE STATEMENTS that make up the compound statement. See NEGATION, CONJUNCTION, DISJUNCTION, CONDITIONAL, and BICONDITIONAL.

TU QUOQUE ARGUMENT

An argument that uses as premises "Person *P* says that '*X*' is true" and "*P* behaves inconsistently with *X*." This argument is fallacious if it concludes that '*X*' is false. The argument can be Strong if it concludes that *P* is acting inconsistently with his or her beliefs.

UNIFORMITY

A rule for evaluating INDUCTIVE GENERALIZATIONS: The greater the likelihood that future or unobserved instances of a POPULATION will be significantly different from present or observed instances, the WEAKER the argument. The greater the likelihood that future or unobserved instances of a population will be very similar to present or observed instances, the STRONGER the argument. See CONSISTENCY, QUANTITY, and VARIETY.

UNIVERSAL GENERALIZATION

A universal generalization is an INDUCTIVE GENERALIZATION that begins with a number of particular observations of instances, and generalizes to a UNIVERSAL STATEMENT. For example, "I've observed 100 crows, and each was black; therefore all crows are black." Compare STATISTICAL GENERALIZATION.

UNIVERSAL STATEMENT

In general, any statement of the form "All *X* are *Y*" or "No *X* are *Y*." See CATEGORICAL STATEMENT, EXISTENTIAL IMPORT, ARISTOTELEAN INTERPRETATION, and MODERN INTERPRETATION. For FALLACIES OF SOUNDNESS associated with universal statements, see FALSE UNIVERSALS, PREJUDICE, and STEREOTYPE. See also UNIVERSAL GENERALIZATION.

UNKNOWN INSTANCE

The unknown instance in an ANALOGICAL ARGUMENT is the item or items our efforts at discovery are aimed at. See KNOWN INSTANCE, KNOWN PROPERTY, UNKNOWN PROPERTY, SIMILARITY, and RELEVANCE.

UNKNOWN PROPERTY

The unknown property in an ANALOGICAL ARGUMENT is the feature or features we are investigating in the UNKNOWN INSTANCE. See KNOWN INSTANCE, KNOWN PROPERTY, UNKNOWN INSTANCE, SIMILARITY, and RELEVANCE.

UNLESS EQUIVALENCE

"Unless" states a CONDITIONAL. This is a valid rule of deductive logic:

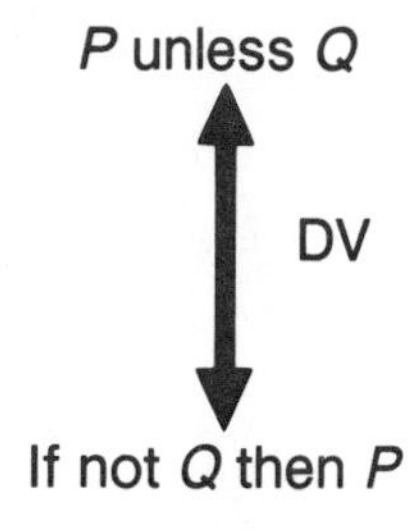

For example, "We'll go on the picnic unless it rains" implies "If it doesn't rain then we'll go on the picnic." See LOGICAL EQUIVALENCE.

UNSOUND

An unsound argument is one that either has false premises or has a DEGREE OF VALIDITY less than STRONG. Contrast SOUND.

VALIDITY

One of the two parameters of the evaluation of an ARGUMENT, and the one of most interest to LOGIC. The validity of an argument is the strength of the support the premises give to the conclusion. See DEGREES OF VALIDITY.

VARIETY

A rule for evaluating INDUCTIVE GENERALIZATIONS: The more variety in the SAMPLE, the STRONGER the argument. The less variety in the sample, the WEAKER the argument. A STRONG argument has sufficient variety. What kind of variety called for depends on the nature of the POPULATION and the PROJECTED PROPERTY. Violations of the variety rule lead to the FALLACY OF BIASED SAMPLING. See CONSISTENCY, QUANTITY, and UNIFORMITY.

VENN DIAGRAMS

A modern method of showing CATEGORICAL SYLLOGISMS to be DEDUCTIVELY VALID or not. Invented by John Venn, these diagrams use a scheme of overlapping circles to represent pictorially the CATEGORICAL STATEMENTS. Venn diagrams assume the MODERN INTERPRETATION of the (A) and (E) categorical statements.

WEAK

A SIMPLE JUSTIFICATION is Weak just in case while supposing its premises to be true, its conclusion has little or no chance of being true. A Weak argument cannot be SOUND. See also FALLACY.

INDEX

This index makes no references to the Key Points or Glossary as these are self-indexed.